Utilizing RapidMiner, Python, and R for Data Mining Applications

Sarawut Ramjan
Thammasat University, Thailand

Jirapon Sunkpho
Thammasat University, Thailand

IGI Global
Scientific Publishing
Publishing Tomorrow's Research Today

Vice President of Editorial Melissa Wagner
Director of Acquisitions Mikaela Felty
Director of Book Development Jocelynn Hessler
Production Manager Mike Brehm
Cover Design Phillip Shickler

Published in the United States of America by
IGI Global Scientific Publishing
701 East Chocolate Avenue
Hershey, PA, 17033, USA
Tel: 717-533-8845
Fax: 717-533-7115
Website: https://www.igi-global.com E-mail: cust@igi-global.com

Library of Congress Cataloging-in-Publication Data

LCCN: 2024059917 (CIP Data Pending)
ISBN13: 9798369360019
Isbn13Softcover: 9798369360026
EISBN13: 9798369360033

British Cataloguing in Publication Data
A Cataloguing in Publication record for this book is available from the British Library.

Table of Contents

Preface

It is with great pleasure that we present the second edition of our book, Utilizing RapidMiner, Python, and R for Data Mining Applications. This edition is a significant expansion and improvement upon the first edition, Data Mining for RapidMiner, thanks to the invaluable suggestions from two esteemed reviewers. Their insights have guided us in refining and enriching the content to better serve our readers.

In this second edition, we have included comprehensive introductions to data mining and essential data concepts. We have also enhanced the sections on software installation and the introduction to RapidMiner. The core chapters on classification, deep learning, clustering, recommendation systems, basic Python programming, and data analytics with Python have been thoroughly rewritten to align with the reviewers' recommendations.

One of the significant enhancements in this edition is the inclusion of new chapters on R programming. We have provided an introductory chapter to R programming, followed by a chapter dedicated to R programming for data scientists. This addition aims to equip our readers with the necessary skills to utilize R, a widely used language in data science, alongside RapidMiner and Python.

This book is authored by Sarawut Ramjan and Jirapon Sunkpho, who bring their extensive expertise and experience in data mining and data science to this work. We are grateful for the support provided by the College of Innovation Book Funding, Thammasat University, which has made this publication possible.

We hope that this expanded and enhanced edition will serve as a valuable resource for students, researchers, and professionals in the field of data mining and data science. Our goal is to provide a comprehensive and practical guide that empowers readers to effectively apply RapidMiner, Python, and R in their data mining projects.

Thank you for choosing our book. We welcome your feedback and look forward to your success in the exciting field of data mining.

ORGANIZATION OF THE BOOK

In *Chapter 1: Introduction to Data Mining – Challenges and Techniques*, we set the foundation for understanding data mining as a transformative tool in today's competitive business landscape. We explore how machine learning techniques are used to uncover valuable patterns and guide strategic decisions. By aligning business objectives with appropriate data mining methods, we emphasize the crucial role of data scientists in navigating and extracting actionable insights from large data sets.

Chapter 2: Data introduces readers to the lifeblood of data mining—data itself. We walk through the process of identifying, classifying, and assessing data types to ensure compatibility with mining techniques. The chapter highlights the importance of data quality, handling missing values, and recognizing outliers using visual tools, all of which lay the groundwork for robust analysis.

In *Chapter 3: Data Pre-Processing and an Example of Data Classification with RapidMiner*, we delve into the essential preparatory steps for data mining, focusing on RapidMiner as a powerful, no-code platform. We guide readers through visual data exploration, feature selection, normalization, and missing value handling. A hands-on classification example enables readers to apply these concepts directly using RapidMiner.

Chapter 4: Classification underscores the importance of supervised learning in predictive analytics. We explain how techniques such as k-Nearest Neighbors, decision trees, and Naïve Bayes can be effectively used to derive insights from data, particularly with RapidMiner. This chapter provides readers with a practical, step-by-step approach to implementing classification in real-world scenarios.

Chapter 5: Deep Learning expands our discussion into neural networks and their application in big data analysis. By introducing Convolutional Neural Networks (CNNs) for image data and Recurrent Neural Networks (RNNs) for time series data, we demonstrate how deep learning can be used for forecasting and classification. The chapter includes guided experiments using RapidMiner to bring theory into practice.

In *Chapter 6: Clustering*, we present unsupervised learning techniques that enable the segmentation of data into meaningful groups. With practical demonstrations of K-Means, Hierarchical Clustering, and DBSCAN, we help readers understand how to label clusters and assess their effectiveness using both subjective and objective methods. RapidMiner again serves as our tool of choice for practical application.

Chapter 7: Association Rule focuses on mining hidden patterns in customer behavior. We walk through the Apriori algorithm and discuss how association rules can inform product bundling and cross-selling strategies. Emphasizing collaboration with domain experts, this chapter also provides a hands-on tutorial in implementing association rule mining via RapidMiner.

In *Chapter 8: Recommendation Systems*, we explore the mechanisms behind content-based and collaborative filtering. From understanding customer purchase history to predicting future preferences, we illustrate how recommendation engines support business goals such as retention and ROI. Using RapidMiner, we walk readers through building and testing effective recommendation models.

Chapter 9: Basic Python Programming introduces Python as a flexible programming language essential for customizing data science workflows. Designed for beginners, we cover syntax, variables, control structures, recursion, and file handling. We also introduce Google Colab as a practical coding environment, setting the stage for Python-based data mining.

In *Chapter 10: Data Analytics with Python*, we dive deeper into the Python ecosystem for data science. We explain how libraries like NumPy, Pandas, Matplotlib, Seaborn, and Scikit-learn support data pre-processing, visualization, and modeling. This chapter equips readers with the tools needed to explore, visualize, and analyze data when off-the-shelf software falls short.

Chapter 11: Introduction to R Programming serves as a beginner's guide to R, introducing its history, core features, and significance in statistics and data analysis. Through guided examples and exercises, readers become familiar with data types, control structures, and data visualization using ggplot2—building a strong foundation for further R-based analysis.

Finally, *Chapter 12: R Programming for Data Scientists* expands upon introductory concepts, guiding readers through more advanced topics such as statistical analysis, data mining techniques, and machine learning integration using R. With real-world examples and case studies, we illustrate how R can solve complex data science challenges, empowering readers to confidently apply R in their own projects.

Sarawut Ramjan
Thammasat University, Thailand

Jirapon Sunkpho
Thammasat University, Thailand

Chapter 1
Introduction to Data Mining: Challenges and Techniques

ABSTRACT

Data mining is a powerful and increasingly popular tool that uses machine learning to uncover patterns in data that can help businesses to stay competitive. Data scientists are trained to understand business objectives and to select the correct techniques for data exploration and pre-processing. After formulating a business question, data mining methods are chosen and evaluated to determine their ability to fit the data set and to answer the query. The results are then reported back to the business owner. Data mining is an essential part of modern business, allowing the organization to keep up with the competition and remain successful. With its growing popularity, the need for data scientists is rapidly increasing.

INTRODUCTION

In today's world, the role of data analysis through data mining is increasingly critical. The digital landscape enables the storage of vast volumes of data, utilizing either cloud technology or databases with extensive memory capacities. Additionally, data is continuously generated by users worldwide in real time and at high speed through social networks. This phenomenon has led to the exponential growth of data, commonly referred to as Big Data, which offers significant opportunities for business professionals globally. For example, analyzing customer purchase trends or forecasting raw material requirements for production necessitates the use of

DOI: 10.4018/979-8-3693-6001-9.ch001

data mining techniques. These techniques are essential for uncovering patterns and predicting outcomes, aiding entrepreneurs in making informed decisions.

Data analysis for business decision-making encompasses various methodologies, including descriptive and inferential statistics. Therefore, data mining should not be seen as a replacement for traditional data analysis methods but rather as an evolution, offering advanced analytical capabilities in conjunction with machine learning technology. This advancement is particularly effective in processing and analyzing large-scale data sets, or Big Data. As a result, data mining has proven to be a reliable tool, producing accurate results that align with specific business queries.

CHALLENGES AND STRATEGIES IN IMPLEMENTING DATA MINING

As the need for problem analysis grows, it has led to the creation of specific roles dedicated to data analysis, known as data scientists. However, data scientists are not exclusively digital technology experts; anyone who possesses data can assume this role. For example, medical technicians, who have access to patient health information and understand the medical industry context, can become data scientists as they are familiar with the questions to ask and the nature of the data in their field.

Many industries now hire data scientists who may not have a deep familiarity with the industry or the specific data they are analyzing. As a result, data scientists often need to consult those who pose the questions, typically management, as well as industry experts, to ensure that their findings align with the facts. This section presents the wide-ranging applications of data across various industries, derived from research papers by the author and various research partners.

- **Detecting Damage in Undersea Oil Pipelines**, due to frequent oil leaks, oil companies conduct costly diving operations to inspect undersea pipelines. Thammasiri and Ramjan (2021) proposed a classification model to detect damage based on key features such as pipeline service life, internal fluid temperature, and equipment height relative to sea level. Feature selection played a crucial role in identifying the most relevant attributes. Their study found that the XGBoost Classifier achieved a 76.2% efficiency rate in classifying damaged areas.
- **Predicting Traffic Accident Hotspots**, governments use historical accident data to prioritize safety measures, though inefficiencies arise when resources are allocated to low-risk areas. Bunjongprasoet and Ramjan (2021) sought to improve accident-prone area prediction by analyzing data from Bangkok, Thailand. Feature selection using the information gain technique revealed

that route characteristics had the most significant impact on accident likelihood, whereas vehicle type had a lesser effect. Their model achieved an 81.62% accuracy rate in predicting accident-prone locations.
- **Sentiment Analysis for Hospital Service Quality**, hospitals aim to improve service quality through various standards, but customer complaints—especially regarding nursing services—remain a challenge. Phoha and Ramjan (2023) developed a sentiment analysis model to assess customer feedback from sources like Facebook pages and other channels. Effective data pre-processing, including removing stop words and word tokenization, was essential. Their research found that the decision tree technique achieved an 81.80% accuracy rate in classifying customer sentiment as satisfied or dissatisfied.

It is evident from the research that data mining techniques are not the primary challenge for data scientists; the real challenges lie in data exploration and the pre-processing stages. While data science offers numerous advantages across various industries, a range of challenges are still encountered by users as outlined by Tanantong (2020).

- **Scalability** – The rapid growth of data from social networks and industries like travel necessitates efficient data management, access, and transfer algorithms (Almasoud, Al-Khalifa, & Al-Salman, 2019).
- **High Dimensionality** – Fields like autonomous vehicles generate vast high-resolution data, requiring advanced exploration and pre-processing techniques for accurate analysis (Lawal et al., 2020).
- **Complex Data** – Organizations store diverse structured and unstructured data, making attribute selection, optimization, and standardization crucial for effective mining (Berman, 2018).
- **Data Ownership & Distribution** – Cloud storage and global networks raise concerns over security, retention, and compliance with regulations like Thailand's PDPA, restricting data use without consent (Jiang, Jiang, & Wang, 2020).

Despite the advancements in data analytics, several challenges persist in its operations. Bias mitigation in algorithms remains a critical concern, as biased models can lead to unfair or inaccurate outcomes in areas such as hiring, lending, and healthcare. Addressing this issue requires techniques like data balancing, algorithmic fairness adjustments, and explainable AI, along with regular audits and diverse training data to ensure fairness and inclusivity in predictive analytics. Another key challenge involves ethical considerations in data mining, particularly regarding privacy, consent, and data security. Organizations must comply with regulations like GDPR and PDPA to responsibly collect and use personal data. Ensuring transparency in data processing, reducing discrimination, and preventing misuse are essential for maintaining public trust and ethical compliance. Additionally, the integration of data mining with emerging technologies such as IoT, blockchain, and AI presents both opportunities and challenges. IoT generates vast real-time data streams, demanding advanced mining techniques for predictive insights. Blockchain enhances data integrity and security in decentralized networks, while AI automates pattern recognition and decision-making, improving efficiency and scalability across various industries. Addressing these challenges is crucial to harnessing the full potential of data analytics in a responsible and effective manner.

DATA MINING TECHNIQUES IN THE DATA ANALYSIS PROCESS

Data mining techniques—classification, numerical prediction, association rule mining, and clustering—are essential for analyzing large datasets (Bramer, 2016). Unlike traditional statistical analysis, data mining leverages Machine Learning (ML) for more precise, data-driven insights (Bell, 2015; Chiarini, Kohli, and Forsgren, 2021). Advances like Deep Learning further enhance pattern recognition in complex datasets, including non-linear structures. These techniques support diverse applications, from tumor pattern analysis in medicine to credit risk assessment and targeted marketing in finance, enabling data-driven decision-making across industries. The data analysis process utilizing data mining techniques, as part of the Knowledge Discovery Process (Cardona, Gomez, and Trujillo, 2014; Kyaw and Limsiroratana, 2019; Gupta, Sahayadhas, and Gupta, 2020), involves several key steps:

- **Data Sources**: Data scientists access multiple data sources simultaneously to assess the potential of these datasets for analysis and to generate results that aptly address specific questions.
- **Data Storage**: Data scientists can gather data from various sources, including in-house databases, business partners, and social networks like Twitter. This data can be stored either as a single dataset or in a combined format by merging data from multiple sources.
- **Data Selectionand Pre-Processing**: In this stage, data scientists employ data processing techniques for data selection. This involves analyzing the relationships between variables in the dataset and the target variables, often consulting experts for insights. Preparation for data mining includes handling missing values and eliminating outliers.

- **Data Mining**: Choosing the right data mining techniques is crucial for obtaining useful results. Data scientists review the suitability of these techniques for the datasets in question, ensuring they can provide answers to the questions posed. If there is a mismatch, they may need to either modify the data analysis method or consider changing the dataset to better suit the analysis.
- **Interpretation**: The quantitative data or data visualizations obtained from data mining (Samasiri, 2020) require interpretation to be understandable to the inquirers. Data scientists must determine whether the questions necessitate the use of data mining techniques or whether simply processing the raw data suffices.

This process reflects the nuanced and multi-faceted nature of data analysis in the modern era where selecting and processing data for specific outcomes is as crucial as the analysis itself. Although the Knowledge Discovery Process is widely-adopted for data analysis, the Cross-industry Standard Process for Data Mining (CRISP-DM) offers a more tailored approach for business-related data analysis (Liu & Ding, 2011). Developed by SPSS Inc. in 2000, CRISP-DM provides a structured framework specifically designed to guide the data mining process in a business context.

- **Business Understanding**: Data scientists collaborate with business stakeholders to define problems where data visualization or mining can provide insights. This process varies by industry and requires consideration of internal factors like budget, resources, and timeframe. Success criteria should be set to ensure actionable results. The choice of technology is also crucial—large datasets may need high-performance computing, while ready-made software can speed up model creation but may be costly compared to open-source alternatives.
- **Data Understanding**: This stage ensures data suitability for analysis, whether from internal or external sources. Data scientists collaborate with stakeholders to verify accuracy, consult experts on data meaning, and use visualization tools to identify outliers or missing values. This process informs effective data cleansing, preparing for the next phase.
- **Data Preparation**: In this stage, a data scientist prepares data for analysis by cleaning, merging, and transforming it into a suitable format. This includes handling missing values, selecting relevant features, and converting data types. The goal is to create a clean, structured dataset ready for data mining techniques.
- **Modeling**: In this phase, data scientists choose suitable data mining techniques, ensuring alignment with business objectives and accuracy. They seg-

ment data for training and testing in Supervised Learning, refining as needed to optimize model performance before full deployment.

- **Model Evaluation**: Data scientists select suitable data mining techniques, prioritizing precision and consistency. If results don't fully align with business questions, predefined success criteria help assess effectiveness. The final evaluation ensures both technical accuracy and business relevance.
- **Deployment**: The deployment phase applies analysis results to business decisions, such as forecasting raw material needs. Data scientists present findings in a clear format for stakeholders, using reports and discussions to address questions. This phase also informs future data collection for improved analysis.

Supervised Learning

In the context of Supervised Learning Data Mining Techniques as discussed by Abdul and Starkey (2020), data scientists are required to identify the target variables, also known as labeled data, for their analysis. The dataset is then split into two distinct segments: the first is utilized for training the machine learning models, and the second is dedicated to testing these models in line with predefined data mining methodologies. The techniques falling under the umbrella of Supervised Learning in data mining include the following.

1. **Classification**

   If the diagnosis is COVID-19, and symptoms are detected as symptomatic with a severe condition, then the patient is classified as a severe patient. If the diagnosis is COVID-19, and symptoms are detected as symptomatic with mild symptoms, then the patient is classified as a symptomatic patient. If the diagnosis is COVID-19, and the patient is detected as asymptomatic, then the patient is classified as an asymptomatic patient.

The classification process is viable only when there is a variable that significantly influences the classification, such as diagnosis, symptoms, and the severity of symptoms in the case of COVID-19. These form the key variables for the classification. The result of the classification is considered the target variable. Classification rules can be effectively represented using a Decision Tree, as demonstrated by Romero et al. (2019). This method graphically illustrates the variables, as shown in Figure 1.

Figure 1. Decision tree diagram: Analyzing COVID-19 patient symptoms

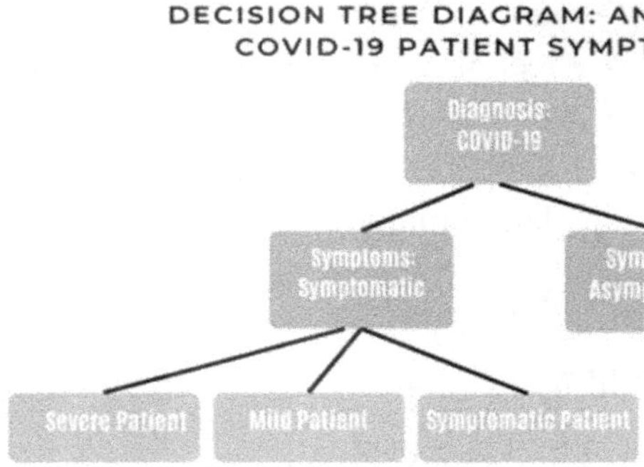

From Figure 1, which illustrates the decision tree for classifying COVID-19 patients based on symptoms, we see a systematic approach to categorizing patient status. The first branch leads to a decision node labeled 'Symptoms: Symptomatic, Severity: Severe,' resulting in the classification 'Patient Status: Severe Patient.' The second branch identifies patients with 'Symptoms: Symptomatic, Severity: Mild,' classifying them as 'Symptomatic Patients.' The third branch categorizes patients as 'Asymptomatic Patients' if they show no symptoms. Beyond these classification rules, the nearest neighbor matching method, as discussed by Atanasovski, Kostov, Arapinoski, and Spirovski (2020), offers an alternative for data categorization. This method bases classification on the proximity to similar data. For example, in the context of car models, if the data attributes of a certain car are similar to those of known luxury cars, it would be classified accordingly as a luxury car, utilizing the principles of nearest neighbor matching.

2. **Numerical Prediction**

Numerical Prediction is a category of Supervised Learning, as outlined by Liu et al. (2021). This approach necessitates the establishment of a target variable and leverages other variables for data analysis. A common application is analyzing students' height using Simple Linear Regression. Additionally, Numerical Prediction encompasses more complex forecasting methods, such as Neural Networks, which utilize multiple variables to predict outcomes. Another notable technique is Deep Learning, particularly well-suited for handling large volumes of data with non-linear characteristics. In implementing these methods, it is essential to partition the datasets into two segments: one for machine learning and the other for testing, specifically tailored for numerical forecasting.

Unsupervised Learning

Unsupervised Learning is a technique in which data scientists do not need to determine the target variables nor to divide the datasets into machine learning and testing parts (Shrestha, Razavi and Prasad, 2020). All data can be processed to achieve the desired results. The data mining techniques classified as Unsupervised Learning are as follows:

1. **Association Rule Mining**

Association Rule Mining is a technique employed to examine the relationships between data, whether for a single variable or for multiple variables. For instance, marketers aiming to optimize their product promotion on Twitter may question which hashtags align best with customer interests. To address such queries, data scientists can apply Association Rule Mining techniques to explore and determine the associative patterns among the data. This approach is exemplified in the work of Tanantong and Ramjan (2021).

$Hashtag_1$, Hashtag $_2$, Hastag$_3$, …, Hashtag $_n$ => {Supply} or
$Hashtag_1$, Hashtag $_2$, Hastag$_3$, …, Hashtag $_n$ => {Demand} or
$Hashtag_1$, Hashtag $_2$, Hastag$_3$, …, Hashtag $_n$ => {Others}

The examples demonstrate that data scientists have the capability to analyze hashtag trends on Twitter, offering valuable insights for marketers. This analysis assists in identifying the most effective hashtags that align with their customers' purchasing interests on the platform. For instance, the hashtag #SellingBlackpink-ConcertTickets, which pertains to product offerings, coupled with #LookingFor-BlackpinkConcertTickets, indicating a desire to purchase, can enable customers to locate relevant Twitter posts more swiftly. Such strategic use of hashtags streamlines the connection between supply and demand within the Twitter community.

2. **Clustering**

Clustering involves grouping data based on two or more variables, as described by Reddy and Aggarwal (2014). In practical applications, data scientists can analyze a dataset comprising various dimensions, such as the width and length of pant legs previously purchased from a factory. The process includes determining the number of desired groups for classification, as illustrated in Figure 2.

Figure 2. Clustering of desired pant sizes for factory production (Tanantong & Ramjan, 2022)

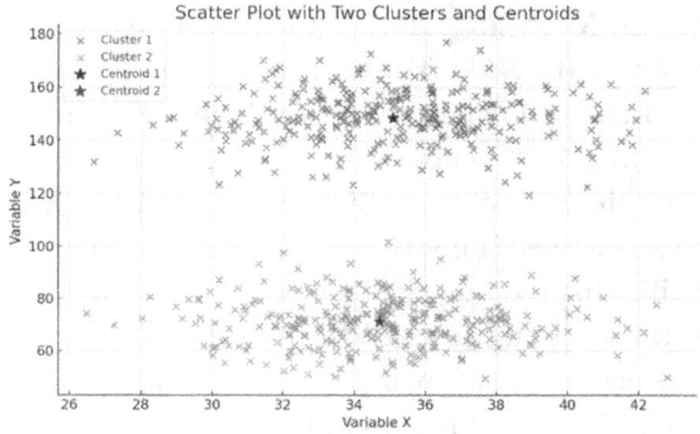

From figure 2, we see how data scientists utilize dimensions of pant leg width (displayed on the x-axis) and pant leg length (on the y-axis) to establish individual data points. These data points are then segmented into two distinct groups. Group 1 is represented in red while Group 2 is shown in blue. Within each group, there is a central point, known as the Centroid, which serves as a key reference. Data scientists use these Centroids to determine the two predominant sizes of pants that the factory should focus on producing.

TOOLS FOR DATA ANALYSIS

In the field of data science, a variety of tools are employed to analyze substantial data volumes. The key stages of data analysis and collection are outlined below:

Data Collection: Data scientists within an organization can directly access internal data sources, subject to authorization. For those requiring public data, such as information from websites or social networks, tools like the Twitter API are useful for extracting data from Twitter (Hernandez-Suarez et al., 2018), and Python Web Scraping is effective for website data extraction (Nigam et al., 2021).

Data Explorationand Preprocessing: Data scientists with a background in digital technology may utilize programming languages like R or Python for data exploration and various data visualizations. These languages are particularly advantageous due to their open-source nature, thus eliminating software costs. Alternatively, data experts may prefer software packages like Microsoft Power

BI, Tableau, or RapidMiner for data exploration. Python can be used for data refinement, merging multiple datasets, and addressing data completeness while RapidMiner facilitates data preparation with built-in models. For simpler data preparation tasks, Microsoft Excel is a viable option.

Data Processing with Data MiningTechniques: Data scientists can opt to program in Python, utilizing libraries for both supervised and unsupervised learning. RapidMiner software supports a wide range of data mining processes and displays results both statistically and visually. Its user-friendliness makes it a popular choice, especially for data scientists with limited programming expertise, facilitating their engagement in data mining tasks.

Data Presentation: In this phase, data scientists can consult data experts to validate the effectiveness of their processing. The results generated through Python or RapidMiner can then be communicated to stakeholders. It is crucial for data scientists to translate these results into insights that answer specific queries. When questions do not necessitate data mining techniques, various software solutions can be employed to develop visual data representations.

Advantages and Limitations of Specialized Data Science Tools: RapidMiner, Python, and R

- **RapidMiner** offers a user-friendly, no-code environment, making it ideal for beginners and business users. Its drag-and-drop interface simplifies data preparation, modeling, and deployment. However, its limited flexibility compared to coding-based tools and higher costs for premium features can be drawbacks for advanced users.
- **Python** is widely used for data science, machine learning, and AI, thanks to its extensive libraries (Pandas, Scikit-learn, TensorFlow). It is highly versatile and scalable, making it suitable for both beginners and experts. However, Python can be slower for computationally heavy tasks compared to compiled languages, and its memory usage can be high when handling large datasets.
- **R** excels in statistical computing and data visualization, with powerful packages like ggplot2 and dplyr. It is particularly favored in academic research and statistical modeling. However, R has a steeper learning curve than Python and may struggle with handling very large datasets due to memory constraints.

Each tool has its strengths, and the choice depends on the project requirements, user expertise, and computational needs. Consequently, this book utilizes RapidMiner software, alongside Python and R, to showcase the practical application of a range of data mining techniques.

CONCLUSION

In conclusion, industries worldwide are recognizing the immense value of employing data mining techniques to address complex business challenges. To fully harness the potential of these techniques, it is essential to cultivate an environment that supports robust data analysis. This includes nurturing the role of data scientists and investing in the necessary software and hardware to process big data efficiently. Data mining techniques are broadly categorized into Supervised Learning, encompassing tasks like numerical classification and forecasting, and Unsupervised Learning, which focuses on identifying correlations and segmentation rules. Among the tools available, RapidMiner has gained prominence for its comprehensive support in every phase of data analysis, enabling data scientists to develop models for data preparation and analysis without the need for extensive programming. Conversely, Python and R programming languages remain integral, especially for aspiring data scientists aiming to enhance their skills and advance to a professional level in this dynamic field.

EXERCISE QUESTIONS

1. Provide an example illustrating how data mining techniques are used across different industries.
2. Outline the challenges associated with scalability in data mining processing.
3. Define Supervised Learning and its significance.
4. Define Unsupervised Learning and its significance.
5. Elaborate on the distinctions between data analysis through programming and utilizing software packages.

REFERENCES

Abdul Aziz, A., & Starkey, A. (2020). Predicting supervise machine learning performances for sentiment analysis using contextual-based approaches. *IEEE Access : Practical Innovations, Open Solutions*, *8*, 17722–17733. DOI: 10.1109/ACCESS.2019.2958702

Almasoud, A. M., Al-Khalifa, H. S., & Al-Salman, A. S. (2019). Handling big data scalability in biological domain using parallel and distributed processing: A case of three biological semantic similarity measures. *BioMed Research International*, *2019*, 1–20. DOI: 10.1155/2019/6750296 PMID: 30809545

Atanasovski, M., Kostov, M., Arapinoski, B., & Spirovski, M. (2020). K-nearest neighbor regression for forecasting electricity demand. *2020 55th International Scientific Conference on Information, Communication and Energy Systems and Technologies (ICEST), 110–113.*

Bell, J. (2015). *Machine learning: Hands-on for developers and technical professionals*. John Wiley & Sons.

Berman, J. J. (2018). *Principles and practice of big data: Preparing, sharing, and analyzing complex information* (2nd ed.). Academic Press/Elsevier.

Bramer, M. (2016). *Principle of data mining* (3rd ed.). Springer-Verlag London Ltd. DOI: 10.1007/978-1-4471-7307-6

Bunjongprasoet, P., & Ramjan, S. (2021). *Prediction road and period of time for road accidents in Bangkok*. Independent Study. College of Innovation: Thammasat University.

Cardona, J. A. S., & Gomez, G. C. H., & Lopez Trujillo, M. (2014). Knowledge discovery process in the open government Colombian model. *2014 9th Computing Colombian Conference (9CCC), 96–102.*

Chiarini, T. M., Kohli, R., & Forsgren, N. (2021). Theories in flux: Reimagining theory building in the age of machine learning. *Management Information Systems Quarterly*, *45*(1), 455–459.

Gupta, A., Sahayadhas, A., & Gupta, V. (2020). Proposed techniques to design speed-efficient data warehouse architecture for fastening knowledge discovery process. *2020 IEEE Third International Conference on Artificial Intelligence and Knowledge Engineering (AIKE),* 200–201. DOI: 10.1109/AIKE48582.2020.00039

Hernandez-Suarez, A., Sanchez-Perez, G., Toscano-Medina, K., Martinez-Hernandez, V., Sanchez, V., & Perez-Meana, H. (2018). A web scraping methodology for bypassing Twitter API restrictions.

Jiang, S., Jiang, T., & Wang, L. (2020). Secure and efficient cloud data deduplication with ownership management. *IEEE Transactions on Services Computing*, *13*(6), 1152–1165.

Kyaw, K. S., & Limsiroratana, S. (2019). Case study: Knowledge discovery process using computation intelligence with feature selection approach. *2019 17th International Conference on ICT and Knowledge Engineering (ICT&KE).*

Lawal, M. M., Ibrahim, H., Sani, N. F. M., & Yaakob, R. (2020). Analyses of indexing techniques on uncertain data with high dimensionality. *IEEE Access : Practical Innovations, Open Solutions*, *8*, 74101–74117. DOI: 10.1109/ACCESS.2020.2988487

Liu, L., & Ding, H. (2011). Modeling China Telecom customer churn prediction based on CRISP-DM. In *2011 International Conference on E-Business and E-Government (ICEE)* (pp. 1–4). IEEE. DOI: 10.1109/ICEBEG.2011.5884504

Liu, Y.-Y., Li, L., Liu, Y.-S., Chan, P.-W., Zhang, W.-H., & Zhang, L. (2021). Estimation of precipitation induced by tropical cyclones based on machine-learning-enhanced analogue identification of numerical prediction. *Meteorological Applications*, *28*(2), e1978. DOI: 10.1002/met.1978

Maslan, A., Mohamad, K. M. B., & Mohd Foozy, F. B. (2020). Feature selection for DDoS detection using classification machine learning techniques. *IAES International Journal of Artificial Intelligence*, *9*(1), 137–145. DOI: 10.11591/ijai.v9.i1.pp137-145

Nigam, H., Biswas, P., Raj, J. S., Iliyasu, A. M., Bestak, R., & Baig, Z. A. (2021). Web scraping: From tools to related legislation and implementation using Python.

Phoha, S., & Ramjan, S. (2023). *Sentiment analysis model for customer classification based on JCI service standards: A case study from Thailand.* Independent Study. College of Innovation: Thammasat University.

Romero, M. P., Parry, J., Prosser, A., Upton, P., Rees, E., Tearne, O., Arnold, M., Chang, Y.-M., Brunton, L. A., Stevens, K., & Drewe, J. A. (2019). Decision tree machine learning applied to bovine tuberculosis risk factors to aid disease control decision making. *Preventive Veterinary Medicine*, 175. PMID: 31812850

Samasiri, P. (2020). Visual representations of different family structures using an interactive data exploration technique. *2020 1st International Conference on Big Data Analytics and Practices (IBDAP), 1–5.*

Shrestha, R. B., Razavi, M., & Prasad, P. W. (2020). An unsupervised machine learning technique for recommendation systems. *2020 5th International Conference on Innovative Technologies in Intelligent Systems and Industrial Applications (CITISIA), 1–9.*

SPSS IncInternational Consortium. (2000). *CRISP-DM 1.0: Free document offers step-by-step guidance for data mining projects*. Business Wire.

Sunkpho, J., & Ramjan, S. (2020). Predicting condominium price in Bangkok using web mining techniques. *Srinakharinwirot Research and Development (Journal of Humanities and Social Sciences), 12*(24).

Tanantong, T. (2021). *Data mining*. Retrieved from https://www.skilllane.com/courses/tuxsa-Data-Mining-Algorithms/chapter

Tanantong, T., & Ramjan, S. (2021). An association rule mining approach to discover demand and supply patterns based on Thai social media data. *International Journal of Knowledge and Systems Science, 12*(2), April–June 2021.

Tanantong, T., & Ramjan, S. (2022). *Data visualization for data science* (1st ed.). Thammasat Press.

Thammasiri, S., & Ramjan, S. (2021). *Corrosion under insulation severity prediction for Carron steel in marine environment using data science methodology*. Independent Study. College of Innovation: Thammasat University.

Chapter 2
Data

ABSTRACT

The initial step for a data scientist when addressing a business question is to identify the data type as not all types can be employed in data mining analyses. Accordingly, the data scientist must select a suitable data type that corresponds to the data mining technique and then classify the data into categorical and continuous types, regardless of the source of the data. Quality control is a significant factor for the data scientist, particularly if data collection is poorly administered or designed, leading to issues like missing values. Once the data scientist has acquired a relevant dataset, they should inspect the outliers associated with each feature to make sure the data are suitable for analysis. Observing outliers through data visualizations, such as scatter plots, is a common practice among data scientists, highlighting the crucial role of data type determination.

INTRODUCTION

While administrators or domain experts in various industries recognize the importance of utilizing data analysis to address organizational challenges and are cognizant of the advancements in data analysis facilitated by data mining techniques, they often struggle to connect the available data with appropriate data processing techniques. In numerous instances, it has been observed that the development of data visualization alone is adequate for addressing questions without necessitating the application of data mining techniques. Conversely, some organizations lack a sufficient amount of data to analyze and effectively respond to posed questions. The primary issue stems from a lack of comprehension among administrators or domain experts within organizations regarding which data can be leveraged and how inquiries should be formulated to yield valuable insights. Many organizations have endeavored to bridge this gap by transforming their domain experts into data scientists, equipping them with a diverse skill set in data analysis. The role of data

DOI: 10.4018/979-8-3693-6001-9.ch002

scientists is indispensable as they possess the ability to utilize existing data for analysis and problem-solving in a timely manner. For instance, in the medical industry, patient data can be utilized to analyze treatments. Therefore, the utilization of data in various forms of data analysis remains a pivotal aspect for students pursuing a career in data science.

ATTRIBUTES

The attributes of the data define the scope of the data object. For example, a data attribute could be gender, with data objects being male, female, or genderless. Data attributes are utilized in various contexts (Inmon and Lindstedt, 2015). When data scientists write programs, data attributes are treated as variables and regarded as features. Data scientists collect data in a dataset comprising features that store multiple records. In data science, these records are referred to as 'instances'. The structure for storing features, data objects, and instances is outlined as follows (Grutter, 2019: Angiulli & Fassetti, 2021).

Table 1. Examples of feature, data object, and instance

First Name	Last Name
Jirapon	Sunkpho
Sarawut	Ramjan
Kom	Campiranon

In Table 1, there are a total of two features, namely the first name and last name. The first name features include Jirapon, Sarawut, and Kom while the last name features consist of Sunkpho, Ramjan, and Campiranon, respectively. When data objects from multiple features are combined, they form instances. From Table 1, there are three instances comprising Jirapon Sunkpho, Sarawut Ramjan, and Kom Campiranon, respectively.

Data Dimensionality refers to the number of features within a dataset (Li, Horiguchi, and Sawaragi, 2020). In data science, the emphasis lies in analyzing data across diverse fields without initially focusing on data storage. The number of dimensions poses a significant consideration for data scientists as they must select only those features conducive to the analysis. Consequently, data scientists aim to diminish the number of dimensions, ensuring they retain only the features essential for data analysis. This approach enables data scientists to streamline the processing of extensive datasets, thereby reducing both time and digital resource requirements.

Resolution serves as a metric utilized to store data objects within each feature. In the realm of data science (Wang et al., 2019), data scientists frequently encounter challenges when collecting datasets from diverse sources, particularly regarding the uniform storage of identical data across various measures. For instance, the feature "height" in dataset A may be recorded in centimeters whereas the same feature in dataset B might be documented in inches. Hence, prior to integrating these datasets, data scientists must engage in Attribute Transformation, altering the format of data objects to conform to a standardized form.

Feature Engineering is the process of selecting, transforming, and creating new features (variables) from raw data to improve a machine learning model's performance (Li, 2024). It involves techniques such as scaling, encoding categorical variables, handling missing values, dimensionality reduction, and feature extraction to enhance the model's ability to learn patterns effectively. Well-engineered features can significantly boost predictive accuracy, making feature engineering a crucial step in data preprocessing.

Data Augmentation is a technique used to artificially increase the size and diversity of a dataset by applying transformations to existing data (Kim et al., 2024). It is commonly used in machine learning and deep learning, especially in computer vision and natural language processing (NLP), to improve model generalization and prevent overfitting. In image processing, data augmentation techniques include rotation, flipping, cropping, scaling, adding noise, and color adjustments. In NLP, methods such as synonym replacement, back-translation, and word shuffling are used to generate variations of text data. For tabular data, augmentation may involve synthetic data generation using techniques like SMOTE (Synthetic Minority Oversampling Technique) for handling class imbalances. By increasing the variability of training data without collecting new samples, data augmentation helps models become more robust and perform better on unseen data.

Ethical concerns play a crucial role in data analysis, as they directly impact data quality and model reliability (Bataineh et al., 2024). Two key ethical challenges in data attributes are bias in data and data privacy protection, both of which influence the fairness and integrity of analytical models.

- **Bias in Data** occurs when datasets reflect imbalanced, incomplete, or prejudiced representations of reality, leading to skewed outcomes in predictive modeling (Parkavi et al., 2018). This bias can arise from historical inequalities, sampling errors, or algorithmic reinforcement of societal prejudices. If left unaddressed, biased data can result in unfair decision-making, particularly in areas such as hiring, lending, and healthcare. Methods to mitigate bias include data balancing, diverse data collection, and bias-aware machine learning techniques to ensure models produce fairer and more representative insights.

- **Data Privacy Protection** is another significant concern in data-driven analysis. As organizations collect and process vast amounts of personal information, ensuring compliance with data protection regulations such as GDPR and PDPA is essential. Sensitive data must be handled with caution to prevent unauthorized access, identity exposure, or misuse (Du, 2021). Techniques such as data anonymization, encryption, and access control mechanisms help safeguard privacy while maintaining the analytical value of the dataset.

To enhance the robustness of data analysis, it is recommended to integrate ethical data handling practices into every stage of data processing. Additionally, real-world case studies can be included to illustrate how ethical considerations impact data quality and model accuracy, providing a more comprehensive perspective on the role of ethical responsibility in data-driven decision-making

DATA TYPE

Various data mining and visualization techniques rely on different types of data, which can either be a single type or a combination of multiple types. Analyzing data to determine compatibility with specific data mining techniques and to address predetermined inquiries poses a significant challenge for data scientists. Data can generally be categorized into two types.

1. CATEGORIAL DATA

Categorical data refers to counted data which is treated as quantitative data without continuity. It encompasses both nominal scales and ordinal scales, each serving distinct purposes (Van et al., 2005).

A nominal scale represents data collected in groupings (Andrews and Messenger, 1973), such as gender, including female, male, and other genders. When data scientists employ a nominal scale in data analysis, they can compare data within the nominal scale; for instance, comparing males and females, as illustrated in the example.

Figure 1. Example of data visualization with a nominal scale

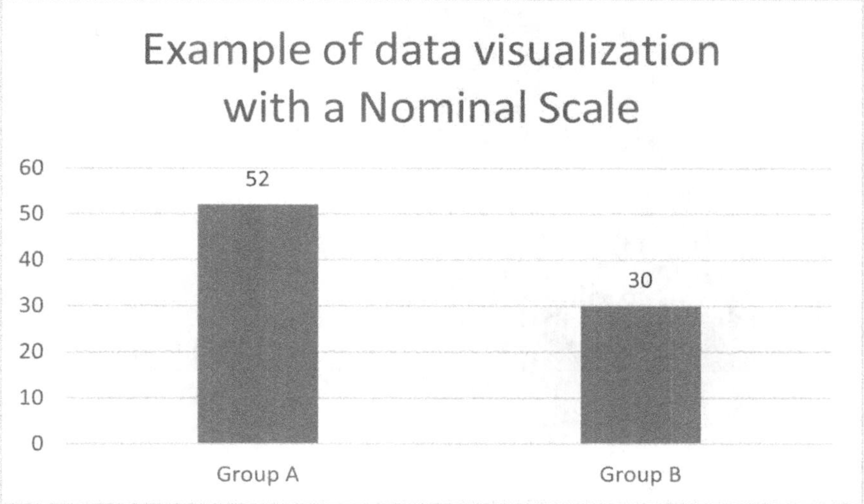

As depicted in Figure 1, data scientists can utilize nominal scales to describe data using the mode, which represents the most frequently occurring data point. For instance, within a range of 0-5, a mode of 3 indicates that the number 3 is the most commonly chosen. Similarly, within a range of 6-10, a mode of 7 suggests that the number 7 is the most frequently chosen. However, it is important to note that data scientists should refrain from performing arithmetic operations such as addition, subtraction, multiplication, division, or averaging on nominal scale data. For instance, interpreting 7.5 males makes no practical sense in data analysis since it is impossible to have a fraction of a person in reality. Additionally, assigning numerical values to letters does not confer them with meaningful numerical properties for calculation purposes. For instance, if Bang Rak District is assigned the value of No. 1 and Sathorn District is assigned the value of No. 2, then adding 1 and 2 to get 3 holds no significance in data interpretation. However, nominal scale data can often be utilized effectively alongside other data types in visualizing data as exemplified below.

Figure 2. An example of the application of a nominal scale with other data

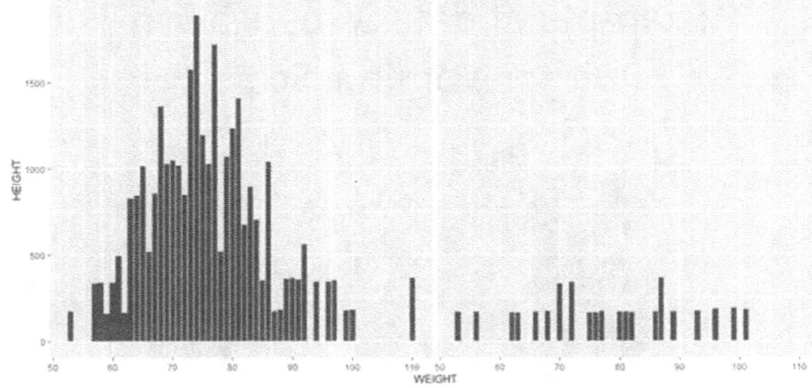

As illustrated in the Figure 2, the nominal scale pertains to the survival and mortality rates of smokers, visualized through a histogram displaying the range of the living and deceased on the x-axis, and the frequency of each on the y-axis.

An ordinal scale involves abstractions represented by ordinal numbers (Yager, 2020). Intention, for instance, is an individual's emotional state. Data scientists can represent this emotion using a Likert Scale ranging from 1 to 5. For example, "no intention to buy" is denoted by 1, while "probably buying" is indicated by 2, with the intensity of buying intent ranging from weak (1) to intense (5). When emotions are represented numerically, data scientists can draw conclusions accordingly. However, it is important to note that if respondents predominantly select number 4, it does not translate into an average value of their emotion. Additionally, interpreting a value like 4.5 as indicative of the level of purchase intention is not meaningful. Nonetheless, data scientists can apply ordinal scales, such as supervised-learning techniques such as regression in data analysis to address predetermined problems; for example, determining whether the purchase intention for product A significantly influences the purchase intention for product B.

2. Continuous Data

Continuous data, as defined by Mesner and Shalizi (2021), refers to a type of streaming data that can take any value within a given range. It is measured and can have an infinite number of possible values between any two points. These types of data allow for the calculation of averages, such as the average salary of employees who have been with the company for more than five years. Data scientists can create visualizations from continuous data as depicted below.

Figure 3. Example of visualization from continuous data

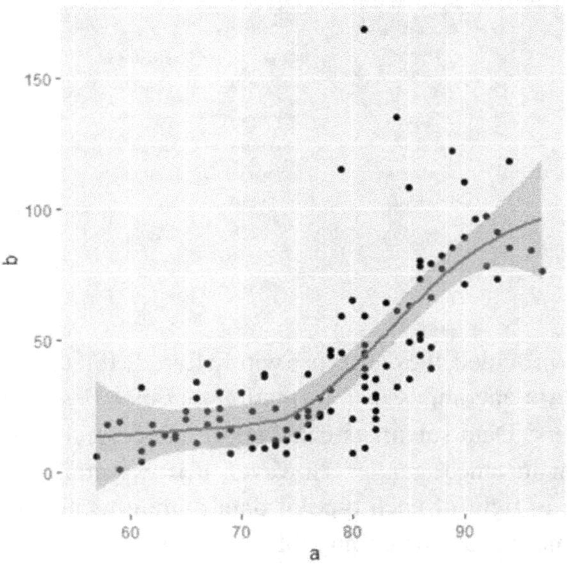

As shown in Figure 3, data scientists generate a scatter plot from continuous data wherein the data along the a-axis represents temperature while the b-axis represents the quantity of ozone. Both sets of data consist of real numbers. Whether the initial data imported by the data scientist originates from categorical or continuous data sources, it is imperative for the data scientist to consider the objectives of the data analysis. Subsequently, appropriate mining techniques can be selected for analyzing the data, and the desired data can be extracted accordingly.

DEFINITION OF DATA TYPES WITHIN THE RAPIDMINER SOFTWARE

This book utilizes RapidMiner software as a tool to experiment with data analysis using various data mining techniques. According to academic classification, data is categorized into categorical data and continuous data. However, RapidMiner provides a method for defining each data type as follows.

Figure 4. Examples of data types within RapidMiner

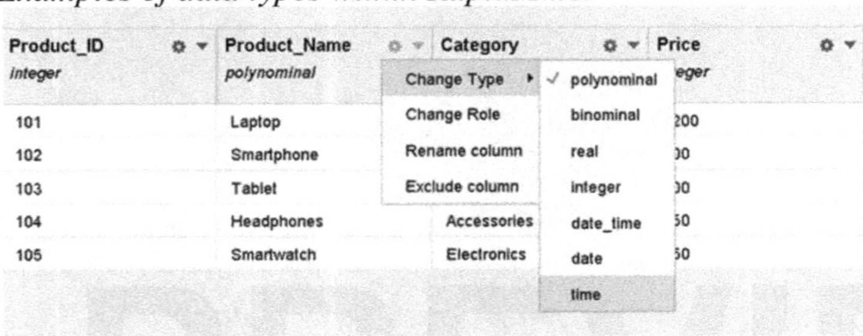

In the example provided, the data types within RapidMiner are divided as follows:

Polynomial data encompasses information that includes both alphabetic characters and numbers. Data scientists can import categorical data and designate it as polynomial, for instance, gender. However, it is essential for data scientists to consider the data in light of each type of data mining technique. Alphabetic and integer data may not always be compatible with the same data mining techniques, even if designated as polynomial.

Binomial data represents a type of data with only two values; "No" can be represented by the number 0, while "Yes" can be represented by the number 1.

Real data comprises real numbers such as temperature, height, or distance. Nonetheless, certain data analysis techniques can analyze both continuous and categorical data, such as linear regression. Examples of such analyses include the examination of correlations between different variables using an ordinal scale analysis, and forecasting outcomes for data with two or more variables through real data analysis.

Integer data consists of whole numbers. Data scientists must exercise caution not to convert letters into integer numbers during quantitative data analysis.

Date_time refers to a period of time, including day, month, year, and duration.

Date denotes specific calendar dates, including day, month, and year.

Time signifies a duration of time.

All Date_time, Date, and Time data are employed in analyzing time-controlled data, such as the Time Series technique. Hence, accurately determining these data types will influence the selection of appropriate techniques and also impact the development of data visualization.

DATA QUALITY

To effectively utilize data mining techniques, it is crucial that the dataset meets the necessary qualifications for analysis. While data mining techniques serve as processing tools, data scientists must meticulously assess and prepare the data, considering its quality across various dimensions to ensure accurate results.

Bias Effective data analysis methods are essential to reducing bias in sample selection (Carlson, Livermore, and Rockmore, 2020). In Thailand, state-owned energy enterprises oversee public data, requiring random sampling to assess citizens' needs or government satisfaction. However, sampling only Bangkok residents can introduce bias, making the data unrepresentative. To mitigate this, population proportions must be considered; for example, Chiang Mai's population density differs from Loei's, making equal sampling across provinces inaccurate. Additionally, discrepancies between sample proportions and actual data, such as overestimating debt default rates, can distort findings.

An outlier is a data point that differs significantly from other observations in a dataset (Li et al., 2019; Jyothi et al., 2020). Outliers can occur due to various reasons such as measurement errors, experimental variability, or genuine deviations in the data. These data points are often considered unusual or abnormal because they fall outside the typical range of values observed in the dataset. Outliers can potentially impact the results of statistical analyses or machine learning models, leading to misleading conclusions if not properly identified and addressed. Detecting and handling outliers is an essential step in data analysis to ensure the accuracy and reliability of the findings.

Figure 5. Exploring data objects that are outliers

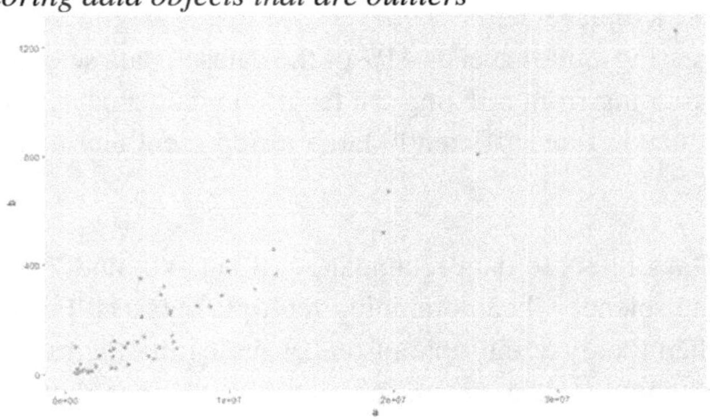

As depicted in Figure 5, the scatter plot utilizes data objects derived from the feature (Shao, et al., 2017). The total population is represented on the x-axis while the features displaying the number of murders are shown on the y-axis. When examining visual data, data scientists should initially ascertain whether a value truly represents an outlier by consulting data experts. This verification process helps confirm whether the value is indeed abnormal or divergent from the majority of data points, thereby reducing the risk of data entry errors.

A Missing Value, in the context of data analysis, refers to a data point that is absent or undefined in a dataset (Montesdeoca et al., 2019). Missing values can occur for various reasons, such as data entry errors, equipment malfunction, or the nature of the data collection process. When dealing with missing values, data analysts must decide how to handle them appropriately as they can impact the accuracy and reliability of statistical analyses or machine learning models. Common approaches to handling missing values include imputation, where missing values are replaced with estimated values based on other observations, or exclusion, where observations with missing values are removed from the analysis altogether. The choice of approach depends on the nature of the data and the specific objectives of the analysis. Once a missing value occurs, data scientists can adopt one of three approaches:

A. When the missing value comprises between 0 and 14% of the dataset, data scientists may choose to remove the instance containing the missing value.
B. If the missing value accounts for between 15 and 40% of the dataset, data scientists can opt to replace the missing values with estimated data. For continuous features, the mean value derived from calculating all data objects can be used to replace the missing value. However, data scientists must consider the type of data before calculating the amended value, ensuring that the average value is not used as a replacement.
C. When the missing value exceeds 41% of the dataset, data scientists should contemplate refraining from utilizing the feature in data analysis. This is because the dataset may not be sufficiently large to represent any meaningful data in the analysis.

Duplicate Data refers to data redundancy (Song, Yu, and Bao, 2019), which can occur in data science when combining multiple datasets. For instance, duplication arises when there are multiple instances indicating the same data, with the only difference being the data owner's email address. When data scientists merge identical data collected from different datasets, duplication occurs. In such cases, data scientists undertake data preparation processes to minimize data redundancy.

Inconsistent Data refers to inaccurate data (Johnny and Trovati, 2020). Instances of inconsistency can occur when users input incorrect information, such as using negative numbers for human height or making typographical errors in names. To mitigate such occurrences, designing an online form that alerts users to potential misinformation before submission can be effective. This proactive approach helps to prevent inaccurate data entry from the outset.

BRIDGING DATA TYPES AND DATA MINING: UNLOCKING THE POWER OF STRUCTURED ANALYSIS

Understanding data types is a foundational pillar in data mining, as different types of data require distinct analytical approaches to extract meaningful insights effectively. The ability to recognize and preprocess these data types correctly determines the success of data-driven decision-making and the overall efficiency of machine learning models.

A. The Impact of Data Types on Data Mining Techniques, numerical data (e.g., temperature, sales figures, or age) is best suited for techniques like statistical analysis, linear regression, and clustering, enabling pattern recognition and predictive modeling. Categorical data (e.g., customer segments or order status) requires preprocessing techniques such as One-Hot Encoding or Label Encoding, ensuring compatibility with machine learning algorithms like Decision Trees and Naïve Bayes Classification. Ordinal data (e.g., satisfaction levels or educational rankings) holds ordered relationships but lacks precise numerical distances; therefore, analytical techniques such as Logistic Regression and Decision Trees effectively accommodate these structured hierarchies. Meanwhile, text data (e.g., customer reviews or social media posts) demands Natural Language Processing (NLP) methods, including tokenization, sentiment analysis, and entity recognition, to extract valuable insights from unstructured content. Understanding these data types and their respective processing techniques is essential for optimizing the accuracy and efficiency of data-driven models.
B. Transforming Raw Data into a Goldmine for Data Mining, data transformation involves converting raw, heterogeneous data into structured formats, enhancing interpretability and model performance. Equally important, data cleaning addresses missing values and outliers, ensuring reliability and preventing distortions in predictive modeling. Additionally, dimensionality reduction techniques, such as Principal Component Analysis (PCA), streamline high-dimensional datasets, improving computational efficiency and model generalization. Together, these

processes optimize data quality, enabling more accurate and efficient data-driven analysis.

C. Aligning Data Mining Techniques with Data Types for Maximum Impact, for continuous numerical data, techniques like regression analysis and clustering uncover trends and segmentations, enabling deeper insights into patterns and relationships. For categorical data, classification models such as Decision Trees and Naïve Bayes facilitate robust pattern recognition, ensuring accurate categorization and decision-making. Meanwhile, for complex data structures like text or images, deep learning methodologies—including Neural Networks and Convolutional Networks—extract intricate patterns beyond the capabilities of traditional analytical approaches, enhancing predictive accuracy and feature extraction.

By mastering the intricate relationships between data types and mining techniques, data scientists can unlock unprecedented levels of insight and predictive power. The synergy between these elements is the key to transforming raw data into strategic intelligence, fueling breakthroughs in business, research, and artificial intelligence.

CASES FROM THE AUTHOR'S RESEARCH

1. The Prediction Condominium Price in Bangkok Using Web Mining Techniques (Sunkpho & Ramjan, 2020)

The sales rate of condominiums in Bangkok, Thailand, particularly among Generation Y and condominium speculators, is notably high. Buyers employ various criteria, such as proximity to sky train or subway stations, and the price of condominiums, which impact both their purchase decision and subsequent selling price. Additionally, the urban environment surrounding the condominium project is a crucial variable influencing pricing considerations. Consequently, the researcher focuses on identifying variables conducive to forecasting condominium prices accurately, tailored to the city's characteristics. This entails defining control variables related to Bangkok condominium pricing. The research methodology involved several stages. First, data collection utilizes Web Crawling from hipflat.co.th, encompassing a comprehensive dataset of 1,465 condominiums with 15 attributes. Subsequently, data exploration, employing correlation analysis, identified the key attributes impacting pricing, including proximity to transportation hubs, return on investment, and rental rate changes. Data preparation involved addressing missing values, with manipulation techniques applied to ensure data integrity. Data modeling utilized five different techniques, with deep learning emerging as the most accurate in forecasting condominium prices. Notably, adjustments were made to enhance efficiency, including the integration of Discretized Process and Distance Measure models. The research identified significant variables influencing condominium prices, such as the construction completion year, the number of floors, the proximity to transportation, and the status of the project owner.

2. Analyzing Factors Influencing Safety Behaviors Among Thai Flight Crews: A Supervised Machine Learning Approach (Maneechaeye & Ramjan, 2022)

While air travel is generally considered the safest mode of transportation, accidents can still occur due to various factors, including pilot error. Adhering strictly to aviation standards is crucial in mitigating the risk of such human errors. This research endeavored to investigate the determinants of safe piloting behavior across organizational, squadron, and individual levels. Qualitative data collection, facilitated by domain experts, offered insights into the overall state of aviation safety in Thailand and instances of pilot behavior deviating from established standards. Drawing upon expert recommendations and existing literature, the researchers developed a questionnaire tool, resulting in a dataset comprising 610 instances. Through exploratory factor analysis, 15 features were categorized into four factors: safety climate, knowledge of aviation safety standards, motivation for safe operation, and pilot compliance with aviation standards. Multiple regression analysis was employed to examine the variables influencing pilot behavior with the dataset split into training and testing sets to evaluate model accuracy. The analysis revealed significant effects of safety climate, knowledge of safety standards, and motivation on pilots' compliance with aviation standards, as evidenced by the mean absolute error (MAE) of 0.47, the mean square error (MSE) of 0.42, the root mean square error (RMSE) of 0.65, and the R-squared value of 0.62.

CONCLUSION

The dataset consists of various features, each of which stores data objects internally. Within each dataset, multiple instances can be found. When utilizing such data for analysis with data mining techniques, data scientists must initially assess the data to determine its type. Different data mining techniques necessitate the use of specific data types. Moreover, for certain types of issues, data visualization alone may suffice without employing data mining techniques. Nevertheless, even in the development of data visualization, data scientists must understand the data types to present the data effectively and to address the identified questions.

EXERCISES AND QUESTIONS

1. Define and provide examples of categorical data.
2. Define and provide examples of continuous data.
3. What types of data can continuous data be defined as in RapidMiner software?
4. Discuss biased data and provide examples.
5. Describe outliers in data objects.

REFERENCES

Andrews, F. M., & Messenger, R. C. (1973). *Multivariate nominal scale analysis: A report on a new analysis technique and a computer program*. University of Michigan.

Angiulli, F., & Fassetti, F. (2021). Uncertain distance-based outlier detection with arbitrarily shaped data objects. *Journal of Intelligent Information Systems*, *57*(1), 1–24. DOI: 10.1007/s10844-020-00624-7

Bataineh, A. Q., Mushtaha, A. S., Abu-AlSondos, I. A., Aldulaimi, S. H., & Abdeldayem, M. (2024). Ethical & legal concerns of artificial intelligence in the healthcare sector. In *2024 ASU International Conference in Emerging Technologies for Sustainability and Intelligent Systems (ICETSIS)* (pp. 491–495). IEEE. DOI: 10.1109/ICETSIS61505.2024.10459438

Carlson, K., Livermore, M. A., & Rockmore, D. N. (2020). The problem of data bias in the pool of published U.S. appellate court opinions. *Journal of Empirical Legal Studies*, *17*(2), 224–261. DOI: 10.1111/jels.12253

Du, J. (2021). Research on enterprise information security and privacy protection in big data environment. In *2021 3rd International Conference on Machine Learning, Big Data and Business Intelligence (MLBDBI)* (pp. 324–327). IEEE. DOI: 10.1109/MLBDBI54094.2021.00067

Grütter, R. (2019). A framework for assisted proximity analysis in feature data. *Journal of Geographical Systems*, *21*(3), 367–394. DOI: 10.1007/s10109-019-00304-3

Inmon, W. H., & Lindstedt, D. (2015). *Data architecture: A primer for the data scientist—Big data, data warehouse, and data vault*. Morgan Kaufmann/Elsevier.

Johnny, O., & Trovati, M. (2020). Big data inconsistencies and incompleteness: A literature review. *International Journal of Grid and Utility Computing*, *5*(5), 705. DOI: 10.1504/IJGUC.2020.110057

Jyothi, P. N., Lakshmi, D. R., & Rao, K. V. S. N. R. (2020). A supervised approach for detection of outliers in healthcare claims data. *Journal of Engineering Science & Technology Review*, *13*(1), 204–213. DOI: 10.25103/jestr.131.25

Kim, W., Yeo, K. M., Jeong, W. C., Park, S. H., Park, J. D., & Moon, Y. B. (2024). Masked background and object image-based data augmentation method. In *2024 15th International Conference on Information and Communication Technology Convergence (ICTC)* (pp. 1329–1331). IEEE. DOI: 10.1109/ICTC62082.2024.10827114

Li, J., Horiguchi, Y., & Sawaragi, T. (2020). Data dimensionality reduction by introducing structural equation modeling to machine learning problems. In *2020 59th Annual Conference of the Society of Instrument and Control Engineers of Japan (SICE)* (pp. 826–831). IEEE. DOI: 10.23919/SICE48898.2020.9240323

Li, K., Li, J., Liu, S., Li, Z., Bo, J., & Liu, B. (2019). GA-iForest: An efficient isolated forest framework based on genetic algorithm for numerical data outlier detection. *Transactions of Nanjing University of Aeronautics & Astronautics*, *36*(6), 1026–1038.

Li, Z. (2024). A feature engineering strategy for data-driven predictive models of educational building's electricity consumption. In *2024 7th International Conference on Advanced Algorithms and Control Engineering (ICAACE)* (pp. 542–546). IEEE. DOI: 10.1109/ICAACE61206.2024.10549389

Maneechaeye, P., & Ramjan, S. (2023). Analyzing factors influencing safety behaviors among Thai flight crews: A supervised machine learning approach. *15th National Conference on Administration and Management.*

Mesner, O. C., & Shalizi, C. R. (2021). Conditional mutual information estimation for mixed, discrete, and continuous data. *IEEE Transactions on Information Theory*, *67*(1), 464–484. DOI: 10.1109/TIT.2020.3024886

Montesdeoca, B., Luengo, J., Maillo, J., García-Gil, D., García, S., & Herrera, F. (2019). A first approach on big data missing values imputation. *IoTBDS 2019 - Proceedings of the 4th International Conference on Internet of Things, Big Data and Security*, 315–323.

Parkavi, A., Jawaid, A., Dev, S., & M. S., V. (2018). The patterns that don't exist: Study on the effects of psychological human biases in data analysis and decision making. In *2018 3rd International Conference on Computational Systems and Information Technology for Sustainable Solutions (CSITSS)* (pp. 193–197). IEEE. DOI: 10.1109/CSITSS.2018.8768554

Shao, L., Mahajan, A., Schreck, T., & Lehmann, D. J. (2017). Interactive regression lens for exploring scatter plots. *Computer Graphics Forum*, *36*(3), 157–166. DOI: 10.1111/cgf.13176

Song, J., Yu, Q., & Bao, R. (2019). The detection algorithms for similar duplicate data. In *2019 6th International Conference on Systems and Informatics (ICSAI)* (pp. 1534–1542). IEEE. DOI: 10.1109/ICSAI48974.2019.9010154

Sunkpho, J., & Ramjan, S. (2020). Predicting condominium price in Bangkok using web mining technique. *Srinakharinwirot Research and Development (Journal of Humanities and Social Sciences), 12*(24).

Wang, J., Sato, K., Guo, S., Chen, W., & Wu, J. (2019). Big data processing with minimal delay and guaranteed data resolution in disaster areas. *IEEE Transactions on Vehicular Technology*, *68*(4), 3833–3842. DOI: 10.1109/TVT.2018.2889094

Yager, R. R. (2020). Ordinal scale-based uncertainty models for AI. *Information Fusion*, *64*, 92–98. DOI: 10.1016/j.inffus.2020.06.010

Chapter 3
Data Pre-Processing and an Example of Data Classification With RapidMiner

ABSTRACT

In this book, the focus is on data mining with RapidMiner. However, it is important to note that there are other essential steps to consider when delving into the realm of data mining. This chapter serves as an introduction to the process of data pre-processing using RapidMiner, allowing readers to practice with a dataset example available on the platform. With RapidMiner, data pre-processing begins with exploring the data visually and then selecting the features that will be analyzed with each data mining technique. Managing missing values in a feature is also a crucial step in this process, which can be achieved by either removing them or replacing them with appropriate values. In addition, RapidMiner allows data scientists to detect outliers and normalize features easily using diagram design without requiring any computer programming skills. To help readers become familiar with the tools offered by RapidMiner, a classification technique will be demonstrated step-by-step.

INTRODUCTION

RapidMiner is a comprehensive tool that supports the entire data science workflow (Mat, Lajis & Nasir, 2018). Data scientists utilize RapidMiner software to import datasets, preparing them for analysis using a variety of data mining techniques (Dai et al., 2016; Samsani, 2016; Phan, Wu & Phan, 2021). In managing missing values and outliers, data scientists have access to a range of data mining models, including

DOI: 10.4018/979-8-3693-6001-9.ch003

both supervised and unsupervised learning methods (Cai et al., 2016; Mandhare & Idate, 2017; Susanti & Azizah, 2017; Abu-Soud, 2019). The software allows for the creation of processing algorithms through model connections, eliminating the need for extensive computer programming. As a result, scientists can easily modify models at each step and conduct reprocessing to enhance processing accuracy. Data Pre-Processing is a crucial step that directly impacts the accuracy and efficiency of Machine Learning and Deep Learning models. Raw data often contains issues such as missing values, outliers, or imbalanced distributions, which can lead to incorrect learning and unreliable model outcomes. Proper data preparation helps reduce model complexity by selecting relevant features (Feature Selection) and reducing dimensionality (Dimensionality Reduction), allowing models to learn faster and lowering computational costs. Additionally, techniques such as normalization and standardization enable models using Gradient Descent to find optimal parameters more efficiently while minimizing bias or overfitting caused by imbalanced or noisy data. Effective Data Pre-Processing also ensures that model results are reliable and can be practically applied in business and research contexts, where accurate data analysis is essential. Most importantly, this process serves as the foundation for all Data Science techniques. Skipping this step can result in ineffective models that are difficult to apply in real-world scenarios. Therefore, readers should thoroughly understand Data Pre-Processing before exploring more advanced models to ensure proper data handling before feeding it into complex machine learning architectures.

DATA PRE-PROCESSING

Data pre-processing is a crucial step in the data analysis pipeline that involves cleaning, transforming, and organizing raw data into a format suitable for analysis. It is often considered the foundation of any data science project as the quality of the data directly impacts the accuracy and reliability of the analysis and the insights derived from it.

The key aspects of data pre-processing

A. **Data Cleaning** involves identifying and rectifying errors or inconsistencies in the dataset. Common tasks include handling missing values (imputation), removing duplicates, correcting inaccuracies, and dealing with outliers. Cleaning the data ensures that it is accurate and reliable for analysis.
B. **Data Transformation** involves converting the raw data into a suitable format for analysis. This may include normalization, where numerical data is scaled to a standard range, and encoding categorical variables into numerical equivalents.

Other transformations include feature scaling, log transformation, and handling skewed distributions to make the data more conducive to analysis.

C. **Feature Selection/Extraction**: In many datasets, there may be a large number of features (variables), some of which may be redundant or irrelevant for analysis. Feature selection involves identifying the most relevant features for the analysis while discarding unnecessary ones. Feature extraction, on the other hand, involves creating new features from existing ones to capture important information more effectively.
D. **Data Integration** involves combining data from multiple sources into a unified dataset for analysis. This may require resolving inconsistencies in naming conventions, data formats, and data structures across different datasets.
E. **Data Reduction**: In cases where the dataset is large and complex, data reduction techniques such as dimensionality reduction may be applied to reduce the number of variables while preserving as much information as possible. This can help to improve the efficiency of analysis and reduce computational overhead.
F. **Data Discretization** involves converting continuous data into discrete intervals or categories. This can simplify analysis and make the data easier to interpret, particularly in the context of machine learning algorithms that require categorical input.

Overall, data pre-processing plays a critical role in ensuring that the data is clean, consistent, and appropriately formatted for analysis. By addressing issues such as missing values, outliers, and irrelevant features, pre-processing lays the groundwork for accurate and meaningful insights to be derived from the data.

Comparing RapidMiner, Python, and R for Data Pre-Processing: Strengths and Limitations

Data pre-processing is a critical step in data science, ensuring that raw data is cleaned, transformed, and prepared for analysis or modeling. RapidMiner, Python, and R are three widely used tools for data pre-processing, each with unique strengths and limitations (Dubey, Jain, Gautam, & Sonare, 2024) Choosing the right tool depends on the specific use case, level of programming expertise, and project complexity. Below is a comparative analysis of these tools based on their capabilities in handling data pre-processing tasks.

A. Ease of Use and Learning Curve
    - **RapidMiner** designed for ease of use, RapidMiner provides a drag-and-drop interface, making it ideal for non-programmers or business users who want to process data without writing code. Users can select

pre-processing operators and visualize their workflows, reducing the need for extensive technical knowledge.

- **Python**, while Python is user-friendly for programmers, requires coding proficiency. Data pre-processing involves using libraries like pandas, numpy, and scikit-learn, making it more flexible but requiring manual scripting (Jafari, 2022). Beginners might face a steep learning curve if they are unfamiliar with Python's syntax.
- **R** is a statistical programming language with a strong emphasis on data manipulation and visualization. Data pre-processing in R relies on packages like dplyr, tidyr, and caret, requiring knowledge of R's functional programming paradigm. While powerful for statisticians, it may not be as intuitive for those unfamiliar with coding.

B. Handling Missing Data and Data Cleansing

- RapidMiner, provides built-in data cleansing operators such as handling missing values, replacing outliers, and normalizing data. These can be applied with simple drag-and-drop actions, making it highly accessible for beginners.
- Python, uses functions like fillna() in pandas for missing values and dropna() for removing null values. Python allows more customization but requires writing scripts to handle missing data efficiently.
- R provides na.omit() for removing missing values and impute() for filling in missing data. R is particularly useful when dealing with complex statistical imputation techniques, making it better suited for researchers and statisticians.

C. Feature Engineering and Transformation

- **RapidMiner** offers a set of built-in feature selection and transformation operators, allowing users to create new variables and transform existing data easily. It provides automated solutions for feature selection, making it useful for those who want an efficient and quick solution without manual coding.
- Python uses scikit-learn for feature selection and transformation (e.g., StandardScaler for normalization). Python allows for complex feature engineering but requires in-depth knowledge of libraries and coding techniques.
- R uses mutate() and select() from the dplyr package for feature engineering. R is strong in statistical transformations, making it preferable for domains requiring advanced transformations, such as econometrics or bioinformatics (Santos, 2023).

A. Scalability and Large Dataset Handling

- **RapidMiner** can handle medium-sized datasets well but struggles with very large datasets unless optimized with external databases or distributed computing frameworks. Performance can slow down when processing millions of rows.
- **Python** with pandas and numpy, Python can handle moderately large datasets, but for truly big data, it requires integration with Dask, Spark, or SQL-based solutions. Python offers better scalability compared to RapidMiner.
- **R** struggles with large datasets in RAM-intensive operations but provides workarounds like data.table for faster data manipulation. However, it is generally less efficient for big data compared to Python.

B. Data Visualization and Pre-Processing Monitoring

- RapidMiner allows users to visualize transformations through its graphical interface. However, its built-in visualization tools are limited compared to R and Python, and more advanced visualizations require external tools.
- Python uses matplotlib and seaborn for customizable visualizations. Python provides more flexibility in plotting data at various pre-processing stages.
- R has ggplot2, one of the most powerful data visualization tools, allowing for detailed exploratory data analysis (EDA) before and after pre-processing. R is best for statistical visualizations.

C. Automation and Integration with Machine Learning Models

- RapidMiner provides automated pre-processing pipelines that can be directly integrated with machine learning models without requiring coding (Bilal et al., 2022). It is particularly useful for business users and beginners who want a streamlined process.
- Python requires manual scripting but offers greater flexibility and control over data pipelines. Users can integrate custom pre-processing functions into machine learning models using scikit-learn.
- R provides automated pipelines via caret but is primarily focused on statistical learning rather than AI-driven automation.

Ultimately, RapidMiner is the best choice for users who prioritize ease of use, automation, and workflow visualization, while Python and R offer greater flexibility for users who prefer coding and deeper customization in data pre-processing tasks.

DATA PRE-PROCESSING USING RAPIDMINER SOFTWARE

To import datasets into a data mining model using RapidMiner software, data scientists have the option to manipulate the data using Microsoft Excel. For instance, Attribute Transformation can be conducted to modify the structure of the data before importing it into RapidMiner software. Additionally, operators within RapidMiner can also be selected. An experiment can be carried out to prepare the data in the following manner:

Figure 1. Using the Titanic sample dataset

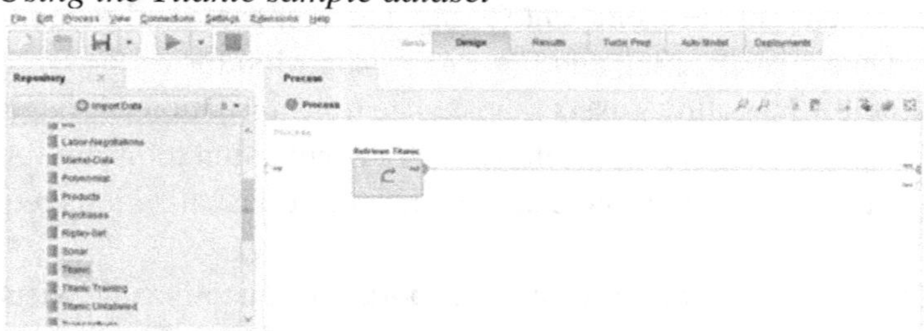

Data scientists have the option to utilize the **Titanic** sample dataset for experimentation. Once the dataset is imported into the process, users can connect the dataset's output to the Result section and execute the model. The resulting outcome is as follows:

Figure 2. Titanic dataset details

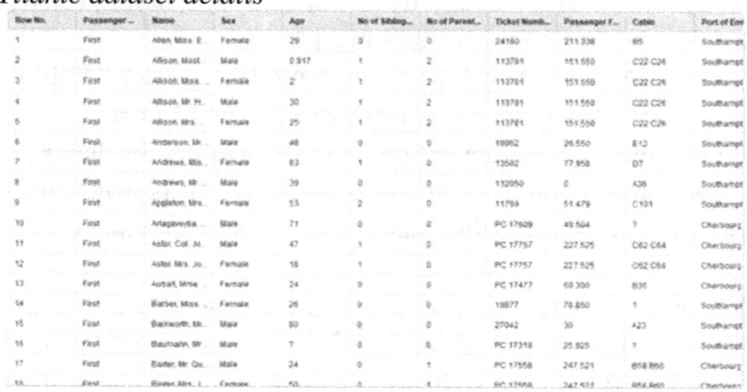

As observed in the dataset details, there are 1,309 records and missing values are evident within the dataset. In RapidMiner, missing values are represented by a question mark. When data scientists access the **Age** statistics section, it provides details about the missing values as depicted below.

Figure 3. The missing value details of age

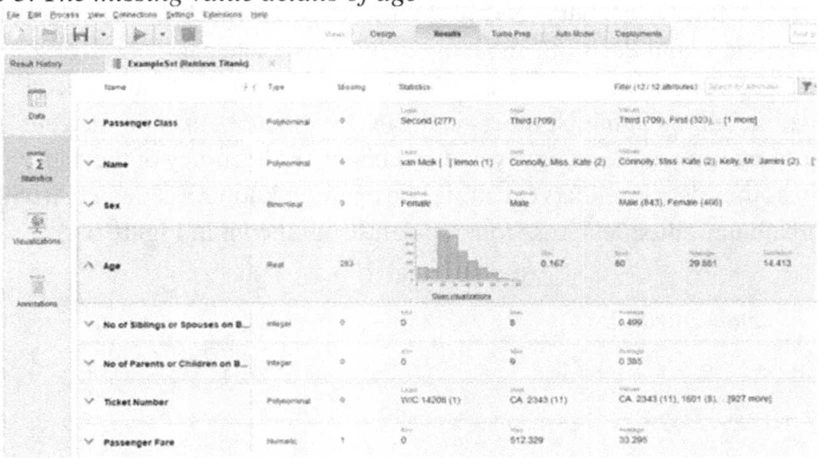

When examining the **Age** variable, it is noted that there are 263 missing values. However, **Age** is an essential attribute for data analysis. Data scientists must address the missing values using various techniques. Subsequently, they can click on the "**Open Visualizations**" button to display the visual information as depicted below.

Figure 4. Visualization of age data

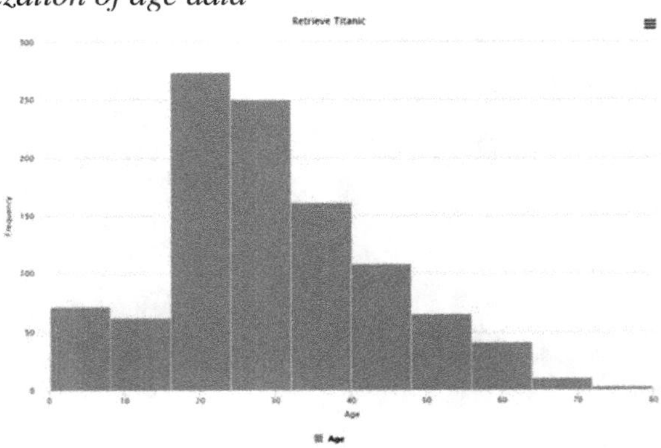

From the image shown in Figure 4, data scientists can examine the data distribution using a histogram visualization, which illustrates age ranges on the x-axis and the frequency of occurrence on the y-axis. When analyzing the Titanic dataset, the focus is on distinguishing characteristics between survivors and casualties of the Titanic shipwreck. Therefore, it is essential for data scientists to carefully consider which features are relevant for data analysis. Some features should be excluded from consideration for two primary reasons. Firstly, attributes such as Passenger Names, Ticket Numbers, and Ports of Embarkation, which denote passengers' destinations, can be disregarded as they do not significantly impact survival rates. Secondly, certain data, including Cabin Numbers and Life Boat Numbers, contain a substantial number of missing values, thereby compromising the accuracy of the data analysis. To address this, data scientists can utilize an operator known as "**Select Attributes**" to eliminate unwanted features from the dataset as shown in Figure 5.

Figure 5. Select attributes

As depicted in Figure 6, data scientists link models from the dataset to the Select Attribute operator and subsequently connect the Select Attribute to the Result section. They can then specify the parameters by choosing the Attribute Filter Type as a subset followed by selecting the desired attributes under "**Select Attributes.**" This procedure is commonly referred to as "**Feature Selection.**"

Figure 6. Feature selection

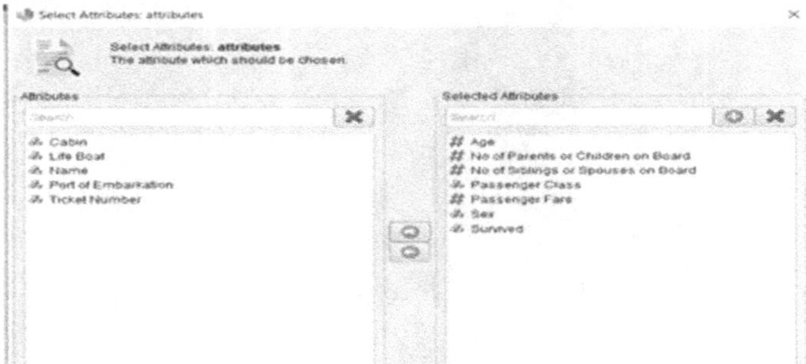

Following the Feature Selection stage, when executing a model within the dataset, only the chosen features remain. This step is crucial for preparing the data before applying data mining techniques as illustrated in Figure 7.

Figure 7. Data sets from feature selection

To perform Feature Selection using models within the RapidMiner software, data scientists have the option to select the desired features while preserving the original dataset. However, it is common for datasets to contain missing values. To handle this, data scientists can utilize the "**Replace Missing Value**" operator to manage the missing data appropriately.

Figure 8. Replacing missing values

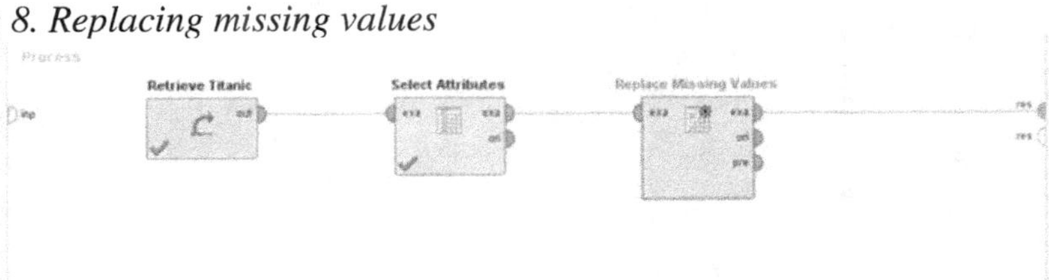

Figure 9. Determining parameters for replacing missing values

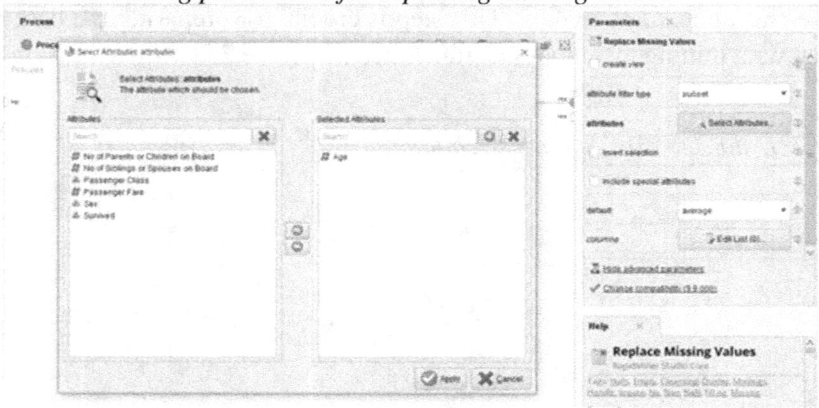

Data scientists have the capability to handle missing values for specific features by configuring the Attribute Filter Type as a subset and then selecting the desired attributes using the "**Select Attributes**" option. In this example, the scientists choose the "**Age**" feature and specify the default value as the average. Consequently, any missing values within the "**Age**" column will be replaced with the mean value as depicted in Figure 10.

Figure 10. Titanic data set after manipulating the missing values

Row No.	Age	Passenger ...	Sex	No of Sibling...	No of Parent...	Passenger F...	Survived
4	30	First	Male	1	2	151.550	No
5	25	First	Female	1	2	151.550	No
6	48	First	Male	0	0	26.550	Yes
7	63	First	Female	1	0	77.958	Yes
8	39	First	Male	0	0	0	No
9	53	First	Female	2	0	51.479	Yes
10	71	First	Male	0	0	49.504	No
11	47	First	Male	1	0	227.525	No
12	18	First	Female	1	0	227.525	Yes
13	24	First	Female	0	0	69.300	Yes
14	26	First	Female	0	0	78.850	Yes
15	80	First	Male	0	0	30	Yes
16	29.881	First	Male	0	0	25.925	No
17	24	First	Male	0	1	247.521	No
18	50	First	Female	0	1	247.521	Yes
19	32	First	Female	0	0	76.292	Yes
20	36	First	Male	0	0	75.242	No
21	37	First	Male	1	1	52.554	Yes

ExampleSet (1,309 examples, 0 special attributes, 7 regular attributes)

When dealing with missing value data manipulation, data scientists must also consider outlier data. In the provided example, this is illustrated through the feature named “**Passenger Fare**”, which represents unusually expensive ticket prices. This outlier data can be identified and examined through visual information as demonstrated below.

Figure 11. Exploring the outlier data

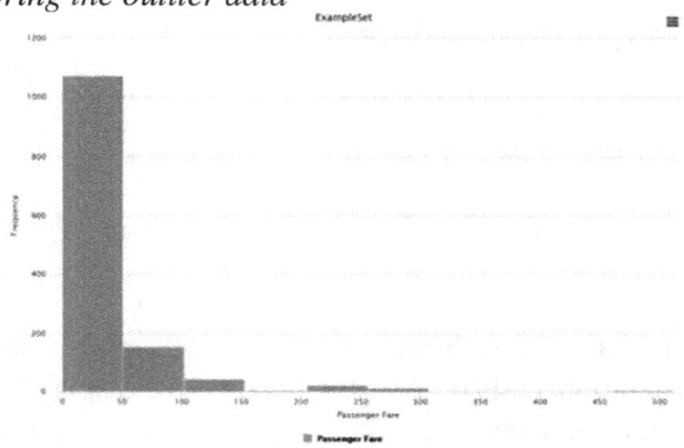

Based on the visual histogram data, data scientists can identify a range of data points that do not cluster with the rest of the dataset and exhibit a low frequency. These data points are typically considered outliers and can be addressed using a model called “**Detect Outlier (Distances)**” as depicted below.

Figure 12. Outlier inspection

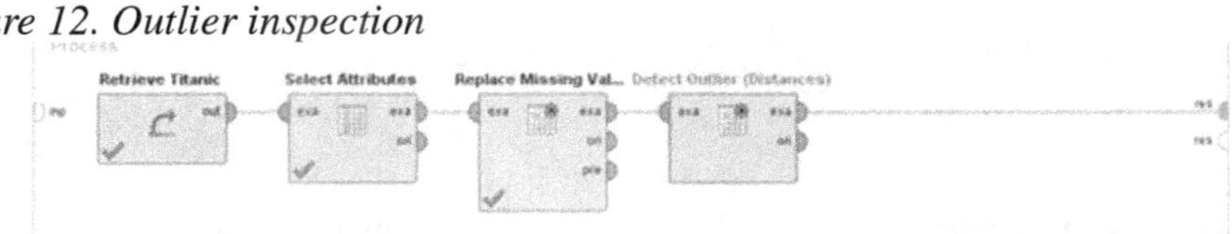

As depicted in Figure 13, data scientists can analyze the outlier data and retrieve the results from the execution as shown below.

Figure 13. Outlier data display

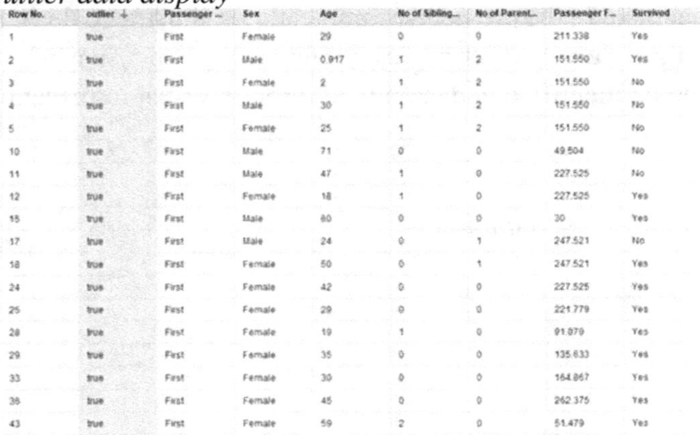

Row No.	outlier ↓	Passenger ...	Sex	Age	No of Sibling...	No of Parent...	Passenger F...	Survived
1	true	First	Female	29	0	0	211.338	Yes
2	true	First	Male	0.917	1	2	151.550	Yes
3	true	First	Female	2	1	2	151.550	No
4	true	First	Male	30	1	2	151.550	No
5	true	First	Female	25	1	2	151.550	No
10	true	First	Male	71	0	0	49.504	No
11	true	First	Male	47	1	0	227.525	No
12	true	First	Female	18	1	0	227.525	Yes
15	true	First	Male	80	0	0	30	Yes
17	true	First	Male	24	0	1	247.521	No
18	true	First	Female	50	0	1	247.521	Yes
24	true	First	Female	42	0	0	227.525	Yes
25	true	First	Female	29	0	0	221.779	Yes
28	true	First	Female	19	1	0	91.079	Yes
29	true	First	Female	35	0	0	135.633	Yes
33	true	First	Female	30	0	0	164.867	Yes
38	true	First	Female	45	0	0	262.375	Yes
43	true	First	Female	59	2	0	51.479	Yes

Regarding the added feature, "**Outlier**" data scientists can ascertain whether the datum qualifies as an outlier. If it does, the feature will display **"True"** indicating the presence of an outlier. Conversely, if it does not meet the criteria for an outlier, the feature will display **"False"**.

Figure 14. Determining the number of outliers

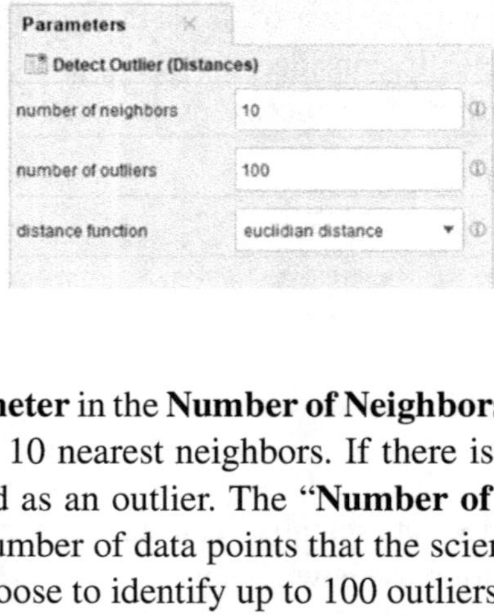

To specify the **parameter** in the **Number of Neighbors**, data scientists compare each data point with its 10 nearest neighbors. If there is a significant difference, the data point is flagged as an outlier. The "**Number of Outliers**" parameter indicates the maximum number of data points that the scientists identify as outliers. In this scenario, they choose to identify up to 100 outliers. Once the outlier data is validated, the scientists can eliminate the outliers from the dataset using a **Filter Examples** model.

Figure 15. Removing outlier data from the datasets

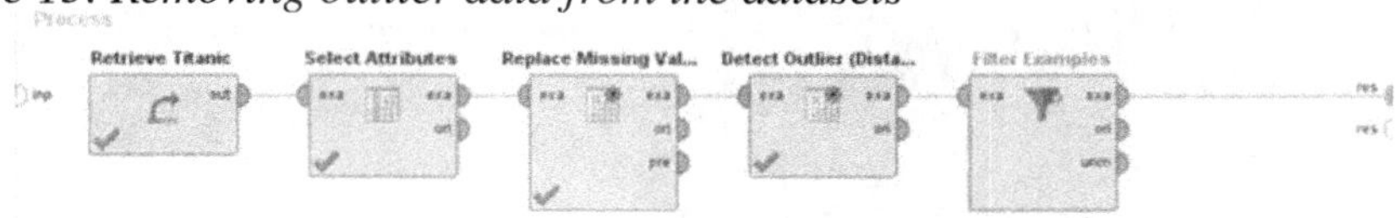

After importing the **Filter Examples** into the process, data scientists specify the conditions for removing the outliers from the dataset by configuring parameters in the **Filters** section. They set the condition for the **Outliers attribute** to be equal to **False.**

Figure 16. Defining conditions to remove outliers from datasets

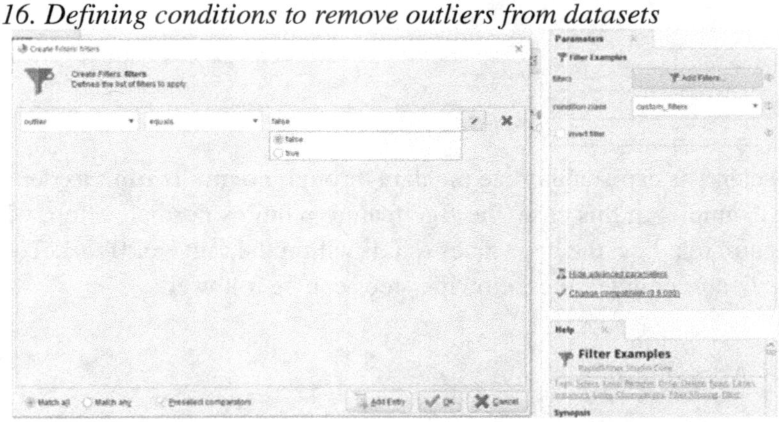

Upon executing the model, the dataset retains only the data where the outlier value is marked as false, effectively storing only data points that are not considered outliers.

Figure 17. Datasets where the outlier data are removed

Row No.	outlier	Passenger ...	Sex	Age	No of Sibling...	No of Parent...	Passenger F...	Survived
1	false	First	Male	48	0	0	26.550	Yes
2	false	First	Female	63	1	0	77.958	Yes
3	false	First	Male	39	0	0	0	No
4	false	First	Female	53	2	0	51.479	Yes
5	false	First	Female	24	0	0	69.300	Yes
6	false	First	Female	26	0	0	78.850	Yes
7	false	First	Male	29.881	0	0	25.925	No
8	false	First	Female	32	0	0	76.292	Yes
9	false	First	Male	36	0	0	75.242	No
10	false	First	Male	37	1	1	52.554	Yes
11	false	First	Female	47	1	1	52.554	Yes
12	false	First	Male	26	0	0	30	Yes
13	false	First	Male	25	0	0	26	No
14	false	First	Male	25	1	0	91.079	Yes
15	false	First	Male	28	0	0	26.550	Yes
16	false	First	Male	45	0	0	35.500	No
17	false	First	Male	40	0	0	31	Yes
18	false	First	Female	58	0	0	26.550	Yes

ExampleSet (1,209 examples, 1 special attribute, 7 regular attributes)

Data scientists can standardize the data through **normalization** as demonstrated in the example. In this case, the Age feature requires normalization, where the scientists aim to adjust the age values to fall within the range of 0 to 1. To execute the normalization model, the following steps can be followed:

Figure 18. Normalization

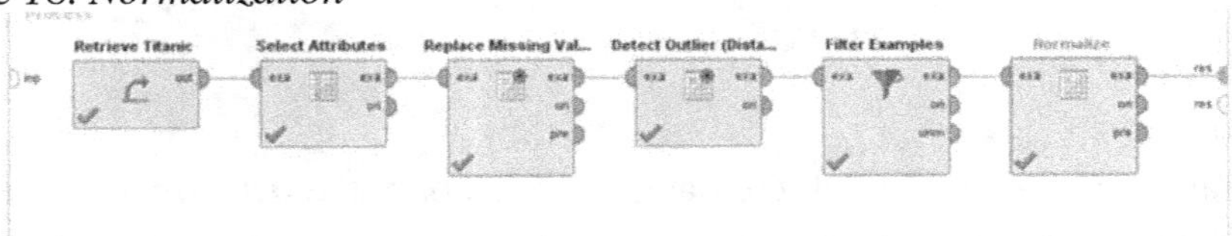

Data scientists can select the type of data processing by adjusting the parameters as illustrated below.

Figure 19. Assigning parameters to normalize

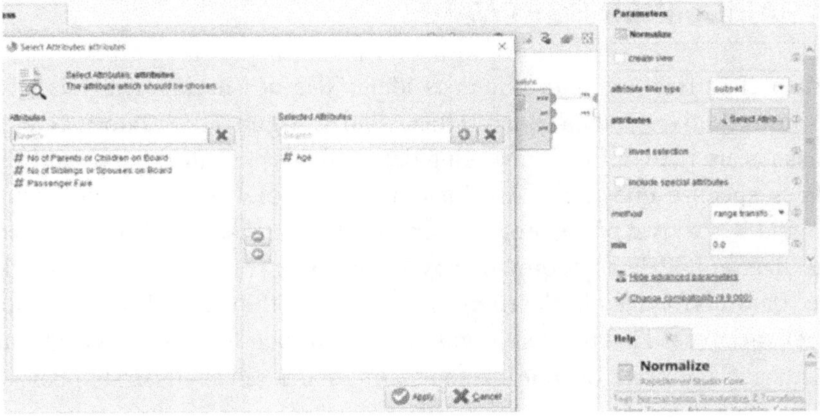

As shown in Figure 19, data scientists choose the **Attribute Filter** Type as a subset and then click the **Select Attribute** button and choose the feature named **Age**. Next, they select the method to adjust the value within Age to Range Transformation, aiming to scale the age data to range from 0 to 1. The outcome of executing this operation is depicted in the image below.

Figure 20. Datasets which are normalized

Row No.	outlier	Age	Passenger ...	Sex	No of Sibling...	No of Parent...	Passenger F...	Survived
1	false	0.685	First	Male	0	0	26.550	Yes
2	false	0.900	First	Female	1	0	77.958	Yes
3	false	0.556	First	Male	0	0	0	No
4	false	0.757	First	Female	2	0	51.479	Yes
5	false	0.341	First	Female	0	0	59.400	Yes
6	false	0.370	First	Female	0	0	78.850	Yes
7	false	0.428	First	Male	0	0	28.925	No
8	false	0.456	First	Female	0	0	76.292	Yes
9	false	0.513	First	Male	0	0	75.242	No
10	false	0.527	First	Male	1	1	52.554	Yes
11	false	0.671	First	Female	1	1	52.554	Yes
12	false	0.370	First	Male	0	0	30	Yes
13	false	0.356	First	Male	0	0	26	No
14	false	0.356	First	Male	1	0	91.079	Yes
15	false	0.399	First	Male	0	0	26.550	Yes
16	false	0.642	First	Male	0	0	38.500	No
17	false	0.570	First	Male	0	0	31	Yes
18	false	0.828	First	Female	0	0	26.550	Yes

ExampleSet (1,209 examples, 1 special attribute, 7 regular attributes)

Hence, during the data survey and preparation phase, researchers must initially explore the data visually. Subsequently, missing values and outlier data are addressed through additional processing (Luengo et al., 2020).

EXAMPLES OF DATA CLASSIFICATION WITH RAPIDMINER SOFTWARE

In data classification, data scientists identify issues in data analysis based on input from executives or data experts (Başarslan & Argun, 2018; Zuo & Guo, 2019). These issues are then defined, involving determining the data sources and datasets to address specific questions. An illustrative example of classification involves examining the survival of passengers from the Titanic disaster. Data scientists may opt to utilize sample datasets provided by RapidMiner software, which include both prepared datasets for machine learning instruction and the original dataset containing the target variables. This process aligns with the principles of supervised learning, where datasets are used for training and testing purposes as illustrated below.

Figure 21. Data analysis using decision tree

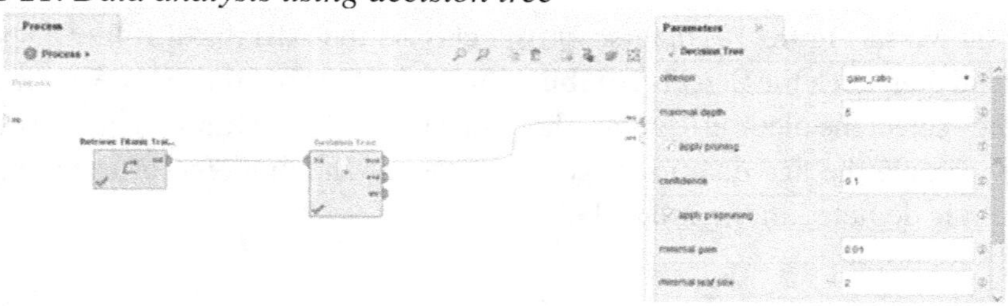

Data scientists employ the **Titanic Training dataset**, available as a sample dataset in RapidMiner software, for conducting various forms of data analysis as illustrated in the example. Utilizing the **Decision Tree model**, a method for categorizing data related to the fatalities and survivors of the Titanic disaster (Yang, 2019), they derive the results depicted in the following model.

Figure 22. Results from decision tree analysis

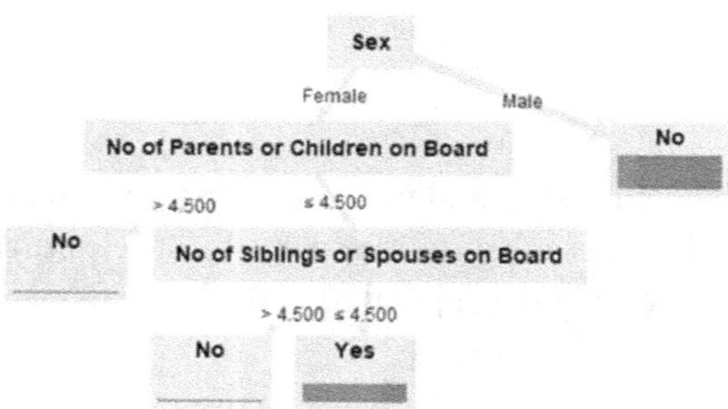

As shown in Figure 23, data scientists configure the parameters to include five leaf nodes. The analysis indicates a higher mortality rate among males compared to females. Subsequently, data scientists proceed to evaluate the model's performance using the Titanic dataset as a sample. In this dataset, the target variable "Survived" is identified for the purpose of data analysis.

Figure 23. Target variables (label)

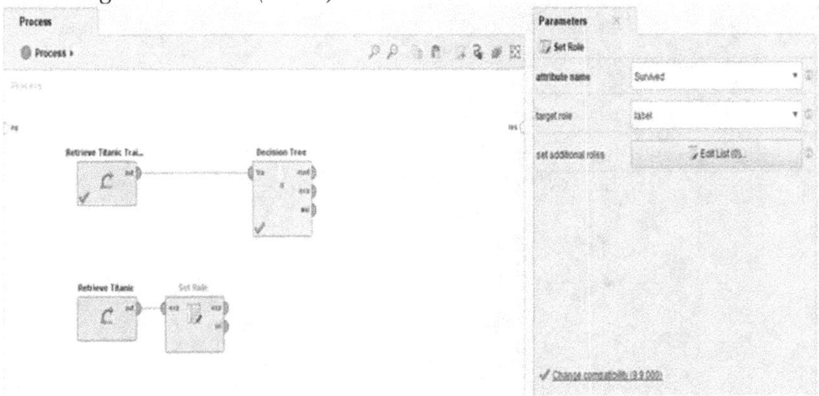

As depicted in the image below, to assess the model's performance, scientists utilize the Set Role operator to designate target variables, with "**Survived**" identified as the label or target variable. Subsequently, the data undergoes analysis leveraging machine learning capabilities through the **Apply Model** operator.

Figure 24. Using the apply model

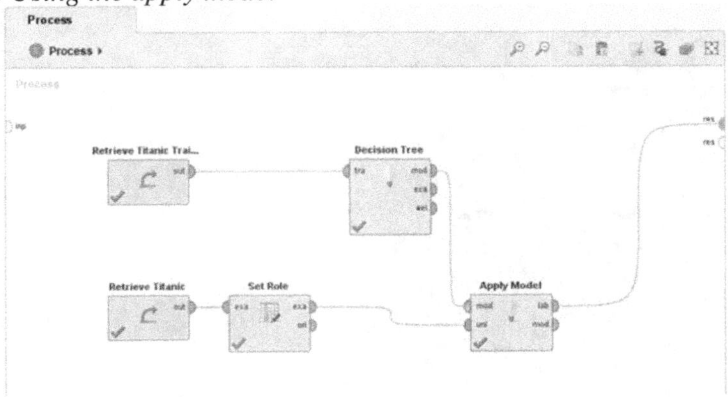

As illustrated in the image below, data scientists utilize the previously-trained **Decision Tree** model to test the Titanic dataset, aiming to determine whether the passengers survived or perished. The outcomes derived from this evaluation are presented below.

Figure 25. Results from decision tree data analysis

Row No.	Survived	prediction(S...	confidence(...	confidence(...	Passenger ...	Name	Sex
1	Yes	Yes	0.756	0.244	First	Allen, Miss. E...	Female
2	Yes	No	0.185	0.815	First	Allison, Mast...	Male
3	No	Yes	0.756	0.244	First	Allison, Miss ...	Female
4	No	No	0.185	0.815	First	Allison, Mr. H...	Male
5	No	Yes	0.756	0.244	First	Allison, Mrs. ...	Female
6	Yes	No	0.185	0.815	First	Anderson, Mr. ...	Male
7	Yes	Yes	0.756	0.244	First	Andrews, Mis...	Female
8	No	No	0.185	0.815	First	Andrews, Mr. ...	Male
9	Yes	Yes	0.756	0.244	First	Appleton, Mrs. ...	Female
10	No	No	0.185	0.815	First	Artagaveytia, ...	Male
11	No	No	0.185	0.815	First	Astor, Col. Jo...	Male
12	Yes	Yes	0.756	0.244	First	Astor, Mrs. Jo...	Female
13	Yes	Yes	0.756	0.244	First	Aubart, Mme ...	Female
14	Yes	Yes	0.756	0.244	First	Barber, Miss ...	Female
15	Yes	No	0.185	0.815	First	Barkworth, Mr. ...	Male
16	No	No	0.185	0.815	First	Baumann, Mr. ...	Male
17	No	No	0.185	0.815	First	Baxter, Mr. Qu...	Male

Data scientists can assess the accuracy of the classification by comparing the actual data employed to train the machine learning model with the predicted outcomes indicating whether each passenger survived or perished. To gauge the classification accuracy, they can utilize the **Performance** model.

Figure 26. Model performance test

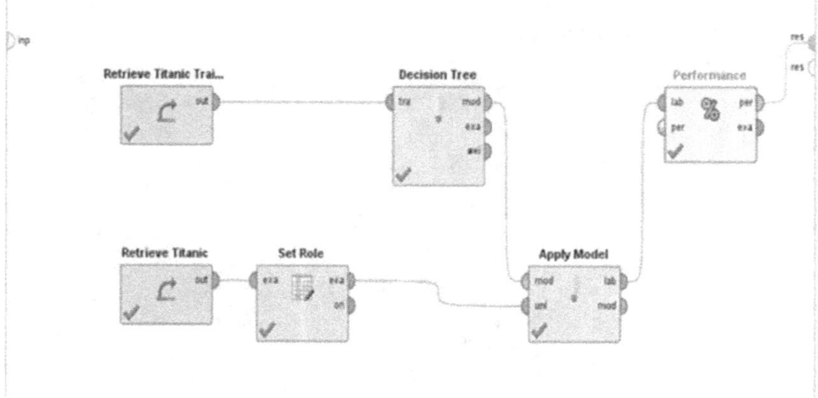

After analyzing the data, data scientists can evaluate the classification accuracy of the machine using the **Performance** model and obtain the following results.

Figure 27. Model accuracy

accuracy: 78.76%

	true Yes	true No	class precision
pred. Yes	338	116	74.45%
pred. No	162	693	81.05%
class recall	67.60%	85.66%	

In the figure, the machine learning classification achieves an efficiency of 78.76 percent, with an error rate of 21.24 percent. In data analysis through classification, data scientists can leverage RapidMiner software for modeling without the necessity of programming (Ghous and Kovács, 2020). By utilizing relevant datasets for machine learning instruction, scientists can conduct efficient data testing. This book introduces various data mining techniques for testing purposes, aiming to provide answers to inquiries using RapidMiner as a data analysis tool.

CONCLUSION

Data science projects typically commence with inquiries posed by business executives or data experts across various industries, such as healthcare or agriculture. Upon receiving these inquiries, data scientists embark on a quest for information sources, which may include internal data as well as external datasets. The collected dataset undergoes thorough scrutiny to assess its suitability for addressing the posed questions, involving processes like data pattern analysis, missing value analysis, and outlier analysis. Subsequently, the dataset undergoes preparation for analysis using data mining techniques, which may involve handling missing values, addressing outliers, and normalizing the data. These techniques are instrumental in generating insights to address the posed questions, and data scientists evaluate the accuracy of the models employed. Throughout this iterative process, data scientists may revisit data preparation to enhance the accuracy of their analysis. Once insights are gleaned, they are presented to the stakeholders who posed the initial questions. Throughout this entire workflow, RapidMiner software serves as a valuable tool, providing support from the inception of the project.

EXERCISES

Handling Missing Values in the Titanic Dataset
Discuss the following:

1. Addressing Outliers in the Titanic Dataset
2. Data Classification with the Decision Tree Model using the Titanic Trained Dataset:
3. Evaluating the Classification Efficiency of the Data using the Titanic Dataset against the Titanic Trained Dataset

REFERENCES

Abu-Soud, S. M. (2019). A novel approach for dealing with missing values in machine learning datasets with discrete values. *2019 International Conference on Computer and Information Sciences (ICCIS)*, 1–5. DOI: 10.1109/ICCISci.2019.8716430

Başarslan, M. S., & Argun, İ. D. (2018). Classification of a bank data set on various data mining platforms. *2018 Electric Electronics, Computer Science, Biomedical Engineerings' Meeting (EBBT)*, 1–4.

Bilal, M., Ali, G., Iqbal, M. W., Anwar, M., Malik, M. S. A., & Kadir, R. A. (2022). Auto-Prep: Efficient and automated data preprocessing pipeline. *IEEE Access : Practical Innovations, Open Solutions, 10*, 107764–107784. DOI: 10.1109/ACCESS.2022.3198662

Cai, S., Sun, R., Hao, S., Li, S., & Yuan, G. (2016). An efficient outlier detection approach on weighted data stream based on minimal rare pattern mining. *China Communications, 16*(10), 83–99. DOI: 10.23919/JCC.2019.10.006

Dai, H., Zhang, S., Wang, L., & Ding, Y. (2016). Research and implementation of big data preprocessing system based on Hadoop. *2016 IEEE International Conference on Big Data Analysis (ICBDA)*, 1–5. DOI: 10.1109/ICBDA.2016.7509802

Dubey, S., Jain, S. K., Gautam, P., & Sonare, S. (2024). Impact of water pollutants in River Narmada using RapidMiner tool. *2024 IEEE 13th International Conference on Communication Systems and Network Technologies (CSNT)*, 808–811. DOI: 10.1109/CSNT60213.2024.10546204

Ghous, H., & Kovács, L. (2020). Efficiency comparison of Python and RapidMiner. *Multidiszciplináris Tudományok, 10*(3), 212–220. DOI: 10.35925/j.multi.2020.3.26

Jafari, R. (2022). *Hands-on data preprocessing in Python: Learn how to effectively prepare data for successful data analytics*. Packt Publishing.

Mandhare, H. C., & Idate, S. R. (2017). A comparative study of cluster-based outlier detection, distance-based outlier detection, and density-based outlier detection techniques. *2017 International Conference on Intelligent Computing and Control Systems (ICICCS)*, 931–935. DOI: 10.1109/ICCONS.2017.8250601

Mat, T. M., Lajis, A., & Nasir, H. (2018). Text data preparation in RapidMiner for short free text answer in assisted assessment. *2018 IEEE 5th International Conference on Smart Instrumentation, Measurement and Application (ICSIMA)*, 1–4.

Phan, Q.-T., Wu, Y.-K., & Phan, Q.-D. (2021). An overview of data preprocessing for short-term wind power forecasting. *2021 7th International Conference on Applied System Innovation (ICASI)*, 121–125.

Samsani, S. (2016). An RST-based efficient preprocessing technique for handling inconsistent data. *2016 IEEE International Conference on Computational Intelligence and Computing Research (ICCIC)*, 1–8. DOI: 10.1109/ICCIC.2016.7919591

Santos, G. R. (2023). *Data wrangling with R: Load, explore, transform and visualize data for modeling with tidyverse libraries*. Packt Publishing.

Susanti, S. P., & Azizah, F. N. (2017). Imputation of missing value using dynamic Bayesian network for multivariate time series data. *2017 International Conference on Data and Software Engineering (ICoDSE)*, 1–5. DOI: 10.1109/ICODSE.2017.8285864

Yang, F.-J. (2019). An extended idea about decision trees. *2019 International Conference on Computational Science and Computational Intelligence (CSCI)*, 349–354. DOI: 10.1109/CSCI49370.2019.00068

Chapter 4
Classification

ABSTRACT

In the world of data mining, classification reigns supreme as a popular technique for supervised learning. Its ability to identify patterns in data by dividing the data into training sets and utilizing machine learning makes it an essential tool in answering critical questions related to data. For instance, classification can aid businesses in identifying customers with high purchasing potential. One of the standout features of classification is K-Nearest Neighbors (k-NN), which allows data to be classified according to the training data set. Decision trees are also commonly used to support decision making by producing easily interpretable diagrams. RapidMiner is an outstanding data mining tool that can employ a range of classification techniques, including k-NN, decision trees, and Naïve Bayes. In this book, readers can follow a step-by-step guide to using these techniques with RapidMiner to achieve effective data classification.

INTRODUCTION

Welcome to our exploration of classification techniques in the fascinating world of data mining. In this chapter, we will begin our journey by delving into foundational methods that serve as the bedrock of classification: k-nearest neighbors (k-NN), decision trees, and Naïve Bayes. These specific techniques offer a solid introduction to classification, particularly for those new to the field. They provide a relatively straightforward understanding, allowing us to grasp essential concepts without getting lost in complex mathematical details. Furthermore, these techniques are incredibly versatile and have applications in various real-world scenarios. From

DOI: 10.4018/979-8-3693-6001-9.ch004

spam filtering to medical diagnosis, their relevance spans across different industries, making them essential tools in the data scientist's toolkit.

Data classification involves categorizing or identifying data, such as classifying customers who may switch mobile phone providers. The outcomes of this analysis yield discrete or categorical data, indicating the clusters or types of data (Vichi, Ritter & Giusti, 2013). In data science, this dataset is referred to as a Class Label. Employing a variable target involves classifying data through supervised learning principles in data processing, by splitting the data into two parts (Mishra & Vats, 2021). Part 1 is for training machines to learn while Part 2 is for testing the model's performance. Data classification techniques are executed as follows.

Figure 1. Data analysis with classification

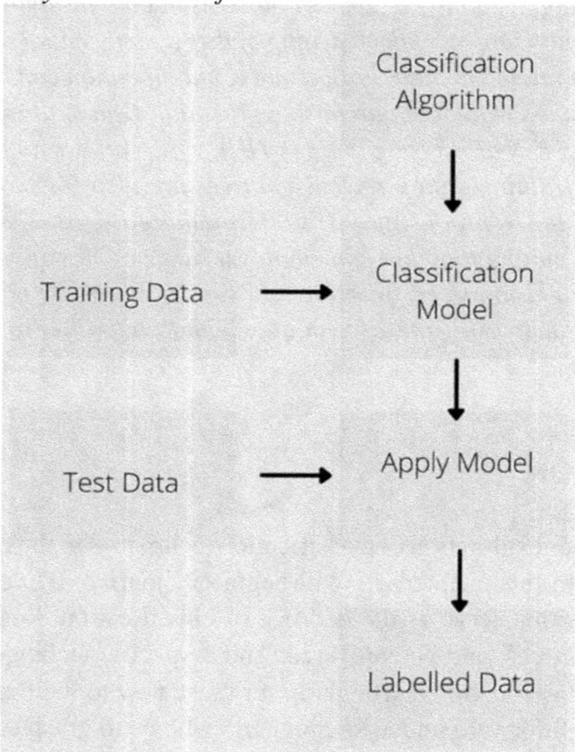

As depicted in Figure 1, data scientists employ classification algorithms like K-Nearest Neighbor (k-NN) or Decision Tree to construct classification models using training data, enabling machines to learn and derive the desired outcomes from data classification (Liu, 2021; Mladenova, 2021). Subsequently, test data are utilized to evaluate the performance accuracy of the model. The test data and the classification results are then compared.

GENERATING TRAINING AND TEST DATA SETS

Before applying data mining techniques, it is essential to generate high-quality training and test datasets, as they impact analysis reliability. This involves defining data requirements, collecting and preparing data, and properly splitting it into subsets. Balanced data, proper documentation, and validation techniques ensure robustness. Following these steps helps data scientists build reliable and well-segmented datasets, forming the foundation for successful data mining.

UNDERSTAND THE DATA REQUIREMENTS

Before diving into the data mining process, it is essential to have a clear understanding of the data requirements. This involves defining the objectives of your analysis and determining the specific variables and features that are crucial for achieving those objectives.

A. **Define analysis objectives** – Clearly state the goal, such as predicting churn, detecting fraud, or optimizing marketing.
B. **Types of insights** – Determine whether the focus is on descriptive (past trends), predictive (future outcomes), or prescriptive (actionable recommendations) insights.
C. **Identify essential variables and features** – Select key dataset variables like demographics, transactions, or behaviors relevant to the analysis.
D. **Consider data sources** – Assess internal and external data sources for quality, reliability, and accessibility to meet analysis objectives.
E. **Address data limitations** – Identify and resolve issues like missing values or discrepancies using data cleaning and imputation techniques.
F. **Consult stakeholders** – Engage domain experts to refine data requirements and analysis goals based on their insights and feedback.

By thoroughly understanding the data requirements, including the analysis objectives and essential variables, you can ensure that your data mining efforts are focused on and aligned with the desired outcomes. This foundational step sets the stage for the subsequent stages of data collection, preparation, and analysis.

DATA COLLECTION AND PREPARATION

Once the data requirements are clearly defined, the next crucial step is to collect and prepare the datasets for analysis. This involves gathering relevant data from appropriate sources and ensuring that the data are clean, consistent, and of high quality.

A. **Gather Relevant Datasets –** Collect data from internal and external sources, ensuring it includes necessary variables for analysis.
B. **Ensure Data Integrity and Quality –** Verify data accuracy, completeness, and reliability through profiling and validation.
C. **Cleanse the Data –** Remove duplicates, handle missing values, and correct inconsistencies to improve data quality.
D. **Normalize and Standardize Data –** Ensure consistency by scaling numerical data and encoding categorical variables appropriately.
E. **Document Data Preparation –** Record all cleaning, normalization, and transformation steps for transparency and reproducibility.
F. **Validate Data Quality –** Check completeness, accuracy, and consistency to confirm data reliability before analysis.
G. **Iterative Process –** Continuously refine data collection and preparation to maintain high data quality throughout analysis.

By rigorously collecting and preparing the datasets, ensuring data integrity and quality, and addressing any inconsistencies or errors, you can lay a solid foundation for the subsequent stages of data analysis and modeling. This ensures that the insights derived from the analysis are accurate, reliable, and actionable.

SPLITTING THE DATA

Once the data has been collected and prepared, the next step is to divide the dataset into two distinct subsets: the training data and the test data. This process is crucial for evaluating the performance of the data mining model and ensuring its generalizability.

A. **Divide the Dataset –** Split data into training and test sets, where training data develop the model, and test data evaluate it.
B. **Training Data –** A larger dataset portion used to teach the model patterns and relationships for predictions.
C. **Test Data –** An independent dataset used to assess model accuracy and generalizability.

D. **Randomization** – Shuffle data before splitting to ensure representativeness and prevent bias.
E. **Split Ratio** – Choose an appropriate ratio (e.g., 70/30, 80/20) based on dataset size and objectives.
F. **Maintain Data Balance** – Use techniques like stratified sampling to preserve class distribution in both subsets.
G. **Document the Splitting Process** – Record split ratio, randomization method, and steps taken for data integrity.
H. **Validation Set (Optional)** – Set aside data for fine-tuning and evaluating model performance during training.

By splitting the dataset into training and test data and following best practices such as randomization and maintaining data balance, data scientists can ensure that their data mining models are effectively trained and rigorously evaluated. This enables the development of robust and reliable models that can generalize well to unseen data.

DATA SPLITTING TECHNIQUES

When splitting data into training and test sets, it is essential to consider various techniques that can influence the performance and generalizability of the data mining models. Here are some common data splitting techniques to explore, each catering to different data characteristics and analysis objectives:

A. **Simple Random Sampling** – Randomly splits data into training and test sets, ensuring each data point has an equal chance of selection.
B. **Stratified Sampling** – Divides data into subgroups to maintain class distribution in both training and test sets, useful for imbalanced data.
C. **Time-Based Splitting** – Splits data chronologically, training on past data and testing on future data, ideal for time-series analysis.
D. **Cross-Validation** – Uses multiple train/test splits (e.g., k-fold) to improve model evaluation, beneficial for small datasets.
E. **Bootstrapping** – Creates multiple samples with replacement to assess model stability and variability in performance.

By exploring different data splitting techniques such as simple random sampling, stratified sampling, time-based splitting, cross-validation, and bootstrapping, data scientists can tailor their approach to match the specific characteristics of the dataset and analysis objectives. Each technique offers unique advantages and considerations, allowing for robust model training and evaluation in diverse scenarios.

CROSS VALIDATION

Cross-validation techniques are invaluable tools for robust model evaluation, particularly when working with limited datasets or aiming for comprehensive performance assessment (Mnich et al., 2020). Two commonly used cross-validation techniques are k-fold cross-validation and leave-one-out cross-validation.

A. **K-Fold Cross-Validation –** Splits data into k folds, training and testing k times with different test sets, then averaging results for reliable performance estimation.
B. **Leave-One-Out Cross-Validation (LOOCV) –** A special k-fold case where each observation serves as a test set once, offering unbiased estimates but being computationally intensive.
C. **Advantages of Cross-Validation –** Provides robust performance assessment, reduces overfitting risk, maximizes data use, and is suitable for various machine learning algorithms.
D. **Considerations and Implementation –** Choosing k, balancing efficiency, and aligning with analysis goals are key; LOOCV ensures unbiased results but demands high computational resources.

In summary, cross-validation techniques such as k-fold cross-validation and leave-one-out cross-validation are powerful tools for robust model evaluation and performance estimation. While optional, they offer significant advantages in terms of reliability, generalizability, and the maximization of available data, making them valuable additions to the data scientist's toolkit.

ASSESSING MODEL ACCURACY IN MACHINE LEARNING

Model accuracy is a fundamental metric in machine learning, reflecting the model's ability to correctly predict or classify instances within a dataset. A comprehensive guide for assessing model accuracy is presented as follows:

A. **Accuracy measures:** the proportion of correctly predicted or classified instances out of the total number of instances in the dataset. It is expressed as a percentage and indicates how well the model performs on unseen data.
B. **A confusion matrix** is a tabular representation that summarizes the performance of a classification model. It consists of four quadrants: true positives (correctly predicted positives), true negatives (correctly predicted negatives), false positives (incorrectly predicted positives), and false negatives (incorrectly predicted negatives). Consider a binary classification problem where we predict whether

an email is spam (positive class) or not spam (negative class). After making predictions on a test dataset, we can construct a confusion matrix:

Table 1. Confusion matrix table

	Predicted Spam	Predicted Not Spam
Actual Spam	120	10
Actual Not Spam	20	450

C. **The accuracy score** is calculated by dividing the total number of correct predictions by the total number of predictions made by the model. It provides an overall measure of how well the model performs across all classes or categories. Using the confusion matrix from Table 5.1, the accuracy score can be calculated as the proportion of correctly predicted instances out of the total number of instances:
   i. Accuracy = (True Positives + True Negatives) / Total Predictions
      1. = (120 + 450) / (120 + 10 + 20 + 450)
      2. = 570 / 600
      3. = 0.95 or 95%

D. **Precision and Recall:** Precision measures the proportion of true positive predictions out of all positive predictions made by the model. Recall, also known as sensitivity, measures the proportion of true positive predictions out of all actual positive instances in the dataset. Precision and recall provide insights into the model's performance for specific classes and help in assessing its effectiveness in different scenarios. Continuing with a binary classification example, precision and recall can be calculated as follows:
   ii. Precision = True Positives / (True Positives + False Positives)
      1. = 120 / (120 + 10)
      2. = 120 / 130
      3. ≈ 0.923 or 92.3%
   iii. Recall = True Positives / (True Positives + False Negatives)
      1. = 120 / (120 + 20)
      2. = 120 / 140
      3. ≈ 0.857 or 85.7%

E. **The F1 score** is the harmonic mean of precision and recall, providing a balanced measure of a model's performance. It ranges from 0 to 1, with higher values indicating better overall performance. Using the precision and recall values obtained above, the F1 score can be calculated as the harmonic mean of precision and recall:

iv. F1 Score = 2 * (Precision * Recall) / (Precision + Recall)

1. = 2 * (0.923 * 0.857) / (0.923 + 0.857)
2. ≈ 0.888 or 88.8%

F. **The Receiver Operating Characteristic (ROC) curve** is a graphical representation of the true positive rate (recall) against the false positive rate (1 - specificity) for different threshold values. The Area Under the ROC Curve (AUC) summarizes the ROC curve's performance, with values closer to 1 indicating better discrimination between classes. Suppose we have a binary classification model that predicts the probability of a patient having a certain disease. By varying the decision threshold, we can plot the ROC curve and calculate the AUC:

Figure 2. ROC curve

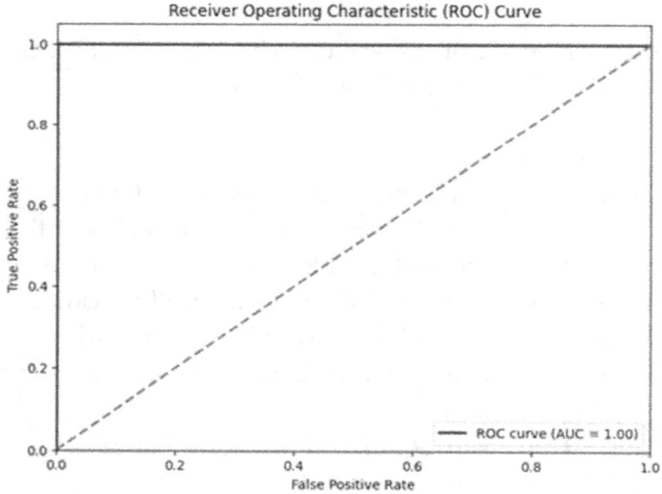

G. **Cross-validation techniques**, such as k-fold cross-validation, help assess the robustness and generalizability of the model's performance across multiple train/test splits. It provides a more reliable estimate of the model's accuracy and helps to identify potential overfitting or bias issues. In k-fold cross-validation, the dataset is divided into k subsets. Each subset is used as the test set once, with the remaining k-1 subsets combined to form the training set. The model's performance is averaged across all k iterations to obtain a more robust estimate of accuracy.

H. **Fine-tuning model hyperparameters**, such as regularization strength or learning rate, can significantly impact model accuracy. Techniques like grid search or random search help to identify the optimal hyperparameter values that maximize model performance. Consider a support vector machine (SVM) model for a classification task. Hyperparameters such as the kernel type and regularization parameter (C) can significantly impact model performance. By performing hyperparameter tuning using techniques like grid search or random search, we can identify the optimal combination of hyperparameter values that maximize accuracy on a validation set.
I. **Domain-Specific Metrics** Depending on the application domain, specific metrics such as mean absolute error (MAE) for regression tasks or the Area Under the Precision-Recall curve (AUC-PR) for imbalanced classification can provide additional insights into model accuracy. In a regression task predicting housing prices, we may use mean absolute error (MAE) as a measure of accuracy. For instance, if the MAE is $10,000, it means that, on average, the model's predictions are off by $10,000 from the actual prices.

By employing these strategies and metrics, data scientists can effectively assess the accuracy of machine learning models, identify areas for improvement, and build more robust and reliable predictive systems.

UNDERSTANDING OVERFITTING AND UNDERFITTING IN MACHINE LEARNING

In the realm of machine learning, overfitting and underfitting are common challenges that arise during the model training process. Each concept is explained as follows:

A. **Overfitting** occurs when a machine learning model learns the training data too well, capturing noise and irrelevant patterns that do not generalize to unseen data. Characteristics of an overfit model include high accuracy on the training data but poor performance on new, unseen data. Overfitting often results from overly complex models that have too many parameters relative to the size of the training data or models that are trained for too many epochs.
B. **Underfitting** occurs when a machine learning model is too simple to capture the underlying patterns and relationships present in the training data. Characteristics of an underfit model include low accuracy on both the training and test data,

indicating a failure to capture the complexity of the underlying data distribution. Underfitting can occur when the model is too simplistic or when insufficient features are used to represent the data adequately.

Addressing Overfitting and Underfitting

A. **Regularization –** L1 (Lasso) and L2 (Ridge) regularization prevent overfitting by penalizing large parameter values, promoting simpler models.
B. **Cross-Validation –** Techniques like k-fold cross-validation assess model generalization, helping detect and address overfitting or underfitting.
C. **Feature Selection –** Dimensionality reduction (e.g., PCA) and feature importance analysis identify relevant features, reducing overfitting risks.
D. **Early Stopping –** Stops training when validation performance declines, preventing models from memorizing training data.
E. **Ensemble Methods –** Techniques like bagging and boosting combine models to improve predictions and reduce overfitting.

By understanding the nuances of overfitting and underfitting and by employing appropriate strategies to address these challenges, data scientists can develop machine learning models that strike the right balance between complexity and generalization, ultimately leading to more accurate and reliable predictions on unseen data.

UNDERSTANDING THE K-NEAREST NEIGHBOR (K-NN) TECHNIQUE

The k-Nearest Neighbor (k-NN) algorithm is a simple yet powerful method used in both classification and regression tasks in machine learning (Thongjor, 2017: Rahman et al., 2021). At its core, the k-NN algorithm operates on the principle of similarity. It assumes that similar data points tend to belong to the same class or have similar numerical values. Given a dataset with labeled examples (for classification) or numerical outcomes (for regression), the k-NN algorithm works as follows:

- For a new, unseen data point, the algorithm identifies the k nearest neighbors in the training dataset based on a chosen distance metric (e.g., Euclidean distance).
- For classification tasks, the algorithm assigns the majority class among the k-nearest neighbors to the new data point.

- For regression tasks, the algorithm calculates the average (or weighted average) of the numerical outcomes of the k nearest neighbors and assigns it to the new data point.

Hyperparameter: The value of k is a hyperparameter that needs to be specified before applying the k-NN algorithm. It determines the number of neighbors considered when making predictions. The choice of k can significantly impact the performance of the model. Smaller values of k may lead to more flexible (less smooth) decision boundaries, potentially increasing the risk of overfitting. Conversely, larger values of k may result in smoother decision boundaries but might lead to underfitting if k is too large.

Distance Metrics: Commonly used distance metrics include Euclidean distance, Manhattan distance, and Minkowski distance. The choice of distance metric depends on the nature of the data and the specific requirements of the problem.

Handling Imbalanced Data: In classification tasks with imbalanced class distributions, the choice of k can significantly impact the model's performance. Techniques such as weighting the contributions of each neighbor or using distance-based voting can help in mitigating the effects of class imbalance.

Pros

- Simple and easy to understand.
- No training phase; the algorithm is instance-based.
- Can be effective for datasets with nonlinear decision boundaries.

Cons

- Computationally expensive during inference, especially for large datasets.
- Sensitive to the choice of distance metric and value of k.
- Performance can degrade in high-dimensional feature spaces (the curse of dimensionality).

Applications k-NN is widely used in various fields, including pattern recognition, recommendation systems, anomaly detection, and medical diagnosis. It is particularly useful when the underlying data distribution is not well understood or when labeled training data are limited.

K-NEAREST NEIGHBOR (K-NN) ALGORITHM

The k-Nearest Neighbors (k-NN) algorithm is a supervised machine learning technique used for classification and regression. It relies on the concept of similarity to make predictions by comparing a new data point with labeled examples in a training dataset. Below is a step-by-step breakdown of how k-NN works, from input data to classification output.

Step 1 Input

- Training dataset with labeled example: $\{(x_1,y_1),(x_2,y_2), \ldots , (x_n,y_n)\}$ where x_1 represents the feature vector of the ith example and y_is its corresponding label.
- New, unseen data point x_{new} for which we want to make predictions.
- Hyperparameter k representing the number of nearest neighbors to consider.

Table 2. Example data set

Height	Weight	Class
4	10	Cat
5	12	Cat
7	15	Cat
9	20	Dog
8	18	Dog
6	13	Dog

New Data Point: (6,14) (6, 14) (6,14) → Predict whether it belongs to "Cat" or "Dog".

Step 2 Calculate Distance Between Data Points

To determine similarity, compute the distance between the new data point x_{new} and every example x_i in the training dataset using a chosen distance metric.

Common Distance Metrics

- **Euclidean Distance:**

$$d(x_{new}, x_i) = \sqrt{(x_{new1} - x_{i1})^2 + (x_{new2} - x_{i2})^2 + \ldots + (x_{newn} - x_{in})^2}$$

- **Manhattan Distance:**

$$d(x_{new}, x_i) = |x_{new1} - x_{i1}| + |x_{new2} - x_{i2}| + \ldots + |x_{newn} - x_{in}|$$

- **Minkowski Distance:** A generalization of Euclidean and Manhattan distances.

Table 3. Example calculation (Euclidean distance for each training point and $\mathbf{x}_{\mathbf{new}}$ *= (6, 14)*

Training Point	Distance Calculation	Euclidean Distance
(4,10)	$\sqrt{6 - 4)^2 + (14 - 10)^2}$	4.47
(5, 12)	$\sqrt{6 - 5)^2 + (14 - 12)^2}$	2.24
(7, 15)	$\sqrt{6 - 7)^2 + (14 - 15)^2}$	1.41
(9, 20)	$\sqrt{6 - 9)^2 + (14 - 20)^2}$	6.71
(8, 18)	$\sqrt{6 - 8)^2 + (14 - 18)^2}$	4.47
(6, 13)	$\sqrt{6 - 6)^2 + (14 - 13)^2}$	1.00

Step 3 Identify the k-Nearest Neighbors

- Sort the training examples by distance from x_{new}.
- Select the top k closest points.
- Choosing $k = 3$, the three nearest neighbors are:
  - o (6,13) → Distance: 1.00 → Class: "Dog"
  - o (7,15) → Distance: 1.41 → Class: "Cat"
  - o (5,12) → Distance: 2.24 → Class: "Cat"

Step 4 Majority Voting for Classification

- Count the class labels of the k nearest neighbors.
- Assign the most frequent class to x_{new}.

Table 4. Voting result (for **k** $=$ *3)*

Class	**Count**
Cat	2
Dog	1

Since the majority class is **"Cat" (2 votes)**, the new data point $x_{new} = (6, 4)$ is classified as "Cat".

Step 5: Output Prediction

The final predicted class for the new data point is "Cat"

The k-Nearest Neighbors (k-NN) algorithm is an intuitive, non-parametric, and instance-based learning method used widely in classification problems. While it is simple and effective, it is computationally expensive for large datasets. Proper feature scaling, choosing the right distance metric, and selecting an appropriate k are crucial for achieving accurate predictions.

UNDERSTANDING DECISION TREES FOR CLASSIFICATION

Decision trees are versatile and intuitive machine learning algorithms used for both classification and regression tasks (Puspitasari et al., 2021). A decision tree is a hierarchical tree-like structure consisting of nodes and branches. Each internal node represents a decision based on a feature, leading to one or more child nodes. Leaf nodes represent the class labels or outcomes.

Algorithm Workflow

Building Phase

- The algorithm selects the best feature to split the dataset based on a chosen criterion, such as Gini impurity or entropy.
- The dataset is partitioned into subsets based on the selected feature's values.
- This process is recursively applied to each subset until certain stopping criteria are met, such as reaching a maximum depth, minimum number of samples, or purity threshold.

Prediction Phase

- To make predictions for a new data point, the algorithm traverses the decision tree from the root node to a leaf node, following the path determined by the feature values of the data point.

- The predicted class label is the majority class of the instances in the leaf node.

Splitting Criteria:

A. **Gini Impurity:** Gini impurity is a measure of the impurity or disorder in a set of labels within a dataset. It quantifies the probability of incorrectly classifying a randomly chosen element if it were randomly labeled according to the distribution of class labels in the dataset.

Mathematically, Gini impurity G for a set of labels with K distinct classes is calculated as:

$$G = 1 - \sum_{i=1}^{K} (p_i)^2$$

Where p_i is the probability of an element belonging to the ith class.

Gini impurity ranges from 0 to 1, where 0 indicates perfect purity (all elements belong to the same class) and 1 indicates maximum impurity (all classes are equally distributed). A lower Gini impurity indicates better purity and more homogeneous class distributions within the dataset.

B. **Entropy** is another measure of impurity or disorder in a set of labels within a dataset. It quantifies the uncertainty or randomness in the distribution of class labels. Entropy is minimized when the data are pure, meaning that all instances belong to the same class.

Mathematically, entropy H for a set of labels with K distinct classes is calculated as:

$$H = -\sum_{i=1}^{K} p_i \log_2(p_i)$$

Where p_i is the probability of an element belonging to the ith class. Entropy also ranges from 0 to 1, where 0 indicates perfect purity (all elements belong to the same class) and 1 indicates maximum impurity (all classes are equally distributed). Similar to Gini impurity, a lower entropy indicates better purity and more homogeneous class distributions within the dataset.

In the diagram, data scientists create a Decision Tree from the attributes consisting of Refund, which means the tax refund, Marital Status, which is the taxpayer's marital status, and Taxable Income, which is the amount of income that has reached the tax threshold. Cheat means entering false data in order to receive a tax refund. Each attribute contains the following data.

C. **Information Gain** measures the reduction in entropy or impurity achieved by splitting the dataset on a particular feature. It quantifies how much uncertainty is removed about the class labels by splitting the data based on that feature.

Mathematically, information gain is calculated as the difference between the entropy of the parent dataset *H*(*P*) and the weighted average of the entropies of the child datasets after the split:

$$Information\ Gain\ =\ H(P) - \sum_{i=1}^{n} \frac{|S_i|}{|S|} H\left(S_i\right)$$

Where:

- *H*(*P*) is the entropy of the parent dataset.
- $|S_i|$ is the number of instances in the ith child dataset after the split.
- $|S|$ is the total number of instances in the parent dataset.
- Information gain ranges from 0 to 1, where a higher information gain indicates a more effective split that results in greater reduction of entropy and better separation of classes.

In decision tree algorithms, the feature with the highest information gain (or lowest Gini impurity) is chosen as the splitting criterion at each node, leading to more informative and discriminative decision boundaries.

Pruning in Decision Trees

Pruning is a technique used to prevent overfitting in decision tree models by removing branches that have little impact on the overall predictive accuracy. While decision trees have a tendency to fit the training data too closely, pruning helps to simplify the tree structure, resulting in a more generalized and interpretable model.

Types of Pruning:

A. **Pre-pruning (Early Stopping)** involves stopping the growth of the decision tree prematurely based on certain criteria. Common stopping criteria include the following:
   - Maximum tree depth: Limiting the maximum depth of the tree prevents it from growing too deep and overfitting the training data.
   - Minimum number of samples per leaf: Stopping the split process when the number of samples in a leaf node falls below a certain threshold prevents overly specific leaf nodes.

- Minimum impurity decrease: Halting node splitting when the decrease in impurity (e.g., Gini impurity or entropy) is below a predefined threshold.

B. **Post-pruning (Cost Complexity Pruning)** involves growing a full decision tree and then removing nodes or branches that contribute little to the overall predictive accuracy. Cost complexity pruning (also known as reduced error pruning) is a common post-pruning technique. The idea behind cost complexity pruning is to iteratively remove nodes with the least impact on tree accuracy while maintaining a balance between model complexity and predictive performance.

Cost Complexity Pruning:

A. **Cost Complexity Measure (Alpha):** The cost complexity measure, denoted by α, quantifies the trade-off between the complexity of the tree and its predictive accuracy. It is calculated as the sum of the impurity of the nodes and a penalty term proportional to the number of leaf nodes. The goal is to determine the optimal value of α that minimizes the cost complexity measure while maximizing predictive accuracy.

B. **Pruning Process**
   - Starting from the full decision tree, nodes are iteratively pruned based on their cost complexity measure.
   - At each iteration, the node with the smallest increase in the cost complexity measure (i.e., the smallest improvement in tree accuracy) is pruned.
   - This process continues until pruning no longer improves the validation accuracy or until a desired level of simplicity is reached.

Benefits of Pruning:

A. **Prevents Overfitting:** Pruning helps to prevent overfitting by simplifying the decision tree structure and reducing its reliance on noisy or irrelevant features.

B. **Improves Generalization**: By removing unnecessary branches, pruning improves the generalization ability of the decision tree, allowing it to make more accurate predictions on unseen data.

C. **Enhances Interpretability**: Pruned decision trees are often simpler and easier to interpret, making them more accessible to users and stakeholders.

Considerations:

A. **Validation Set**: Pruning decisions should be based on a separate validation set to ensure that the pruned tree generalizes well to new data.
B. **Optimal Pruning Strategy**: The optimal pruning strategy may vary depending on the dataset and problem at hand. Experimentation and validation are key to determining the most effective pruning approach.
C. **Trade-off between Complexity and Accuracy**: Pruning involves finding the right balance between model complexity and predictive accuracy. A more complex tree may fit the training data better but is more likely to overfit while a simpler tree may generalize better but may sacrifice some predictive accuracy.

Pruning is a crucial step in the construction of decision trees, helping to create models that strike the right balance between complexity and accuracy, leading to more robust and interpretable predictive models.

Decision trees offer interpretability, mimicking human decision-making processes and making it easy to understand and interpret learned decision rules, providing insights into important features for classification and their contribution to final decisions. They are simple to understand, handle both numerical and categorical features, and are robust to outliers and missing values due to their non-parametric nature. However, they are prone to overfitting, especially with deep trees, lack smooth decision boundaries, and are sensitive to small variations in training data. Despite these disadvantages, decision trees find wide applications in healthcare, finance, marketing, and more, serving as powerful and interpretable tools for classification tasks with a balance between complexity and predictive performance, enabling effective real-world problem-solving for data scientists.

DECISION TREE ALGORITHM

The Decision Tree algorithm is a supervised machine learning technique used for classification and regression. It splits data into subsets based on feature values to create a tree-like structure that can be used for decision-making. Below is a step-by-step breakdown of how a decision tree works, from input data to classification output, using the Play Tennis dataset as an example.

Step 1 Input Data

Training Dataset, set of labeled examples where features represent weather conditions, and the target variable is Play Tennis (Yes/No).

Table 5. Play tennis dataset

Outlook	Temperature	Humidity	Windy	Play Tennis
Sunny	Hot	High	False	No
Sunny	Hot	High	True	No
Overcast	Hot	High	False	Yes
Rainy	Mild	High	False	Yes
Rainy	Cool	Normal	False	Yes
Rainy	Cool	Normal	True	No
Overcast	Cool	Normal	True	Yes
Sunny	Mild	High	False	No
Sunny	Cool	Normal	False	Yes
Rainy	Mild	Normal	False	Yes
Sunny	Mild	Normal	True	Yes
Overcast	Mild	High	True	Yes

- New Data Point, a previously unseen instance with certain weather conditions, for which we want to predict Play Tennis (Yes/No).
- Decision Rule, the decision tree will learn rules from the dataset to classify new examples

Step 2 Choose the Root Node

- Calculate the entropy of the target variable (Play Tennis) before splitting.
- Compute the information gain for each feature (Outlook, Temperature, Humidity, Windy).
- The feature with the highest information gain becomes the root node.

1. Entropy Calculation for Play Tennis

$$H(PlayTennis) = -\frac{9}{14}\, log_2\left(\frac{9}{14}\right) - \frac{5}{14}\, log_2\left(\frac{5}{14}\right)$$

2. Information Gain for the Feature "Outlook"

We split the dataset based on "Outlook" and calculated the weighted entropy after the split.

$$H(PlayTennis \mid Outlook) = \frac{5}{14} \times H(Sunny) + \frac{4}{14} \times H(Overcast) + \frac{5}{14} \times H(Rainy)$$

$$IG(Outlook) = H(PlayTennis) - H(PlayTennis \mid Outlook)$$

Since Outlook has the highest information gain, it becomes the root node.

Step 3 Split the Data Based on the Root Node (Outlook)

After selecting **Outlook** as the root node, the dataset is divided into three subsets based on the values including Sunny, Overcast, and Rainy.

Table 6. New subsets after splitting – sunny

Outlook	**Temperature**	**Humidity**	**Windy**	**Play Tennis**
Sunny	Hot	High	False	No
Sunny	Hot	High	True	No
Sunny	Mild	High	False	No
Sunny	Cool	Normal	False	Yes
Sunny	Mild	Normal	True	Yes

Table 7. New subsets after splitting – overcast

Outlook	**Temperature**	**Humidity**	**Windy**	**Play Tennis**
Overcast	Hot	High	False	Yes
Overcast	Cool	Normal	True	Yes
Overcast	Mild	High	True	Yes

Table 8. New subsets after splitting – rainy

Outlook	Temperature	Humidity	Windy	Play Tennis
Rainy	Mild	High	False	Yes
Rainy	Cool	Normal	False	Yes
Rainy	Cool	Normal	True	No
Rainy	Mild	Normal	False	Yes

- Overcast Subset: All instances belong to "Yes," so this branch stops here (pure leaf node).
- Sunny & Rainy Subsets: Continue splitting based on remaining features.

Step 4 Recursively Split the Remaining Data

For each subset, repeat the following:

- Calculate entropy and information gain for the remaining features.
- Select the best feature for the next split.
- Repeat the process until all subsets contain only one class or meet the stopping condition.
- Next Best Splits:
- For Sunny, "Humidity" provides the highest information gain, so it becomes the next split.
- For Rainy, "Windy" gives the best split.

Step 5 Build the Final Decision Tree

After splitting all branches, the final decision tree is:

Figure 3. Fig x decision tree after splitting all branches

```
                    [Outlook]
                  /     |      \
           Sunny    Overcast  Rainy
            /  \        |         /   \
       High  Normal  Yes     Windy   Not Windy
      /   \         (Pure)   /   \
    No    Yes               No     Yes
```

Example Prediction

If Outlook = Sunny and Humidity = High, follow the tree:

- "Sunny" → Check "Humidity"
- "Humidity = High" → No (Don't Play Tennis)

If Outlook = Rainy and Windy = False, follow the tree:

- "Rainy" → Check "Windy"
- "Windy = False" → Yes (Play Tennis)

Step 6 Output Prediction

The final tree classifies new instances based on learned rules. For any given weather conditions, follow the tree structure to get the predicted outcome.

Table 9. Example new data point

Outlook	Temperature	Humidity	Windy
Sunny	Cool	High	False

Prediction Result is "No" that means "Don't play Tennis"

The Decision Tree algorithm is a powerful classification tool that offers interpretability, flexibility, and efficiency. It provides rule-based predictions, making it easier to understand compared to black-box models. While susceptible to overfitting, proper tuning can make it a robust classifier for many real-world applications.

UNDERSTANDING NAÏVE BAYES CLASSIFIER

Naïve Bayes is a data mining technique that utilizes the Bayesian Classifier, employing probabilities to classify data across the entire dataset. (Rabiul Alam et al., 2021). Naïve Bayes is a simple yet effective probabilistic classifier based on Bayes' theorem with strong independence assumptions between features. A detailed overview of Naïve Bayes is presented below:

A. Bayes' Theorem

Naïve Bayes classifier is based on Bayes' theorem, which describes the probability of a hypothesis given the evidence. Mathematically, it is represented as:

$$\mathrm{P}(he) = \frac{P(e|h) \bullet P(h)}{P(e)}$$

Where:

- P(he) is the probability of hypothesis h given evidence e.
- P(eh) is the probability of evidence e given hypothesis h.
- P(h) is the prior probability of hypothesis h.
- P(e) is the prior probability of evidence e.

B. Naïve Assumption: Naïve Bayes classifier assumes that all features are independent of each other given the class label. This is a strong and often unrealistic assumption, but it simplifies the calculation and makes the classifier computationally efficient.

C. Types of Naïve Bayes Classifiers

- Gaussian Naïve Bayes: Assumes that the features follow a Gaussian (normal) distribution.
- Multinomial Naïve Bayes: Suitable for features with discrete counts, often used in text classification with term frequencies.

- Bernoulli Naïve Bayes: Similar to multinomial Naïve Bayes but considers binary features (presence or absence).

D. Model Training

- During training, Naïve Bayes calculates the prior probabilities of each class and the conditional probabilities of each feature given the class.
- For continuous features, Gaussian Naïve Bayes estimates the mean and standard deviation of each feature and for each class.
- For discrete features, multinomial or Bernoulli Naïve Bayes calculates the likelihood of each feature value given each class.

E. To make predictions, Naïve Bayes calculates the posterior probability of each class given the input features using Bayes' theorem. It selects the class with the highest posterior probability as the predicted class for the input instance.

Naïve Bayes offers several advantages, including simplicity and ease of implementation, requiring minimal training data to estimate parameters, and exhibiting efficiency in both training and prediction phases. It performs well in numerous real-world scenarios, particularly with high-dimensional data. However, it comes with limitations such as the strong independence assumption, which may not always hold true in real-world datasets, leading to poor performance when features are highly correlated and an inability to capture complex relationships between features. Despite these limitations, Naïve Bayes finds applications in various domains such as text classification (e.g., spam filtering, sentiment analysis), document categorization, medical diagnosis, recommendation systems, and fraud detection.

Let's consider a simple example of text classification using the Naïve Bayes classifier to determine whether an email is spam or not based on the presence of certain words.

Example Scenario

Suppose we have a dataset of emails labeled as spam or non-spam (ham). Each email is represented by a bag-of-words model, where the presence or absence of specific words is used as a feature for classification.

Table 10. Email dataset

Email	Label
Buy now, limited time offer!	Spam
Free gift for you, click here!	Spam
Meeting scheduled for tomorrow.	Ham
Reminder: appointment at 2 PM.	Ham
Congratulations, you've won a prize!	Spam
Important update: please review document.	Ham

Steps to Calculate Naïve Bayes Probability

A. **Preprocessing:** Convert text data into a bag-of-words representation. Calculate the frequency of each word in spam and non-spam emails.
B. **Calculate Class Probabilities:** Calculate the prior probability of each class (spam and ham):

- $P(Spam) = \frac{Number\ of\ spam\ emails}{Total\ number\ of\ emails}$

- $P(Ham) = \frac{Number\ of\ ham\ emails}{Total\ number\ of\ emails}$

C. **Calculate Conditional Probabilities**: For each word in the vocabulary, calculate the conditional probability of that word given the class:

- $P(Word \mid Spam) = \frac{Frequency\ of\ word\ in\ spam\ emails}{Total\ number\ of\ words\ in\ spam\ emails}$

- $P(Word \mid Ham) = \frac{frequency\ of\ word\ in\ ham\ emails}{Total\ number\ of\ words\ in\ ham\ emails}$

D. Prediction

- Given a new email with words $w_1, w_2, \ldots, w_n$, calculate the probability of it being spam or ham using Bayes' theorem:

o $P(\text{Spam} \mid w_1, w_2, \ldots, w_n) \propto P(\text{Spam}) \times \prod_{i=1}^{n} P(w_i|\text{Spam})$

o $P(\text{Ham} \mid w_1, w_2, \ldots, w_n) \propto P(\text{Ham}) \times \prod_{i=1}^{n} P(w_i|\text{Ham})$

- Normalize the probabilities to sum up to 1.

- Assign the label with the highest probability as the predicted class for the email.

Calculation Example

Let's demonstrate the calculation of Naïve Bayes probabilities for the example email "Limited time offer, buy now!" based on dataset from table 5.3.

A. **Preprocessing**, Convert text data into a bag-of-words representation. Calculate the frequency of each word in spam and non-spam emails.

B. **Calculate Class Probabilities**

- $P(Spam) = \frac{3}{6} = 0.5$
- $P(Ham) = \frac{3}{6} = 0.5$

C. **Calculate Conditional Probabilities**: For each word in the vocabulary, calculate the conditional probability of that word given the class. Let's assume:

- $P(\text{limited}|\text{Spam}) = 0.67$
- $P(\text{time}|\text{Spam}) = 0.33$
- $P(\text{offer}|\text{Spam}) = 0.67$
- $P(\text{buy}|\text{Spam}) = 0.67$
- $P(\text{limited}|\text{Ham}) = 0$
- $P(\text{time}|\text{Ham}) = 0$
- $P(\text{offer}|\text{Ham}) = 0$
- $P(\text{buy}|\text{Ham}) = 0$

D. **Prediction:** Given the new email "Limited time offer, buy now!", calculate the probability of it being spam or ham:

- $P(\text{Spam}|\text{"Limited time offer, buy now!}) \propto P(\text{Spam})$

$\times P(\text{limited}|\text{Spam}) \times P(\text{time}|\text{Spam}) \times P(\text{offer}|\text{Spam}) \times P(\text{buy}|\text{Spam})$

- $\propto 0.5 \times 0.67 \times 0.33 \times 0.67 \times 0.67$
- $\propto 0.038$
- $P(\text{Ham}|$"Limited time offer, buy now!) $\propto P(\text{Ham})$

$\times P(\text{limited}|\text{Ham}) \times P(\text{time}|\text{Ham}) \times P(\text{offer}|\text{Ham}) \times P(\text{buy}|\text{Ham})$

- $\propto 0.5 \times 0 \times 0 \times 0 \times 0$
- $\propto 0$

E. **Normalize the probabilities**:
$P(\text{Spam}|$"Limited time offer, buy now!) $= \frac{0.038}{0.038 + 0} = 1$

Assign the label with the highest probability as the predicted class. In this case, the email "Limited time offer, buy now!" is predicted to be spam. Based on the Naïve Bayes classifier, the email "Limited time offer, buy now!" is classified as spam.

In conclusion, Naïve Bayes is a powerful and widely used classification algorithm known for its simplicity, efficiency, and effectiveness in handling high-dimensional data. By making strong independence assumptions between features, Naïve Bayes can efficiently estimate class probabilities even with limited training data. Despite its simplicity, Naïve Bayes performs well in many real-world scenarios, including text classification, document categorization, medical diagnosis, recommendation systems, and fraud detection. However, its performance may be hindered by violations of the independence assumption and the inability to capture complex relationships between features. Overall, Naïve Bayes remains a valuable tool in the machine learning toolkit, offering a balance between computational efficiency and competitive performance in various classification tasks.

OTHER METHODS FOR CLASSIFICATION

Besides k-NN, decision trees, and Naïve Bayes, other classification techniques like SVM, logistic regression, random forests, and ensemble methods (boosting, bagging) provide a broader perspective. Understanding these methods helps in selecting the right approach based on data characteristics and analysis goals, setting the stage for deeper exploration in later chapters.

SVM, or Support Vector Machine is a supervised learning algorithm used for classification and regression tasks in machine learning (Jamalludin et al, 2021). It is particularly well-suited for classification tasks and is widely employed in various fields, including text and image classification, bioinformatics, finance, and more. SVM works by finding the optimal hyperplane that separates data points belonging to different classes in feature space. The algorithm aims to maximize the margin, which is the distance between the hyperplane and the nearest data points (known as support vectors). SVM is known for its effectiveness in handling high-dimensional data and its ability to handle both linearly separable and nonlinearly separable data through the use of kernel functions. With its versatility and robust performance, SVM remains a popular choice for classification tasks across different domains.

Logistic regression is a statistical method used for binary classification tasks in machine learning (Thangakumar & Kommina, 2020). Despite its name, logistic regression is actually a classification algorithm rather than a regression one. It models the probability that a given input belongs to a particular class using the logistic function, also known as the sigmoid function. In logistic regression, the output is transformed using the logistic function to ensure it falls between 0 and 1, representing probabilities. This output can then be interpreted as the probability of the input belonging to the positive class (class 1). Logistic regression models the relationship between one or more independent variable (feature) and a binary dependent variable (target) by estimating coefficients for each feature. These coefficients are learned during the training process, typically using optimization algorithms such as gradient descent. Despite its simplicity, logistic regression is widely used due to its interpretability, efficiency, and effectiveness in many classification tasks. It is commonly used in various fields such as healthcare (e.g., predicting disease outcomes), finance (e.g., credit risk assessment), and marketing (e.g., customer churn prediction).

Random Forest is a popular ensemble learning technique used for classification, regression, and other tasks in machine learning. It operates by constructing a multitude of decision trees during training and outputting the mode (classification) or mean prediction (regression) of the individual trees. Random Forest works as follows:

- Bootstrap Sampling (Bagging): Random Forest starts by creating multiple bootstrap samples (random samples with replacement) from the original dataset. Each sample is used to train a separate decision tree.
- Random Feature Selection: For each tree in the forest, only a random subset of features is considered at each split. This helps to introduce diversity among the trees and prevents overfitting.

- Decision Tree Training: Each decision tree in the forest is trained independently using the bootstrap samples and random feature subsets.
- Voting (Classification) or Averaging (Regression): During prediction, the Random Forest aggregates the predictions of all individual trees to make a final prediction. For classification tasks, it uses majority voting among the trees while for regression tasks, it computes the average prediction.

Random Forest offers several advantages: It is robust to overfitting due to its ensemble nature and the use of random feature subsets. It can handle high-dimensional data and large datasets effectively. It provides an estimate of feature importance, allowing insights into the most influential features.

Random Forest is commonly used in various applications such as classification and regression problems in finance, healthcare, and bioinformatics. It is valued for its robustness, scalability, and ability to produce reliable predictions across different domains and datasets.

Each classification technique has its unique advantages and drawbacks, making them suitable for different applications. k-NN is simple and effective for small datasets but struggles with large-scale data due to its computational cost. Naïve Bayes is ideal for high-dimensional data and text classification but assumes feature independence, which may not always hold. Decision Trees offer high interpretability and work well with structured data, but they can be overfit without proper pruning. SVM performs exceptionally well for small, high-dimensional datasets and can handle non-linearly separable data using kernel functions, but it is computationally expensive for large datasets. Logistic Regression is best for binary classification problems and works efficiently with large datasets, though it assumes linear separability, which limits its flexibility. Selecting the right algorithm depends on the specific dataset characteristics and problem requirements.

Different classification techniques perform best under specific dataset conditions. Naïve Bayes and SVM are well-suited for imbalanced datasets, whereas k-NN and Decision Trees perform better with well-distributed classes. For high-dimensional data, SVM and Naïve Bayes are the preferred choices, while k-NN, Decision Trees, and Logistic Regression work best with low-dimensional datasets. Small datasets benefit from k-NN, SVM, and Decision Trees, while Naïve Bayes, Logistic Regression, and Decision Trees scale well for large datasets. Decision Trees and Naïve Bayes handle categorical data efficiently, while SVM, k-NN, and Logistic Regression perform better with numerical features. When dealing with complex feature interactions, Decision Trees and SVM are more effective, and for non-linearly separable data, SVM with kernel tricks and Decision Trees are the best choices. If interpretability is a priority, Decision Trees and Logistic Regression provide clear, understandable results, making them ideal for regulated industries and applications requiring transparency.

The choice of a classification algorithm should align with the dataset structure and classification objective. k-NN is a great choice for small datasets with well-defined clusters, while Naïve Bayes excels in text classification and high-dimensional data processing. Decision Trees are highly interpretable and work well with structured data, making them suitable for decision-making applications. SVM is ideal for high-dimensional and complex datasets, particularly when the data is not linearly separable. Logistic Regression is efficient for binary classification tasks with linearly separable data and is widely used in medical diagnoses and fraud detection. When handling large and complex datasets, ensemble learning techniques such as Random Forest or XGBoost may be more effective than using a single classifier. Selecting the most appropriate model requires understanding the dataset characteristics and balancing accuracy, interpretability, and computational efficiency.

DATA CLASSIFICATION WITH RAPIDMINER SOFTWARE

The data classification experiment conducted with RapidMiner software involves three methods: k-Nearest Neighbors (k-NN), Decision Tree, and Naïve Bayes.

1. K-NN DATA MINING TECHNIQUE

Data scientists can conduct k-NN data mining classification experiments using the Golf dataset within RapidMiner.

Figure 4. Sample dataset: Golf

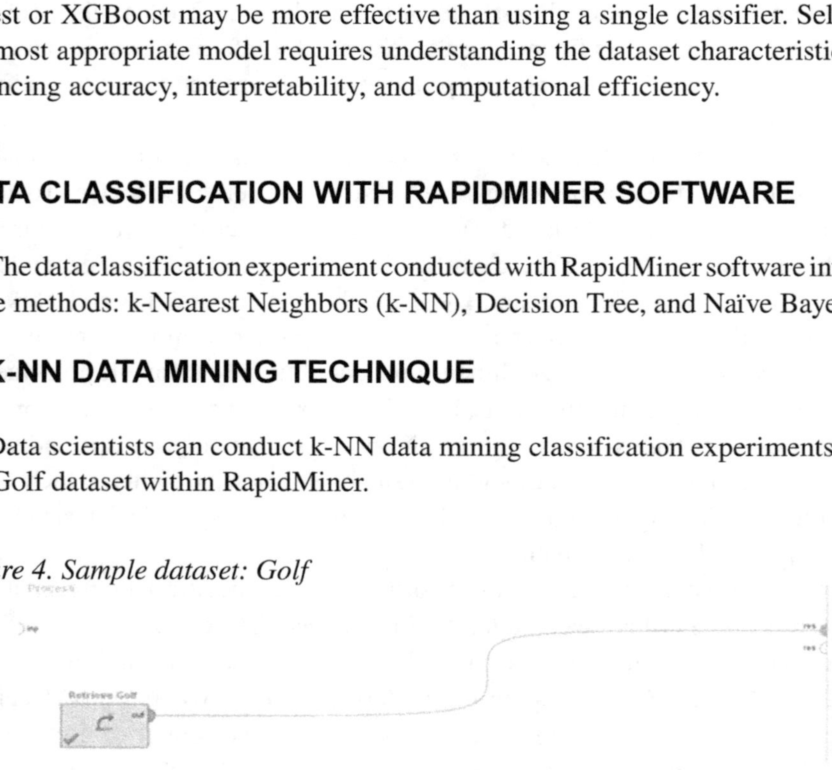

By incorporating a sample dataset named 'Golf' into the model, the dataset includes attributes such as "Play" indicating whether to play golf or not, "Outlook" representing weather conditions, "Temperature", "Humidity", and "Wind". These attributes serve to classify the data and determine the decision whether or not to play golf. Within the dataset, the instances are structured as follows:

Figure 5. Details of golf dataset

Row No.	Play	Outlook	Temperature	Humidity	Wind
1	no	sunny	85	85	false
2	no	sunny	80	90	true
3	yes	overcast	83	78	false
4	yes	rain	70	96	false
5	yes	rain	68	80	false
6	no	rain	65	70	true
7	yes	overcast	64	65	true
8	no	sunny	72	95	false
9	yes	sunny	69	70	false
10	yes	rain	75	80	false
11	yes	sunny	75	70	true
12	yes	overcast	72	90	true
13	yes	overcast	81	75	false
14	no	rain	71	80	true

Next, the data scientist can proceed by right-clicking, selecting "Insert Building Block," and opting for "Nominal Cross Validation" to partition the data into a training set and a test set.

Figure 6. Using nominal cross validation

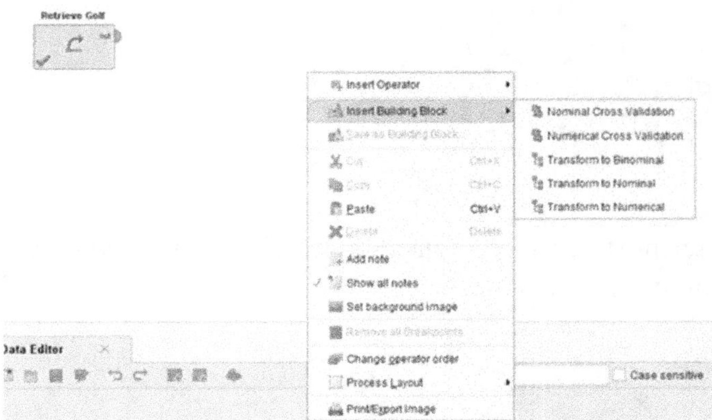

Figure 7. Bringing cross-validation into the model

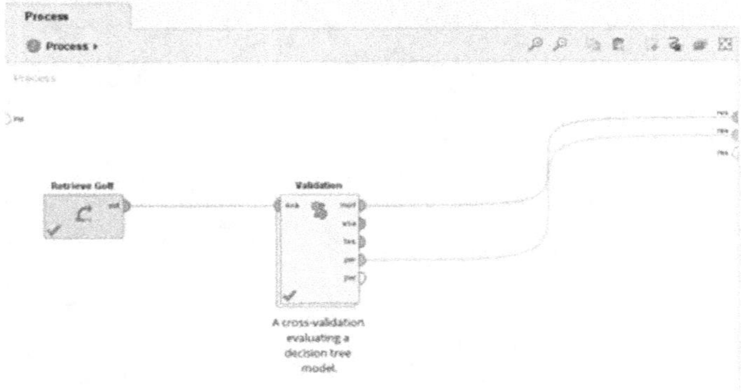

Following this, the data scientist can establish a connection between the Golf dataset and the Validation operator, linking the outcomes of machine learning to the performance testing results. Within the Validation operator, the Decision Tree data mining technique is set as the default option.

Figure 8. Default validation

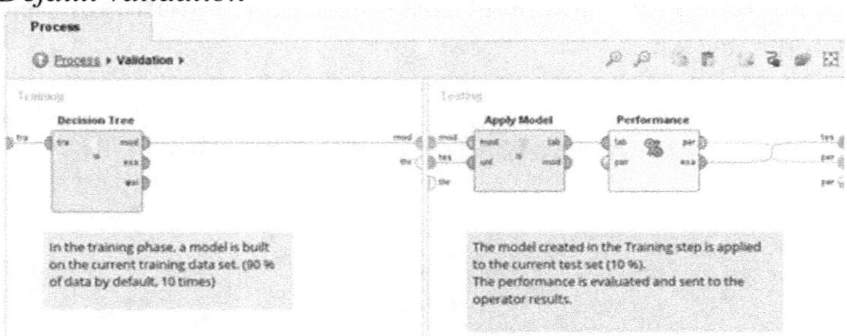

The data scientist can then replace the Decision Tree model with the k-NN model as follows:

Figure 9. Using the k-NN technique for data classification

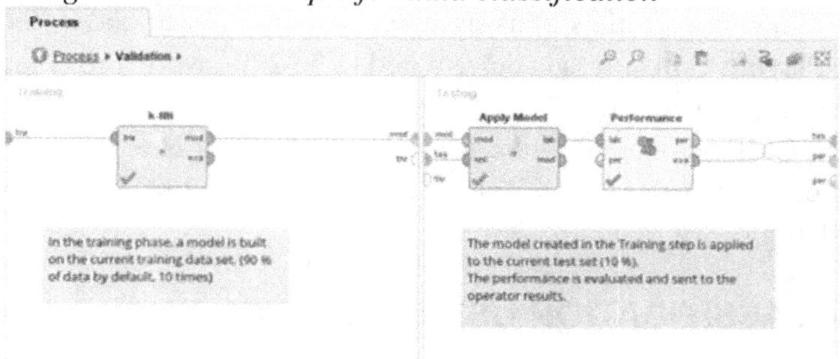

To utilize the k-NN model, the data scientist needs to specify the value of k, which represents the number of neighbors considered during distance analysis. In this example, the value of k is set to 3.

Figure 10. Setting k number

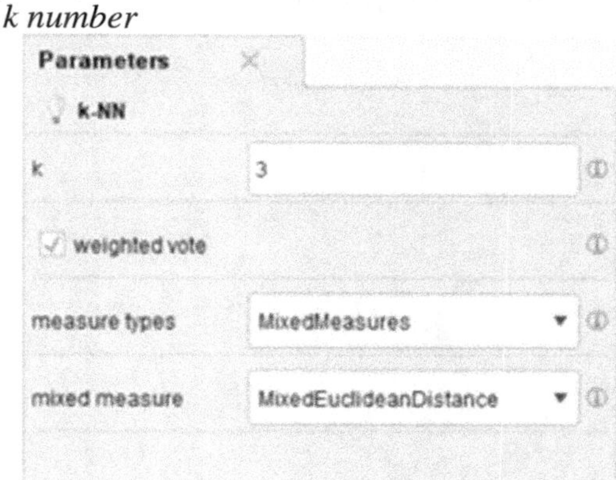

Subsequently, the data scientist can conduct data processing experiments using the k-NN data mining technique to obtain the following results.

Figure 11. Results of data processing with k-NN data mining technique

accuracy: 55.00% +/- 43.78% (micro average: 57.14%)

	true no	true yes	class precision
pred. no	1	2	33.33%
pred. yes	4	7	63.64%
class recall	20.00%	77.78%	

In Figure 10, RapidMiner software displays data using precision and recall techniques, allowing scientists to assess the accuracy of each class. The accuracy of the "Not Playing Golf" class is determined to be 20%, while the "Playing Golf" class achieves an accuracy of 77.8%. Moreover, the accuracy of classified data for "Not Playing Golf" is 33.33% while for "Playing Golf" it is 63.64%. Overall, the accuracy is calculated to be 55%, which can be attributed to the relatively small size of the dataset.

2. DATA CLASSIFICATION USING DECISION TREE

Based on the previous datasets, such as Golf and Cross Validation, when data scientists need to analyze data using Decision Tree, they can utilize Nominal Cross Validation, where the default setting is configured to the Decision Tree as illustrated below.

Figure 12. Using the decision tree defaulted to nominal cross validation

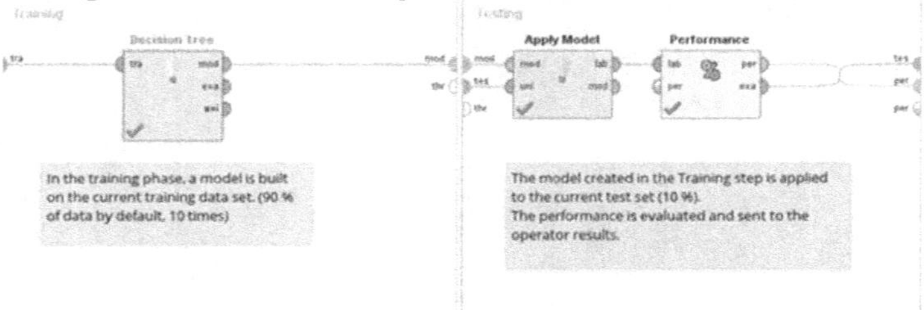

Figure 13. Adjusting parameters to create a decision tree model

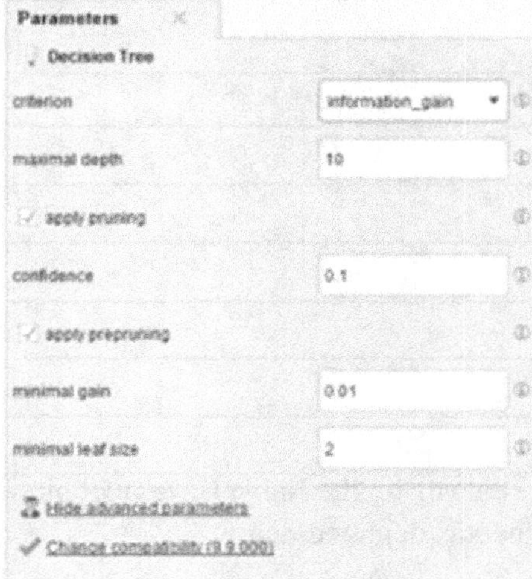

The data scientist has the option to adjust the parameter criterion to "Information Gain" to select the most appropriate attributes for creating a Decision Tree. The outcome of this processing is as follows:

Figure 14. Results from decision tree processing

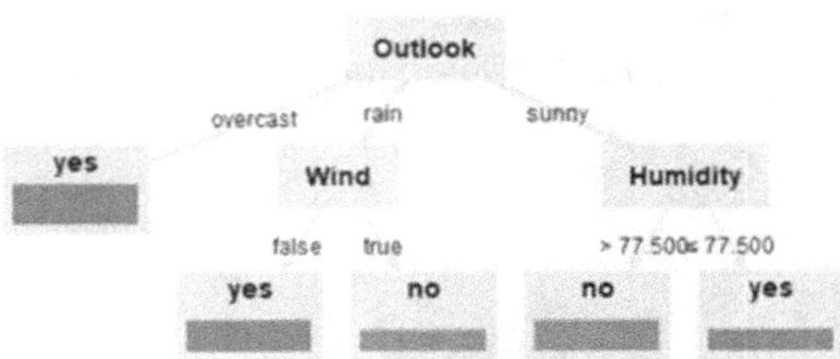

The data scientist can utilize the results obtained from Decision Tree processing to make informed decisions regarding whether to play golf or not.

3. DATA CLASSIFICATION USING NAÏVE BAYES

After the data scientist has conducted data classification experiments with k-NN and Decision Tree, another technique that can be used to classify data with Rapid-Miner software is Naïve Bayes, leveraging the Golf and Nominal Cross Validation datasets as depicted below.

Figure 15. Data classification using naïve bayes

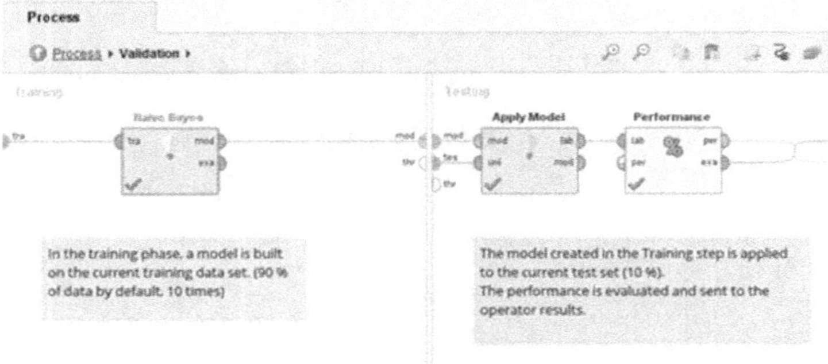

After processing the data using the Naïve Bayes technique, the results of the data classification are obtained as depicted below.

Figure 16. Results from naïve bayes processing

accuracy: 50.00% +/- 47.14% (micro average: 57.14%)

	true no	true yes	class precision
pred. no	1	2	33.33%
pred. yes	4	7	63.64%
class recall	20.00%	77.78%	

The data scientist can classify the data based on the probabilities of each class. In this experiment, the accuracy of the data analysis is 50.0%.

CONCLUSION

The data mining techniques discussed in this book primarily fall under the category of unsupervised learning. To effectively utilize these techniques, the data scientist first divides the dataset into two parts: one for training the machine learning model and the other for testing its performance. The book provides examples of three prominent data mining techniques: k-Nearest Neighbors (k-NN), Decision Tree, and Naïve Bayes. In the case of k-NN, classification involves calculating distances between the data of interest and the dataset used for analysis. This method classifies data by considering the proximity to similar instances in the dataset. Decision Tree, on the other hand, constructs a diagram based on attributes or features, employing techniques such as Information Gain for classification. By incorporating the dataset into the Decision Tree, data scientists can derive appropriate classification results. Lastly, Naïve Bayes facilitates probabilistic analysis of data classification by processing the desired data along with the dataset. RapidMiner software provides a convenient platform for implementing k-NN, Decision Tree, or Naïve Bayes techniques, allowing data scientists to quickly classify data. Additionally, the Cross Validation model is employed to partition the dataset into two subsets: one for training the machine learning model and the other for evaluating the effectiveness of data classification.

EXERCISES

1. Clarify the distinction between clustering and classification.
2. Explain cross validation and its implementation in RapidMiner software.
3. Define the concept of k-Nearest Neighbors (k-NN).
4. Detail the considerations for results derived from Decision Tree analysis in data analysis.
5. Investigate research on the use of classification in data analysis and provide a concise overview.

REFERENCES

Jamalludin, M. D., Muljono, F., Shidik, G. F., & Fanani, A. Z. Purwanto, & Al Zami, F. (2021). Implementation of feature selection using gain ratio towards improved accuracy of support vector machine (SVM) on YouTube comment classification. *2021 International Seminar on Application for Technology of Information and Communication (ISemantic)*, 28–31.

Junaidi, A., Tanjung, N. A. F., Wijayanto, S., Lasama, J., & Iskandar, A. R. (2021). Overfitting problem in images classification for egg incubator using convolutional neural network. *2021 9th International Conference on Cyber and IT Service Management (CITSM)*, 1–7.

Karthik, M. G., & Krishnan, M. B. M. (2021). Detecting internet of things attacks using post pruning decision tree-synthetic minority over sampling technique. *International Journal of Intelligent Engineering & Systems*, *14*(4), 105–114. DOI: 10.22266/ijies2021.0831.10

Khan, S. A., & Ali Rana, Z. (2019). Evaluating performance of software defect prediction models using area under precision-recall curve (AUC-PR). *2019 2nd International Conference on Advancements in Computational Sciences (ICACS)*, 1–6.

Liu, L. (2021). Design of human resource management information system based on decision tree algorithm. *2021 Global Reliability and Prognostics and Health Management (PHM-Nanjing)*, 1–6.

Mishra, A., & Vats, A. (2021). Supervised machine learning classification algorithms for detection of fracture location in dissimilar friction stir welded joints. *Frattura e Integrita Strutturale*, *15*(58), 242–253. DOI: 10.3221/IGF-ESIS.58.18

Mladenova, T. (2021). A feature-weighted rule for the k-nearest neighbor. *2021 5th International Symposium on Multidisciplinary Studies and Innovative Technologies (ISMSIT)*, 493–497.

Mnich, K., Polewko-Klim, A., Kitlas Golinska, A., Lesinski, W., & Rudnicki, W. R. (2020). Super learning with repeated cross validation. *2020 International Conference on Data Mining Workshops (ICDMW)*, 629–635. DOI: 10.1109/ICDMW51313.2020.00089

Mohan, L., Jain, S., Suyal, P., & Kumar, A. (2020). Data mining classification techniques for intrusion detection system. *2020 12th International Conference on Computational Intelligence and Communication Networks (CICN)*, 351–355.

Puspitasari, D. I., Kholdani, A. F. R., Dharmawati, A., Rosadi, M. E., & Dhuhita, W. M. P. (2021). Stroke disease analysis and classification using decision tree and random forest methods. *2021 Sixth International Conference on Informatics and Computing (ICIC)*, 1–4. Alam, M. G. R., Hussain, S., Islam Mim, M. M., & Islam, M. T. (2021). Telecom customer behavior analysis using naïve Bayes classifier. *2021 IEEE 4th International Conference on Computer and Communication Engineering Technology (CCET)*, 308–312. DOI: 10.1109/ICIC54025.2021.9632906

Rahman, B., Warnars, H. L. H. S., Sabarguna, B. S., & Budiharto, W. (2021). Heart disease classification model using k-nearest neighbor algorithm. *2021 Sixth International Conference on Informatics and Computing (ICIC)*, 1–4. DOI: 10.1109/ICIC54025.2021.9632918

Song, H., Fu, Y., Saket, B., & Stasko, J. (2021). Understanding the effects of visualizing missing values on visual data exploration. *2021. IEEE Visualization Conference : VIS*, 161–165.

Thangakumar, J., & Kommina, S. B. (2020). Ant colony optimization-based feature subset selection with logistic regression classification model for education data mining. *International Journal of Advanced Science and Technology*, *29*(3), 5821–5834.

Thongjor, N. (2017). Understanding the data classification: k-nearest neighbours. Retrieved August 9, 2021, from https://www.babelcoder.com/blog/articles/k-nearest-neighbors

Vichi, M., Ritter, G., & Giusti, A. (2013). *Classification and data mining*. Springer Verlag.

Zhang, H., Zhang, L., & Jiang, Y. (2019). Overfitting and underfitting analysis for deep learning-based end-to-end communication systems. *2019 11th International Conference on Wireless Communications and Signal Processing (WCSP)*, 1–6.

Chapter 5
Deep Learning

ABSTRACT

Neural network and deep learning techniques are essential tools for data scientists when analyzing big data for forecasting and classification. In supervised learning, data sets are divided into training sets and test sets, and neural network repeatedly adjusts the weight of data to better represent the actual data. This book offers a practical guide to performing a neural network experiment with RapidMiner, which readers can follow step-by-step. For big data, especially non-linear data, deep learning can be employed. This chapter introduces two types of deep learning: Convolutional Neural Networks (CNN) for picture analysis, and Recurrent Neural Networks (RNN) for sequential or time series data. The book provides a demonstration of both techniques using RapidMiner, making it accessible to readers who wish to deepen their understanding of these powerful tools.

INTRODUCTION

In the early days of artificial intelligence (AI), there was a strong drive to develop AI systems capable of human-like responses. However, this endeavor faced challenges due to the requirement of high-performance computing technology and vast amounts of experimental data. As technology advanced, particularly with the advent of high-performance computing technologies such as GPUs and high-speed networks (Telikani, Shahbahrami, & Gandomi, 2021), data scientists gained the ability to utilize data mining techniques on such platforms and to collect big data for experimentation. Deep learning techniques have emerged as a powerful tool for analyzing unstructured data, including images, sounds, and text (Fernando et al., 2021; Hongyi Zhu, Samtani, Brown, & Hsinchun Chen, 2021). Within deep learning, there are two primary types: Convolutional Neural Networks (CNNs) and Recurrent Neural Networks (RNNs) (Lakshmi Devi & Samundeeswari V, 2021; Snineh et al., 2021). These models leverage pre-configured data processing alongside neural

DOI: 10.4018/979-8-3693-6001-9.ch005

network techniques. Artificial Neural Networks (ANNs) are a data mining technique capable of both classification and numerical predictions, falling under supervised learning (Thankachan, Prakash & Jothi, 2021). Before testing data, machines must first be trained to learn. Unlike other data mining techniques that classify data with linear planes, neural networks allow for classification of data closely aligned with real-world facts through Non-Linear Functions. Neural networks find application in pattern recognition tasks like user face recognition for identification or authentication (Ghorpade & Koneru, 2021) and forecasting tasks such as predicting stock price trends (Chinnarasri, Nonsawang & Supharatid, 2012).

This book delves into the principles of artificial neural networks and deep learning, encompassing both CNN and RNN formats.

ARTIFICIAL NEURAL NETWORK (ANN)

1. CONCEPTUAL WORK OF ARTIFICIAL NEURAL NETWORKS

Artificial Neural Networks (ANNs) are computational models inspired by the biological neural networks present in the human brain. ANNs consist of interconnected nodes, known as neurons, organized in layers (Chow and Cho, 2007: Aggarwal, 2018). Each neuron receives input signals, processes them, and then produces an output signal. The strength of the connections between neurons, known as weights, determines the influence of one neuron's output on another's input (Ramirez-Hernandez et al., 2020: Guo, Zhang and Chen, 2021).

Architecture of Artificial Neural Networks

- The **Input Layer** is the first layer of neurons in the network receives input data. Each neuron represents a feature or attribute of the input data.
- The **Hidden Layers** are intermediate layers between the input and output layers that perform complex transformations on the input data through weighted combinations and activation functions.
- The **Output Layer** is the final layer of neurons that produces the network's output. The number of neurons in the output layer depends on the type of task (e.g., classification, regression).

Figure 1. Artificial neural network

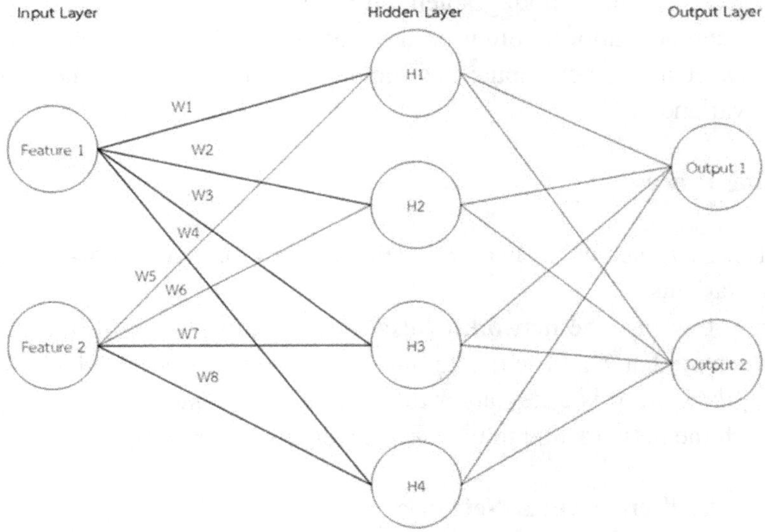

Activation Functions

Activation functions are crucial components of neural networks, introducing non-linearity to enable the network to learn complex patterns in the data. There are several common activation functions used in neural networks:

A. Sigmoid Function
   - The sigmoid function maps input values to the range [0, 1].
   - It is often employed in binary classification tasks, where the output represents probabilities of belonging to a certain class.
   - The sigmoid function has a smooth gradient, making it suitable for gradient-based optimization algorithms like backpropagation.

B. ReLU (Rectified Linear Unit) Function
   - The ReLU function sets negative input values to zero and leaves positive values unchanged.
   - It is widely used in hidden layers due to its computational efficiency and effectiveness in overcoming the vanishing gradient problem.
   - The ReLU function is simple and computationally efficient, making it a popular choice in many neural network architectures.

C. Tanh (Hyperbolic Tangent) Function
   - The tanh function is similar to the sigmoid function but maps input values to the range [-1, 1].

- Like the sigmoid function, tanh is also commonly used in neural networks for its smooth gradient properties.
- Tanh activation is often used in the hidden layers of neural networks, especially when inputs are standardized to have zero mean and unit variance.

Training Process

- ANNs are trained using an optimization algorithm, typically gradient descent or its variants.
- During training, the network adjusts its weighting based on the difference between predicted and actual outputs, minimizing a predefined loss function.
- Backpropagation is a key algorithm used to propagate the error backwards through the network and to update the weights accordingly.

Types of Artificial Neural Networks

- Feedforward Neural Networks (FNNs): Information flows in one direction, from input to output, without cycles or loops, which is suitable for tasks like classification and regression.
- Recurrent Neural Networks (RNNs) allow connections between neurons to form cycles, enabling them to process sequences of data. RNNs are commonly used in tasks like natural language processing and time series prediction.
- Convolutional Neural Networks (CNNs) are designed for processing structured grid-like data, such as images. CNNs leverage convolutional layers to extract hierarchical features from the input data.

Artificial Neural Networks (ANNs) are widely used in image recognition, NLP, speech processing, finance, healthcare, and autonomous systems. However, they require large, labeled datasets, intensive computation, and are prone to overfitting, necessitating techniques like regularization and dropout. Despite these challenges, ANNs are powerful tools for learning complex patterns and advancing AI, but they require careful design and evaluation for optimal performance.

2. DATA ANALYSIS WITHIN ARTIFICIAL NEURAL NETWORK

Let's consider a simple example of an Artificial Neural Network (ANN) processing for a regression task. Suppose we have a dataset containing information about houses, such as their size (in square feet) and the corresponding sale price (in thousands of dollars). We want to train an ANN to predict the sale price of a house based on its size.

A. **Data Preparation:** We start by preprocessing the dataset, which involves normalizing the input features (size) and the target variable (sale price) to ensure they are within a similar scale.
B. **Network Architecture:** For this example, we will create a simple feedforward neural network with one input neuron (for size), one hidden layer with two neurons, and one output neuron (for predicted sale price). We will use ReLU activation functions in the hidden layer and a linear activation function in the output layer for regression.
C. **Training:** We initialize the weights and biases of the neural network randomly. We use a gradient descent optimization algorithm along with backpropagation to update the weights and biases iteratively, minimizing the Mean Squared Error (MSE) loss between the predicted sale prices and the actual sale prices in the training dataset.
D. **Forward Pass:** Given a house size as input, we perform a forward pass through the network to compute the predicted sale price. The input size is multiplied by the weights connecting the input layer to the hidden layer and is passed through the ReLU activation function. The output of the hidden layer is then multiplied by the weights connecting the hidden layer to the output layer and passed through the linear activation function to obtain the predicted sale price.
E. **Backward Pass:** we calculate the gradient of the loss function with respect to the network's parameters (weights and biases) using backpropagation. We update the weights and biases in the network based on the gradient descent algorithm to minimize the loss function.
F. **Evaluation:** After training the network on a portion of the dataset, we evaluate its performance on a separate validation set. We calculate metrics such as Mean Absolute Error (MAE) or Mean Squared Error (MSE) to assess how well the network predicts the sale prices of houses it has not seen during training.

By iteratively adjusting the weights and biases through the training process, the neural network learns to map house sizes to their corresponding sale prices, effectively performing regression. The accuracy of the predictions depends on factors such as the network architecture, the size of the dataset, and the quality of the features.

Let's demonstrate the calculation process for a simple neural network with one input neuron, one hidden layer with two neurons, and one output neuron for a regression task. We will use the following notation:

x: Input Feature (house size)

h_1, h_2: Outputs of the hidden layer neurons
w_{ij}: Weight connecting neuron *i* in the input layer to neuron *j* in the hidden layer
b_j: Bias term for neuron *j* in the hidden layer
v_j: Weight connecting neuron *j* in the hidden layer to the output neuron
c: Bias term for the output neuron
ReLU(*z*): Rectified Linear Unit activation function
$\hat{y}$: Predicted sale price

Let's assume the following parameters and initial values:

- $w_{11} = 0.5, w_{12} = 0.8$
- $b_1 = 0.2, b_2 = 0.3$
- $v_1 = 0.6, v_2 = 0.7$
- $c = 0.4$

Suppose we have a house with a size $x = 1500$ square feet.

A. Forward Pass

- **Input Layer to hidden Layer**

o $h_1 = \text{ReLU}(w_{11} \times x + b_1) = \text{ReLU}(0.5 \times 1500 + 0.2) = \text{ReLU}(750 + 0.2) = \text{ReLU}(750.2)$

$= 750.2$

o $h_2 = \text{ReLU}(w_{12} \times x + b_2) = \text{ReLU}(0.8 \times 1500 + 0.3) = \text{ReLU}(1200 + 0.3) = \text{ReLU}(1200.3)$

$= 1200.3$

- **Hidden Layer to Output Layer**

o $\hat{y} = v_1 \times h_1 \times v_2 \times h_2 + c$

o $\hat{y} = 0.6 \times 750.2 \times 0.7 \times 1200.3 + 0.4$

o $\hat{y} = 450.12 + 840.21 + 0.4$

o $\hat{y} = 1290.3$

Thus, the predicted sale price for a house with a size of 1500 square feet is approximately \$1290.73.

B. Backward Pass

In the backward pass, we compute the gradient of the loss function with respect to each parameter (weights and biases) in the neural network using the chain rule of calculus. We then update the parameters in the opposite direction of the gradient to minimize the loss function. Let's consider the Mean Squared Error (MSE) loss function for simplicity:

$$L(\hat{y}, y) = \frac{1}{2}(y - \hat{y})^2$$

Where $\hat{y}$ is the predicted sale price, and y is the actual sale price from the training data.

Using the chain rule, the gradients for the parameters in the backward pass are computed as follows:

A. Output Layer

- $\frac{\partial L}{\partial \hat{y}} = \left(\hat{y} - y\right)$
- $\frac{\partial \hat{y}}{\partial v_j} = h_j$
- $\frac{\partial \hat{y}}{\partial c} = 1$

B. Hidden Layer

- $\frac{\partial L}{\partial h_j} = (\hat{y} - y) \times v_j$
- $\frac{\partial h_j}{\partial w_{ij}} = x_i$ (where x_i is the input feature)
- $\frac{\partial h_i}{\partial b_j} = 1$

C. Update Rule

- $v_j = v_j - \alpha \times \frac{\partial L}{\partial \hat{y}} \times \frac{\partial \hat{y}}{\partial v_j}$
- $c = c - \alpha \times \frac{\partial L}{\partial \hat{y}} \times \frac{\partial \hat{y}}{\partial c}$
- $w_{ij} = w_{ij} - \alpha \times \frac{\partial L}{\partial h_j} \times \frac{\partial h_j}{\partial w_{ij}}$

- $b_j = b_j - \alpha \times \frac{\partial L}{\partial h_j} \times \frac{\partial h_i}{\partial b_j}$

where α is the learning rate, controlling the step size during parameter updates.

Using the forward pass result from the previous example, let's assume the actual sale price y for the house with a size of 1500 square feet is $1300 thousand. The gradients and parameter updates can be calculated accordingly.

- $\frac{\partial L}{\partial \hat{y}} = \left(\hat{y} - y\right) = (1290.73 - 1300) = -9.27$
- $\frac{\partial \hat{y}}{\partial v_1} = h_1 = 750.2$
- $\frac{\partial \hat{y}}{\partial v_2} = h_2 = 1200.3$
- $\frac{\partial h_i}{\partial b_j} = 1$
- $\frac{\partial L}{\partial h_1} = (\hat{y} - y) \times v_1 = -9.27 \times 0.6 = -5.562$
- $\frac{\partial L}{\partial h_2} = (\hat{y} - y) \times v_2 = -9.27 \times 0.7 = -6.489$

Using these gradients, we can update the weights and biases accordingly to improve the network's performance in subsequent iterations of training.

In conclusion, Artificial Neural Networks (ANNs) are powerful computational models inspired by the structure and function of the human brain. They have found wide-ranging applications across various domains, including image recognition, natural language processing, financial forecasting, healthcare, and autonomous vehicles. ANNs introduce non-linearity to data processing, allowing them to learn complex patterns and make predictions from input data. By adjusting the weights and biases through iterative training processes such as forward and backward passes, ANNs can effectively approximate complex functions and make accurate predictions. Despite their effectiveness, ANNs come with challenges such as the need for large amounts of labeled training data, computational intensity, and the risk of overfitting. However, with advancements in hardware technologies and optimization algorithms, ANNs continue to be at the forefront of machine learning research and applications, driving innovations and breakthroughs in various fields.

3. ANALYZING DATA WITH ARTIFICIAL NEURAL NETWORK USING RAPIDMINER SOFTWARE

Data scientists can import the desired dataset for both classification and numerical forecasting into RapidMiner software and then proceed to create an artificial neural network model as depicted in the following figure.

Figure 2. Starting neural net

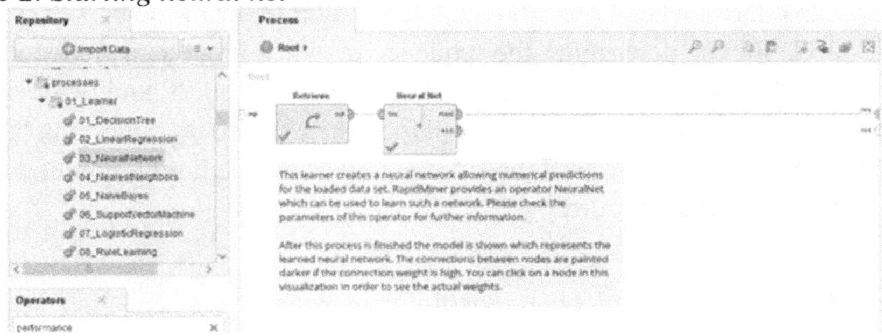

Data scientists can initiate the utilization of the Artificial Neural Network model through the sample process within RapidMiner software, named “NeuralNetwork.” This process facilitates the preparation of an entire numerical dataset and employs a Neural Net model to extract and analyze the data. Data scientists can determine the parameters as follows:

Figure 3. Parameters of the neural network

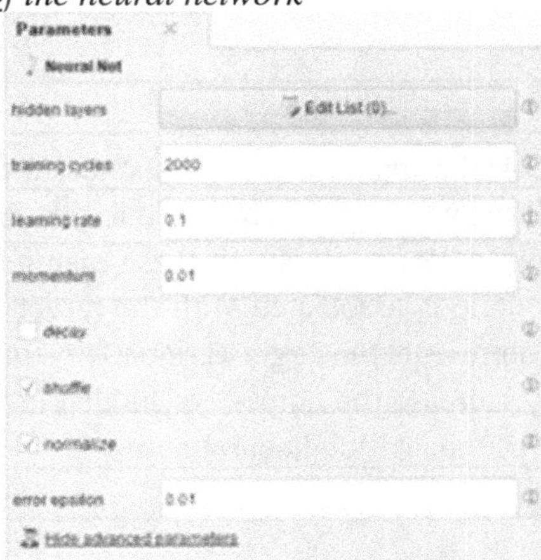

From the provided figure, data scientists can specify several parameters for the Artificial Neural Network model. Firstly, they can determine the number of hidden layers, which influences the network's capacity to learn complex patterns from the data. Next, the Training Cycle parameter is defined to specify the number of iterations or epochs during the training process, indicating the number of times the machine undergoes the learning phase. The learning rate, ranging from 0 to 1, determines the step size of weight adjustments during training while Momentum indicates the influence of previous weight adjustments on the current round. Additionally, scientists can choose whether to adjust the learning rate over time by selecting the Decay option. Shuffle determines the sequence in which input data are fed into the model, Normalization scales the data to a range between 0 and 1, and Error Epsilon sets a threshold for the model to stop training when the error value falls below a predefined threshold. Once configured, scientists can execute the model, and the results will be generated accordingly.

Figure 4. Executing the results of an artificial neural network

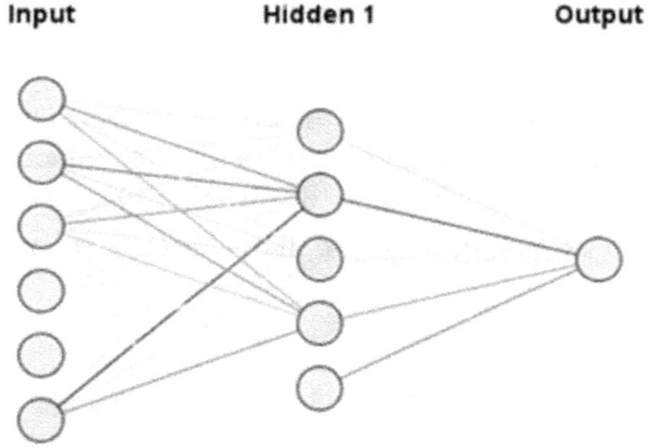

As shown in Figure 4, the input node corresponds to the number of features utilized in the data analysis, which in this instance is five features. The neural network generates five input nodes to represent these features, alongside additional bias nodes. The output node is associated with the target variable, where in this example, a single node represents the target variable. Scientists have the flexibility to adjust and potentially increase the number of hidden layers, thereby enhancing the analysis complexity of the artificial neural network.

Figure 5. Adding a hidden layer to an artificial neural network

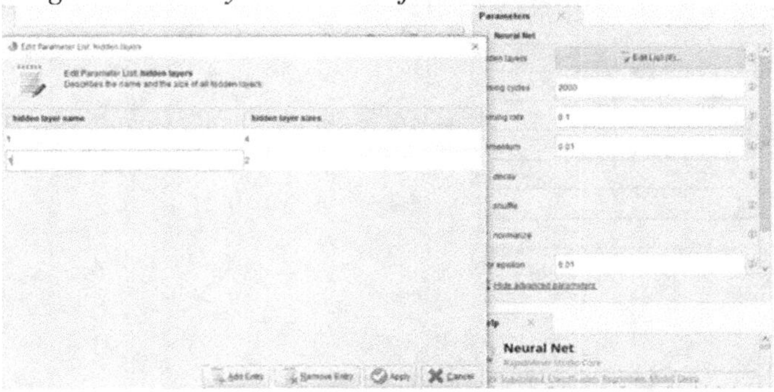

Data scientists can press the "Edit List" button to add hidden layers by specifying the number of hidden nodes. In the figure below, scientists define two hidden layers. Layer 1 is configured with four hidden nodes while layer 2 is determined to have two hidden nodes. Upon execution, the results are generated accordingly.

Figure 6. Adding hidden layers

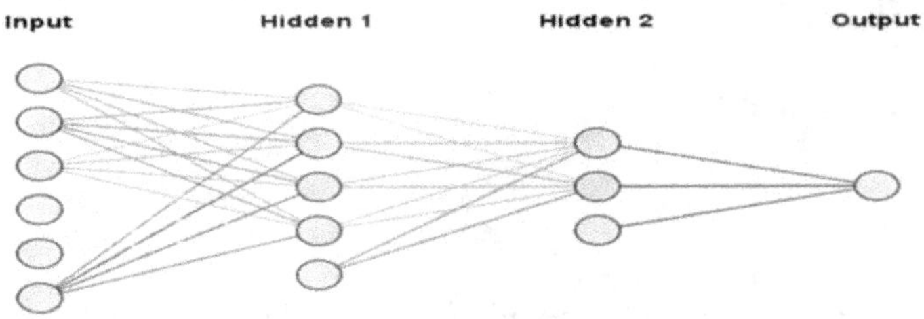

As shown in Figure 6, when data scientists set the nodes in layer 1 to 4, additional bias nodes are automatically added. Similarly, in layer 2, two additional bias nodes are set. When data scientists aim to classify data using artificial neural networks, they can conduct experiments using a sample dataset within RapidMiner software, such as the Iris dataset. This dataset contains information about the sizes of Iris flower petals. By leveraging this dataset, experiments can be conducted to identify the species of Iris flowers based on the provided data.

Figure 7. Iris classification experiment

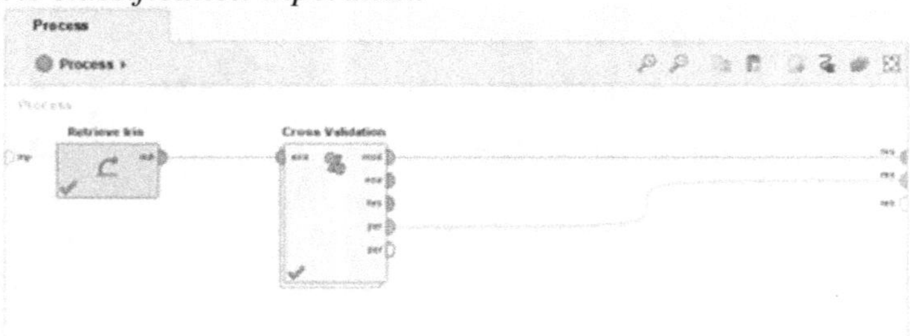

As shown in Figure 7, data scientists import the Iris dataset into the process. Subsequently, the Cross Validation model is employed to partition the data into two subsets: one for training the machine learning model and the other for testing the classification of Iris species. The results of these two parts, including the neural network model and its classification accuracy, are interconnected within the Cross Validation framework.

Figure 8. Processing results with neural net

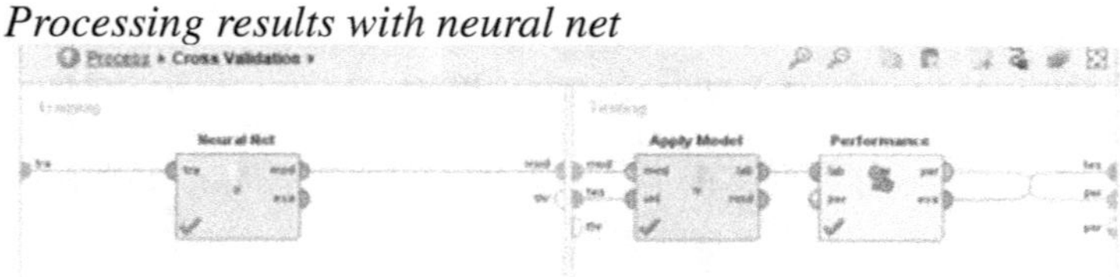

As shown in Figure 8, the Cross Validation model utilizes the Neural Net model to train the machine learning algorithm on data pertaining to the width and length of Iris petals. This training process aims to enable the model to accurately identify different Iris flower species and construct a neural network accordingly. Subsequently, the Apply Model component is employed to apply the trained model and to generate classifications for Iris flowers based on their petal width and length. Finally, in the concluding section, the accuracy of Iris flower species classification is analyzed and evaluated.

Figure 9. Neural network for iris flower species identification

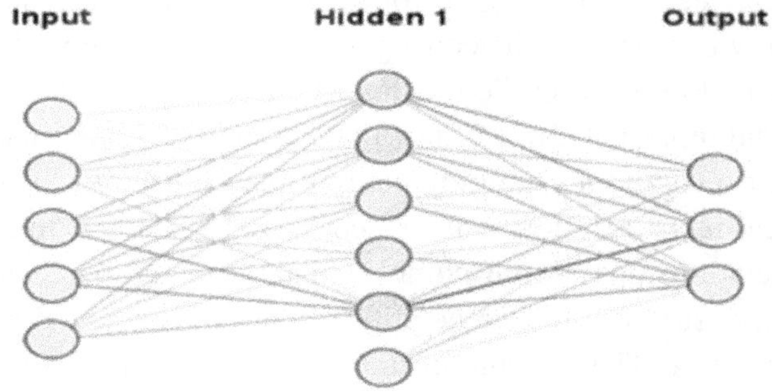

As depicted in Figure 9, the ANN comprises four input features, representing the width and length of the Iris flower. Additionally, there is one hidden layer composed of five nodes, along with three output nodes corresponding to the three types of Iris flower. The accuracy of data classification is shown in Figure 10.

Figure 10. Accuracy of data classification with an artificial neural network

accuracy: 97.33% +/- 3.44% (micro average: 97.33%)

	true Iris-setosa	true Iris-versicolor	true Iris-virginica	class precision
pred. Iris-setosa	50	0	0	100.00%
pred. Iris-versicolor	0	47	1	97.92%
pred. Iris-virginica	0	3	49	94.23%
class recall	100.00%	94.00%	98.00%	

After analyzing the accuracy of Iris data classification, it is observed that the ANN achieves an accuracy of 97.33%. Data scientists have the capability to adjust the number of hidden layers to enhance the complexity of data processing for the ANN. However, the effectiveness of using additional hidden layers for high-precision data analysis is contingent upon the characteristics of the dataset. Notably, the accuracy does not necessarily increase with the addition of more hidden layers. Therefore, it is imperative for data scientists to adequately prepare the data for analysis and conduct various data analysis experiments to attain the most accurate results.

4. DEEP LEARNING

Deep learning is a subset of machine learning that involves training ANNs to learn from large amounts of data in an unsupervised or supervised manner. It is inspired by the structure and function of the human brain, particularly the interconnected neurons that process and transmit information. The term "deep" refers to the multiple layers of interconnected nodes, or neurons, within the neural network. At its core, deep learning revolves around the concept of hierarchical feature learning. Instead of manually extracting features from data, deep learning algorithms automatically learn hierarchical representations of the input data, gradually transforming it from raw data into abstract and meaningful features at each layer of the neural network. This hierarchical representation enables deep learning models to capture intricate patterns and relationships within complex datasets, making them exceptionally powerful for tasks such as image recognition, natural language processing, speech recognition, and more. The key components of deep learning include the following:

A. Artificial Neural Networks (ANNs): Deep learning models are typically built using ANNs, which are composed of interconnected layers of nodes. Each node, or neuron, performs simple computations on its input data and passes the result to the next layer. ANNs can vary in architecture, including feedforward neural networks, convolutional neural networks (CNNs), recurrent neural networks (RNNs), and more.
B. Training with Backpropagation: Deep learning models are trained using an optimization algorithm called backpropagation. During training, the model's predictions are compared to the ground truth labels, and the difference, or error, is propagated backwards through the network to adjust the model's weights and biases. This iterative process minimizes error and improves the model's performance over time.
C. Activation Functions introduce non-linearity to the neural network, allowing it to capture complex relationships in the data. Common activation functions include sigmoid, ReLU (Rectified Linear Unit), tanh (Hyperbolic Tangent), and softmax, each serving different purposes depending on the architecture and task.
D. Optimization Algorithms such as stochastic gradient descent (SGD), Adam, and RMSprop, are used to update the model's parameters during training and find the optimal set of weights and biases that minimize the loss function.
E. Deep Learning Frameworks such as TensorFlow, PyTorch, Keras, and MXNet, provide tools and libraries for building, training, and deploying deep learning models efficiently.

Overall, deep learning has revolutionized the field of artificial intelligence by enabling machines to learn complex patterns and representations from data, leading to remarkable advancements in a wide range of applications across industries.

4.1 Convolutional Neural Networks (CNN)

Convolutional Neural Network (CNN) is a specialized type of ANN designed to process and analyze structured grid-like data, such as images and videos (Sriwiboon, 2020). CNNs are particularly adept at capturing spatial hierarchies and patterns in data, making them incredibly effective for tasks such as image recognition, object detection, and image classification. At the core of CNNs are convolutional layers, which apply convolution operations to input data using learnable filters or kernels. These filters enable the network to extract features from the input data by detecting patterns such as edges, textures, and shapes. Additionally, CNNs typically include pooling layers, which downsample the feature maps obtained from the convolutional layers to reduce the computational complexity and to extract the most relevant information.

One of the key advantages of CNNs is their ability to automatically learn hierarchical representations of features through the network's architecture. As the data flow through successive convolutional and pooling layers, the network learns to detect increasingly complex patterns and features at different levels of abstraction. This hierarchical feature learning enables CNNs to achieve remarkable performance on tasks such as image classification and object detection. Furthermore, CNNs often incorporate other layers such as activation functions (e.g., ReLU), normalization layers (e.g., BatchNormalization), and fully connected layers to further enhance their representational power and predictive performance. Additionally, modern CNN architectures, such as ResNet, VGG, and Inception, leverage advanced design principles and techniques to achieve state-of-the-art results on challenging visual recognition tasks.

Overall, CNNs have revolutionized the field of computer vision and image processing, enabling machines to achieve human-level performance on a wide range of visual tasks. Their versatility, scalability, and effectiveness make CNNs indispensable tools in various domains, including healthcare, autonomous vehicles, surveillance, and entertainment.

Feature extraction in image processing refers to the process of identifying and extracting meaningful information or patterns from images. It plays a crucial role in various computer vision tasks, such as object detection, image classification, and image segmentation. Feature extraction techniques aim to represent images in a way that captures important characteristics while reducing the complexity of the data. There are several methods for feature extraction in image processing, including the following:

- Pixel Intensity Features: Basic features that describe the intensity of pixels in an image, such as mean intensity, standard deviation, and histogram-based features.
- Edge Detection: Edge detection algorithms identify boundaries between objects in an image by detecting abrupt changes in pixel intensity. Common edge detection methods include the Sobel, Prewitt, and Canny edge detectors.
- Texture Analysis: Texture features describe the spatial arrangement of pixels in an image and capture information about patterns, such as roughness, smoothness, and regularity. Texture analysis techniques include gray-level co-occurrence matrices (GLCM), local binary patterns (LBP), and Gabor filters.
- Corner Detection: Corner detection algorithms identify key points or corners in an image where there is a significant change in brightness or intensity. Harris corner detection and FAST (Features from Accelerated Segment Test) are popular corner detection methods.
- Scale-Invariant Feature Transform (SIFT): SIFT is a feature detection and description algorithm that detects and describes local features in an image, which are invariant to changes in scale, rotation, and illumination.
- Convolutional Neural Networks (CNNs): CNNs automatically learn hierarchical features from images through convolutional layers. These learned features can capture complex patterns and structures in the images and are often used in deep learning-based image processing tasks.

After extracting features from images, they are typically represented as feature vectors, which can then be used as input to machine learning algorithms for tasks such as classification, clustering, or regression. Feature extraction is a critical step in image processing pipelines and significantly impacts the performance and accuracy of computer vision systems.

A filter matrix, in the context of image processing and convolutional neural networks (CNNs), refers to a matrix or kernel used to perform convolution operations on an input image. In image processing, convolution involves applying a filter matrix to an input image to extract specific features or to perform various operations such as blurring, sharpening, edge detection, or noise reduction. The filter matrix slides over the image, and at each position, the element-wise product between the filter and the corresponding patch of the image is computed, and the results are then summed to produce a single output value. This process is repeated for every position in the image, resulting in a filtered output image. In the context of CNNs, filter matrices are also known as convolutional filters or kernels. These filters are the learnable parameters of the convolutional layers in the network. During the training process, the CNN learns to adjust the values of these filter matrices to extract meaningful features from the input images. Each filter captures specific patterns or features present in the images, such as edges, textures, or shapes.

The size and values of the filter matrix determine the nature of the features extracted from the input image. Commonly used filter sizes in CNNs include 3x3, 5x5, and 7x7. The values of the filter matrix are adjusted through the training process via backpropagation, where the network learns to optimize the filters to improve the performance of the model on a given task, such as image classification or object detection. In summary, a filter matrix is a key component in image processing and CNNs, used to extract features from input images through convolution operations. It plays a crucial role in tasks such as feature extraction, image enhancement, and pattern recognition.

Let's consider an example of Convolutional Neural Network (CNN) processing with a dataset of handwritten digits, such as the famous MNIST dataset. The MNIST dataset consists of 28x28 pixel grayscale images of handwritten digits (0-9) and corresponding labels.

A. **Dataset Preparation:** the MNIST dataset contains a training set of 60,000 images and a test set of 10,000 images. Each image is a grayscale 28x28 pixel array, and each pixel value ranges from 0 to 255, representing the intensity of the pixel. The goal is to train a CNN to classify these images into their respective digit classes (0-9).
B. **Model Architecture:** We will build a simple CNN architecture consisting of convolutional layers, pooling layers, and fully connected layers. The convolutional layers will extract features from the input images, while the pooling layers will downsample the feature maps. Finally, fully connected layers will perform classification based on the extracted features.
C. **Training the CNN:** We will train the CNN using the training set of handwritten digit images and their corresponding labels. During training, the CNN will learn to recognize patterns and features associated with each digit class through backpropagation and optimization algorithms like stochastic gradient descent. The training process involves iteratively adjusting the parameters (weights and biases) of the CNN to minimize the prediction error.
D. **Evaluating the CNN:** After training, we will evaluate the performance of the CNN using the test set of images. The CNN will make predictions on the test images, and we will compare these predictions with the ground truth labels to measure the accuracy of the model. Additionally, we can visualize the CNN's predictions and inspect any misclassifications to gain insights into its performance.
E. **Example Results:** Upon evaluation, the CNN achieves an accuracy of over 99% on the MNIST test set, demonstrating its effectiveness in accurately classifying handwritten digits. We can further analyze the CNN's performance by examining

its confusion matrix, precision, recall, and other evaluation metrics to gain a deeper understanding of its strengths and weaknesses.

Let's consider a simple example of convolutional neural network (CNN) processing with a small dataset of grayscale images. For demonstration purposes, we will use a toy dataset consisting of 3x3 pixel images with values ranging from 0 to 255.

Figure 11. Example grayscale image dataset for CNN demonstration

```
Image 1:
[[100, 150, 200],
 [120, 140, 180],
 [90, 110, 130]]

Image 2:
[[80, 90, 100],
 [110, 120, 130],
 [150, 160, 170]]
```

Let's define a simple CNN architecture with one convolutional layer and one max-pooling layer:

A. Convolutional Layer
   - Filter size: 2x2
   - Stride: 1
   - Padding: None (valid convolution)

B. Max-Pooling Layer:
   - Pool size: 2x2
   - Stride: 2

Now, let's perform the forward pass of this CNN architecture on the given dataset:

C. Convolutional Layer:
   - Apply a 2x2 filter/kernel to each 3x3 image to produce feature maps:
     - o Feature map 1 (Image 1):

[[(100W11 + 150W12 + 120W21 + 140W22), (150W11 + 200W12 + 140W21 + 180W22)],
[(120W11 + 140W12 + 90W21 + 110W22), (140W11 + 180W12 + 110W21 + 130W22)]]

- o Feature map 2 (Image 2):

[[(80W11 + 90W12 + 110W21 + 120W22), (90W11 + 100W12 + 120W21 + 130W22)],
[(110W11 + 120W12 + 150W21 + 160W22), (120W11 + 130W12 + 160W21 + 170W22)]]

D. Max-Pooling Layer:

- Apply max-pooling with a 2x2 window to each feature map:
    - o Max-pooled feature map 1:
    - o [[(200), (180)]]
    - o [[(180), (130)]]
    - o Max-pooled feature map 2:
    - o [[(120), (130)]]
    - o [[(160), (170)]]

These max-pooled feature maps are the outputs of the CNN for the given dataset. They represent the extracted features after the convolution and max-pooling operations. The values within these feature maps will then be flattened and passed through fully connected layers for further processing, such as classification or regression.

4.2 Recurrent Neural Networks (RNN)

Recurrent Neural Networks (RNN) are a type of artificial neural network designed to handle sequential data by incorporating feedback loops (Sabau et. al., 2021). Unlike feedforward neural networks, which process input data in a single pass, RNNs can maintain internal state or memory, allowing them to capture temporal dependencies and patterns in sequential data. At each time step, an RNN receives an input vector and produces an output vector while also updating its internal state based on both the current input and the previous state. This recurrent connection enables RNNs to model sequences of arbitrary lengths and capture long-term dependencies in the data. One of the key features of RNNs is their ability to handle input sequences of varying lengths, making them well-suited for tasks such as natural language processing (NLP), speech recognition, time series analysis, and handwriting recognition. RNNs can learn to generate sequences of text, predict the next word in a sentence, classify sentiment in a text document, or forecast future values in a time series.

Figure 12. RNN architecture

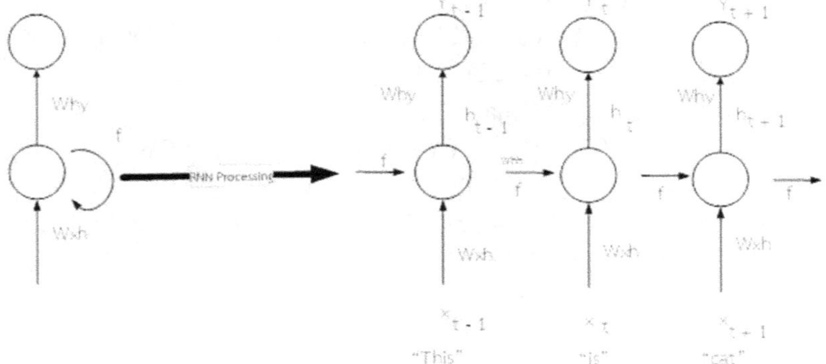

However, traditional RNNs suffer from the vanishing gradient problem where gradients become extremely small during backpropagation through time, leading to difficulties in learning long-range dependencies. To address this issue, several variants of RNNs have been developed, including Long Short-Term Memory (LSTM) networks and Gated Recurrent Units (GRU), which incorporate specialized memory cells and gating mechanisms to better preserve and update information over time. Overall, RNNs are powerful tools for modeling sequential data and have been widely used in various applications across fields such as natural language processing, speech recognition, and time series prediction. Their ability to capture temporal dependencies makes them an essential component of many deep learning architectures.

Consider a dataset containing daily temperature recordings from a weather station over several years. The goal is to use a Recurrent Neural Network (RNN) to predict the temperature for the next day based on historical temperature data.

A. **Data Pre-processing**: The dataset consists of a sequence of daily temperature measurements. Each data point includes the temperature value and the date. Before training the RNN, the data must be pre-processed by scaling the temperature values and encoding the dates into a format suitable for input to the RNN.
B. **Sequence Creation**: Next, the dataset is divided into sequences of fixed length, with each sequence containing a window of past temperature measurements as input and the temperature measurement for the next day as the target output. For example, we may create sequences of length 30, where each input sequence contains temperature readings for the past 30 days and the corresponding output is the temperature for the next day.

C. **Model Architecture**: The RNN model architecture consists of an input layer, one or more recurrent layers (such as LSTM or GRU), and an output layer. The input to the model is a sequence of temperature measurements, and the output is the predicted temperature for the next day. The model is trained using back-propagation through time (BPTT), where gradients are computed and updated across the entire sequence.
D. **Training**: The RNN is trained on the pre-processed dataset using stochastic gradient descent (SGD) or another optimization algorithm. During training, the model learns to capture temporal dependencies in the data and make accurate predictions based on the input sequence.
E. **Prediction**: Once the RNN is trained, it can be used to make predictions on new, unseen data. Given a sequence of past temperature measurements, the RNN predicts the temperature for the next day. This prediction can be compared to the actual temperature measurement to evaluate the model's performance.
F. **Evaluation**: The performance of the RNN model is evaluated using metrics such as mean squared error (MSE) or root mean squared error (RMSE) on a validation set or test set. These metrics quantify the difference between the predicted temperatures and the actual temperatures, providing insight into the model's accuracy and generalization ability.

By training an RNN on historical temperature data and using it to predict future temperatures, we demonstrate the ability of RNNs to model temporal dependencies and to make sequential predictions in time series data. Let's consider a simplified example to demonstrate how a Recurrent Neural Network (RNN) processes sequential data. We will use a toy dataset consisting of a sequence of numbers:

Dataset: [1, 2, 3, 4, 5, 6, 7, 8, 9, 10]

Objective: The task is to predict the next number in the sequence.

A. **Data Pre-processing:** In this simple example, no pre-processing is required as the dataset is already in a suitable format.
B. **Sequence Creation:** We will create input-output pairs or sequences of fixed length. Let's say we choose a sequence length of 3. So, the input sequences and their corresponding outputs will be as follows:

Table 1. Example dataset for RNN processing

Input (X)	Output (y)
[1, 2, 3]	4
[2, 3, 4]	5
[3, 4, 5]	6
[4, 5, 6]	7
[5, 6, 7]	8
[6, 7, 8]	9
[7, 8, 9]	10

C. **Model Architecture:** We will use a simple RNN model with one recurrent layer and a single output neuron. Each input sequence will be fed into the RNN, and the model will learn to predict the next number in the sequence.

D. **Training:** The RNN is trained using the input-output pairs generated from the dataset. During training, the model learns to capture patterns in the sequential data and make accurate predictions.

E. **Prediction:** Once trained, the RNN can be used to predict the next number in the sequence given an input sequence. For example, if we input the sequence [8, 9, 10], the model should predict the next number, which is 11.

Let's assume the trained RNN model has learned the following weights and biases:

- Weight matrix connecting the input to the hidden layer: W_input_hidden = [[0.1], [0.2], [0.3]]
- Weight matrix connecting the hidden layer to the output: W_hidden_output = [0.4]
- Bias term for the hidden layer: b_hidden = 0.1
- Bias term for the output: b_output = 0.2

Now, let's calculate the prediction for the input sequence [8, 9, 10]:

A. Forward Pass

- Input sequence: [8, 9, 10]
- Hidden state at time step 1:

  h_1 = tanh(W_input_hidden * [8; 9; 10] + b_hidden)

  $= \tanh([0.1 * 8 + 0.2 * 9 + 0.3 * 10] + 0.1)$

  $\approx \tanh(3.2 + 0.1) \approx \tanh(3.3)$

  ≈ 0.9975

- Hidden state at time step 2:

  $h\_2 = \tanh(W\_input\_hidden * [9; 10; y\_1] + b\_hidden)$
  $= \tanh([0.1 * 9 + 0.2 * 10 + 0.3 * 0.9975] + 0.1)$
  $\approx \tanh(3.7 + 0.1) \approx \tanh(3.8)$
  ≈ 0.9984
- Output prediction

  $y\_pred = W\_hidden\_output * h\_2 + b\_output$
  $= [0.4] * 0.9984 + 0.2$
  $\approx 0.3994 + 0.2$
  ≈ 0.5994

B. **Result:** The predicted next number in the sequence after [8, 9, 10] is approximately 0.5994.

This is a simplified example to demonstrate the calculation process of an RNN. In practice, RNNs are applied to more complex sequential data and tasks, such as natural language processing and time series prediction.

In conclusion, Recurrent Neural Networks (RNNs) are a powerful class of neural network designed to handle sequential data by maintaining internal memory. They have shown remarkable success in various tasks such as natural language processing, time series prediction, and sequence generation. RNNs excel at capturing temporal dependencies and patterns in sequential data, making them well-suited for tasks where the order of data points matters. Despite their effectiveness, RNNs have certain limitations, including difficulties in learning long-term dependencies and vanishing/exploding gradient problems. Nevertheless, advancements such as Long Short-Term Memory (LSTM) and Gated Recurrent Unit (GRU) architecture have mitigated some of these challenges, enhancing the capabilities of RNNs. Overall, RNNs remain a fundamental tool in the field of deep learning, offering valuable insights and solutions for a wide range of sequential data analysis tasks.

CURRENT TRENDS AND CHALLENGES IN DEEP LEARNING

Deep Learning has significantly evolved in recent years, driving breakthroughs in various domains, from computer vision to natural language processing. Among the most impactful developments are **Generative Adversarial Networks (GANs), Transformer Models, and Reinforcement Learning (RL)**. These techniques have expanded the capabilities of AI beyond traditional supervised learning, enabling generative modeling, efficient sequence processing, and autonomous decision-making. However, despite these advancements, deep learning still faces several challenges when applied in real-world industrial settings.

A. Generative Adversarial Networks (GANs)

GANs, introduced by Ian Goodfellow in 2014, consist of two neural networks, the **generator** and the **discriminator**, competing against each other in a zero-sum game (Miller, 2019). This approach has led to impressive advancements in image synthesis, style transfer, and data augmentation. Industries such as **fashion, gaming, and healthcare** leverage GANs to generate synthetic images for design prototyping, create realistic avatars, and enhance medical imaging. However, training GANs is notoriously unstable, requiring extensive hyperparameter tuning and large computational resources. Moreover, ethical concerns, such as the generation of deepfake content, pose societal risks (Jaleel & Ali, 2022:John & Sherif, 2022)

B. Transformer Models

Transformers have revolutionized the field of **natural language processing (NLP)** and beyond (Panopoulos et al., 2023). The self-attention mechanism in models like **BERT, GPT, and T5** allows efficient handling of long-range dependencies, making them superior to traditional recurrent neural networks (RNNs) (Salıcı & Ölçer, 2024). Industries such as **finance, customer service, and e-commerce** use Transformer models for chatbots, automated document analysis, and fraud detection. However, the high computational cost and data requirements of these models present challenges for deployment in resource-constrained environments. Efforts to create lightweight models, such as **DistilBERT and ALBERT**, aim to address these limitations (Choi et al., 2021: Damatie et al., 2024).

C. Reinforcement Learning (RL)

Reinforcement Learning enables **autonomous decision-making** by training agents through trial and error using reward signals (Pecioski et al., 2023). Applications range from **robotics and autonomous vehicles** to **financial portfolio management and healthcare optimization**. Despite its potential, RL models are difficult to train in real-world environments due to sample inefficiency, lack of generalization, and the need for well-designed reward functions. Additionally, RL often requires expensive simulations or real-world interactions, making implementation costly and time-consuming.

D. Challenges of Deep Learning in Industry

While deep learning models have demonstrated remarkable success in research settings, their real-world deployment comes with numerous challenges:

1. **Data Quality and Availability**, many industries struggle with insufficient or biased data, impacting model performance and fairness.
2. **Computational Costs**, high-end GPUs and TPUs are essential for training large models, making deep learning inaccessible for smaller enterprises.
3. **Model Interpretability**, many deep learning models act as black boxes, making it difficult to explain decisions in regulated industries like healthcare and finance.
4. **Scalability and System Integration**, deploying deep learning models in production requires robust integration with existing IT infrastructure and scalability solutions.
5. **Ethical and Environmental Concerns**, the carbon footprint of training large models is a growing concern, necessitating research into more energy-efficient AI models.

Deep learning continues to push technological boundaries, with GANs, Transformers, and Reinforcement Learning leading the way. However, the path to real-world adoption is filled with challenges, from computational demands to ethical considerations. By addressing these issues through better model optimization, responsible AI practices, and hybrid approaches combining deep learning with traditional methods, industries can unlock the full potential of AI-driven solutions.

5. USING CNN DEEP LEARNING TECHNIQUES WITH RAPIDMINER SOFTWARE

In order to employ deep learning techniques within RapidMiner, although the software provides basic models like Deep Learning H2O, data scientists need to install the Deep Learning ND4J extension in RapidMiner if they intend to work with CNN and RNN models.

Figure 13. Installing extensions

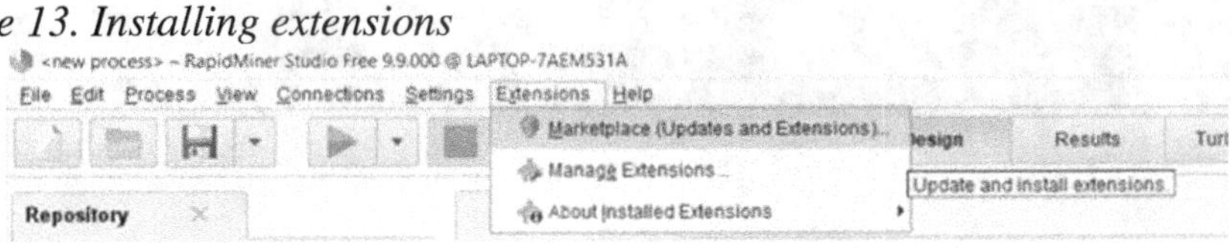

As depicted in Figure 13, data scientists can install extensions by selecting the "Extensions" menu and then choosing "Marketplace (Updates and Extensions)."

Figure 14. Searching for extensions and installing it

When accessing the RapidMiner Marketplace, scientists should navigate to the search bar and look for "ND4J," and then proceed to click on "Search." Once they identify the extensions related to machine learning models, they should select all three extensions - ND4J, Deep Learning, and Image Handling - by clicking on them for installation and then by pressing "Install Packages." Upon completion of the installation process, data scientists must restart the RapidMiner software.

In order to develop models using CNN deep learning techniques, this book utilized a sample image dataset from the website http://yann.lecun.com/exdb/mnist/. The dataset, known as MNIST – JPG - Training, consists of a total of 10,000 instances (Beohar and Rasool, 2021; LeCun, Cortes, and Burges, 2021), as demonstrated in the provided example.

Figure 15. Sample data within the experimental dataset

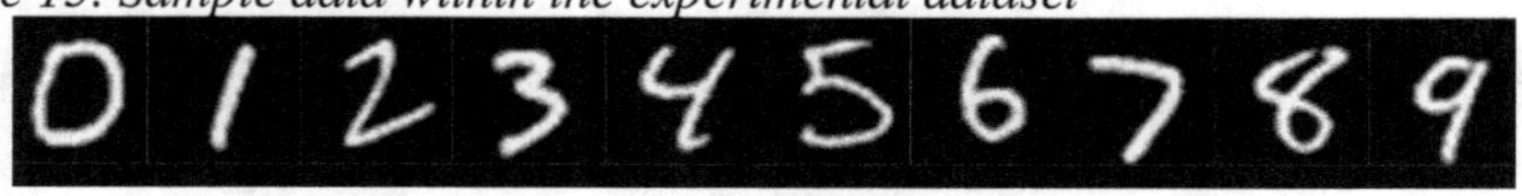

From the image dataset, data scientists can utilize RapidMiner software to model CNN machine learning. The process is outlined as follows:

Figure 16 Model of CNN learning techniques

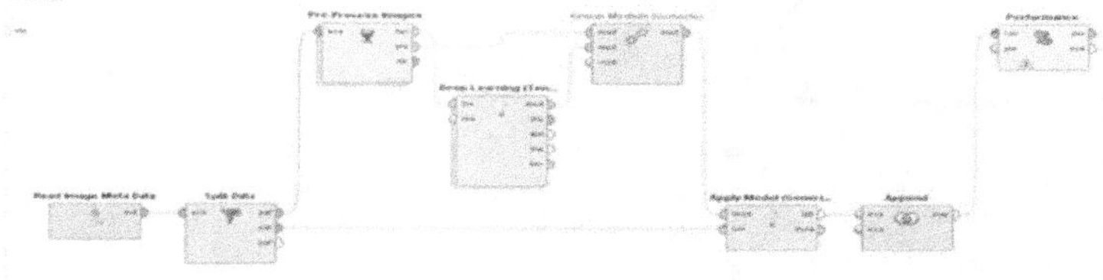

As shown in Figure 16, data scientists begin by importing the MNIST – JPG – Training dataset into the model using "Read Image Meta Data," and they then split the data into two parts using "Split Data." The dataset is divided into two parts: 80% for training the machine learning models and 20% for testing the accuracy of the model. Next, the data for machine learning is imported into the "Pre-Process Image" module to be transformed into a Tensor object in vector form, which allows the "Deep Learning (Tensor)" model to process it. The data from the "Pre-Process Image" and the "Deep Learning (Tensor)" are then fed into the "Group Model (Generic)," allowing the "Pre-Process Image" to be co-processed with the "Deep Learning (Tensor)." The accuracy of the processing is then verified using the "Apply Model (Generic)." The "Append" model is subsequently utilized to compare the datasets from forecasting before sending them to the "Performance" module in order to demonstrate the accuracy of all data classification processing.

Within "Deep Learning (Tensor)," data scientists can utilize models to define CNN-based processing, which includes Convolutional Operation, Pooling, and Fully-Connected layers, as illustrated below.

Figure 17. Setting convolutional operator model, pooling and fully-connected

As shown in Figure 17, data scientists can specify parameters for each section to establish CNN processing as outlined below:

Figure 18. Setting parameters to add convolutional layer

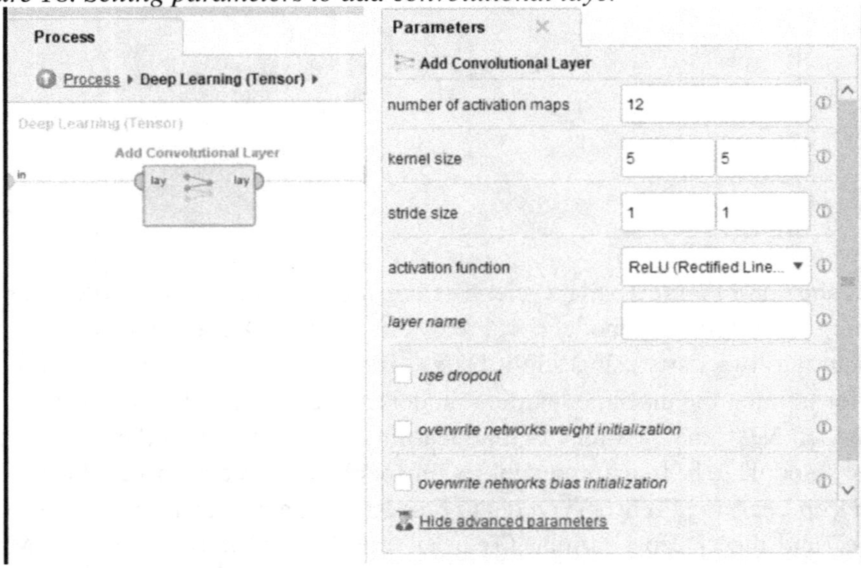

The data scientists set the Size of the Feature Map to a frequency of 12, ensuring coverage of the important areas in the image by configuring the Number of Activation Maps to 12. They specify the size of the Filter Matrix as 5 x 5 and set the movement of the Filter Matrix to detect every row and column by establishing the Stride Size as 1 x 1.

Figure 19. Setting parameters to add pooling layer

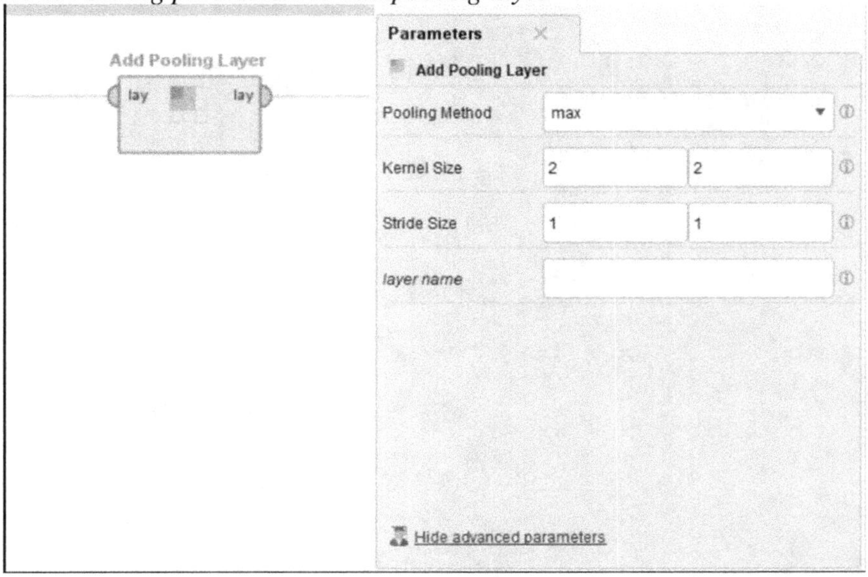

As shown in Figure 19, scientists can choose the method for reducing the data size by setting the Pooling Method to Max. They can then adjust the size of the Filter Matrix by setting the Kernel Size to 2 x 2 and configure the movement of the Filter Matrix to detect every row and column with a Stride Size of 1 x 1.

Figure 20. Setting parameters to add fully-connected layer

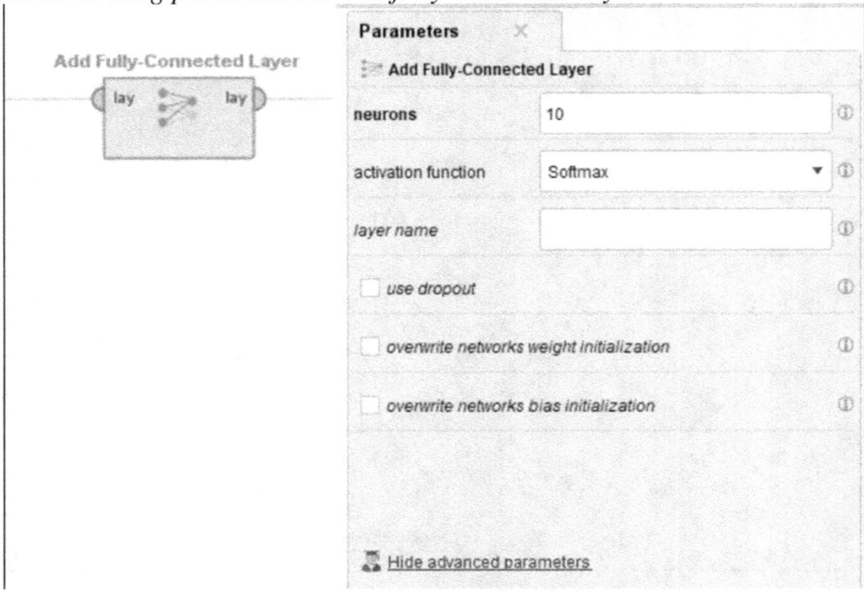

When classifying the data, the number of neurons must match the number of data types. In this scenario, the image data ranges from 0 to 9. Therefore, if there are 10 data types in total, data scientists need to configure the number of neurons to 10 and set the Activation Function to the Softmax format by adding a Fully-Connected Layer. This adjustment is necessary to transform the data into feature forms that can be processed by artificial neural networks.

In each section of the model, data scientists can specify parameters to ensure that the model performs the processing suitable for the task at hand.

Figure 21. Setting parameters to read image meta data

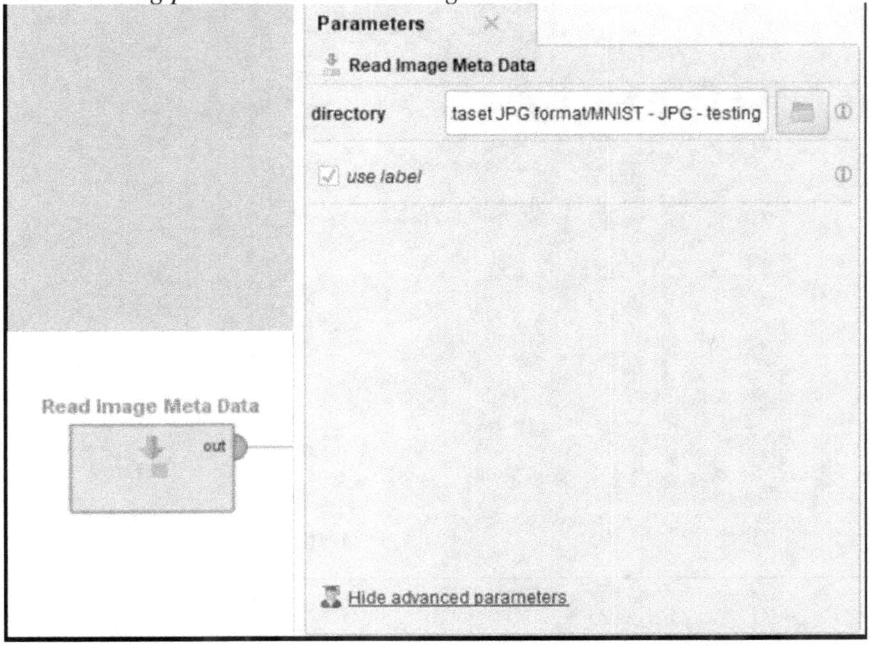

Data scientists can utilize the "Read Image Meta Data" function to import image data into models. They accomplish this by configuring the Directory parameter to indicate the data source. This is achieved by selecting the folder button and providing the source address of the dataset. Subsequently, the target variables are designated by selecting "Use Label." In the dataset employed in this experiment, there are subfolders labeled 0 through 9. Therefore, the target variables for each subfolder are set based on their respective folder names, ranging from 0 to 9.

Figure 22. Setting parameters to split data

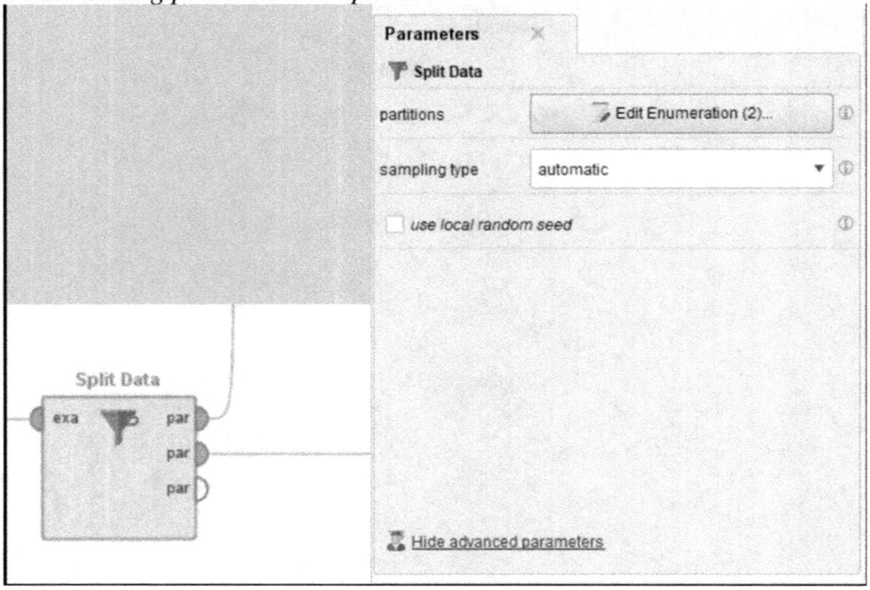

Data scientists can partition the data into two segments—one for training machine learning models and the other for testing—by configuring the Partitions section. They accomplish this by clicking on the "Edits Enumeration" button.

Figure 23. Partition setting to divide the dataset

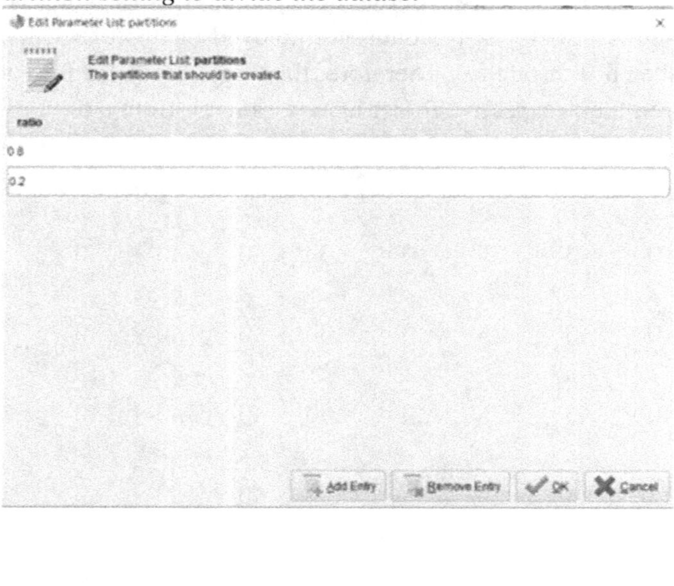

Data scientists can specify the proportions of the data by selecting "Add Entry" and then setting Part 1 to 0.8 and Part 2 to 0.2. Following this, scientists can define parameters for pre-processing images by setting the Path parameter as "Path."

Figure 24. Setting parameters to pre-process images

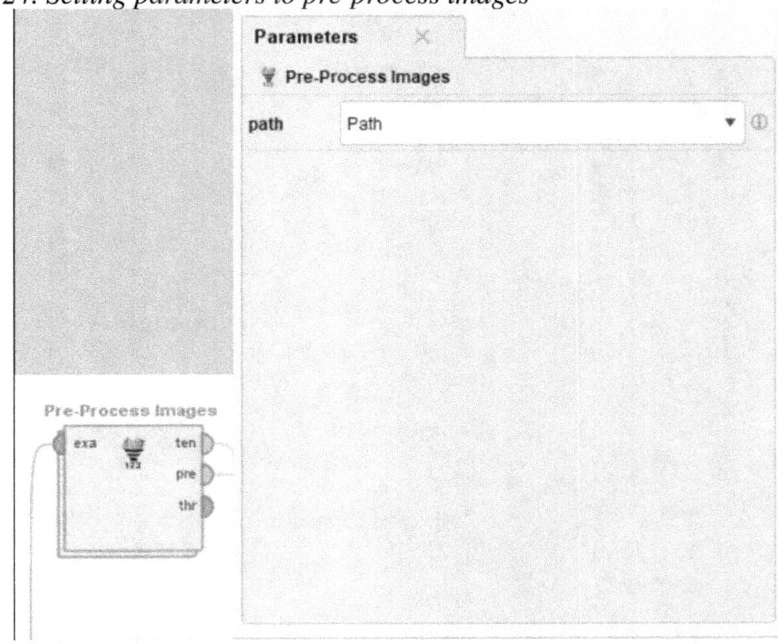

Following this, data scientists can define a model within the Pre-Process Images module to manipulate image data as follows:

Figure 25. Path setting within pre-process images

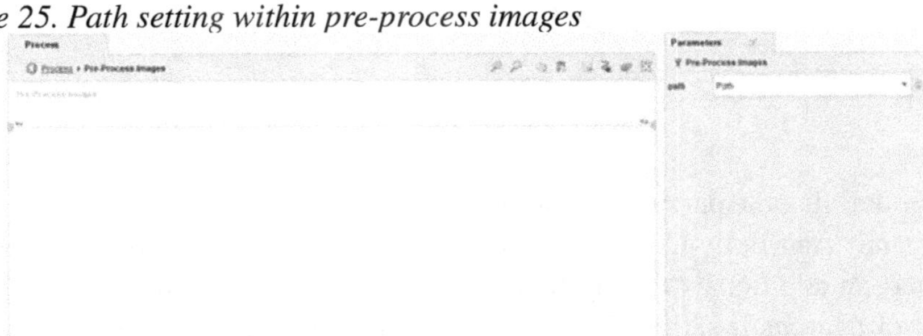

Additionally, parameters for Deep Learning (Tensor) are determined, which also processes the data through Convolutional Operations, Pooling, and Fully-Connected layers.

Figure 26. Setting parameters to deep learning (tensor)

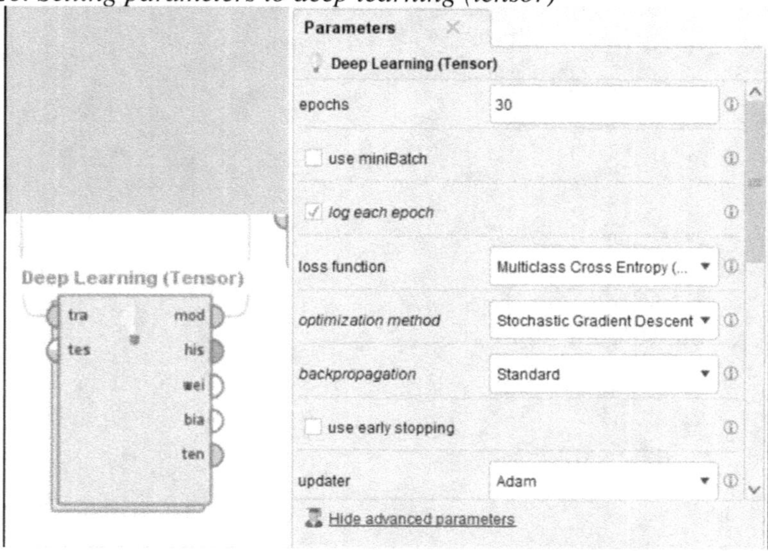

As shown in Figure 26, data scientists set the Epochs to 30, which represents the number of times the dataset teaches the machine to learn. Then, within Deep Learning (Tensor), the structure of the processing can be defined as follows.

Figure 27. Determining the number of neural for each add full-connected layer

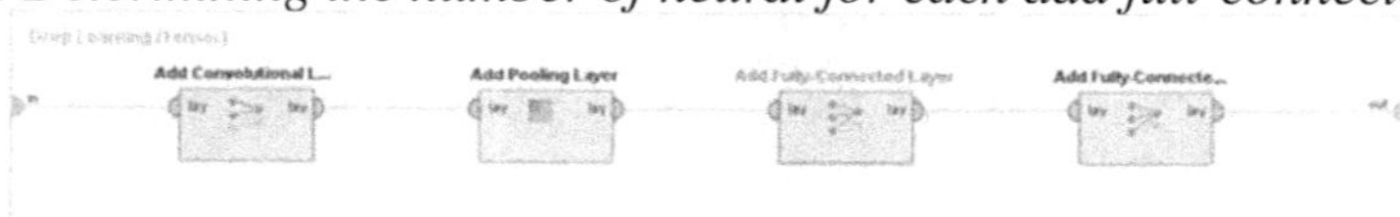

After defining the parameters for the "Add Convolutional Layer," "Add Pooling Layer," and "Add Fully-Connected Layer" as in the previous step, data scientists can insert an additional "Add Fully-Connected Layer" before the final step. The number of neurons is set to 100 to reduce the data from the "Add Pooling Layer" before passing it to the "Add Fully-Connected Layer." The number of neurons is then adjusted to 10, corresponding to the number of data types ranging from 0 to 9. Once the deep learning model has been created and the parameters have been assigned to each model, data scientists can execute the model. The resulting output is as follows.

Figure 28. Processing result

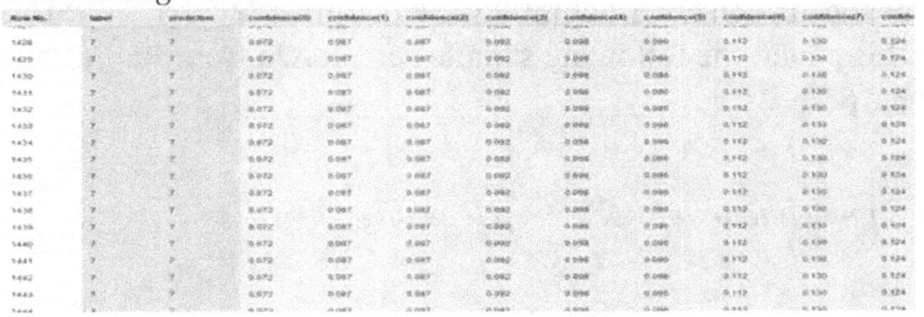

The processing results provide a comparison between the actual data and the outcomes obtained through classification using a CNN-type deep learning model. For instance, if the real datum is the number 7, and the classification result is also the number 7, it indicates a successful classification. However, this experiment utilized a dataset comprising only 10,000 instances, with 8,000 instances allocated for training the machine learning model and 2,000 instances for testing the model. This resulted in an efficiency of 10.30% for training the machine learning model, and only 7 out of 10 categories were correctly classified.

Figure 29. Accuracy of data processing

accuracy: 10.30%

	true 0	true 1	true 2	true 3	true 4	true 5	true 6	true 7	true 8	true 9	class prec...
pred. 0	0	0	0	0	0	0	0	0	0	0	0.00%
pred. 1	0	0	0	0	0	0	0	0	0	0	0.00%
pred. 2	0	0	0	0	0	0	0	0	0	0	0.00%
pred. 3	0	0	0	0	0	0	0	0	0	0	0.00%
pred. 4	0	0	0	0	0	0	0	0	0	0	0.00%
pred. 5	0	0	0	0	0	0	0	0	0	0	0.00%
pred. 6	0	0	0	0	0	0	0	0	0	0	0.00%
pred. 7	195	227	206	202	196	178	192	206	195	202	10.30%
pred. 8	0	0	0	0	0	0	0	0	0	0	0.00%
pred. 9	0	0	0	0	0	0	0	0	0	0	0.00%
class recall	0.00%	0.00%	0.00%	0.00%	0.00%	0.00%	0.00%	100.00%	0.00%	0.00%	

CNN-type deep learning techniques are well-suited for analyzing large datasets for classification and machine learning training. Consequently, data scientists often utilize GPU processing to expedite the processing time. Additionally, handling a substantial number of instances and employing vast amounts of data can enhance the accuracy of CNN-type deep learning models.

6. THE USE OF RNN DEEP LEARNING TECHNIQUES WITH RAPIDMINER SOFTWARE

When data scientists encounter challenges in analyzing data to predict outcomes, particularly from time series data, they can turn to Recurrent Neural Networks (RNN). In this paper, the following samples are drawn from RapidMiner software for testing purposes.

Figure 30. Sample model of RNN deep learning

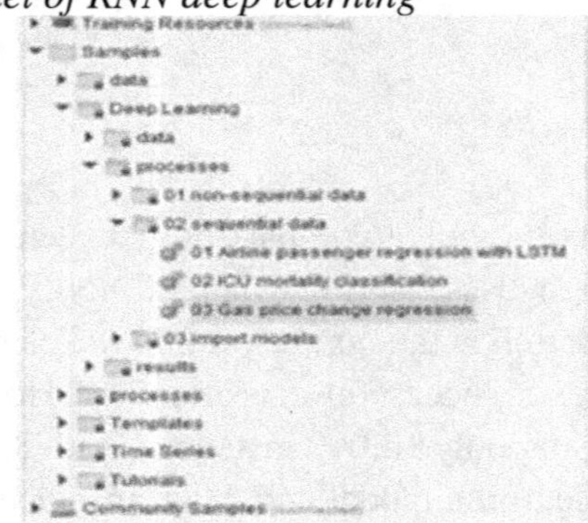

The sample model pertains to forecasting oil prices. Within the dataset, the features include the sequence of oil price changes, the rate of change, the date of change, and oil prices. The dataset comprises 10,000 instances. The daily oil price and each sequence of change are dependent on the price from the previous day.

Figure 31. Gas Station dataset within RapidMiner software

Row No.	id	change	date	price
1	2	0	2016/08/26	1269
2	3	150	2016/08/26	1269
3	4	-120	2016/08/26	1419
4	5	40	2016/08/26	1299
5	6	-40	2016/08/26	1339
6	7	-10	2016/08/26	1299
7	8	-20	2016/08/26	1289
8	9	80	2016/08/26	1269
9	10	-60	2016/08/26	1349
10	1	90	2016/08/27	1289
11	2	-30	2016/08/27	1379
12	3	-40	2016/08/27	1349
13	4	-30	2016/08/27	1309
14	5	60	2016/08/27	1279
15	6	-40	2016/08/27	1339
16	7	0	2016/08/27	1299

Based on the provided datasets, data scientists can employ Recurrent Neural Networks (RNN) to forecast oil prices, leveraging the continuous and correlated nature of the data. Models can be developed following the provided example.

Figure 32. Sample model of RNN deep learning

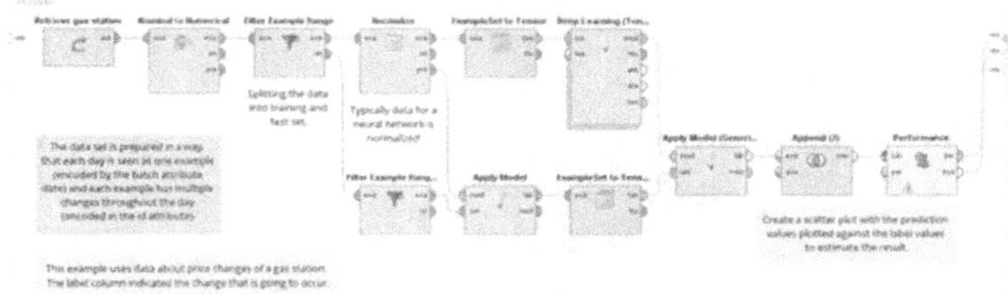

The Gas Station dataset is first imported into the model. Then, the nominal data are converted to numerical data using "Nominal to Numerical" so that it can be processed by ANN techniques. The dataset is then split into two parts: one for training the machine learning model and the other for testing its performance using "Filter Example Range." Next, the "Normalize" model is applied to scale the numbers in the dataset for training the machine learning model to be between 0 and 1. The data are then transformed into vector format using "Example Set to Tensor" to prepare the data for processing with "Deep Learning (Tensor)." The testing data are fed into "Apply Model" to evaluate the model's performance. Subsequently, both the training and testing data are processed using "Apply Model" and then converted into vector format using "Example Set to Tensor." The results are then combined using "Append" to determine the accuracy. Within "Deep Learning (Tensor)," the model connection is defined according to the RNN technique.

Figure 33. RNN connection

The model incorporates an LSTM Layer to enable it to consider the results of previous data along with the current data. This allows the model to remember processing results that are distant from the current data, enhancing its ability to accurately predict results based on the sequential relationships within the data. Subsequently, an "Add Fully-Connected" layer is utilized to compile the data into features that can be processed by artificial neural networks. The outcomes of the data processing are presented as follows.

Figure 34. Results from CNN deep learning processing

Row No.	label	prediction	price
1	-0.421	0.115	-0.688
2	-0.000	0.151	-1.198
3	0.316	0.170	-1.198
4	-0.105	0.107	-0.815
5	-0.211	0.136	-0.943
6	-0.316	0.182	-1.198
7	-0.000	0.250	-1.580
8	1.579	0.251	-1.580
9	-0.737	-0.058	0.332
10	0.105	0.042	-0.561
11	-0.632	0.031	-0.433
12	0.421	0.171	-1.198
13	0.737	0.081	-0.688
14	-1.158	-0.070	0.204
15	-0.526	0.182	-1.198
16	0.316	0.285	-1.835
17	-0.105	0.225	-1.453

As shown in Figure 34, data scientists utilize Time Series data to analyze correlations from previous data in order to forecast oil prices. The LSTM technique is employed to co-process data from distant time points, thereby enhancing efficiency. However, the analysis of the data using the sample models reveals an accuracy measured in Root Mean Squared Error form of 0.546, as depicted below.

Figure 35. Root Mean Squared Error values from oil price forecast

root_mean_squared_error

root_mean_squared_error: 0.546 +/- 0.000

As shown in Figure 35, the Root Mean Squared Error value is 0.546. It is likely that the model made incorrect predictions due to the limited dataset size of only 10,000 instances used for machine learning. Therefore, when encountering problems that necessitate processing with RNN to identify data relationships and sequences, it is important to consider having a sufficient amount of data as another crucial condition.

CONCLUSION

The Artificial Neural Network (ANN) data mining technique is highly effective for data classification tasks. Data scientists leverage features within a dataset to classify data by assigning labels through machine learning functionality. Consequently, existing datasets can be utilized to train machine learning models and to create artificial neural networks. The accuracy of the model is then assessed using separate test datasets to ensure reliable results. Scientists can continually test and refine the accuracy of the model and extend the use of artificial neural networks to classify data in other datasets, such as analyzing borrowers' bank refinance capabilities based on borrowers' historical data. Two prominent deep learning techniques, Convolutional Neural Networks (CNN) and Recurrent Neural Networks (RNN), are employed. CNN is particularly suitable for tasks requiring data classification while RNN is utilized for predicting time series data, such as oil prices.

Through experiments with both CNN and RNN, it has been observed that the quantity of data used for machine learning significantly impacts the efficiency and accuracy of data classification and prediction techniques. Processing large datasets also necessitates GPU processing to reduce processing time. Therefore, data scientists must be equipped with on-premises digital resources to effectively implement data mining techniques for Big Data processing.

EXERCISES

1. Obtain sample datasets from the internet for classification purposes.
2. Perform feature selection based on the datasets obtained in step 1 and then handle missing values and outliers.

3. Utilize an artificial neural network model to classify the data from step 2 and demonstrate the accuracy of the model in the analysis.
4. Identify data analysis problems requiring Convolutional Neural Network (CNN) processing.
5. Locate a suitable dataset for data analysis based on the problems identified in step 4.
6. Develop an analysis model using RapidMiner software based on the dataset obtained in step 5.
7. Summarize the results of the experiment and evaluate the accuracy of the analysis from step 6.
8. Define problems for data analysis that necessitate processing with Recurrent Neural Networks (RNN).
9. Find a suitable dataset for data analysis based on the problems identified in step 8.
10. Develop an analysis model using RapidMiner software based on the dataset obtained in step 9.
11. Summarize the results of the experiment and assess the accuracy of the analysis from step 10.

REFERENCES

Aggarwal, C. C. (2018). *Neural networks and deep learning: A textbook*. Springer. DOI: 10.1007/978-3-319-94463-0

Beohar, D., & Rasool, A. (2021). Handwritten digit recognition of MNIST dataset using deep learning state-of-the-art artificial neural network (ANN) and convolutional neural network (CNN). *2021 International Conference on Emerging Smart Computing and Informatics (ESCI)*, 542–548. DOI: 10.1109/ESCI50559.2021.9396870

Chinnarasri, C., Nonsawang, S., & Supharatid, S. (2012). *Application of artificial neural networks for river stage forecasting in Hatyai. King Mongkut's University of Technology Thonburi*. KMUTT.

Choi, H., Kim, J., Joe, S., & Gwon, Y. (2021). Evaluation of BERT and ALBERT sentence embedding performance on downstream NLP tasks. *2020 25th International Conference on Pattern Recognition (ICPR)*, 5482–5487. DOI: 10.1109/ICPR48806.2021.9412102

Chow, T. W. S., & Cho, S.-Y. (2007). *Neural networks and computing: Learning algorithms and applications*. Imperial College Press. DOI: 10.1142/p487

Damatie, E. M., Eleyan, A., & Bejaoui, T. (2024). Real-time email phishing detection using a custom DistilBERT model. *2024 International Symposium on Networks, Computers and Communications (ISNCC)*, 1–6. DOI: 10.1109/ISNCC62547.2024.10759011

Fernando, T., Gammulle, H., Denman, S., Sridharan, S., & Fookes, C. (2021). Deep learning for medical anomaly detection - A survey. *ACM Computing Surveys*, *54*(7), 1–37. DOI: 10.1145/3464423

Ghorpade, V. G., & Koneru, V. S. (2021). Pattern recognition neural network model for experimental-based compressive strength graded self-compacting concrete. *Materials Today: Proceedings*, *43*(2), 795–799. DOI: 10.1016/j.matpr.2020.06.175

Guo, C., Zhang, M., & Chen, H. (2021). Suitability of low-field nuclear magnetic resonance (LF-NMR) combining with back-propagation artificial neural network (BP-ANN) to predict printability of polysaccharide hydrogels 3D printing. *International Journal of Food Science & Technology*, *56*(5), 2264–2272. DOI: 10.1111/ijfs.14844

Jaleel, Q., & Ali, I. H. (2022). Facial behavior analysis-based DeepFake video detection using GAN discriminator. *2022 International Conference on Data Science and Intelligent Computing (ICDSIC)*, 36–40. DOI: 10.1109/ICDSIC56987.2022.10075660

John, J., & Sherif, B. V. (2022). Comparative analysis on different DeepFake detection methods and semi-supervised GAN architecture for DeepFake detection. *2022 Sixth International Conference on I-SMAC (IoT in Social, Mobile, Analytics and Cloud) (I-SMAC)*, 516–521. DOI: 10.1109/I-SMAC55078.2022.9987265

Lakshmi Devi, R., & Samundeeswari, V. V. (2021). Detection and automated classification of brain tumor types in MRI images using convolutional neural network with grid search optimization. *2021 Fifth International Conference on I-SMAC (IoT in Social, Mobile, Analytics and Cloud) (I-SMAC)*, 1280–1284. DOI: 10.1109/I-SMAC52330.2021.9640670

LeCun, Y., Cortes, C., & Burges, J. C. C. (2021). The MNIST database of handwritten digits. Retrieved from http://yann.lecun.com/exdb/mnist/

Miller, A. I. (2019). Ian Goodfellow's generative adversarial networks: AI learns to imagine. In *The artist in the machine: The world of AI-powered creativity* (pp. 87–98). MIT Press. DOI: 10.7551/mitpress/11585.003.0015

Panopoulos, I., Nikolaidis, S., Venieris, S. I., & Venieris, I. S. (2023). Exploring the performance and efficiency of transformer models for NLP on mobile devices. *2023 IEEE Symposium on Computers and Communications (ISCC)*, 1–4. DOI: 10.1109/ISCC58397.2023.10217850

Pecioski, D., Gavriloski, V., Domazetovska, S., & Ignjatovska, A. (2023). An overview of reinforcement learning techniques. *2023 12th Mediterranean Conference on Embedded Computing (MECO)*, 1–4. DOI: 10.1109/MECO58584.2023.10155066

Ramirez-Hernandez, J., Juarez-Sandoval, O.-U., Hernandez-Gonzalez, L., Hernandez-Ramirez, A., & Olivares-Dominguez, R.-S. (2020). Voltage control based on a back-propagation artificial neural network algorithm. *2020 IEEE International Autumn Meeting on Power, Electronics and Computing (ROPEC)*, 1–6. DOI: 10.1109/ROPEC50909.2020.9258699

Sabau Popa, C. D., Popa, D. N., Bogdan, V., & Simut, R. (2021). Composite financial performance index prediction – A neural networks approach. *Journal of Business Economics and Management*, *22*(2), 277–296. DOI: 10.3846/jbem.2021.14000

Salıcı, M., & Ölçer, Ü. E. (2024). Impact of transformer-based models in NLP: An in-depth study on BERT and GPT. *2024 8th International Artificial Intelligence and Data Processing Symposium (IDAP)*, 1–6. DOI: 10.1109/IDAP64064.2024.10710796

Snineh, S. M., Amrani, N. E. A., Youssfi, M., Bouattane, O., & Daaif, A. (2021). Detection of traffic anomaly in highways by using recurrent neural network. *2021 Fifth International Conference on Intelligent Computing in Data Sciences (ICDS)*, 1–6. DOI: 10.1109/ICDS53782.2021.9626741

Sriwiboon, N. (2020). Improvement the performance of the chest X-ray image classification with convolutional neural network model by using image augmentations technique for COVID-19 diagnosis. *The Journal of King Mongkut's University of Technology North Bangkok*, *31*(1), 109–117. DOI: 10.14416/j.kmutnb.2020.10.002

Telikani, A., Shahbahrami, A., & Gandomi, A. H. (2021). High-performance implementation of evolutionary privacy-preserving algorithm for big data using GPU platform. *Information Sciences*, *579*, 251–265. DOI: 10.1016/j.ins.2021.08.006

Thankachan, T., Prakash, K. S., & Jothi, S. (2021). Artificial neural network modeling to evaluate and predict the mechanical strength of duplex stainless steel during casting. *Sadhana*, *46*(4), 1–12. DOI: 10.1007/s12046-021-01742-w

Chapter 6
Clustering

ABSTRACT

Clustering is employed to divide a data set into an appropriate number of groups. Clustering is a form of unsupervised learning, which means a data scientist can bring labelled features of interest into the mining model. Furthermore, after dividing the data set, the data scientist can label each cluster. In business, clustering is used to analyze a customer or product segment that matches a target market. This chapter introduces clustering techniques including K-Means, Hierarchical Clustering, and DBSCAN, as well as techniques to indicate the efficiency of the clustering analysis. Data scientists can assess the efficiency of clustering analysis in two ways. Firstly, subjective measurement is where a data scientist consults a domain expert to confirm the efficiency of the cluster analysis, and secondly, data scientists can use objective measurements that test the efficiency of the cluster analysis result based on calculations. This chapter demonstrates cluster analysis adoption with RapidMiner so that readers can follow the process step-by-step.

INTRODUCTION

A clustering technique is a method used in data mining to organize similar data points into groups or clusters based on their characteristics or attributes. It is an unsupervised learning approach, meaning that it does not require predefined labels or target variables (Govindaraj et al., 2020; Abbas et al., 2021). Instead, it automatically identifies patterns and structures within the data, grouping together data points that are more similar to each other while keeping dissimilar points apart. Clustering finds applications in various fields, including customer segmentation, anomaly detection, pattern recognition, and image segmentation, among others. Therefore, clustering finds applications across various industries, such as customer segmentation based on purchasing behaviors (Punhani et al., 2021). Customers within the same group typically exhibit similar purchasing behaviors and expected price ranges. Cluster-

DOI: 10.4018/979-8-3693-6001-9.ch006

ing facilitates the design of tailored marketing strategies for each customer group. Additionally, it aids in diagnosing cancer stages based on tumor sizes in patients' organs (Kumar, Ganapathy & Kang, 2021).

K-MEANS CLUSTERING

K-Means clustering is widely used for various applications, including customer segmentation, image compression, anomaly detection, and more (Ginting, 2021: Puspasari et al., 2021). Its simplicity, scalability, and efficiency make it suitable for analyzing large datasets with high-dimensional features. In this chapter, we explore the principles, implementation, and applications of K-Means clustering, providing insights into its strengths, limitations, and practical considerations for effective usage. Through examples and case studies, we illustrate how K-Means clustering can be applied to real-world datasets to uncover hidden patterns, to gain insights, and to support decision-making processes across different domains.

K-MEANS CLUSTERING ALGORITHM

The K-Means clustering algorithm is an iterative, centroid-based technique used for partitioning a dataset into a predetermined number of clusters, denoted by 'K'. The algorithm aims to minimize the within-cluster sum of squares, also known as inertia or distortion, which measures the compactness of the clusters. K-Means is a simple and efficient algorithm that is widely used for clustering tasks in various domains. However, it has some limitations, such as sensitivity to initial centroid placement and the requirement to specify the number of clusters 'K' in advance. Nevertheless, K-Means remains a popular choice for clustering large datasets due to its scalability and computational efficiency.

THE KEY CHARACTERISTICS OF THE K-MEANS ALGORITHM

A. Cluster Centroids: In the context of K-Means clustering, a centroid represents the center or average point of a cluster. It is a multidimensional point that summarizes the characteristics of the data points assigned to the cluster.

Initialization: At the beginning of the K-Means algorithm, 'K' centroids are initialized. Typically, these centroids are randomly selected from the dataset although alternative initialization strategies, such as K-Means++, can be used to improve convergence.

Assignment Step (Expectation): During each iteration of the algorithm, every data point is assigned to the nearest centroid based on a distance metric, commonly Euclidean distance. This step determines which cluster each data point belongs to.

Update Step (Maximization): Once all data points are assigned to clusters, the centroids are updated to better represent the center of their respective clusters. The update is done by calculating the mean (average) of all data points assigned to each cluster. Mathematically, the centroid of a cluster 'C' is computed as the average of the data points in that cluster:

$$Centroid(C) = \frac{1}{|C|} \sum_{x \in C^x}$$

Where: *Centroid*(*C*) represents the centroid of cluster 'c'.

$|c|$ denotes the number of data points in cluster 'c'.

x represents a data point in cluster 'c'.

$\sum_{x \in C^x}$ denotes the summation of all data points in cluster 'c'.

Iteration: The assignment and update steps are repeated iteratively until the centroids stabilize, meaning that there are no significant changes in their positions between iterations, or until a maximum number of iterations is reached.

Convergence: Convergence occurs when the centroids no longer change significantly between iterations. At this point, the algorithm stops, and the final cluster centroids represent the center of each cluster.

Usage: After the K-Means algorithm converges, the centroids can be used for various purposes, such as interpreting the characteristics of each cluster, making predictions for new data points by assigning them to the nearest centroid, or for visualizing the clusters in lower-dimensional space.

Let's illustrate the calculation of cluster centroids using a simple example dataset. Suppose we have a dataset consisting of two-dimensional points:

$$Dataset = \{(x_1, y_1), (x_2, y_2), \ldots., (x_n, y_n)\}$$

Now, let's consider a scenario where we perform K-Means clustering on this dataset and end up with three clusters, denoted as C_1, C_2, and C_3. After several iterations, our clusters may look something like this:

Cluster C_1: (2,4),(3,5),(2,3)
Cluster C_2: (7,6),(6,8),(8,7)
Cluster C_3: (10,2),(11,1),(9,3)

To calculate the centroids for each cluster, we take the mean of the coordinates for all data points within the cluster.

For Cluster $\boldsymbol{C_1}$

- x – coordinates: (2+3+2)/3 = 2.33
- y – coordinates: (4+5+3)/3 = 4.00

So, the centroid for C_1 is approximately (2.33, 4.00)
For Cluster $\boldsymbol{C_2}$

- x – coordinates: (7+6+8)/3 = 7.00
- y – coordinates: (6+8+7)/3 = 7.00

So, the centroid for C_2 is approximately (7.00, 7.00)

For Cluster $\boldsymbol{C_3}$

- x – coordinates: (10+11+9)/3 = 10.00
- y – coordinates: (2+1+3)/3 = 2.00

So, the centroid for C_3 is approximately (10.00, 20.00)

These calculated centroids represent the center points of their respective clusters. They summarize the characteristics of the data points within each cluster and are used to update the clusters in subsequent iterations of the K-Means algorithm.

In summary, cluster centroids are crucial components of the K-Means clustering algorithm, representing the center of each cluster and are updated iteratively based on the mean of the data points assigned to the cluster. They play a vital role in the formation and interpretation of clusters in the dataset.

B. Euclidean Distance is a commonly used metric in mathematics to measure the straight-line distance between two points in a multi-dimensional space. In the context of K-Means clustering, Euclidean distance is used to quantify the similarity or dissimilarity between data points and cluster centroids. The Euclidean distance between two points P and Q in n – dimensional space is calculated using the following formula:

$$Euclidean\ Distance(P, Q) = \sqrt{\sum_{i=1}^{n} (q_i - p_i)^2}$$

Where: P and Q are two data points in n – dimensional space
p_i and q_i are the coordinates of points P and Q along the i-th dimension, respectively.

n denotes the number of dimensions.

Application in K-Means: In the context of K-Means clustering, Euclidean distance is used to determine the similarity between each data point and each cluster centroid. The algorithm assigns each data point to the cluster whose centroid is closest to it in terms of Euclidean distance. The Euclidean distance metric is essential in determining the similarity between data points and centroids, enabling the K-Means clustering algorithm to assign data points to the nearest centroid efficiently.

Euclidean distance plays a crucial role in K-Means clustering by quantifying the distance between data points and cluster centroids. It enables the algorithm to partition the dataset into clusters by assigning each data point to the nearest centroid based on similarity in feature space.

C. Objective Function: The objective of K-Means clustering is to partition a given dataset into k clusters in such a way that the within-cluster sum of squares (WCSS) is minimized. WCSS represents the sum of squared distances between each data point and its assigned centroid. Mathematically, the objective function for K-Means clustering can be expressed as:

$$WCSS = \sum_{i=1}^{k} \sum_{x \in C_i} \|x - \mu_i\|^2$$

Where: k is the number of clusters.
C_i represents the i-th cluster.
x denotes a data point in cluster C_i.
μ_i denotes the centroid of cluster C_i.
$\|x - \mu_i\|^2$ represents the squared Euclidean distance between data point x and centroid μ_i

Let's demonstrate the calculation of the objective function, which is the within-cluster sum of squares (WCSS), with a simple example dataset and a set of centroids.

Dataset = $\{(2,3),(4,5),(7,9),(10,11)\}$

Additionally, let's consider that we have three cluster centroids:

$Centroid_1 = (3,4)$, $Centroid_2 = (6,8)$, $Centroid_3 = (9,10)$

Now, let's calculate the WCSS for this dataset and these centroids.

For cluster $\boldsymbol{C_1}$

$$WCSS_1 = \sum_{x \in C_1} \|x - Centroid_1\|^2$$

$$= \|(2,3) - (3,4)\|^2 = \|(-1,-1)^2 = 1^2 + 1^2 = 2$$

$$= \|(4,5) - (3,4)\|^2 = \|(1,1)^2 = 1^2 + 1^2 = 2$$

So, for cluster $C_1 WCSS_1 = 2 + 2 = 4$.

For cluster $\boldsymbol{C_2}$

$$WCSS_2 = \sum_{x \in C_2} \|x - Centroid_2\|^2$$

$= \| (7,9) - (6,8)\|^2 = \| (1,1)\ ^2 = 1^2 + 1^2 = 2$

So, for cluster $C_2 WCSS_2 = 2$.

For cluster $\boldsymbol{C_3}$

$$WCSS_3 = \sum_{x \in C_3} \|x - Centroid_3\|^2$$

$= \| (10,11) - (9,10)\|^2 = \| (1,1)\ ^2 = 1^2 + 1^2 = 2$

So, for cluster $C_3 WCSS_3 = 2$.

Now, the total WCSS is the sum of the WCSS for each cluster:

Total $WCSS = WCSS_1 + WCSS_2 + WCSS_3 = 4 + 2 + 2 = 8$

Therefore, the total within-cluster sum of squares (WCSS) for this example dataset and centroids is 8.

Explanation:

Minimizing Squared Distances: The objective of the K-Means algorithm is to minimize the sum of squared distances between each data point and its assigned centroid within each cluster. By minimizing these squared distances, the algorithm aims to ensure that data points are clustered around their respective centroids, making the clusters compact and well-separated.

Iterative Optimization: K-Means clustering is an iterative optimization algorithm. It starts with an initial set of centroids and iteratively updates them to minimize the WCSS. During each iteration, data points are assigned to the nearest centroid based on their squared distances, and the centroids are recalculated based on the mean of the data points assigned to each cluster.

Convergence: The algorithm continues to iterate until convergence, meaning that there is no significant improvement in the WCSS between iterations or until a predefined number of iterations is reached.

Impact of the Number of Clusters: The number of clusters (k) is a crucial parameter in K-Means clustering. Choosing an appropriate number of clusters is essential as it directly affects the WCSS. Increasing the number of clusters typically decreases the WCSS, but too many clusters may lead to overfitting and less meaningful clusters.

The objective function of K-Means clustering, to minimize the within-cluster sum of squares (WCSS), serves as a guiding principle for the algorithm to partition the dataset into compact and well-separated clusters. By minimizing the squared distances between data points and centroids, K-Means aims to create clusters that accurately represent the underlying structure of the data.

D. **Convergence:** In K-Means clustering, convergence refers to the point at which the algorithm reaches a stable state where further iterations do not significantly change the centroids' positions. Convergence is a crucial aspect of the algorithm as it indicates that the clustering process has effectively partitioned the dataset into clusters, and further iterations are unlikely to improve the clustering solution significantly.

    Stabilization of Centroids: The primary indicator of convergence in K-Means clustering is the stabilization of centroids. Initially, the centroids are randomly initialized or selected from the dataset. As the algorithm iterates, centroids are recalculated based on the mean of the data points assigned to each cluster. With each iteration, centroids move closer to the centers of their respective clusters.

    No Significant Change: Convergence occurs when the centroids no longer change significantly between iterations. This means that the difference in the positions of centroids from one iteration to the next becomes negligible. While minor fluctuations may still occur due to the algorithm's iterative nature, these changes are considered insignificant if they do not alter the overall clustering solution substantially.

    Maximum Number of Iterations: In addition to centroid stabilization, convergence may also be determined by reaching a maximum number of iterations. To prevent infinite looping and to ensure computational efficiency, K-Means algorithms often impose a limit on the number of iterations. If the algorithm reaches this maximum number of iterations without converging, it terminates, and the current clustering solution is considered final.

    Implications of Convergence: Achieving convergence in K-Means clustering signifies that the algorithm has successfully partitioned the dataset into clusters, and the resulting centroids represent the centers of these clusters. It indicates that further iterations are unlikely to improve the clustering solution significantly and that the algorithm has found a stable solution.

In K-Means clustering, convergence can be mathematically expressed using an equation that measures the change in centroids between successive iterations. One common method to determine convergence is to calculate the Euclidean distance between the centroids in the current iteration and their corresponding centroids in the previous iteration. If this distance falls below a predefined threshold, the algorithm is considered to have converged. It is denoted as follows:

C_t as the set of centroids in iteration t.
C_{t-1} as the set of centroids in the previous iteration $t - 1$
$d(C_t, C_{t-1})$ as the Euclidean distance between the centroids in iterations t and $t - 1$.

The equation for convergence can be written as:

$$d(C_t, C_{t-1}) < Threshold$$

Where *Threshold* is a predefined value that determines when the algorithm should stop iterating.

Now, let's demonstrate this with a simple example dataset and iterations of the K-Means algorithm. Suppose we have the following dataset with two-dimensional points:

$$\text{Dataset} = \{(2,3),(4,5),(7,9),(10,11)\}$$

Additionally, let's consider that we have three cluster centroids:

$$Centroid_1 = (3,4),\ Centroid_2 = (6,8),\ Centroid_3 = (9,10)$$

We will perform iterations of the K-Means algorithm and calculate the Euclidean distance between centroids in successive iterations until convergence.

Iteration 1:
New centroids: $Centroid_1 = (3.0,4.0)$, $Centroid_2 = (6.25,7.5)$, $Centroid_3 = (10.0,11.0)$
Iteration 2:
New centroids: $Centroid_1 = (3.5,4.0)$, $Centroid_2 = (6.5,7.0)$, $Centroid_3 = (10.0,11.0)$

Let's calculate the Euclidean distance between centroids in successive iterations:

$$d\left(Centroid_2^{(2)}, Centroid_2^{(1)}\right) = \sqrt{(6.25 - 6.5^2 + (7.5 - 7.0)^2}$$

$$= \sqrt{0.0625 + 0.25} = \sqrt{0.3125} \approx 0.56$$

Suppose our threshold for convergence is 0.5. Since the Euclidean distance between centroids in successive iterations is less than the threshold, the algorithm is considered to have converged. This demonstrates the calculation of convergence in the K-Means algorithm using the Euclidean distance between centroids in successive iterations. If this distance falls below a predefined threshold, the algorithm stops iterating, indicating convergence.

Convergence is a critical criterion in K-Means clustering, indicating the algorithm's effectiveness in partitioning the dataset into clusters. When the centroids stabilize and no longer change significantly between iterations or when a maximum number of iterations is reached, the algorithm is considered to have converged, and the clustering solution is finalized.

HIERARCHICAL CLUSTERING

Hierarchical clustering is a popular method used in unsupervised learning for clustering data points into groups based on their similarities (Rezaeijo, 2021: Zhou et al., 2021). Unlike k-means clustering, which requires the number of clusters to be specified beforehand, hierarchical clustering does not require a predetermined number of clusters. Instead, it creates a hierarchical tree of clusters, known as a dendrogram, where the number of clusters can be determined based on the structure of the dendrogram or by using a cutoff threshold.

There are two main types of hierarchical clustering:

Agglomerative (bottom-up): This is the most common approach to hierarchical clustering. It starts by considering each data point as a single cluster and then iteratively merges the closest pairs of clusters until all points belong to a single cluster. The distance between clusters can be measured using various metrics such as Euclidean distance, Manhattan distance, or cosine similarity.

Divisive (top-down): In contrast to agglomerative clustering, divisive hierarchical clustering starts with all data points in a single cluster and recursively splits clusters into smaller clusters until each cluster contains only one data point. While conceptually simpler, divisive clustering can be computationally expensive and less commonly used compared to agglomerative clustering.

The process of hierarchical clustering typically involves the following steps:

1. Compute pairwise distances and then calculate the distance or dissimilarity between each pair of data points based on a chosen distance metric.
2. Create initial clusters and treat each data point as a single cluster.
3. Merge or split clusters and iteratively merge (agglomerative) or split (divisive) clusters based on their proximity, forming a dendrogram.
4. Determine the number of clusters and decide on the appropriate number of clusters based on the dendrogram structure or by setting a cutoff threshold on the distance.
5. Assign data points to clusters based on the determined number of clusters and assign each data point to its corresponding cluster.

Hierarchical clustering is widely used in various fields such as biology (for gene expression analysis), image processing, social network analysis, and customer segmentation in marketing. It offers flexibility and interpretability, allowing for a hierarchical organization of clusters that can be visualized and analyzed to gain insights into the structure of the data.

Let's demonstrate hierarchical clustering with a simple example dataset of points in a 2-dimensional space:

Consider the following dataset with 6 data points:

Data points:

A(2, 10), B(2, 5), C(8, 4), D(5, 8), E(7, 5), F(6, 4)

We can visualize these data points on a 2-dimensional scatter plot. Each data point represents a location in the 2-dimensional space.

Figure 1. Example dataset of points in a 2-dimensional space

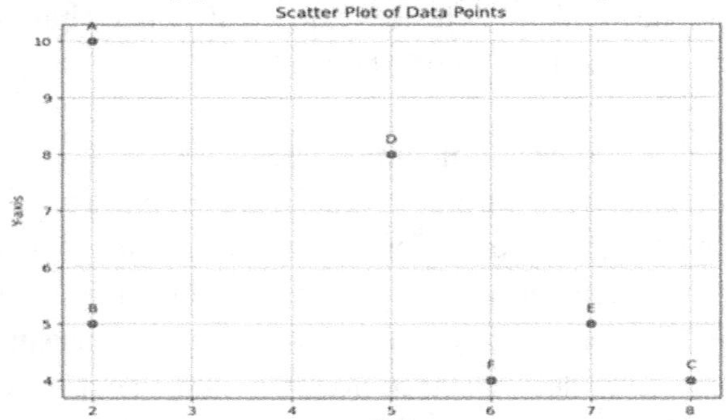

Now, let's perform hierarchical clustering using the Euclidean distance as the similarity measure. We'll use the agglomerative approach, starting with each data point as its own cluster and then iteratively merging clusters based on their pairwise distances.

Here's a step-by-step demonstration of the hierarchical clustering process:

1. Initialization, start with each data point as its own cluster.
2. Calculate Distance Matrix, compute the pairwise distances between all data points.
3. Merge Closest Clusters, identify the two closest clusters based on the distance matrix and merge them into a single cluster.
4. Update Distance Matrix, recalculate the distances between the new cluster and all other clusters.
5. Repeat Steps 3-4, continue merging the closest clusters and updating the distance matrix until only one cluster remains.

Let's illustrate these steps with our example dataset:

1. Initialization, each data point is considered as an individual cluster: {A}, {B}, {C}, {D}, {E}, {F}.
2. Calculate Distance Matrix, compute the pairwise distances between all data points.
3. Merge Closest Clusters, let's say the closest clusters are {B} and {F}. We merge them into a new cluster {B, F}.
4. Update Distance Matrix, recalculate the distances between the new cluster {B, F} and all other clusters.
5. Repeat Steps 3-4, continue merging the closest clusters and updating the distance matrix until only one cluster remains.

Finally, we can visualize the hierarchical clustering process using a dendrogram, which illustrates the sequence of cluster merges. The dendrogram will show how the data points are grouped into clusters at each step of the process, providing insights into the hierarchical structure of the data.

Figure 2. Hierarchical clustering process using a dendrogram

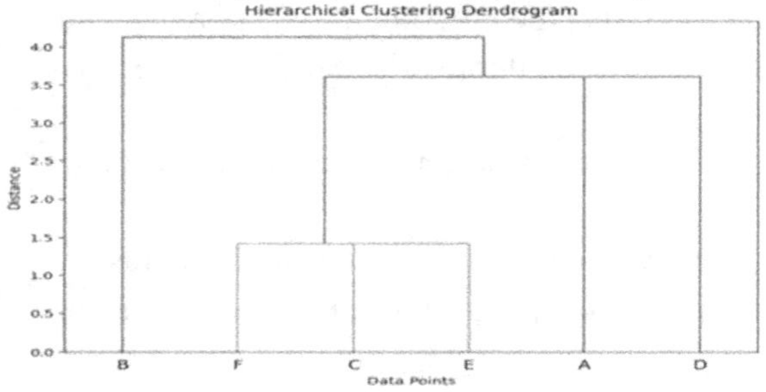

Hierarchical Clustering Real-World Implementation

Hierarchical Clustering is an algorithm suited for organizing data into a tree-like structure (dendrogram), allowing for flexible group selection based on data hierarchy. In **biological taxonomy and DNA clustering**, scientists use it to classify living organisms by grouping DNA sequences of bacteria or viruses, such as tracking the evolution of COVID-19 variants. In **customer segmentation**, businesses leverage Hierarchical Clustering to categorize customers based on purchasing behavior, distinguishing between high- and low-spending customers or frequent and occasional buyers, using dendrograms to determine the optimal number of segments. In **document classification and topic modeling**, it helps categorize large datasets like research papers, news articles, or blogs by clustering similar topics, such as AI, healthcare, or economics, improving search engine relevance. Additionally, in **image segmentation and face recognition**, Hierarchical Clustering is applied in systems like Google Photos and Apple Photos to group similar faces automatically, enhancing facial recognition and photo organization.

In conclusion, hierarchical clustering is a powerful technique for grouping data points based on their similarity or distance. It allows us to explore the inherent structure within the data and to identify natural clusters without requiring prior knowledge of the number of clusters. By constructing a hierarchical tree-like structure called a dendrogram, hierarchical clustering provides insights into the relationships between data points and the formation of clusters at different levels of granularity. This method is particularly useful when dealing with small to moderate-sized datasets and when the underlying structure of the data is not well-defined. However, hierarchical clustering can be computationally intensive for large datasets and may not always produce optimal results, especially when the data contains noise or outliers. Overall, hierarchical clustering is a valuable tool in exploratory data analysis and can aid in understanding the underlying patterns and structures present in the data.

DBSCAN

DBSCAN, which stands for Density-Based Spatial Clustering of Applications with Noise, is a popular clustering algorithm used in machine learning and data mining (Wafa et al, 2021). Unlike traditional clustering algorithms like K-means, DBSCAN does not require the user to specify the number of clusters beforehand, making it particularly useful for datasets with complex structures or varying cluster densities. The key idea behind DBSCAN is to group together closely packed data points based on their density. It defines clusters as dense regions of data points separated by regions of lower density, and it identifies outliers as data points that lie in low-density regions.

DBSCAN operates by iteratively expanding clusters from a seed point, based on two parameters: epsilon (ε), which defines the radius within which neighboring points are considered part of the same cluster, and minPts, which specifies the minimum number of points required to form a dense region. During the clustering process, DBSCAN categorizes each data point as one of three types: core points, border points, or noise points (outliers). Core points are those that have at least minPts neighboring points within a distance of ε while border points have fewer neighbors but lie within the ε-distance of a core point. Noise points, on the other hand, are neither core nor border points and are considered outliers.

DBSCAN's ability to handle noise and outliers, its robustness to varying cluster densities, and its parameter-free nature make it a versatile and widely used clustering algorithm in various applications, including spatial data analysis, image segmentation, anomaly detection, and more. However, it may struggle with datasets of high dimensionality or irregularly shaped clusters, and the choice of ε and minPts parameters can significantly impact its performance. Here are the main steps of the DBSCAN algorithm:

1. Parameter Setup
    - ε (epsilon), The maximum radius of the neighborhood around a data point.
    - MinPts: The minimum number of points required to form a dense region (including the point itself).
2. Core Point Identification

For each data point P in the dataset

- Count the number of points within distance ε of point P. If this count is greater than or equal to MinPts, mark P as a core point.
- If P is a core point, identify all its neighboring points within distance ε

3. Cluster Expansion

For each core point P and its neighboring points

- If a neighboring point is also a core point, recursively explore its neighborhood and add all reachable points to the same cluster as P.
- If a neighboring point is not yet assigned to any cluster, assign it to the same cluster as P.

4. Noise Point Identification, any point that is not a core point and does not belong to any cluster is considered a noise point (outlier).

This process forms clusters of varying shapes and sizes based on density connectivity. Points that are not reachable from any core point (i.e., they are not within distance ε of any core point) and do not have sufficient neighbors (i.e., they are not core points themselves) are labeled as noise points.

The key equations involved in DBSCAN are the distance calculation between points to determine neighbors and the decision rule to classify points as core, border, or noise points based on the ε and MinPts parameters. However, the algorithm itself is not typically represented by a single mathematical equation but rather by a series of logical steps as outlined above. Let's illustrate DBSCAN with a simple example dataset and perform the calculations step by step.

Consider the following dataset:
A(2, 10), B(2, 5), C(8, 4), D(5, 8), E(7, 5), F(6, 4)
Let's assume ε = 3 and MinPts = 2
Let's go through the steps:

1. **Calculate Distances**

Distance(A, B) = $\sqrt{((2\text{-}2)^2 + (10\text{-}5)^2)} = \sqrt{25} = 5$
Distance(A, C) = $\sqrt{((2\text{-}8)^2 + (10\text{-}4)^2)} = \sqrt{36 + 36} = \sqrt{72} \approx 8.49$
Distance(A, D) = $\sqrt{((2\text{-}5)^2 + (10\text{-}8)^2)} = \sqrt{9 + 4} = \sqrt{13} \approx 3.61$
Distance(A, E) = $\sqrt{((2\text{-}7)^2 + (10\text{-}5)^2)} = \sqrt{25 + 25} = \sqrt{50} \approx 7.07$
Distance(A, F) = $\sqrt{((2\text{-}6)^2 + (10\text{-}4)^2)} = \sqrt{16 + 36} = \sqrt{52} \approx 7.21$
Distance(B, C) = $\sqrt{((2\text{-}8)^2 + (5\text{-}4)^2)} = \sqrt{36 + 1} = \sqrt{37} \approx 6.08$
Distance(B, D) = $\sqrt{((2\text{-}5)^2 + (5\text{-}8)^2)} = \sqrt{9 + 9} = \sqrt{18} \approx 4.24$
Distance(B, E) = $\sqrt{((2\text{-}7)^2 + (5\text{-}5)^2)} = \sqrt{25} = 5$
Distance(B, F) = $\sqrt{((2\text{-}6)^2 + (5\text{-}4)^2)} = \sqrt{16 + 1} = \sqrt{17} \approx 4.12$
Distance(C, D) = $\sqrt{((8\text{-}5)^2 + (4\text{-}8)^2)} = \sqrt{9 + 16} = \sqrt{25} = 5$
Distance(C, E) = $\sqrt{((8\text{-}7)^2 + (4\text{-}5)^2)} = \sqrt{1 + 1} = \sqrt{2} \approx 1.41$
Distance(C, F) = $\sqrt{((8\text{-}6)^2 + (4\text{-}4)^2)} = \sqrt{4} = 2$

Distance(D, E) = $\sqrt{((5-7)^2 + (8-5)^2)} = \sqrt{4 + 9} = \sqrt{13} \approx 3.61$
Distance(D, F) = $\sqrt{((5-6)^2 + (8-4)^2)} = \sqrt{1 + 16} = \sqrt{17} \approx 4.12$
Distance(E, F) = $\sqrt{((7-6)^2 + (5-4)^2)} = \sqrt{1 + 1} = \sqrt{2} \approx 1.41$

2. **Identify Core Points**, A, B, C, D, E, and F all have at least 2 neighbors within distance $\varepsilon = 3.61$, so all points are core points.
3. **Expand Clusters**
   - Start with an arbitrary core point (e.g., A) and add its neighbors recursively.
   - Repeat this process for all core points until no more points can be added to any cluster.
4. **Identify Noise Points**: Since all points are core points and can be reached from each other, there are no noise points.

This completes the DBSCAN clustering process. The clusters formed will depend on the distance parameter ε and the minimum points parameter MinPts. The final clustering result will be the groups of points that are densely connected to each other.

DBSACN Real-World Implementation

DBSCAN is well-suited for clustering complex-shaped data with varying densities without requiring a predefined number of clusters. It is also effective at detecting noise and outliers. In **fraud detection**, banks and credit card companies use DBSCAN to identify suspicious transactions, such as unusually large withdrawals or transactions across multiple countries in a short period. In **traffic flow analysis**, DBSCAN helps city planners analyze GPS data from taxis and other vehicles to detect high-traffic zones and anomalies like accidents or unexpected stops. In **earthquake epicenter detection**, geologists utilize DBSCAN to pinpoint the center of seismic activity by distinguishing core tremors from less affected regions. Additionally, in **user behavior analysis in apps**, DBSCAN is used by gaming and app companies to differentiate normal users from those exhibiting unusual behavior, such as using bots or engaging in fraudulent transactions.

In conclusion, DBSCAN (Density-Based Spatial Clustering of Applications with Noise) is a powerful clustering algorithm that is effective in identifying clusters of varying shapes and sizes in spatial data. Unlike traditional clustering algorithms, DBSCAN does not require the user to specify the number of clusters beforehand and can automatically detect outliers as noise. By utilizing the concepts of core points, border points, and noise points, DBSCAN can effectively partition the data space into dense regions separated by areas of lower density. This flexibility and robustness make DBSCAN a valuable tool in various applications such as spatial data analysis, image segmentation, and anomaly detection. However, it is important to tune the parameters of DBSCAN appropriately, such as the epsilon (ε) neighborhood size and the minimum number of points required to form a dense region (MinPts), to achieve optimal clustering results. Overall, DBSCAN offers a versatile and efficient approach to clustering spatial data, making it a popular choice for data mining and machine learning applications.

CLUSTERING TECHNIQUES COMPARISION

Clustering is a fundamental technique in machine learning and data mining, used to group similar data points based on their characteristics. Among the various clustering algorithms, **K-Means, Hierarchical Clustering**, and **DBSCAN** are widely applied in different domains. Each technique has its own strengths and weaknesses, making them suitable for different types of datasets and real-world applications. This table provides a comparative analysis of these three clustering techniques by highlighting their advantages, disadvantages, limitations, and ways to address their challenges. Understanding these differences will help practitioners choose the most appropriate clustering method based on their specific use case.

Table 1. Clustering techniques comparison between K-means, hierarchical clustering and DBSCAN

Clustering Technique	Advantages	Disadvantages	Limitations	How to Resolve the Limitation
K-Means	Efficient for large datasets, easy to implement, and works well with spherical clusters.	Requires specifying the number of clusters in advance, sensitive to outliers and initial centroid selection.	Fails with non-spherical clusters and highly imbalanced cluster sizes.	Use the Elbow Method or Silhouette Score to determine the optimal number of clusters; normalize data to reduce sensitivity to outliers.
Hierarchical Clustering	Does not require the number of clusters to be predefined, produces a dendrogram for visual analysis.	Computationally expensive for large datasets, difficult to scale, and sensitive to noise.	Becomes inefficient with large datasets and may not clearly define cluster boundaries.	Apply an optimized version such as agglomerative clustering with linkage strategies; use hybrid approaches to combine clustering methods.
DBSCAN	Can detect arbitrarily shaped clusters and outliers, does not require specifying the number of clusters.	Struggles with clusters of varying density, sensitive to parameter selection (epsilon and minPts).	May misclassify points in datasets with varying densities or poor parameter tuning.	Fine-tune epsilon and minPts parameters through domain knowledge or automatic tuning; preprocess data to remove noise.

Selecting the right clustering technique depends on the dataset's characteristics and the desired outcomes. **K-Means** is efficient and scalable but struggles with non-spherical clusters and requires predefining the number of clusters. **Hierarchical Clustering** provides flexibility in determining the number of clusters but becomes computationally expensive for large datasets. **DBSCAN** excels at detecting arbitrarily shaped clusters and outliers but requires careful parameter tuning. By understanding the advantages and limitations of each method and applying suitable optimizations, data analysts can improve clustering effectiveness and derive meaningful insights from their data.

ANALYZING THE EFFICIENCY OF DATA CLUSTERING

Analyzing the efficiency of data clustering involves evaluating the quality and performance of clustering algorithms applied to a dataset. Several metrics and techniques can be employed for this purpose:

1. **Evaluation Metrics:** Various metrics, such as silhouette score, Davies-Bouldin index, and Calinski-Harabasz index, can be used to quantitatively measure the quality of clustering results. These metrics assess factors such as cluster cohesion, separation, and overall compactness to provide insights into the effectiveness of clustering algorithms.
   A. **Silhouette Score** is a metric used to calculate the goodness of a clustering technique by measuring the distance between data points within clusters and the distance between clusters themselves. It quantifies the separation distance between the resulting clusters and provides insight into the optimal number of clusters for a given dataset. Mathematically, the silhouette score s for a single data point i is calculated as:

$$s_i = \frac{b_i - a_i}{\max(a_i b_i)}$$

Where: a_i is the average distance from the data point i to other data points within the same cluster.

b_i is the smallest average distance from the data point i to data points in any other cluster, where i is not a member.

The silhouette score for the entire dataset is the mean of the silhouette scores of all individual data points and ranges from -1 to 1:

- A score close to +1 indicates that the data point is well-clustered, with a clear separation from neighboring clusters.
- A score close to 0 suggests that the data point lies close to the decision boundary between two clusters.
- A score close to -1 indicates that the data point may have been assigned to the wrong cluster.

In general, a higher silhouette score implies better clustering results with values closer to 1 indicating more distinct and well-separated clusters.

Suppose we have a dataset with five data points and two clusters:

- Cluster 1: Points A, B, and C
- Cluster 2: Points D and E

The pairwise distances between the data points are as follows:

- Distance between A and B: 2
- Distance between A and C: 4
- Distance between A and D: 5
- Distance between A and E: 6
- Distance between B and C: 3
- Distance between B and D: 4
- Distance between B and E: 5
- Distance between C and D: 3
- Distance between C and E: 4
- Distance between D and E: 1

Now, let's calculate the Silhouette Score for each data point:

For point A:

$$a(A) = \frac{2+4}{2} = 3$$

$$b(A) = 1$$

$$s(A) = \frac{1-3}{\max\{1,3\}} = -\frac{2}{3}$$

Similarly, compute $s(B)$, $s(C)$, $s(D)$, and $s(E)$ using the same process.

After calculating the Silhouette Score for each data point, the average is computed to obtain the overall Silhouette Score for the dataset.

B. **Davies-Bouldin Index (DBI)** is a metric used to evaluate the clustering quality of a dataset. It measures the average similarity between each cluster and its most similar cluster, relative to the average dissimilarity within clusters. Mathematically, the DBI is defined as follows:

$$DBI = \frac{1}{n} \sum_{i=1}^{n} \max j \neq i \left(\frac{S_i + S_j}{d\left(c_i c_j\right)} \right)$$

Where: n is the number of clusters.

S_i is the average distance between each point in cluster i and the centroid of cluster i.
$d(c_i c_j)$ is the distance between the centroids of clusters i and j.
The term $\max j \neq i \left(\frac{S_i + S_j}{d(c_i c_j)} \right)$ represents the similarity between clusters i and j.

A lower DBI indicates better clustering where a value closer to zero suggests tighter clusters with greater separation between them.

To calculate the DBI for a dataset, compute the average similarity between each cluster and its most similar cluster, then take the mean of these values across all clusters. To demonstrate the calculation of the Davies-Bouldin Index (DBI) with an example dataset, we will consider a dataset with three clusters:

Cluster 1: Points (2, 2), (3, 3), (4, 4)
Cluster 2: Points (7, 7), (8, 8), (9, 9)
Cluster 3: Points (15, 15), (16, 16), (17, 17)

First, we need to compute the centroids of each cluster. we then calculate the average distance between each point in a cluster and its centroid as well as the distance between centroids of different clusters. Finally, we compute the DBI using these distances.

Let's calculate it step by step:

1. Calculate Centroids:
   - Centroid of Cluster 1: (3, 3)
   - Centroid of Cluster 2: (8, 8)
   - Centroid of Cluster 3: (16, 16)
2. Calculate Average Distance within Clusters:
   - Cluster 1:

o Distance from (2, 2) to (3, 3): $\sqrt{(3-2)^2 + (3-2)^2} = \sqrt{2}$

o Distance from (3, 3) to (3, 3): $\sqrt{(3-3)^2 + (3-3)^2} = 0$

o Distance from (4, 4) to (3, 3): $\sqrt{(4-3)^2 + (4-3)^2} = \sqrt{2}$

o Average distance: $(\sqrt{2} + 0 + \sqrt{2})/3 = \frac{2\sqrt{2}}{3}$

- Cluster 2:

o Distance from (7, 7) to (8, 8): $\sqrt{(8-7)^2 + (8-7)^2} = \sqrt{2}$

o Distance from (8, 8) to (8, 8): $\sqrt{(8-8)^2 + (8-8)^2} = 0$

o Distance from (9, 9) to (8, 8): $\sqrt{(9-8)^2 + (9-8)^2} = \sqrt{2}$

o Average distance: $(\sqrt{2} + 0 + \sqrt{2})/3 = \frac{2\sqrt{2}}{3}$

- Cluster 3:

o Distance from (15, 15) to (16, 16): $\sqrt{(16-15)^2 + (16-15)^2} = \sqrt{2}$

o Distance from (16, 16) to (16, 16): $\sqrt{(16-16)^2 + (16-16)^2} = 0$

o Distance from (17, 17) to (16, 16): $\sqrt{(17-16)^2 + (17-16)^2} = \sqrt{2}$

o Average distance: $(\sqrt{2} + 0 + \sqrt{2})/3 = \frac{2\sqrt{2}}{3}$

3. Calculate Distance between Centroids:

- Distance between Cluster 1 and Cluster 2 centroids: $\sqrt{(8-3)^2 + (8-3)^2}$ $= 5\sqrt{2}$

- Distance between Cluster 1 and Cluster 3 centroids: $\sqrt{(16-3)^2 + (16-3)^2}$ $= 13\sqrt{2}$

- Distance between Cluster 2 and Cluster 3 centroids: $\sqrt{(16-8)^2 + (16-8)^2}$

$= 8\sqrt{2}$

4. Calculate DBI:

For Cluster 1:

$$R_1 = \frac{2\sqrt{2}/3 + 5\sqrt{2}}{13\sqrt{2}} = \frac{2}{39}$$

For Cluster 2:

$$R_2 = \frac{2\sqrt{2}/3 + 5\sqrt{2}}{8\sqrt{2}} = \frac{2}{24} = \frac{1}{12}$$

For Cluster 3:

$$R_3 = \frac{2\sqrt{2}/3 + 8\sqrt{2}}{13\sqrt{2}} = \frac{2}{39}$$

5. Average DBI:

$$DBI = \frac{1}{3}\left(\frac{2}{39} + \frac{1}{12} + \frac{2}{39}\right)$$

$$DBI = \frac{1}{3}\left(\frac{79}{468}\right)$$

$$DBI \approx 0.056$$

So, the Davies-Bouldin Index (DBI) for this example dataset is approximately 0.056.

C. **Calinski-Harabasz Index (also known as the Variance Ratio Criterion)** is a metric used to evaluate the clustering quality of a dataset. It measures the ratio of between-cluster dispersion to within-cluster dispersion, aiming to find clusters that are both compact and well-separated. Mathematically, the Calinski-Harabasz Index is defined as follows:

$$CH = \frac{Tr(B_k)}{Tr(W_k)} \times \frac{N-k}{k-1}$$

Where: CH is the Calinski-Harabasz Index.

$Tr(B_k)$ is the trace of the between-cluster scatter matrix.
$Tr(W_k)$ is the trace of the within-cluster scatter matrix.
N is the total number of data points.
k is the number of clusters.

A higher CH value indicates better clustering, with a larger ratio of between-cluster dispersion to within-cluster dispersion. It suggests that the clusters are more compact and well-separated. To calculate the Calinski-Harabasz Index for a dataset, compute the scatter matrices for both within-cluster and between-cluster dispersion, and then apply the formula to derive the index. To calculate the Calinski-Harabasz Index (CH) for a given dataset, you need to compute the scatter matrices for both within-cluster and between-cluster dispersion and then apply the formula. Let's consider an example dataset with six data points and two features:

Data Points: [(2, 10), (2, 5), (8, 4), (5, 8), (7, 5), (6, 4)]

Let's assume these data points are clustered into two clusters:

Cluster 1: {(2, 10), (2, 5), (8, 4)}
Cluster 2: {(5, 8), (7, 5), (6, 4)}

Now, we compute the centroid of each cluster:

Centroid 1: (4, 6.33)
Centroid 2: (6, 5.67)

Next, we calculate the within-cluster scatter matrix (W) for each cluster. For simplicity, let's use the Euclidean distance as the distance metric.

For Cluster 1
W1 = sum of squared distances from each point to the centroid
$= [(2 - 4)^2 + (10 - 6.33)^2 + (2 - 4)^2 + (5 - 6.33)^2 + (8 - 4)^2 + (4 - 6.33)^2]$
$= [4.6533 + 5.5977 + 4.6533 + 3.2977 + 16.5977 + 4.5977]$
$= 39.3974$
For Cluster 2
W2 = sum of squared distances from each point to the centroid
= [(5-6)2 + (8-5.67)2 + (7-6)2 + (5-6)2 + (6-6)2 + (4-5.67)2]
$= [1 + 6.6249 + 1 + 1 + 0 + 2.0577]$
$= 11.6826$

Then, we calculate the between-cluster scatter matrix (B) as the sum of squared distances between the centroids and the overall centroid:

$B = [(4 - 5)^2 + (6.33 - 5.67)^2] + [(6 - 5)^2 + (5.67 - 5.67)^2]$
$= [1 + 0.4353] + [1 + 0]$
$= 2.4353$

Now, we can calculate the Calinski-Harabasz Index (CH) using the formula:

$CH = (Tr(B\_k))/(Tr(W\_k)) \times (N - k)/(k - 1)$

$= (2.4353 / (39.3974 + 11.6826)) * ((6 - 2) / (2 - 1))$
$= (2.4353 / 51.08) * (4 / 1)$
≈ 0.1903

So, the Calinski-Harabasz Index for this example dataset with two clusters is approximately 0.1903.

2. **Visualization Techniques: Visualizing clustered data using techniques like scatter plots,** heatmaps, and dendrograms can offer intuitive insights into the structure and characteristics of the clusters formed. Visual inspection allows for

the identification of any patterns, outliers, or inconsistencies in the clustering results.

3. **Comparative Analysis:** Comparing the results of different clustering algorithms applied to the same dataset can help to identify the most suitable algorithm for the specific data characteristics and clustering objectives. This comparative analysis may involve assessing factors such as computational efficiency, scalability, and robustness across various algorithms.
4. **Parameter Tuning:** Fine-tuning the parameters of clustering algorithms, such as the number of clusters (k) or distance thresholds, can significantly impact clustering performance. Conducting sensitivity analysis or parameter optimization techniques, such as grid search or random search, can help to identify optimal parameter configurations for improved clustering efficiency.
5. **Domain-Specific Considerations:** Understanding domain-specific requirements and constraints is crucial for evaluating the efficiency of data clustering. Domain experts may provide valuable insights into the relevance and interpretability of clustering results in real-world applications, ensuring that the clustering solution aligns with domain-specific objectives and constraints.

By employing a combination of these techniques, data analysts and researchers can comprehensively analyze the efficiency of data clustering algorithms and make informed decisions regarding algorithm selection, parameter tuning, and interpretation of clustering results.

DATA CLUSTERING USING RAPIDMINER SOFTWARE

To utilize the K-Means clustering functionality in RapidMiner for clustering, this book employs the Iris flower dataset to cluster the Iris flower data of each cultivar, including Setosa, Versicolor, and all Virginica, totaling 150 instances. K-Means falls under unsupervised learning, where data scientists can import the datasets into the model without labeling the target variables or training the machine. The experimental process is outlined as follows:

Figure 3. Importing the Irish flower dataset into the model

As shown in Figure 3, data scientists can import the Iris flower dataset into the RapidMiner software for experimentation. The Iris flower dataset comprises the following information.

Figure 4. Irish flower data set

Row No.	id	label	a1	a2	a3	a4
1	id_1	Iris-setosa	5.100	3.500	1.400	0.200
2	id_2	Iris-setosa	4.900	3	1.400	0.200
3	id_3	Iris-setosa	4.700	3.200	1.300	0.200
4	id_4	Iris-setosa	4.600	3.100	1.500	0.200
5	id_5	Iris-setosa	5	3.600	1.400	0.200
6	id_6	Iris-setosa	5.400	3.900	1.700	0.400
7	id_7	Iris-setosa	4.600	3.400	1.400	0.300
8	id_8	Iris-setosa	5	3.400	1.500	0.200
9	id_9	Iris-setosa	4.400	2.900	1.400	0.200
10	id_10	Iris-setosa	4.900	3.100	1.500	0.100
11	id_11	Iris-setosa	5.400	3.700	1.500	0.200
12	id_12	Iris-setosa	4.800	3.400	1.600	0.200
13	id_13	Iris-setosa	4.800	3	1.400	0.100
14	id_14	Iris-setosa	4.300	3	1.100	0.100
15	id_15	Iris-setosa	5.800	4	1.200	0.200
16	id_16	Iris-setosa	5.700	4.400	1.500	0.400
17	id_17	Iris-setosa	5.400	3.900	1.300	0.400
18	id_18	Iris-setosa	5.100	3.500	1.400	0.300

ExampleSet (150 examples, 2 special attributes, 4 regular attributes)

Figure 5. Using K-means clustering

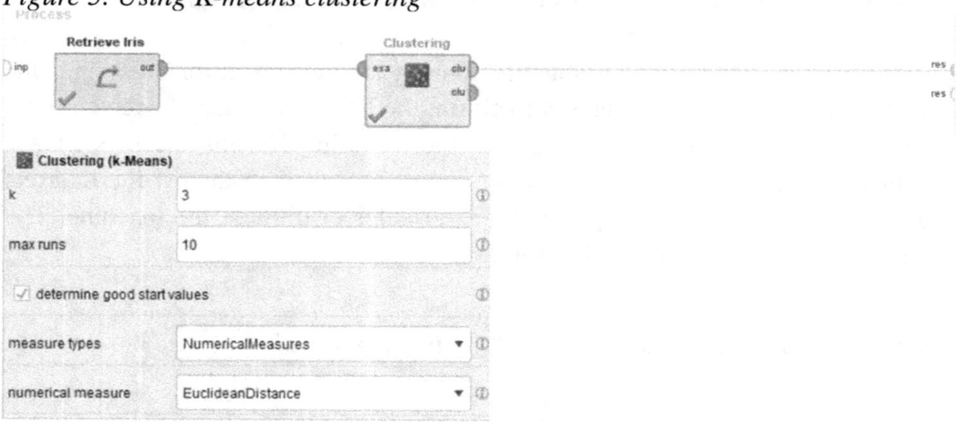

As shown in Figure 5, data scientists utilize the K-Means Clustering model to cluster the data, setting the number of clusters to 3. The distance between the data points is calculated using the Euclidean distance method. The results of the initial clustering are as follows.

Figure 6. The number of data objects organized in each cluster

Cluster Model

```
Cluster 0: 50 items
Cluster 1: 38 items
Cluster 2: 62 items
Total number of items: 150
```

As shown in Figure 6, the datasets are divided into three clusters as defined. Cluster 0 comprises a total of 50 data objects, Cluster 1 includes 38 data objects, and Cluster 2 encompasses 62 data objects. Within each cluster, the clustered data are visually represented as shown below.

Figure 7. Data results after K-means clustering

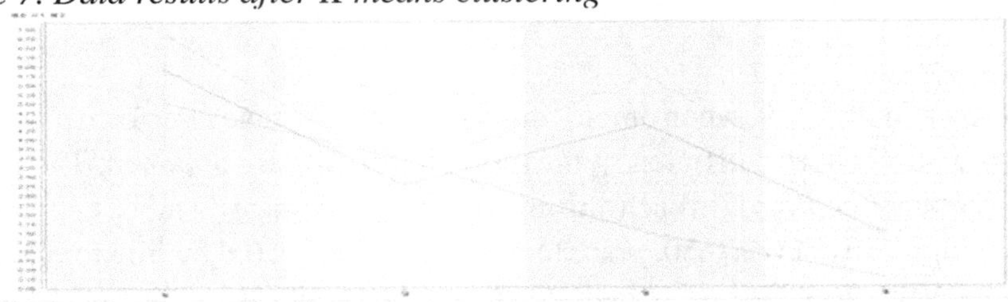

Data scientists can utilize the visualized data to consult a data specialist to evaluate the effectiveness of the data clustering, considering the distances between clusters, their distinct separations, and the internal cohesion. The Iris flower cultivars are evidently segregated into three clusters, each exhibiting notable differences in the sizes of flowers and sepals within their respective species.

To reaffirm the efficacy of data clustering, data scientists may opt to conduct further analysis.

Figure 8. Measuring clustering efficiency with cluster distance performance

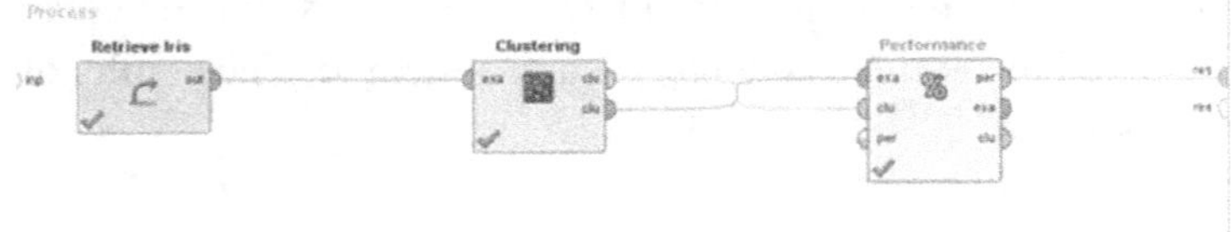

As shown in Figure 8, data scientists utilize Cluster Distance Performance to evaluate the effectiveness of data clustering. This involves assessing the average distance between data objects within each cluster as well as the average distance between the centroids of each cluster. The overall performance metrics are as follows.

Figure 9. Evaluation of clustering efficiency result

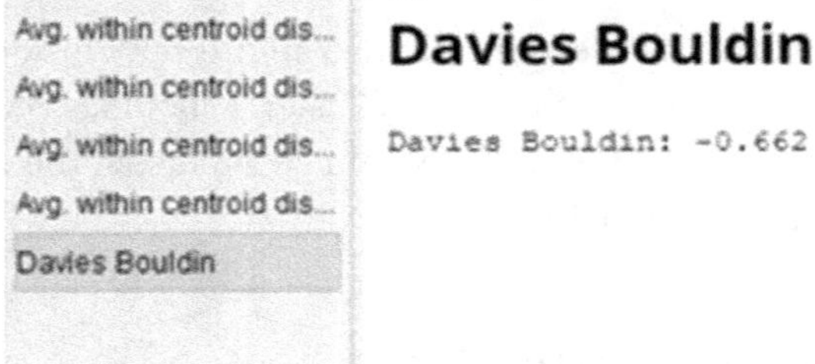

As shown in Figure 9, when employing the Cluster Distance Performance model to evaluate the clustering efficiency, the following results are obtained: The average distance between centroids in each cluster is 0.52. The average distance between data objects within Cluster 0 is 0.30. For Cluster 1, this value is 0.62 while for Cluster 2, it is 0.64. Lastly, the efficiency calculated using the Davies Bouldin method is 0.66.

Based on all of the results, it can be observed that each pair of clusters exhibits good distances between their centroids, indicating appropriate separation between the clusters. Moreover, within each cluster, the distance between the centroid and data objects is not excessively high, suggesting a moderate grouping effect. The Davies Bouldin method of calculation further reflects the clustering efficiency at a moderate level.

CONCLUSION

Clustering serves as a valuable tool for categorizing quantitative data and finds applications in diverse domains like customer segmentation and disease classification. Data scientists can leverage RapidMiner software to import quantitative datasets and to employ clustering techniques such as K-Means Clustering or DBSCAN for data clustering. An effective clustering outcome is characterized by well-clustered data within each group while ensuring clear separation between clusters. RapidMiner offers models alongside visualization tools to facilitate the evaluation of clustering efficiency by data experts.

EXERCISES

1. Provide a concise overview of the K-Means Clustering algorithm.
2. Elaborate on the distinction between Manhattan Distance and Euclidean Distance computations.
3. Detail the process of interpreting outcomes derived from Centroid analysis.
4. Present instances of scenarios well-suited for data examination using K-Means.
5. Conduct a literature review to identify research employing K-Means Clustering for data analysis and summarize its key findings briefly.

REFERENCES

Abbas, A., Prayitno, P., Butarbutar, F., Nurkim, N., Prumanto, D., Dewadi, F. M., Hidayati, N., & Windarto, A. P. (2021). Implementation of clustering unsupervised learning using K-means mapping techniques. *IOP Conference Series. Materials Science and Engineering*, *1088*(1), 012004. DOI: 10.1088/1757-899X/1088/1/012004

Bayram, E., & Nabiyev, V. (2020). Image segmentation by using K-means clustering algorithm in Euclidean and Mahalanobis distance calculation in camouflage images. *2020 28th Signal Processing and Communications Applications Conference (SIU)*, 1–4.

Ben Ncir, C.-E., Hamza, A., & Bouaguel, W. (2021). Parallel and scalable Dunn Index for the validation of big data clusters. *Parallel Computing*, *102*, 102. DOI: 10.1016/j.parco.2021.102751

Ginting, S. W., Hartati, R. S., Sudarma, M., & Swamardika, I. B. A. (2021). Clustering of earthquake and volcanic eruption trauma survivor groups using K-means algorithm. *2021 International Conference on Smart-Green Technology in Electrical and Information Systems (ICSGTEIS)*, 69–73. DOI: 10.1109/ICSGTEIS53426.2021.9650357

Govindaraj, V., Thiyagarajan, A., Rajasekaran, P., Zhang, Y., & Krishnasamy, R. (2020). Automated unsupervised learning-based clustering approach for effective anomaly detection in brain magnetic resonance imaging (MRI). *IET Image Processing*, *14*(14), 3516–3526. DOI: 10.1049/iet-ipr.2020.0597

Haviluddin, I. M., Putra, G. M., Puspitasari, N., Setyadi, H. J., Dwiyanto, F. A., Wibawa, A. P., & Alfred, R. (2020). A performance comparison of Euclidean, Manhattan and Minkowski distances in K-means clustering. *2020 6th International Conference on Science in Information Technology (ICSITech)*, 184–188.

Kumar, P., Ganapathy, G., & Kang, J.-J. (2021). A hybrid mod K-means clustering with mod SVM algorithm to enhance the cancer prediction. *International Journal of Internet. Broadcasting and Communication*, *13*(2), 231–243.

Punhani, R., Arora, V. P. S., Sabitha, S., & Kumar Shukla, V. (2021). Application of clustering algorithm for effective customer segmentation in e-commerce. *2021 International Conference on Computational Intelligence and Knowledge Economy (ICCIKE)*, 149–154. DOI: 10.1109/ICCIKE51210.2021.9410713

Puspasari, B. D., Damayanti, L. L., Pramono, A., & Darmawan, A. K. (2021). Implementation K-means clustering method in job recommendation system. *2021 7th International Conference on Electrical, Electronics and Information Engineering (ICEEIE)*, 1–6.

Rezaeijo, S. M., Hashemi, B., Mofid, B., Bakhshandeh, M., Mahdavi, A., & Hashemi, M. S. (2021). The feasibility of a dose painting procedure to treat prostate cancer based on mpMR images and hierarchical clustering. *Radiation Oncology (London, England)*, *16*(1), 1–16. DOI: 10.1186/s13014-021-01906-2 PMID: 34544468

Wafa, H. A., Aminuddin, R., Ibrahim, S., Mangshor, N. N. A., & Wahab, N. I. F. A. (2021). A data visualization framework during pandemic using the Density-Based Spatial Clustering with Noise (DBSCAN) machine learning model. *2021 IEEE 11th International Conference on System Engineering and Technology (ICSET)*, 1–6.

Wijaya, Y. A., Kurniady, D. A., Setyanto, E., Tarihoran, W. S., Rusmana, D., & Rahim, R. (2021). Davies Bouldin Index algorithm for optimizing clustering case studies mapping school facilities. *TEM Journal*, *10*(3), 1099–1103. DOI: 10.18421/TEM103-13

Zhou, Y., Yan, S., Wang, C., Zheng, K., & Zhu, L. (2021). Position monitoring system based on hierarchical clustering. *2021 26th IEEE Asia-Pacific Conference on Communications (APCC)*, 111–114.

Chapter 7
Association Rule

ABSTRACT

Businesses are increasingly seeking to understand consumer behavior and purchasing habits in order to analyze the relationship between different products purchased by customers. By leveraging the Association Rule mining technique, businesses can identify complementary products and bundle them together to increase sales. This chapter provides an overview of Association Rule mining, a form of unsupervised learning that enables data scientists to analyze the relationship between data items in a dataset. The chapter explains the Apriori algorithm, a feature of Association Rule mining, and highlights how data scientists can collaborate with domain experts to achieve business objectives such as product matching and testing the efficiency of Association Rule results. Readers can follow a step-by-step guide to experience the Association Rule mining technique using RapidMiner, enabling them to develop their understanding of this valuable analytical tool.

INTRODUCTION

In the vast ocean of data that engulfs various industries today, the ability to sift through and find meaningful patterns is not just an advantage but a necessity. Data mining, the process of discovering patterns and knowledge from large amounts of data, serves as a cornerstone in this quest. Among the myriad techniques that form the body of data mining, Association Rule mining stands out for its simplicity and powerful application across domains. Association Rule mining is a technique to identify underlying relationships between different items within large datasets. Historically, its roots can be traced back to the early 1990s, evolving from simple market basket analysis to a broad application spectrum. This method focuses on discovering rules that define how the presence of one set of items in transactions often implies the presence of other items, quantified through measures such as support, confidence, and lift (Ren, 2021: Yingzhuo & Xuewen, 2021). The applications of Association

DOI: 10.4018/979-8-3693-6001-9.ch007

Rule mining are vast and varied. Retailers use it for market basket analysis to understand the purchasing behavior of customers. It also finds applications in cross-marketing, catalog design, fraud detection, and even in healthcare management for identifying patterns in treatment procedures and patient records (Toumi, Gribaa, & Ben Abdessalem Karaa, 2021). At the heart of Association Rule mining lie three key metrics: support, which measures how frequently an itemset appears in the dataset; confidence, which assesses how often items A and B are purchased together; and lift, which evaluates the strength of a rule over the random co-occurrence of A and B. The discovery of frequent itemsets is often achieved through algorithms such as the Apriori algorithm, serving as a foundation for generating association rules (Paruechanon & Sriurai, 2019: Hong & Nan 2021: Salman & Sadkhan, 2021). Despite its usefulness, Association Rule mining faces challenges, particularly in handling large datasets efficiently and in the discovery of meaningful rules without overwhelming users with too much information. Scalability and efficiency remain at the forefront of these challenges, driving ongoing research and development efforts. Recent advances in Association Rule mining have focused on improving algorithm efficiency, integrating machine learning techniques for better prediction capabilities, and expanding its application scope. The future of Association Rule mining looks promising, with potential expansions into predictive analysis and other advanced data mining techniques. Association Rule mining is a fundamental technique in data mining that offers profound insights into data patterns. Its applications span various industries, highlighting its versatility and effectiveness in extracting valuable information from vast datasets. As we delve deeper into the nuances of this technique in the subsequent chapters, the foundational knowledge provided here sets the stage for a comprehensive understanding of Association Rule mining.

ASSOCIATION RULE

Association Rule learning is a machine learning technique used to discover interesting relationships, or associations, between variables in large datasets. It is often applied in market basket analysis, where the goal is to identify patterns of co-occurrence among items purchased together by customers. (Zhang & Zhang, 2002). The most common algorithm used for Association Rule learning is the Apriori algorithm. This algorithm works by identifying frequent itemsets, which are sets of items that frequently occur together in the dataset. From these frequent itemsets, association rules are generated. An association rule is typically in the form of "if {X} then {Y}", where X and Y are sets of items.

Two key measures are used to evaluate the strength of association rules:

A. Support: The support of an itemset is the proportion of transactions in the dataset that contain that itemset. For an association rule, the support is the proportion of transactions that contain both X and Y.
B. Confidence: The confidence of an association rule {X} -> {Y} is the proportion of transactions containing X that also contain Y. It measures the reliability of the inference made by the rule.

Association Rule learning has various applications beyond market basket analysis, including the following:

A. Recommender systems: recommending products or items based on the historical behavior of users.
B. Cross-selling: suggesting additional products or services to customers based on their previous purchases.
C. Health informatics: identifying associations between medical conditions, symptoms, and treatments.
D. Fraud detection: discovering patterns of fraudulent behavior in financial transactions.
E. Association Rule learning is particularly useful for exploratory data analysis and can provide valuable insights into the underlying structure of large datasets. However, it is important to note that association does not imply causation, and additional analysis may be needed to validate the discovered relationships.

Association Rule processing involves several steps, which can be described using equations and mathematical notation. Let's break down the process into key equations.

A. **Support Calculation:** support ($supp(X)$) of an itemset X is defined as the proportion of transactions containing X out of the total number of transactions N.

$$supp(X) = \frac{Transactions\ containing\ X}{N}$$

Where: *Transactions containing* X is the count of transactions that contain the itemset X.

N is the total number of transactions in the dataset.

B. **Frequent Itemset Generation:** Frequent itemsets are those whose support exceeds a predefined minimum support threshold *minsupp*.
C. **Association Rule Generation:** Association rules are generated from frequent itemsets. For a frequent itemset X, an association rule can be represented as $X \rightarrow Y$, where Y is a subset of X.

Let X and Y be disjoint subsets of items such that $X \cup Y$ is a frequent itemset. The confidence of the association rule $X \rightarrow Y$ is calculated as:

$$\text{conf}(X \rightarrow Y) = \frac{supp(X \cup Y)}{supp(X)}$$

Where: $supp(X \cup Y)$ is the support of the combined itemset $X \cup Y$.
$supp(X)$ is the support of itemset X.

D. **Rule Pruning:** association rules with confidence below a specified minimum confidence threshold minconf are pruned.

These equations outline the fundamental steps involved in Association Rule processing. The support and confidence measures play crucial roles in determining the significance of itemsets and association rules, respectively. By setting appropriate support and confidence thresholds, one can control the quality and quantity of the discovered rules.

Let's demonstrate an association rule calculation with a simple example dataset. Consider a transaction dataset from a grocery store.

Table 1. Example dataset from a grocery store

Transaction ID	Items
1	Bread, Milk
2	Bread, Diapers, Beer, Eggs
3	Milk, Diapers, Beer, Coke
4	Bread, Milk, Diapers, Beer
5	Bread, Milk, Diapers, Coke

Let's go through each step:

A. **Calculate Support for Itemsets**

We will calculate the support for each individual item and itemset. The support for an item X is calculated as:

$$supp(X) = \frac{Transactions\ containing\ X}{N}$$

For example, the support for the item "Bread" is:

$supp("Bread") = \frac{4}{5} = 0.8$

B. **Generate Frequent Itemsets**

We will set a minimum support threshold, say minsupp = 0.4. Any itemset with support greater than or equal to this threshold is considered frequent.

Frequent Itemsets:

{Bread} (support = 0.8)
{Milk} (support = 0.6)
{Diapers} (support = 0.6)
{Beer} (support = 0.6)

C. **Generate Association Rules:** for each frequent itemset, we generate association rules. For example, from the itemset {Bread, Milk}, we can generate two rules:

D.
Bread -> Milk
Milk -> Bread

We calculate the confidence for each rule:

$$\text{conf}(X \rightarrow Y) = \frac{supp(X \cup Y)}{supp(X)}$$

For example, the confidence for the rule Bread -> Milk is:

$$\text{conf(Bread} \rightarrow \text{Milk)} = \frac{\text{supp(Bread, Milk)}}{\text{supp(Bread)}} = \frac{0.6}{0.8} = 0.75$$

E. **Prune the rules based on confidence**: we set a minimum confidence threshold, say

minconf = 0.6. Any rule with confidence greater than or equal to this threshold is considered significant. So, the significant association rules are:

F.
Bread -> Milk (confidence = 0.75)
Milk -> Bread (confidence = 1.0)

Diapers -> Beer (confidence = 1.0)
Beer -> Diapers (confidence = 1.0)

These are the association rules generated from the example dataset, along with their corresponding confidence. They represent patterns of association between items in the transactions.

In conclusion, Association Rule learning is a valuable tool for exploratory data analysis, providing actionable insights into patterns of association within datasets. By leveraging these insights, businesses can make informed decisions to optimize processes, enhance customer experiences, and drive strategic initiatives.

APRIORI ALGORITHM

The Apriori algorithm is a classic and fundamental algorithm for Association Rule mining in transactional databases (Baby & Reddy, 2021: Hodijah & Setijohatmo, 2021). It efficiently discovers frequent itemsets and generates association rules from transaction data. Developed by Rakesh Agrawal and Ramakrishnan Srikant in 1994, the Apriori algorithm remains widely used due to its simplicity and effectiveness (Agrawal & Srikant, 1994). The key concepts are as follows:

A. **Frequent Itemsets:** an itemset is considered frequent if it appears in a sufficient number of transactions, surpassing a predefined support threshold.
B. **Support Count:** the number of transactions in which an itemset appears.
C. **Support:** the proportion of transactions containing a particular itemset out of the total number of transactions.
D. **Apriori Principle:** the principle states that if an itemset is frequent, then all of its subsets must also be frequent. This property is leveraged to reduce the search space while generating frequent itemsets.

The algorithm steps are presented as follows:

A. **Generate Candidate Itemsets:** start by identifying frequent individual items (itemsets of size 1). Then, iteratively generate candidate itemsets of larger sizes based on the frequent itemsets found in the previous iteration.
B. **Prune Infrequent Itemsets:** remove candidate itemsets that are subsets of infrequent itemsets, as they cannot be frequent themselves due to the Apriori principle.
C. **Count Support:** scan the transaction database to count the support of each candidate itemset

D. **Identify Frequent Itemsets:** filter out candidate itemsets whose support does not meet the minimum support threshold, resulting in a set of frequent itemsets.
E. **Generate Association Rules:** from the frequent itemsets, generate association rules with confidence exceeding a specified threshold. Association rules are generated by considering all possible combinations of items within frequent itemsets.

Let's demonstrate Apriori algorithm processing with an example dataset from Table 8.1. Given a minimum support threshold of 2, and a minimum confidence threshold of 0.5, the Apriori algorithm would proceed as follows:

Identify frequent itemsets:

{Bread}, {Milk}, {Diapers}, {Beer} are frequent itemsets.
Generate association rules from frequent itemsets:
Bread -> Milk, Diapers -> Beer, etc.
Prune rules based on confidence threshold.

The Apriori algorithm offers several advantages. Firstly, it demonstrates efficiency by employing candidate generation and pruning strategies, effectively navigating the search space, which renders it suitable for handling large datasets. Secondly, it showcases scalability, effortlessly managing large transactional databases despite its straightforward approach. Thirdly, the interpretability of association rules generated by Apriori aids in decision-making processes, making it user-friendly and accessible.

However, the algorithm also presents certain limitations. It can incur memory and computational overhead, particularly noticeable with datasets containing a large number of unique items. Additionally, the need for tuning is paramount as selecting appropriate support and confidence thresholds is crucial for deriving meaningful results. Moreover, handling sparse data poses a challenge as identifying frequent itemsets becomes more difficult in datasets with a high degree of sparsity.

Despite these limitations, the Apriori algorithm remains a foundational technique in Association Rule mining. Its significance persists as it forms the basis for more advanced algorithms and approaches in this field, contributing to ongoing developments and applications in data mining and analytics.

RULE INTERESTINGNESS

Rule interestingness refers to the measure of how valuable or informative an association rule is in a given context. In the context of Association Rule mining, where large amounts of data are analyzed to discover interesting relationships between variables, assessing the interestingness of generated rules is crucial for identifying those that are truly meaningful and actionable (Bing, Yiming & Lee, 2001: Glass, 2013: Greco, Słowiński & Szczęch, 2016). There are several factors that contribute to the interestingness of an association rule:

A. **Support:** the support of a rule indicates how frequently the items in the rule occur together in the dataset. Rules with higher support values are generally considered more interesting as they represent more common patterns in the data. Let's demonstrate support calculation using an example dataset from Table 1.

We will calculate the support for individual items and itemsets. Suppose we are interested in calculating the support for the item "Bread".

1. **Calculate Support for Individual Items**

The support for an item is the proportion of transactions containing that item out of the total number of transactions.

Support (supp(X)) of an item X is calculated as:

$$supp(X) = \frac{Transactions\ containing\ X}{N}$$

Where N is the total number of transactions

For item "Bread", the support is calculated as:

$$\text{supp}(\text{"}Bread\text{"}) = \frac{4}{5} = 0.8$$

2. **Calculate Support for Itemsets:** similarly, we can calculate the support for itemsets of size greater than 1. For example, the support for the itemset {Bread, Milk} is the proportion of transactions containing both "Bread" and "Milk".

$$\text{supp}\left(\text{"Bread, Milk"}\right) = \frac{3}{5} = 0.6$$

Here, 3 out of 5 transactions contain both "Bread" and "Milk".

By calculating the support for individual items and itemsets, we can identify frequent itemsets that meet a predefined minimum support threshold. In this example, if we set a minimum support threshold of 0.4, the item "Bread" and the itemset {Bread, Milk} would both be considered frequent. These frequent itemsets form the basis for generating association rules using algorithms like Apriori.

B. **Confidence** measures the reliability or strength of the association between the antecedent (the items on the left-hand side of the rule) and the consequent (the items on the right-hand side). Rules with higher confidence values are typically more interesting because they indicate a stronger relationship between the items. Let's illustrate a confidence calculation using the same example dataset from Table 8.1. We will focus on calculating the confidence for the association rule "Bread -> Milk", which implies that if a transaction contains "Bread", it is likely to contain "Milk" as well.

1. **Calculate Support for Itemsets:** before calculating confidence, we need to calculate the support for both the antecedent (left-hand side) and the consequent (right-hand side) of the rule. We have already calculated the support for individual items and itemsets in the previous example.

Support of "Bread": supp("Bread") = 0.8
Support of "Bread, Milk": supp("Bread, Milk") = 0.6

2. **Calculate Confidence:** confidence ($\text{conf}(X \rightarrow Y)$) measures the conditional probability of finding the consequent (Y) in transactions containing the antecedent (X).

Confidence for the rule "Bread -> Milk" is calculated as:

$$\text{conf}(\text{"Bread"} \rightarrow \text{"Milk"}) = \frac{\text{supp("Bread, Milk")}}{\text{supp("Bread")}}$$

Substituting the support values:

$$\text{conf}(\text{"Bread"} \rightarrow \text{"Milk"}) = \frac{0.6}{0.8} = 0.75$$

This means that in 75% of the transactions containing "Bread", "Milk" is also present.

3. **Interpretation:** a confidence of 0.75 indicates that when "Bread" is purchased, there is a 75% chance that "Milk" will also be purchased. This implies a relatively strong association between the two items.

By calculating confidence for association rules, we can assess the reliability of the rules and prioritize those with higher confidence values for further analysis or action. Confidence, along with support, plays a crucial role in determining the interestingness of association rules in the context of Association Rule mining.

C. **Lift** measures the ratio of the observed support of the rule to the expected support if the antecedent and consequent were independent of each other. A lift value greater than 1 indicates that the antecedent and consequent are positively correlated, making the rule more interesting. Lift measures how much more likely the consequent (Y) is to occur in transactions containing the antecedent (X) compared to its expected occurrence if X and Y were independent. Let's demonstrate the lift calculation using the same example dataset from Table 8.1.

We will focus on calculating the lift for the association rule "Bread -> Milk", which implies that if a transaction contains "Bread", it is likely to contain "Milk" as well.

1. **Calculate Support for Itemsets:** before calculating lift, we need to calculate the support for both the antecedent (left-hand side) and the consequent (right-hand side) of the rule. We have already calculated the support for individual items and itemsets in the previous examples.
   Support of "Bread": supp("Bread") = 0.8
   Support of "Milk": supp("Milk") = 0.6
   Support of "Bread, Milk": supp("Bread, Milk") = 0.6
2. **Calculate Lift:**
   Lift ($\text{lift}(X \rightarrow Y)$) measures the ratio of the observed support of the rule to the expected support if X and Y were independent.
   Lift for the rule "Bread -> Milk" is calculated as:
   $$\text{lift}(\text{Bread} \rightarrow \text{Milk}) = \frac{\text{supp}(\text{Bread, Milk})}{\text{supp}(\text{Bread}) \times \text{supp}(\text{Milk})}$$

Substituting the support values:

$$\text{lift}(\text{"Bread"} \rightarrow \text{"Milk"}) = \frac{0.6}{0.8 \times 0.6} = \frac{0.6}{0.48} \approx 1.25$$

3. **Interpretation:** a lift of approximately 1.25 indicates that the likelihood of purchasing "Milk" when "Bread" is purchased is 1.25 times higher than if the purchases were independent. A lift value greater than 1 suggests a positive association between the items while a lift value less than 1 indicates a negative association.

By calculating lift for association rules, we can assess the significance of the association between items and identify rules with stronger associations for further analysis or action. Lift provides valuable insights into the dependency between items beyond what can be inferred from support and confidence alone.

D. **Conviction** measures the ratio of the expected frequency that the consequent occurs without the antecedent to the observed frequency of incorrect predictions. Higher conviction values indicate that the consequent is highly dependent on the antecedent, making the rule more interesting. Let's demonstrate a conviction calculation using the same example dataset from Table 8.1.

We will focus on calculating the conviction for the association rule "Bread -> Milk", which implies that if a transaction contains "Bread", it is likely to contain "Milk" as well.

1. **Calculate Support for Itemsets:** before calculating conviction, we need to calculate the support for both the antecedent (left-hand side) and the consequent (right-hand side) of the rule. We have already calculated the support for individual items and itemsets in the previous examples.
   Support of "Bread": supp("Bread") = 0.8
   Support of "Milk": supp("Milk") = 0.6
   Support of "Bread, Milk": supp("Bread, Milk") = 0.6

Calculate Conviction: Conviction (conv(X → Y)) measures the ratio of the expected frequency that the consequent occurs without the antecedent to the observed frequency of incorrect predictions.

Conviction for the rule "Bread -> Milk" is calculated as:

$$\text{conv}(\text{"Bread"} \rightarrow \text{"Milk"}) = \frac{\text{supp}(\text{"Bread"}) \times (1 - \text{supp}(\text{"Milk"})}{(1 - \text{supp}(\text{"Bread, Milk"})}$$

Substituting the support values:

$$\text{conv}(\text{"Bread"} \rightarrow \text{"Milk"}) = \frac{0.8 \times (1 - 0.6)}{(1 - 0.6)} = \frac{0.8 \times 0.4}{0.4} = 0.8$$

2. **Interpretation**, A conviction of 0.8 indicates that the consequent "Milk" is 0.8 times more likely to occur without the antecedent "Bread" than it is to be incorrectly predicted given "Bread". A conviction value greater than 1 suggests a strong dependency between the antecedent and consequent, indicating that the consequent is highly dependent on the antecedent.

By calculating conviction for association rules, we can evaluate the strength of dependency between items and identify rules with significant associations for further analysis or action. Conviction provides additional insights into the dependency between items beyond what can be inferred from support, confidence, and lift measures alone.

3. **Interest Measures:** various other interest measures, such as leverage, the Jaccard coefficient, and the Kulczynski measure, can also be used to assess the interestingness of association rules by capturing different aspects of the relationships between items.

Overall, rule interestingness provides a means to prioritize and evaluate the relevance of association rules discovered from data mining algorithms. By considering multiple factors such as support, confidence, lift, and other interest measures, analysts can identify the most informative and actionable rules for further analysis or decision-making purposes.

PERFORMANCE TRADE-OFFS IN ASSOCIATION RULE EVALUATION: PRECISION, RECALL, AND SUPPORT

In association rule mining, evaluating the quality of generated rules involves trade-offs among **precision, recall, and support**, which impact the usefulness and relevance of the rules.

Table 2. Trade-offs between precision, recall, and support in association rule evaluation

Measure	Definition	Trade-offs & Considerations
Precision	The proportion of discovered rules that are truly relevant.	**Higher precision** ensures more reliable rules but may lead to fewer rules being discovered. **Increasing precision** can reduce recall because stricter thresholds filter out more rules.
Recall	The proportion of all relevant rules that are correctly discovered.	**Higher recall** means more relevant rules are found but may include more false positives. **Optimizing for recall** can decrease precision, as more weak rules might be accepted.
Support	The frequency of an itemset occurring in the dataset.	**Higher support** rules are more general but may miss rare but valuable patterns. **Lowering the support threshold** increases recall but may lead to noisy or less significant rules.

Balancing precision and recall is crucial, as prioritizing one can negatively impact the other. High support thresholds tend to highlight common patterns, while lower support thresholds allow rare but potentially valuable rules to emerge. The ideal balance depends on the specific application. For instance, in market basket analysis, high recall is preferred to capture diverse purchasing behaviors, whereas in medical diagnosis, high precision is essential to minimize false positives. Ultimately, the optimal trade-off is determined by the analysis objective and the acceptable level of false positives or false negatives in decision-making.

ANALYZING ASSOCIATION RULES WITH RAPIDMINER SOFTWARE

In this data analysis experiment utilizing association rules, the sample dataset utilized is termed "shopping.csv," housing purchase data. Data scientists import this dataset, named "shopping.csv," into the RapidMiner software. The dataset comprises Boolean data objects, with "True" indicating a purchase and "False" indicating no purchase. It encompasses 13 features and 786 instances. Consequently, data scientists must categorize each attribute into binomial values. In the unsupervised learning process, data scientists are not required to define the target variables, as illustrated in Figure 1.

Figure 1. Importing the shopping.csv dataset into RapidMiner software

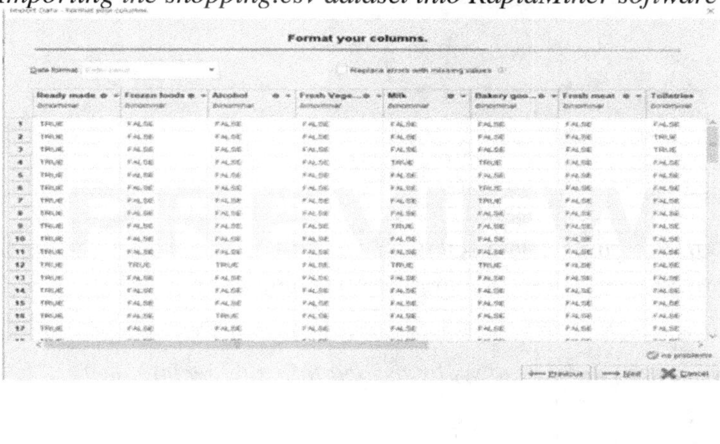

Furthermore, the data scientists construct the model by importing the "shopping.csv" dataset into the FP-Growth model, utilized for analyzing association rules with the goal of generating a tree diagram and minimizing the creation of a large number of frequent item sets in the Apriori algorithm. Subsequently, the minimum support value is established. Initially set at 0.95 in RapidMiner, it is then adjusted to 0.2, as depicted in the illustration below.

Figure 2. Beginning data analysis with the association rule technique

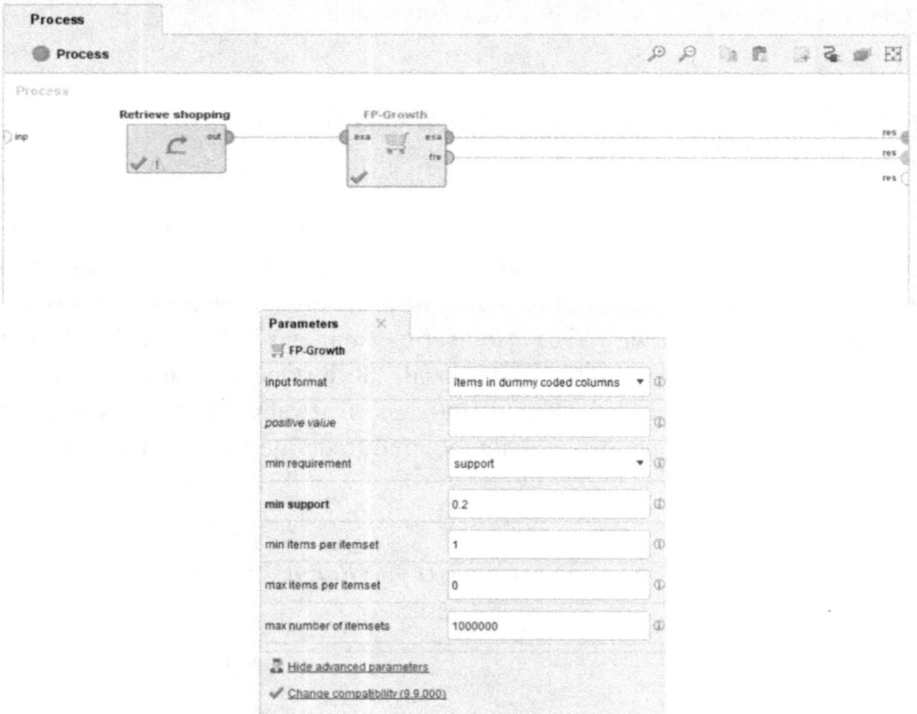

As shown in Figure 2, data scientists can link a model from “shopping.csv” to the FP-Growth model and configure the minimum support at 0.2.

Figure 3. Results of data analysis by association rule technique

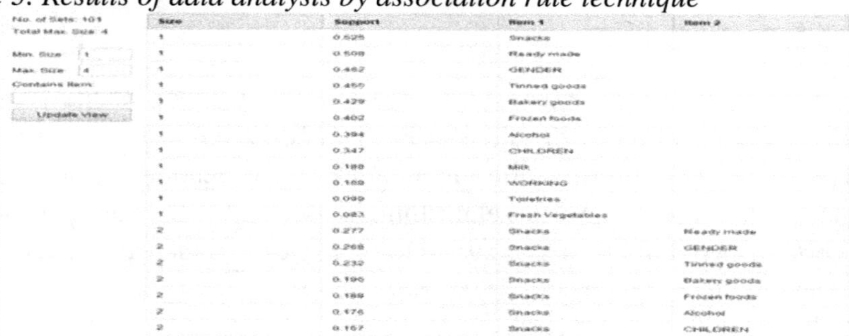

In this figure, the Association Rule technique is applied to the "shopping.csv" dataset. RapidMiner software has generated item sets ranging from 1-ItemSet to 4-ItemSet, with each item set representing a support value indicating the frequency of occurrence in the data.

However, when considering all attributes within the dataset, some data may be irrelevant to the frequency of customer purchases. Data scientists need to connect to the Select Attributes model to choose specific attributes that are related to the frequency of customer purchases.

Figure 4. Selecting only the attribute needed for data analysis

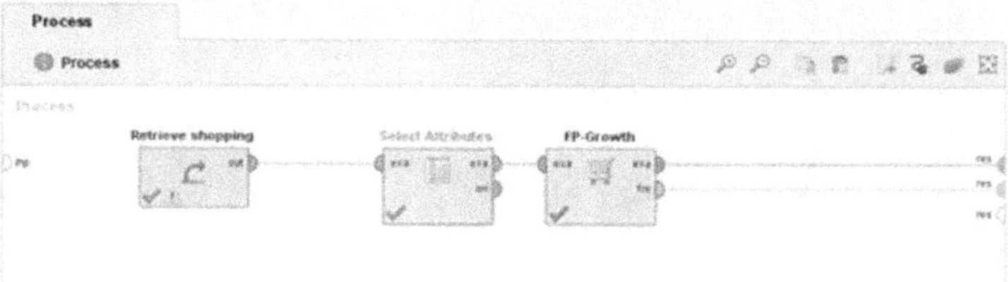

Data scientists utilize the Select Attribute model to isolate attributes pertinent to the frequency of customer purchases. This is achieved by configuring the parameters as a subset and then selecting specific attributes: Children, Gender, and Working. These attributes are chosen and placed into the designated box on the right within the Select Attributes interface.

Figure 5. Determining parameters to select attribute models

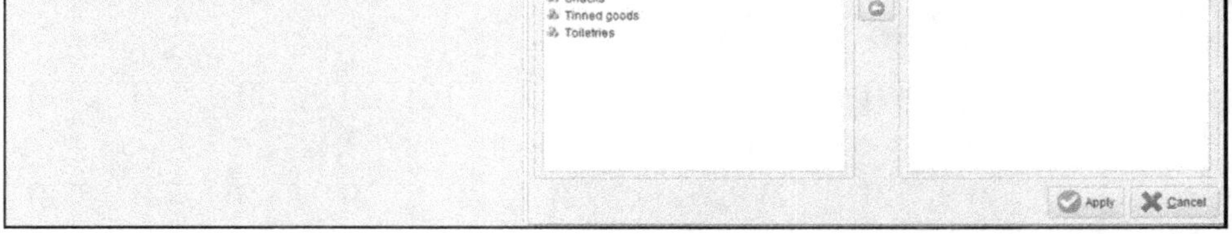

After defining the parameters, data scientists can opt to select "Invert Selection." This action informs the RapidMiner software to utilize the remaining attributes that were not specifically chosen for the data analysis. The resulting output after selecting the attributes appears as follows:

Figure 6. Results after selecting attributes

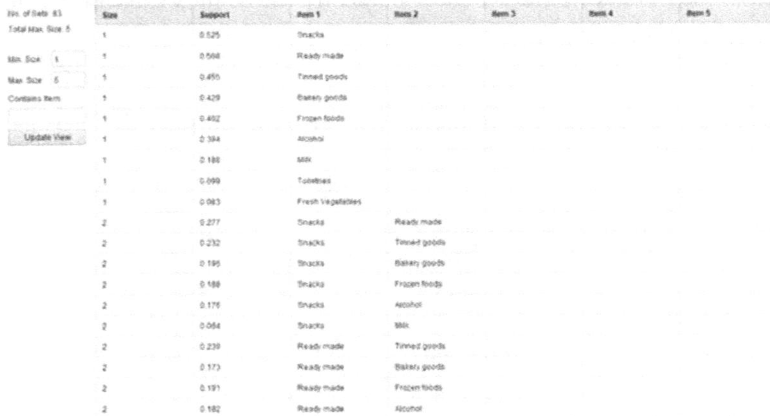

No. of Sets: 83
Total Max. Size: 5
Min. Size: 1
Max. Size: 5
Contains Item:
Update View

Size	Support	Item 1	Item 2	Item 3	Item 4	Item 5
1	0.525	Snacks				
1	0.508	Ready made				
1	0.455	Tinned goods				
1	0.429	Bakery goods				
1	0.402	Frozen foods				
1	0.394	Alcohol				
1	0.188	Milk				
1	0.099	Toiletries				
1	0.083	Fresh Vegetables				
2	0.277	Snacks	Ready made			
2	0.232	Snacks	Tinned goods			
2	0.195	Snacks	Bakery goods			
2	0.188	Snacks	Frozen foods			
2	0.176	Snacks	Alcohol			
2	0.064	Snacks	Milk			
2	0.239	Ready made	Tinned goods			
2	0.173	Ready made	Bakery goods			
2	0.191	Ready made	Frozen foods			
2	0.182	Ready made	Alcohol			

After data scientists have selected only the necessary attributes for data analysis, RapidMiner can utilize the Association Rule technique to generate more frequent item sets, extending up to a 5-ItemSet.

Once the frequent item set has been established, data scientists proceed to employ all item sets in creating association rules. This process is facilitated by the Create Association Rules model, which links the FP-Growth model to the association rule display, as demonstrated below.

Figure 7. Creating association rules using create association rules

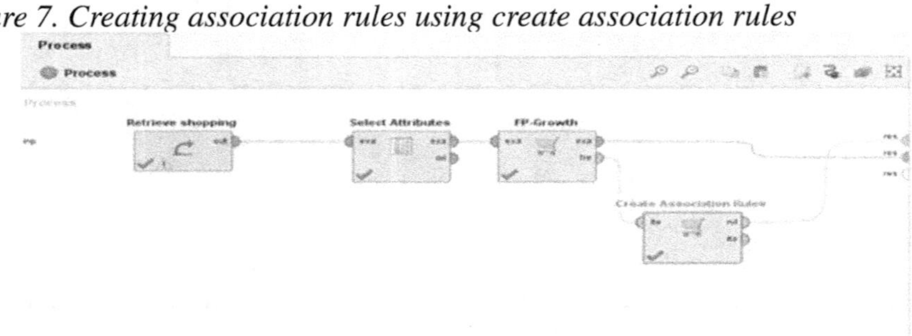

To utilize the Create Association Rules model for generating association rules, data scientists can define parameters to measure the efficiency of strong and valuable association rules, thereby supporting decision-making. The parameters can be set as follows:

Figure 8. Selecting a metric for measuring the efficiency of the association rules

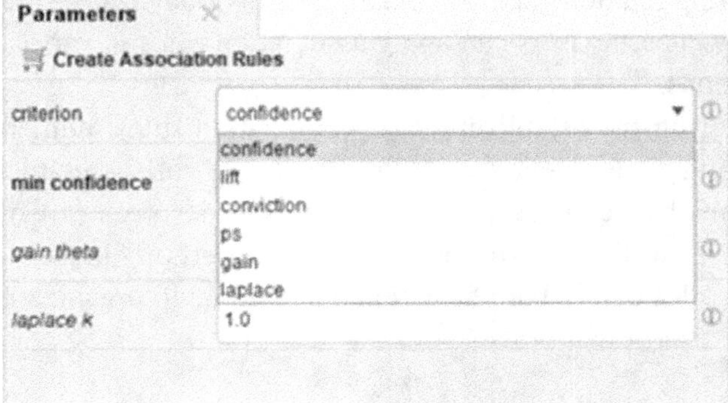

As shown in Figure 8, data scientists can select measures such as Confidence, Lift, and Conviction. They can also specify the minimum value of minimum confidence. The resulting output is as follows.

Figure 9. Results from creating association rules

No.	Premises	Conclusion	Support	Confidence	LaPlace	Gain	p-s	Lift
4	Tinned goods, Bakery goods, Alcohol, Milk	Frozen foods	0.056	0.830	0.989	-0.079	0.029	2.065
5	Fresh Vegetables	Tinned goods	0.069	0.831	0.987	-0.097	0.031	1.824
6	Frozen foods, Milk	Bakery goods	0.090	0.835	0.984	-0.126	0.044	1.948
7	Bakery goods, Fresh Vegetables	Tinned goods	0.050	0.848	0.992	-0.067	0.023	1.861
8	Frozen foods, Fresh Vegetables	Tinned goods	0.043	0.850	0.993	-0.059	0.020	1.866
9	Frozen foods, Fresh Vegetables	Bakery goods	0.043	0.850	0.993	-0.059	0.021	1.982
10	Tinned goods, Alcohol, Milk	Bakery goods	0.067	0.856	0.989	-0.090	0.034	1.994
11	Frozen foods, Alcohol, Milk	Bakery goods	0.073	0.864	0.989	-0.095	0.037	2.014
12	Tinned goods, Frozen foods, Milk	Bakery goods	0.071	0.875	0.991	-0.092	0.036	2.041
13	Tinned goods, Frozen foods, Alcohol, Milk	Bakery goods	0.056	0.898	0.994	-0.069	0.029	2.094

Ias shown in Figure 9, data scientists can interpret the outcome of the rule. For instance, in Association Rule No. 5, when a customer purchases Fresh Vegetables, they are likely to also purchase Tinned Goods. The confidence value associated with this rule is 0.81, indicating a strong and reliable relationship based on quantitative measures.

CONCLUSION

Data scientists can leverage RapidMiner software to analyze datasets using association rules. Suitable data for such analysis typically comprise categorical data, such as product types, gender, and address. The objective of association rules is to examine the correlations between the frequency of occurrence of such data and reveal the resulting relationships. For example, individuals who purchase wine may also tend to buy cheese. Users can apply association rules in various business and industry operations.

However, during the establishment of association rules, numerous rules may emerge, requiring data scientists to discern strong rules suitable for decision-making. This involves considering quantitative metrics such as Confidence, Lift, and Conviction, as well as consulting knowledge experts. This process ensures that the association rules derived are factual and beneficial to organizations.

EXERCISES

1. Outline the objectives of data analysis using association rules.
2. Clarify the distinction between Confidence and Support.
3. Define the concept of frequent itemsets.
4. Provide an example illustrating the need for association rules in data analysis.
5. Locate a research paper utilizing association rules in data analysis and provide a concise summary.

REFERENCES

Agrawal, R., & Srikant, R. (1994). Fast algorithms for mining association rules. *Proceedings of the 20th International Conference on Very Large Data Bases (VLDB)*, Santiago, Chile, September 12–15.

Baby, S. S., & Reddy, S. L. (2021). End-to-end product recommendation system with improvements in Apriori algorithm. *2021 Third International Conference on Inventive Research in Computing Applications (ICIRCA)*, 1357–1361. DOI: 10.1109/ICIRCA51532.2021.9544981

Bing, L., Yiming, M., & Lee, R. (2001). Analyzing the interestingness of association rules from the temporal dimension. *Proceedings 2001 IEEE International Conference on Data Mining (ICDM 2001)*, 377–384. DOI: 10.1109/ICDM.2001.989542

Glass, D. H. (2013). Confirmation measures of association rule interestingness. *Knowledge-Based Systems*, *44*, 65–77. DOI: 10.1016/j.knosys.2013.01.021

Greco, S., Słowiński, R., & Szczęch, I. (2016). Measures of rule interestingness in various perspectives of confirmation. *Information Sciences*, *346–347*, 216–235. DOI: 10.1016/j.ins.2016.01.056

Hodijah, A., & Setiyohatmo, U. T. (2021). Analysis of frequent itemset generation based on trie data structure in Apriori algorithm. *Telkomnika*, *19*(5), 1553–1564. DOI: 10.12928/telkomnika.v19i5.19273

Hong, G., & Nan, G. (2021). Research and application of a multidimensional association rules mining algorithm based on Hadoop. *2021 IEEE International Conference on Parallel & Distributed Processing with Applications, Big Data & Cloud Computing, Sustainable Computing & Communications, Social Computing & Networking (ISPA/BDCloud/SocialCom/SustainCom)*, 636–643. DOI: 10.1109/ISPA-BDCloud-SocialCom-SustainCom52081.2021.00093

Paruechanon, P., & Sriurai, W. (2019). Applying association rule to risk analysis for student-dropout in Information Technology program. *Journal of Science and Science Education*, *1*(2), 123–133.

Ren, X. (2021). Application of Apriori association rules algorithm to data mining technology to mining e-commerce potential customers. *2021 International Wireless Communications and Mobile Computing (IWCMC)*, 1193–1196.

Salman, W. A. K., & Sadkhan, S. B. (2021). Proposed association rules mining algorithm for sensors data streams. *2021 1st Babylon International Conference on Information Technology and Science (BICITS)*, 76–81.

Toumi, A., Gribaa, N., & Ben Abdessalem Karaa, W. (2021). Mining biomedical texts based on statistical method and association rules. *2021 International Conference of Women in Data Science at Taif University (WiDSTaif)*, 1–4. DOI: 10.1109/WiDSTaif52235.2021.9430200

Yingzhuo, X., & Xuewen, W. (2021). Research on community consumer behavior based on association rules analysis. *2021 6th International Conference on Intelligent Computing and Signal Processing (ICSP)*, 1213–1216.

Zhang, C., & Zhang, S. (2002). *Association rule mining: Models and algorithms.* Springer Berlin Heidelberg. DOI: 10.1007/3-540-46027-6

Chapter 8
Recommendation Systems

ABSTRACT

Recommendation systems are critical tools used by marketing departments to provide customers with product recommendations. Data scientists also use recommendation system analysis to assess the effectiveness of product and service suggestions. There are two types of recommendation systems: content-based and collaborative filtering. Content-based recommendations are based on the customer's purchase history while collaborative filtering suggests a product based on purchasing behavior. Collaborative filtering can be divided into content-based filtering, which suggests products based on similar purchasing behavior, and item-based filtering, which suggests products based on their attributes. User-based and item-based nearest-neighbor collaborative filtering and probabilistic methods are used to analyze data and to provide product suggestions. Businesses rely on recommendation systems to achieve various objectives such as customer retention and increased ROI. RapidMiner can analyze data following the principles of the recommendation system, as demonstrated step-by-step in this chapter.

INTRODUCTION

In today's digital age, recommendation systems have emerged as indispensable tools for guiding users through the vast array of content and products available online. These systems leverage advanced algorithms and data-driven approaches to analyze user preferences and behaviors, ultimately delivering personalized recommendations tailored to individual tastes and interests. Recommendation systems play a crucial role in enhancing user experience and engagement across various digital platforms, including e-commerce websites, streaming services, social media platforms, and more. By providing users with relevant and personalized recommendations, these

DOI: 10.4018/979-8-3693-6001-9.ch008

systems help to alleviate the challenge of information overload and assist users in discovering content and products that align with their preferences. With the exponential growth of digital content and products available online, users often find themselves overwhelmed by the sheer volume of choices. Recommendation systems address this issue by intelligently filtering and curating content based on user preferences, thereby simplifying the decision-making process and improving user satisfaction. By delivering personalized recommendations, recommendation systems contribute to increased user engagement and retention on digital platforms. Users are more likely to spend time exploring recommended content or products that resonate with their interests, leading to higher levels of engagement and potentially driving revenue through increased sales and conversions. One of the key benefits of recommendation systems is their ability to provide personalized experiences for users. By analyzing user data and behavior, these systems can tailor recommendations to each individual user by considering their preferences, past interactions, and demographic information. This level of personalization enhances user satisfaction and loyalty, fostering a deeper connection between users and digital platforms.

RECOMMENDATION SYSTEM

A recommendation system is a computational tool or algorithm designed to suggest relevant items or content to users based on their preferences, past interactions, or similarities with other users (Aditya et al, 2021: Chen & Qin, 2021: Wayan Priscila Yuni Praditya, Erna Permanasari, Hidayah, 2021). These systems are widely used in various online platforms such as e-commerce websites, streaming services, social media platforms, and news websites to enhance user experience, increase engagement, and drive sales. Recommendation systems utilize techniques such as collaborative filtering, content-based filtering, matrix factorization, and machine learning algorithms to generate personalized recommendations tailored to individual user preferences and behavior. They play a crucial role in helping users discover new products, services, or content that they may find interesting or useful, thereby improving customer satisfaction and loyalty.

TYPES OF RECOMMENDATION SYSTEMS

A. Collaborative Filtering

Collaborative filtering generates personalized recommendations by analyzing user preferences (Emon et al., 2021; Khatter et al., 2021). It assumes that users with similar past preferences will have similar future choices and works without requiring item attributes. While effective, it faces challenges like the "cold start" problem, popularity bias, and difficulty recommending niche items. Widely used in e-commerce, streaming, and social media, collaborative filtering enhances user engagement and satisfaction.

1. User-Based Collaborative Filtering

In user-based collaborative filtering, recommendations are generated by identifying users with similar preferences and recommending items that these similar users have liked or interacted with in the past (Adeniyi, Wei & Yongquan, 2016: Riswanto, Suparyanto & Robi'In, 2019). This approach relies on computing similarity metrics between users, such as cosine similarity or the Pearson correlation coefficient.

The basic equation for user-based collaborative filtering involves computing the similarity between users based on their interactions with items. One common similarity metric used in user-based collaborative filtering is the cosine similarity. The cosine similarity between two users μ_i and μ_j is calculated as follows:

$$\text{sim}(\mu_i, \mu_j) = \frac{\sum_{k \in I_{ij}} r_{ik} \bullet r_{jk}}{\sqrt{\sum_{k \in I_{ij}} r_{ik}^2} \bullet \sqrt{\sum_{k \in I_{ij}} r_{jk}^2}}$$

Where:

$\text{sim}(\mu_i, \mu_j)$ is the cosine similarity between users μ_i and μ_j.
I_{ij} represents the set of items that both users μ_i and μ_j have interacted with.
r_{ik} and r_{jk} denote the ratings or interactions of users μ_i and μ_j with item k respectively.

Once the similarity between users is computed, recommendations for a target user μ_t can be generated by selecting items that similar users have interacted with positively and that μ_t has not yet interacted with. Let's consider a simplified example dataset where users have rated movies on a scale of 1 to 5. We will calculate the cosine similarity between two users μ_1 and μ_2 based on their ratings for three movies (items) A, B, and C.

Table 1. Example dataset for user-based collaborative filtering

Users	**Movie A**	**Movie B**	**Movie C**
User 1	4	5	3
User 2	3	4	5

For user μ_1 and μ_2, we will calculate the similarity based on movies A, B, and C.

1. Calculate the dot product of ratings for shared items.

$r_{1A} \bullet r_{2A} = 4 \bullet 3 = 12$

$r_{1B} \bullet r_{2B} = 5 \bullet 4 = 20$

$r_{1C} \bullet r_{2C} = 3 \bullet 5 = 15$

2. Calculate the sum of squares of ratings for each user.

$\Sigma_{k \in I_{ij}} r_{ik}^2$ for user 1:

$r_{1A}^2 + r_{1B}^2 + r_{1C}^2 = 4^2 + 5^2 + 3^2 = 16 + 25 + 9 = 50$

$\Sigma_{k \in I_{ij}} r_{jk}^2$ for user 2:

$r_{2A}^2 + r_{2B}^2 + r_{2C}^2 = 3^2 + 4^2 + 5^2 = 9 + 16 + 25 = 50$

3. Calculate the square root of the sums of squares.

$\sqrt{\Sigma_{k \in I_{ij}} r_{ik}^2}$ for user 1: $\sqrt{50}$

$\sqrt{\Sigma_{k \in I_{ij}} r_{jk}^2}$ for user 2: $\sqrt{50}$

4. Compute the cosine similarity.

$$\text{sim}(\mu_1, \mu_2) = \frac{12}{\sqrt{50} \bullet \sqrt{50}} = \frac{12}{50} = 0.24$$

Therefore, the cosine similarity between users μ_1 and μ_2 is 0.24. This calculation indicates a moderate level of similarity between the two users based on their ratings for movies A, B, and C.

Collaborative filtering remains a cornerstone technique in recommendation systems, offering personalized recommendations based on user preferences and behaviors. Despite its challenges, collaborative filtering continues to be widely used and researched, driving innovation in the field of recommendation systems.

2. Item-Based Collaborative Filtering

Item-based collaborative filtering generates recommendations by identifying items similar to those a user has interacted with (Kusumawardhani, Nasrun & Setianingsih, 2019; Lourenco & Varde, 2020; Padhy, Singh & Vetrivelan, 2022). It calculates similarity between items using metrics like cosine similarity, which is also used in user-based collaborative filtering. Despite differences in context, both approaches rely on shared interactions to compute similarity.

Let's consider a simplified example dataset where users have rated movies on a scale of 1 to 5. We will calculate the cosine similarity between two movies (items) A and B based on the ratings provided by users.

Table 2. Example dataset for item-based collaborative filtering

Users	Movie A	Movie B
User 1	4	5
User 2	3	4
User 3	5	3

Using the cosine similarity formula for items A and B.

$$\mathrm{sim}(A,B) = \frac{\sum_{u \in U_{AB}} r_{uA} \bullet r_{uB}}{\sqrt{\sum_{u \in U_{AB}} r_{uA}^2} \bullet \sqrt{\sum_{u \in U_{AB}} r_{uB}^2}}$$

Where:

$\mathrm{sim}(A,B)$ is the cosine similarity between movies A and B.
U_{AB} represents the set of users who have rated both movies A and B.
r_{uA} and r_{uB} denote the ratings of users for movies A and B respectively.

1. Calculate the dot product of ratings for shared users.

$r_{1A} \bullet r_{1B} = 4 \bullet 5 = 20$

$r_{2A} \bullet r_{2B} = 3 \bullet 4 = 12$

$r_{3A} \bullet r_{3B} = 5 \bullet 3 = 15$

2. Calculate the sum of squares of ratings for each movie.

$\Sigma_{u \in U_{AB}} r^2_{uA}$ for movie A:

$r^2_{1A} + r^2_{2A} + r^2_{3A} = 4^2 + 3^2 + 5^2 = 16 + 9 + 25 = 50$

$\Sigma_{u \in U_{AB}} r^2_{uB}$ for movie B:

$r^2_{1B} + r^2_{2B} + r^2_{3B} = 5^2 + 4^2 + 3^2 = 25 + 16 + 9 = 50$

3. Calculate the square root of the sums of squares.

$\sqrt{\Sigma_{u \in U_{AB}} r^2_{uA}}$ for Movie A: $\sqrt{50}$

$\sqrt{\Sigma_{u \in U_{AB}} r^2_{uB}}$ for Movie B: $\sqrt{50}$

4. Compute the cosine similarity.

$$\text{sim}(A, B) \frac{20}{\sqrt{50} \bullet \sqrt{50}} = \frac{20}{50} = 0.4$$

Therefore, the cosine similarity between movies *A* and *B* is 0.4. This calculation indicates a moderate level of similarity between movies A and B based on the ratings provided by users.

B. Content-Based Filtering

Content-based filtering is a popular recommendation technique used in recommendation systems to generate personalized recommendations based on the attributes or characteristics of items (Tai, Sun & Yao 2021). Unlike collaborative filtering methods that rely on user interactions, content-based filtering focuses on the intrinsic features of items themselves. It recommends items to users that are similar to those they have interacted with positively in the past, based on shared characteristics or attributes. The algorithm for content-based filtering involves several steps:

- **Item Representation:** Each item (e.g., movie, product, article) is represented using a set of attributes or features. These attributes could include metadata such as genre, keywords, actors, directors (for movies), or product attributes (for e-commerce). Each item *i* represented by a vector of attributes or features $X_i = [x_{i1,} x_{i2,} \ldots, x_{in,}]$, where *n* is the number of attributes/features. These attributes could include metadata such as genre, keywords, or other descriptive characteristics of the item.
- **User Profile Creation:** A user profile is created based on the items they have interacted with positively in the past. The user profile captures the user's preferences and interests based on the attributes of the items they have liked, rated, or viewed. A user profile P_u is created based on the items the user has interacted with positively in the past. The user profile captures the user's preferences and interests based on the attributes of the items they have liked, rated, or viewed.
- **Similarity Calculation:** The similarity between items is calculated based on their attributes or features. Various similarity metrics can be used, such as cosine similarity or Jaccard similarity, to measure the similarity between item profiles and the user profile. The similarity between items *i* and *j* is calculated based on their attribute vectors using a similarity metric such as cosine similarity or Jaccard similarity.

  Cosine similarity:$\text{sim}(i,j) = \frac{X_i \bullet X_j}{\|X_i\| \bullet \|X_j\|}$

  Jaccard similarity (for binary attributes):$\text{sim}(i,j) = \frac{|X_i \cap X_j|}{|X_i \cup X_j|}$
- **Recommendation Generation:** recommendations are generated by selecting items that are most similar to those the user has interacted with positively and that match the user's preferences based on the attributes of the items.

In the example, recommendations for user *u* are generated in this way, the predicted preference score for item *i* by user *u* is as follows :

$$\hat{r}_{ui} = \frac{\sum_{j \in I_u} \text{sim}(i,j) \bullet r_{uj}}{\sum_{j \in I_u} \text{sim}(i,j)}$$

Where:

I_u represents the set of items interacted with positively by user *u*.
r_{ui} denotes the rating or interaction of user *u* with item *j*.

This equation calculates a weighted average of the ratings of similar items, where the weights are determined by the similarity between items and the user's preferences. The predicted preference score $\hat{r}_{ui}$ represents the estimated rating or preference of user u for item j.

By following these steps and equations, content-based filtering generates personalized recommendations for users based on the attributes of items and the user's preferences.

Example: consider a movie recommendation system where movies are represented by attributes such as genre, director, and actors. If a user has interacted positively with movies of a particular genre or director in the past, content-based filtering would recommend other movies with similar attributes. For example, if a user enjoys action movies directed by Christopher Nolan, the system recommends other action movies directed by Christopher Nolan or featuring similar actors. Let's consider a simplified example dataset where movies are represented by genre attributes. We will calculate the cosine similarity between two movies (items), A and B, based on their genre attributes, and then generate recommendations for a user based on their preferences.

Table 3. Example dataset for content-based filtering

Movies	Genre1	Genre2	Genre3
Movie A	1	0	1
Movie B	0	1	1

Table 4. User preferences

User	Movie A	Movie B
User 1	1	0

Using the cosine similarity formula for items A and B.

$$\text{sim}(A, B) = \frac{X_A \cdot X_B}{\|X_A\| \cdot \|X_B\|}$$

1. Calculate the dot product of the genre attribute vectors for movies A and B.

$$X_A \cdot X_B = (1 \times 0) + (0 \times 1) + (1 \times 1) = 0 + 0 + 1 = 1$$

2. Calculate the Euclidean norms of the genre attribute vectors for movies A and B:

$$\|X_A\| = \sqrt{1^2 + 0^2 + 1^2} = \sqrt{2}$$

$$\|X_B\| = \sqrt{0^2 + 1^2 + 1^2} = \sqrt{2}$$

3. Calculate the cosine similarity.

$$\text{sim}(A, B) \frac{1}{\sqrt{2} \bullet \sqrt{2}} = \frac{1}{2} = 0.5$$

Therefore, the cosine similarity between movies A and B based on their genre attributes is 0.5. Next, let's generate recommendations for User 1 based on their preferences:

$$\hat{r}_{1A} = \frac{\text{sim}(A,A) \times 1 + \text{sim}(A,B) \times 0}{\text{sim}(A,A) + \text{sim}(A,B)}$$

$$\hat{r}_{1B} = \frac{\text{sim}(B,A) \times 1 + \text{sim}(B,B) \times 0}{\text{sim}(B,A) + \text{sim}(B,B)}$$

Using the calculated similarity ($\text{sim}(A, B) = 0.5$), we can substitute into the equations:

$$\hat{r}_{1A} = \frac{1 \times 1 + 0.5 \times 0}{1 + 0.5} = \frac{1}{1.5} \approx 0.67$$

$$\hat{r}_{1B} = \frac{0.5 \times 1 + 1 \times 0}{0.5 + 1} = \frac{0.5}{1.5} \approx 0.33$$

Therefore, the predicted preference scores for User 1 are approximately 0.67 for Movie A and 0.33 for Movie B. These scores represent the estimated preferences of User 1 for each movie based on their genre attributes and the cosine similarity between items. In this example, Movie A is predicted to be more preferred by User 1 when compared to Movie B.

Content-based filtering does not rely on user interactions, making it suitable for cold-start scenarios where there is limited user data. It can recommend niche or novel items that have not yet gained popularity among users but match the user's preferences based on item attributes. On the other hand, content-based filtering is limited by the quality of item attributes and the accuracy of similarity metrics. If item attributes are poorly defined or incomplete, the recommendations may be less relevant. It may suffer from the "filter bubble" phenomenon, where users are only exposed to items similar to those they have interacted with in the past, limiting serendipitous discovery.

Content-based filtering offers a powerful approach to generating personalized recommendations based on item attributes and user preferences. By focusing on the intrinsic features of items, content-based filtering helps to alleviate some of the limitations of collaborative filtering methods and provides users with tailored recommendations that match their interests and preferences.

C. Hybrid Approaches

Hybrid approaches for recommendation systems combine multiple recommendation techniques, such as collaborative filtering, content-based filtering, and other methods, to improve recommendation accuracy and address the limitations of individual techniques. These hybrid approaches leverage the strengths of different recommendation techniques while mitigating their weaknesses, resulting in more effective and personalized recommendations.

1. **Collaborative-Content Hybrid:** this approach combines collaborative filtering and content-based filtering methods. It leverages user-item interactions as well as item attributes to generate recommendations. By considering both user preferences and item characteristics, this hybrid approach can provide more diverse and accurate recommendations.
2. **Weighted Hybrid:** in this approach, recommendations from different recommendation techniques are combined using weighted averaging or other aggregation methods. Each recommendation technique is assigned a weight based on its performance or relevance to the user. By adjusting the weights dynamically, the system can adapt to different user preferences and recommendation scenarios.
3. **Feature Combination:** this approach combines the features extracted from collaborative filtering and content-based filtering methods into a single feature vector. Machine learning models, such as neural networks or decision trees, are then trained on this combined feature vector to predict user preferences and generate recommendations. By leveraging the complementary information from different recommendation techniques, this approach can improve recommendation accuracy.
4. **Cascade Hybrid:** in the cascade hybrid approach, recommendations from one recommendation technique are used to filter or augment the recommendations generated by another technique. For example, collaborative filtering may be used to generate initial recommendations, which are then filtered or enhanced using content-based filtering methods. This sequential processing helps to improve recommendation relevance and coverage.

5. **Context-Aware Hybrid:** this approach incorporates contextual information, such as user demographics, location, or time of day, into the recommendation process. Contextual factors are used to personalize recommendations and to adapt them to the user's current situation or preferences. By considering contextual information, the hybrid recommendation system can generate more relevant and timely recommendations.
6. **Ensemble methods:** combine multiple recommendation algorithms into a single predictive model. Techniques such as bagging, boosting, or stacking are used to aggregate predictions from different recommendation algorithms. Ensemble methods can help reduce overfitting and improve recommendation robustness by leveraging the diversity of individual recommendation models.

Overall, hybrid approaches for recommendation systems offer a flexible and effective way to leverage the strengths of different recommendation techniques while addressing their limitations. By combining collaborative filtering, content-based filtering, and other methods, hybrid recommendation systems can provide more accurate, diverse, and personalized recommendations to users.

THE KEY ALGORITHMIC TECHNIQUES USED IN RECOMMENDATION SYSTEMS

A. Matrix Factorization

Matrix factorization is a popular technique used in collaborative filtering-based recommendation systems. The basic idea behind matrix factorization is to decompose the user-item interaction matrix into two lower-dimensional matrices: one representing users and the other representing items. These matrices are then multiplied to approximate the original interaction matrix. By capturing latent factors or features that represent user preferences and item characteristics, matrix factorization can effectively model user-item relationships and generate personalized recommendations. Common matrix factorization techniques include Singular Value Decomposition (SVD), Alternating Least Squares (ALS), and Stochastic Gradient Descent (SGD). Let's explore the algorithm of matrix factorization:

1. **Problem formulation:** given a user-item interaction matrix R, where each entry r_{ui} represents the rating or interaction of user u with item i, the goal of matrix factorization is to find two lower-dimensional matrices U (user matrix) and I (item matrix) such that their product approximates the original interaction matrix R.

2. **Objective Function:** matrix factorization typically involves minimizing a loss function that quantifies the difference between the original interaction matrix R and the product of the user and item matrices U and I. The loss function can be formulated as the sum of squared differences between the observed ratings and the predicted ratings:

$$\text{minimize} \sum_{(u,i)\in \Omega} \left(r_{ui} - \hat{r}_{ui} \right)^2$$

Where

Ω represents the set of observed user-item interactions,
r_{ui} is the observed rating, and
$\hat{r}_{ui}$ is the predicted rating computed as the dot product of the corresponding user and item vectors $\hat{r}_{ui} = U_u \bullet I_i$.

The optimization problem is typically solved using iterative optimization algorithms such as Alternating Least Squares (ALS) or Stochastic Gradient Descent (SGD). These algorithms alternate between updating the user and item matrices to minimize the loss function iteratively until convergence.

- **Alternating Least Squares (ALS):** the user and item matrices are alternately updated while keeping the other matrix fixed. The optimization problem is decomposed into two subproblems: one for updating the user matrix U and the other for updating the item matrix I. These subproblems can be solved efficiently using least squares optimization techniques.
- **Stochastic Gradient Descent (SGD):** the user and item matrices are updated iteratively using gradient descent based on randomly sampled user-item interactions. The gradients of the loss function with respect to the user and item matrices are computed, and the matrices are updated in the direction of the negative gradient to minimize the loss function.

Regularization: to prevent overfitting and to improve generalization, regularization terms are often added to the objective function. Regularization penalizes large values of the user and item matrices, encouraging them to be sparse and preventing the model from fitting noise in the data.

Let's demonstrate how matrix factorization works with a simplified example dataset. Suppose we have a user-item interaction matrix representing movie ratings, and we want to apply matrix factorization to approximate this matrix with lower-dimensional matrices capturing latent factors.

Table 5. Example dataset for matrix factorization

User	Movie A	Movie B	Movie C	Movie D
User 1	4	5	0	0
User 2	0	3	4	0
User 3	5	0	0	3
User 4	0	4	0	5

1. **Initialization:** we start by initializing the user matrix U and the item matrix I with random values. Let's assume we have two latent factors, so the dimensions of U and I are 4×2 and 4×2 respectively.
2. **Optimization (Alternating Least Squares):** we iteratively update the user and item matrices to minimize the loss function, alternately fixing one matrix while optimizing the other. Let's assume we update the matrices for a fixed number of iterations.
3. **Updating User Matrix**U : for each user u, we update the corresponding row in the user matrix U using least squares optimization. For example, for User 1:
   - We consider the ratings of User 1 for movies A and B (4 and 5) and their corresponding latent factors in the item matrix I.
   - Using least squares optimization, we update the latent factors of User 1 in the user matrix to minimize the difference between the observed ratings and the predicted ratings based on the dot product of the user and item vectors.
4. **Updating Item Matrix** for each item , we update the corresponding row in the item matrix using least squares optimization. For example, for Movie A:
   - We consider the ratings of all users for Movie A and their corresponding latent factors in the user matrix
   - Using least squares optimization, we update the latent factors of Movie A in the item matrix to minimize the difference between the observed ratings and the predicted ratings based on the dot product of the user and item vectors.
5. **Prediction:** once the user and item matrices are optimized, we can predict the ratings for all users and items by taking the dot product of the corresponding user and item vectors. For example, to predict the rating of User 2 for Movie A:
   - We take the dot product of the latent factors of User 2 and Movie A in the user and item matrices, respectively.

6. **Evaluation:** we evaluate the performance of the matrix factorization model using metrics such as root mean square error (RMSE) or mean absolute error (MAE) by comparing the predicted ratings with the observed ratings in the original user-item interaction matrix.

By iteratively updating the user and item matrices and minimizing the loss function, matrix factorization allows us to approximate the original user-item interaction matrix with lower-dimensional matrices capturing latent factors. This enables us to generate personalized recommendations efficiently and accurately.

Matrix factorization is an effective technique for recommendation systems, allowing them to capture complex patterns in user-item interactions and to generate personalized recommendations. By decomposing the user-item interaction matrix into lower-dimensional matrices, matrix factorization provides a compact representation of user preferences and item characteristics, enabling efficient computation and accurate recommendation generation.

B. Nearest Neighbor Methods

Nearest neighbor methods such as k-Nearest Neighbors (k-NN), are used in both collaborative filtering and content-based recommendation systems. In collaborative filtering, nearest neighbor methods identify similar users or items based on their interaction patterns and recommend items that similar users have interacted with positively. In content-based filtering, nearest neighbor methods compute the similarity between items based on their attributes or features and recommend items that are most similar to those the user has interacted with in the past. Nearest neighbor methods are intuitive and easy to implement, making them popular choices for recommendation systems. Let's break down the content and demonstrate it with an example dataset.

1. Equation for k-Nearest Neighbors (k-NN) Similarity

The equation for calculating the similarity between two items and using k-NN can be represented by various similarity metrics such as cosine similarity, Pearson correlation coefficient, or Jaccard similarity. Let's use cosine similarity as an example:

Where:

represents the cosine similarity between items and
denotes the set of users who have interacted with both items and
and are the ratings or interactions of users with items and respectively.

2. Demonstration with an Example Dataset

Suppose we have a simplified example dataset representing movie ratings:

Table 6. Example dataset for k-Nearest Neighbors (k-NN)

User	Movie A	Movie B	Movie C
User 1	5	4	0
User 2	0	3	4
User 3	4	0	5

Let's calculate the cosine similarity between Movie A and Movie B using k-NN:

- Calculate the dot product of ratings for shared users.
- Calculate the sum of squares of ratings for each movie.

for Movie A:

for Movie B:

- Calculate the square root of the sums of squares.

for Movie A

for Movie B

- Compute the cosine similarity.

We calculated the cosine similarity (0.733) between Movie A and Movie B based on user ratings, indicating moderate similarity. This allows recommendation systems to suggest similar items—if a user likes Movie A, Movie B may be recommended. This process scales to large datasets using indexing, caching, and parallelization for efficiency. k-NN similarity plays a key role in recommendation systems, enhancing user engagement and content discovery through personalized suggestions.

C. Deep Learning

Deep learning approaches have gained popularity in recommendation systems due to their ability to automatically learn complex patterns and representations from large-scale data. Deep learning models, such as neural networks, can capture non-linear relationships between users and items and then generate personalized recommendations. One common approach is to use neural network architectures, such as Multi-Layer Perceptrons (MLPs) or Recurrent Neural Networks (RNNs), to model user-item interactions directly from raw data (e.g., user-item interaction sequences, textual data, or image data). Deep learning-based recommendation systems can handle sparse and high-dimensional data efficiently and provide accurate recommendations even in cold-start scenarios. Let's break down the content and demonstrate it with an example dataset using a deep learning approach, specifically a Multi-Layer Perceptron (MLP) architecture for recommendation systems.

1. Equation for MLP-based Recommendation

In an MLP-based recommendation system, we use neural network architectures to model user-item interactions directly from raw data. The neural network takes as input the features representing users and items and learns to predict user preferences for items. The output of the neural network represents the predicted ratings or preferences of users for items.

The equation for predicting the preference of user for item using an MLP can be represented as follows:

Where:

is the predicted preference of user for item .
is the feature vector representing the interaction between user and item .
represents the parameters (weights and biases) of the MLP.
is the activation function of the MLP.

2. Demonstration with an Example Dataset

Suppose we have an example dataset representing movie ratings:

Table 7. Example dataset for deep learning

User	Movie A	Movie B	Movie C	Movie D
User 1	5	4	0	0
User 2	0	3	4	0
User 3	4	0	0	5

Let's represent this dataset as input features for the MLP. We will assume one-hot encoding for simplicity:

- For User 1 interacting with Movie A, the input feature vector would be [1, 0, 0, 0] (indicating interaction with Movie A and no interaction with other movies).
- Similarly, we construct input feature vectors for all user-item interactions in the dataset.

We then train the MLP using these input features and the corresponding observed ratings as targets. The MLP learns to capture the complex relationships between users and items, and once trained, it can predict the preferences of users for items.

1. **Prediction:** after training, we can use the trained MLP to predict the preferences of users for items. For example, we can predict the preference of User 2 for Movie A by passing the corresponding input feature vector through the trained MLP.
2. **Evaluation:** we evaluate the performance of the MLP-based recommendation system using metrics such as mean squared error (MSE) or mean absolute error (MAE) by comparing the predicted preferences with the observed ratings in the original dataset.

In summary, the MLP-based recommendation system utilizes neural network architectures to model user-item interactions and predict user preferences for items, offering the capability to handle sparse and high-dimensional data efficiently and to provide accurate recommendations even in cold-start scenarios.

Overall, these algorithmic techniques play a crucial role in recommendation systems by enabling them to model user preferences, capture item characteristics, and generate personalized recommendations. By leveraging matrix factorization, nearest neighbor methods, and deep learning approaches, recommendation systems can provide users with relevant, diverse, and engaging recommendations across various domains and applications.

MEASUREMENT FOR RECOMMENDATION SYSTEMS

In the realm of recommendation systems, measurement plays a crucial role in evaluating the effectiveness, accuracy, and performance of recommendation algorithms. Measurement metrics provide insights into how well a recommendation system is performing in terms of user satisfaction, engagement, and the relevance of recommendations.

A. Key Metrics for Evaluating Recommendation Systems

1. **Accuracy metrics** assess the accuracy of recommendations by comparing predicted ratings or preferences with observed ratings in the dataset. Common accuracy metrics include Mean Squared Error (MSE), Root Mean Squared Error (RMSE), Mean Absolute Error (MAE), and Precision-Recall.
2. **Relevance metrics** evaluate the relevance of recommended items to users' interests and preferences. Metrics such as Precision, Recall, F1-score, and Hit Rate measure how well the recommended items align with users' expectations and needs.
3. **Diversity metrics** quantify the diversity of recommendations by assessing the variety and coverage of recommended items. Metrics like Intra-List Diversity, Inter-List Diversity, and Novelty measure how diverse and novel the recommended items are, aiming to enhance serendipity and exploration in recommendations.
4. **Serendipity metrics** evaluate the unexpectedness and surprise factor of recommended items. Metrics such as Surprise, Unexpectedness, and Serendipity Index measure the degree to which recommended items deviate from users' past preferences and introduce new and interesting content.
5. **Coverage metrics** assess the coverage of the recommendation system by measuring the proportion of items that are recommended to users. Metrics like Catalog Coverage and User Coverage evaluate the extent to which the entire item catalog or user base is covered by recommendations.
6. **Robustness metrics** gauge the stability and reliability of recommendation algorithms under different conditions, such as changes in data distribution or system parameters. Metrics like Stability, Robustness, and Sensitivity measure the resilience of recommendation systems to variations and perturbations.

B. Evaluation Techniques for Recommendation Systems

1. **Offline evaluation** involves assessing recommendation algorithms using historical data without user interaction. Algorithms are evaluated based on predefined metrics using offline datasets, allowing for controlled experiments and benchmarking.
2. **Online evaluation** involves testing recommendation algorithms in live environments with real users. Algorithms are deployed in production systems, and their performance is measured based on user interactions, feedback, and engagement metrics, providing real-world insights into algorithm performance.
3. **Cross-validation techniques**, such as k-fold cross-validation or holdout validation, partition the dataset into training and test sets to evaluate recommendation algorithms' generalization performance and prevent overfitting.

C. Considerations and Challenges

1. **Cold-Start Problem:** recommendation systems face challenges when dealing with new users or items with limited interaction data, known as the cold-start problem. Measurement techniques should account for the cold-start scenario and assess the system's ability to provide accurate recommendations in such cases.
2. **Dynamic Environments:** recommendation systems operate in dynamic environments where user preferences, item availability, and system conditions change over time. Measurement techniques should adapt to these changes and evaluate the system's performance in evolving scenarios.

Measurement is a critical aspect of recommendation systems, providing valuable insights into system performance, user satisfaction, and recommendation quality. By employing a diverse set of metrics and evaluation techniques, recommendation systems can be effectively evaluated, optimized, and improved to deliver personalized and relevant recommendations to users. Ongoing research and advancements in measurement methodologies continue to enhance the effectiveness and impact of recommendation systems in various domains and applications.

RECOMMENDATION SYSTEM WITH RAPIDMINER

Data scientists have the capability to analyze the Recommendation System using RapidMiner software by downloading additional installations from Extensions and selecting Marketplace (Updates and Extensions) as depicted below.

Figure 1. Accessing marketplace to download additional installation

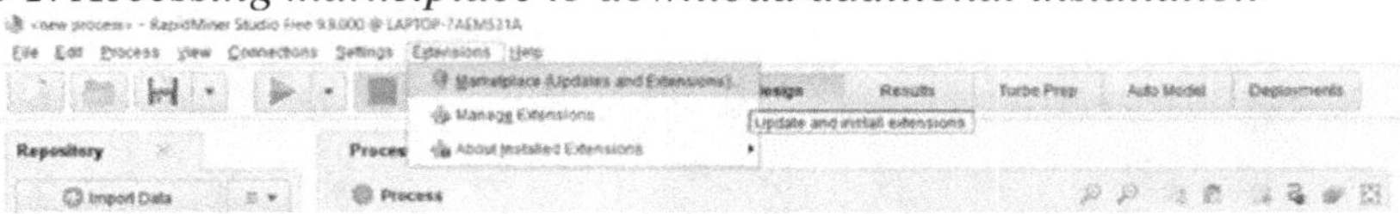

Following this, scientists can proceed by searching for the Recommender Extension, opting for installation, and subsequently clicking the "Install Packages" button.

Figure 2. Recommender extension installation

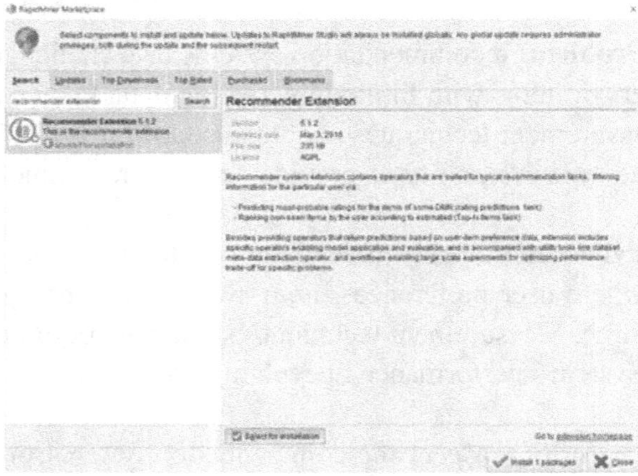

Throughout the software installation process, RapidMiner will prompt for license confirmation. Data scientists can select "I accept the terms of all license agreements" and then proceed by selecting "Install packages."

Figure 3. License agreement

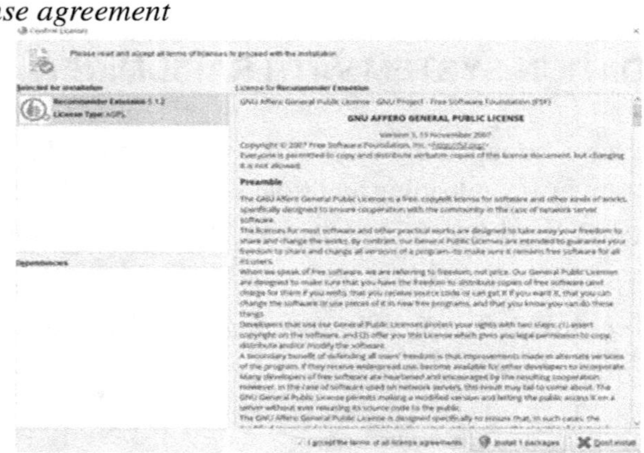

After the installation, data scientists can import the "Ratings.csv" dataset into the RapidMiner software. This dataset contains information on the fondness level each reader has for the books, totaling 10,000 instances, as follows.

Figure 4. Importing ratings dataset into RapidMiner software

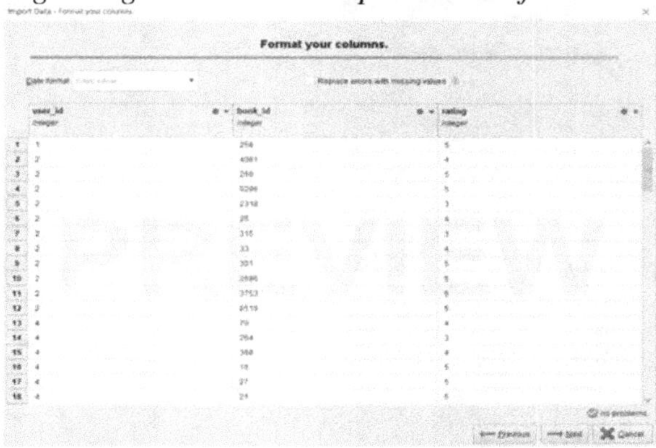

Subsequently, scientists can designate the role of each attribute, enabling them to import and process the data for item recommendation as follows.

Figure 5. Setting roles for the dataset

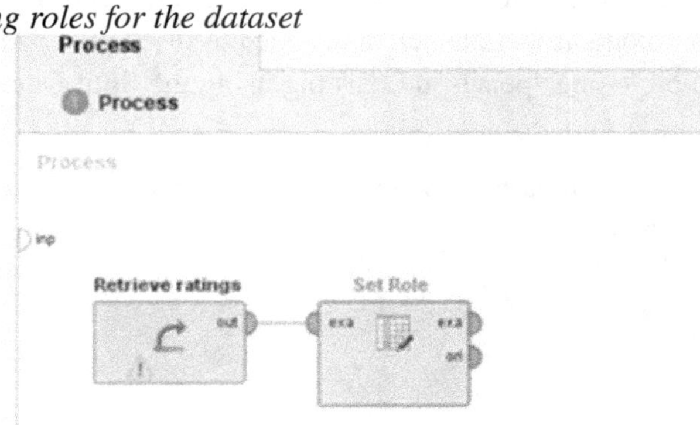

The data scientists can choose “Edit List (2)” to set roles for the data within the dataset.

Figure 6. Setting roles on data for item recommendation processing

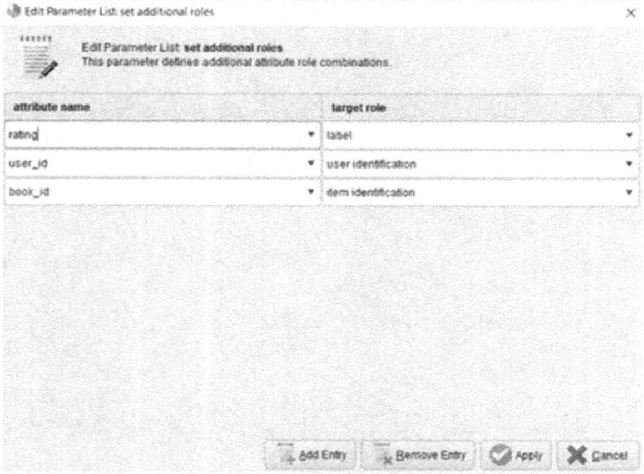

As shown in Figure 6, data scientists should define "rating" as the label or target variable, set "user_id" as the user identification, and set "book_id" as the item identification. This enables the data to be processed with the Item Recommendation model.

For data recommendation, data scientists need to divide the data into two parts based on the principle of Supervised Learning using the Split Data model.

Figure 7. The data are divided into two sections; for teaching machine learning and for testing the model

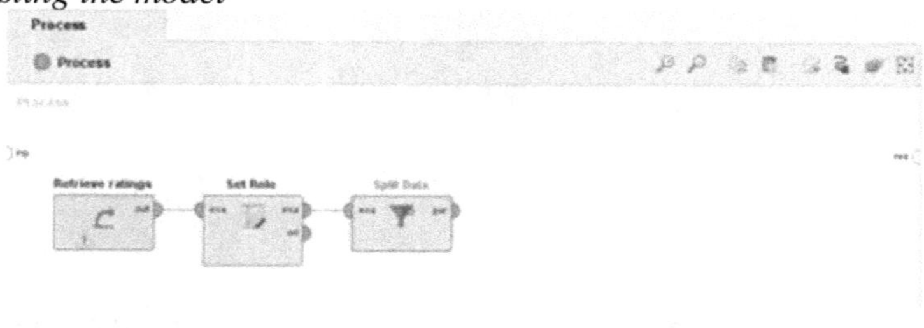

As shown in Figure 7, data scientists utilize the Split Data tool to partition the data into two segments: 80% for training machine learning models and 20% for evaluating the model's performance.

Figure 8. Dividing the dataset into two parts using split data

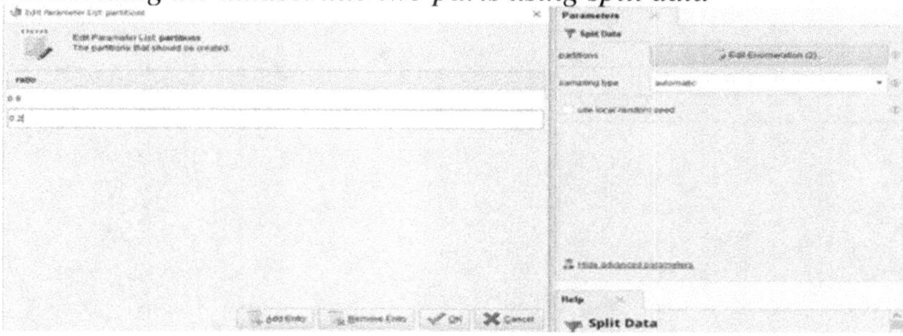

As shown in Figure 8, scientists can click on the "Edit Enumeration" button (2) and subsequently specify the proportion as 0.8 for training the machine learning model, and 0.2 for testing the model.

Figure 9. Forecasting and testing data for recommendation

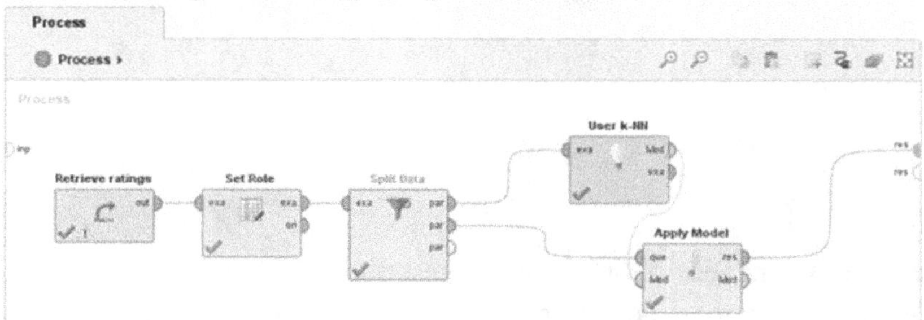

As shown in Figure 9, data scientists connect the Split Data model, with 80% of the data designated for training machine learning, to the User K-NN model under the Recommender implementation to predict missing data. Subsequently, 20% of the data allocated for testing is connected to the forecasted data, and both are fed into the Apply Model (Item Recommendation) for analysis using the Recommendation System. The results of the data analysis are presented in Figure 10 below.

Figure 10. Results from data analysis using recommendation system

Row No.	user_id	item_id	rank
1	2	8	1
2	2	2	2
3	2	11	3
4	2	24	4
5	2	4	5
6	2	21	6
7	2	32	7
8	2	18	8
9	2	5	9
10	2	27	10
11	2	35	11
12	2	10	12
13	2	115	13
14	2	101	14
15	2	94	15
16	2	80	16

The Recommendation System can suggest books for each reader. For instance, the system may recommend 100 books to Reader 2, utilizing user_id number 2 and the number of books in the Item_id suggested by the model. Subsequently, the efficacy of the recommendation can be assessed using the Performance (Item Recommendation) model as follows.

Figure 11. Testing the efficiency of the recommendation system using performance

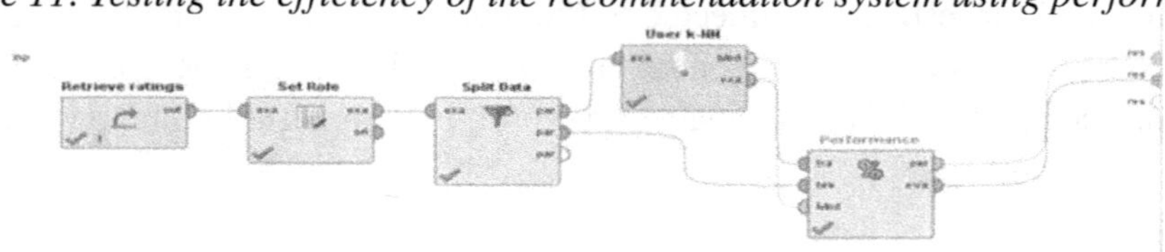

Data scientists can evaluate the efficiency of the system by linking the machine-learning model from K-NN learning to the Performance model. Next, they can connect the forecasted results from User K-NN to the Performance training data.

Subsequently, 20 percent of the data are reserved for testing and are connected to the Performance Test to conduct analysis. The efficiency testing results are displayed in the table below.

Figure 12. Results of the recommendation system efficiency

Row No.	AUC	prec@5	prec@10	prec@15	NDCG	MAP
1	0.820	0.137	0.098	0.082	0.377	0.115

The test result obtained using a model within the RapidMiner software includes Rank Accuracy, which represents the percentage of accuracy provided by the Recommendation System to the users. For instance, if the prec@5 value is 0.137, it indicates an accuracy of 20 percent.

CONCLUSION

In conclusion, the recommendation system plays a pivotal role in facilitating personalized experiences for users by suggesting relevant items based on their preferences and behavior. Throughout this chapter, we have delved into various aspects of recommendation systems, including different algorithms such as collaborative filtering, content-based filtering, and hybrid approaches. We have explored the utilization of machine learning techniques, such as k-Nearest Neighbors (k-NN) and deep learning, in building recommendation models. Additionally, we have discussed the importance of measurement and evaluation metrics in assessing the effectiveness and performance of recommendation systems. Furthermore, we have provided a practical demonstration using RapidMiner software, showcasing the process of building and evaluating recommendation models. From setting up the environment to importing datasets, setting roles, and testing model efficiency, we have illustrated the steps involved in implementing a recommendation system using a real-world example. Overall, recommendation systems continue to evolve and play a crucial role in various domains such as e-commerce, content streaming, and social media platforms. By leveraging advanced algorithms and data analysis techniques, recommendation systems have the potential to enhance user engagement, satisfaction, and overall experience. As technology advances and data availability increases, the future of recommendation systems holds promising prospects for delivering more accurate, personalized, and relevant recommendations to users worldwide.

EXERCISES

1. Describe the concept of User-Based Recommendation.
2. Describe the concept of Item-Based Collaborative Filtering.
3. Differentiate between User-Based Filtering and Item-Based Filtering.
4. Provide examples of scenarios where Recommendation Systems are needed to offer users recommendations and solutions.
5. Research and summarize studies utilizing Recommendation Systems.

REFERENCES

Adeniyi, D. A., Wei, Z., & Yongquan, Y. (2016). Automated web usage data mining and recommendation system using K-Nearest Neighbor (KNN) classification method. *Applied Computing & Informatics, 12*(1), 90–108. DOI: 10.1016/j.aci.2014.10.001

Aditya, G. M., Hoode, A., Anvesh Rai, K., Biradar, G., Ajay Kumara, M., Manoj Kumar, M. V., Prashanth, B. S., Sneha, H. R., & Shivadarshan, S. L. (2021). Machine learning-based platform and recommendation system for food ordering services within premises. *2021 2nd Global Conference for Advancement in Technology (GCAT)*, 1–8.

Chen, Q., & Qin, J. (2021). Research and implementation of movie recommendation system based on deep learning. *2021 IEEE International Conference on Computer Science, Electronic Information Engineering and Intelligent Control Technology (CEI)*, 225–228. DOI: 10.1109/CEI52496.2021.9574461

Emon, M. I., Shahiduzzaman, M., Rakib, M. R. H., Shathee, M. S. A., Saha, S., Kamran, M. N., & Fahim, J. H. (2021). Profile-based course recommendation system using association rule mining and collaborative filtering. *2021 International Conference on Science & Contemporary Technologies (ICSCT)*, 1–5. DOI: 10.1109/ICSCT53883.2021.9642633

Gong, S., Ye, H.-W., & Zhu, X. (2009). Item-based collaborative filtering recommendation using self-organizing map. *2009 Chinese Control and Decision Conference (CCDC)*, 4029–4031. DOI: 10.1109/CCDC.2009.5192713

Kamukwamba, Y., & Chunxiao, L. (2021). A novel algorithm using content-based filtering technology in Apache Spark for big data analysis. *2021 4th International Conference on Artificial Intelligence and Big Data (ICAIBD)*, 22–26.

Khatter, H., Arif, S., Singh, U., Mathur, S., & Jain, S. (2021). Product recommendation system for e-commerce using collaborative filtering and textual clustering. *2021 Third International Conference on Inventive Research in Computing Applications (ICIRCA)*, 612–618. DOI: 10.1109/ICIRCA51532.2021.9544753

Kusumawardhani, N. K., Nasrun, M., & Setianingsih, C. (2019). Web recommended system library book selection using item-based collaborative filtering method. *2019 IEEE International Conference on Engineering, Technology and Education (TALE)*, 1–8. DOI: 10.1109/TALE48000.2019.9225960

Lourenco, J., & Varde, A. S. (2020). Item-based collaborative filtering and association rules for a baseline recommender in e-commerce. *2020 IEEE International Conference on Big Data (Big Data)*, 4636–4645. DOI: 10.1109/BigData50022.2020.9377807

Padhy, S. K., Singh, A. K., & Vetrivelan, P. (2022). Item-based collaborative filtering blockchain for secure movie recommendation system. *Lecture Notes in Electrical Engineering*, *792*, 937–948. DOI: 10.1007/978-981-16-4625-6_93

Riswanto, E., Robi'in, B., & Suparyanto, . (2019). Mobile recommendation system for culinary tourism destination using KNN (K-nearest neighbor). *Journal of Physics: Conference Series*, *1201*(1), 012039. DOI: 10.1088/1742-6596/1201/1/012039

Tai, Y., Sun, Z., & Yao, Z. (2021). Content-based recommendation using machine learning. *2021 IEEE 31st International Workshop on Machine Learning for Signal Processing (MLSP)*, 1–4.

Wayan Priscila Yuni Praditya, N., Erna Permanasari, A., & Hidayah, I. (2021). Designing a tourism recommendation system using a hybrid method (collaborative filtering and content-based filtering). *2021 IEEE International Conference on Communication, Networks and Satellite (COMNETSAT)*, 298–305. DOI: 10.1109/COMNETSAT53002.2021.9530823

Yadalam, T. V., Gowda, V. M., Kumar, V. S., Girish, D., & M., N. (2020). Career recommendation systems using content-based filtering. *2020 5th International Conference on Communication and Electronics Systems (ICCES)*, 660–665.

Chapter 9
Basic Python Programming

ABSTRACT

The availability of off-the-shelf tools for data mining has made it easier to process data. However, in many cases, such software packages are not flexible enough to allow for algorithmic improvements. Therefore, data scientists need to write computer programs to customize processing methods in tandem with the software packages. This chapter introduces Python, a programming language that provides libraries that support data science work. The content includes Python programming syntax, such as variables, structured programming, decision making programming, recursive programming, data structure handling, and file handling. Additionally, the chapter introduces Google Colab as a tool for programming experiments. It provides a crucial foundation for data science students who are going to process data using Python programming data mining techniques in the next chapter. Although data scientists do not need a deep understanding of computer programming, learning computer languages is nevertheless important, and this chapter caters to beginners.

INTRODUCTION

Various industries today prioritize data science, recognizing its crucial role in decision-making (Raschka & Mirajalili, 2018). Whether in the medical, automotive, or scientific sectors, data scientists are in high demand, either recruited externally or developed within organizations. Regardless of industry, organizations follow a similar data analysis process, including defining questions, seeking resources, exploring and preprocessing data, applying mining techniques, and presenting results to stakeholders. Numerous tools facilitate data exploration, preparation, and mining, with Python being a widely used option. Python offers an extensive library for visualization, data preparation, and mining techniques, while its algorithms enable

DOI: 10.4018/979-8-3693-6001-9.ch009

large-scale data processing without limitations. As an open-source tool, Python helps organizations reduce digital resource costs (Sneeringer, 2016; Reges, Obourn & Stepp, 2019). Consequently, Python has become an essential tool for beginners in data science (Bowles, 2015; Joshi, 2017). Developed by Guido van Rossum in 1980, Python is a high-level programming language designed to resemble human language, making it ideal for beginners (Sunkpho & Ramjan, 2020; Tanantong & Ramjan, 2022). Its easy-to-remember syntax allows for both structural and object-oriented programming (Hill, 2015; Bader, 2018; Mueller, 2018; Lubanovic, 2019). Additionally, Python's open-source nature enables global developer collaboration without licensing costs (Stewart, 2017; Zelle, 2010).

Software developers can use editors like Google Colab to write Python code and interpreters to convert it into an executable format for digital devices. The execution process follows these steps:

1. Developers write commands in a software editor.
2. The interpreter translates Python commands for digital devices.
3. Digital devices process commands.
4. Commands are executed as instructed.
5. Developers verify the operation's accuracy.

Python's case sensitivity is important, as it differentiates between uppercase and lowercase characters (e.g., "dX" vs. "DX"). While developers and data scientists have distinct roles, data scientists can start their Python journey with basic commands for data analysis, making it a valuable tool in the field.

1. Variables

Data scientists have the ability to analyze data by organizing it into variables within Python. These variables serve as containers that hold data for purposes such as transfer, processing, and display. Data scientists can determine the data containing variables. In the example, the data scientists assign all three variables. Variable 1 stores the first data which is number 8; and variable 2 stores the second which is number 5. The numbers in variable 1 and variable 2 are then combined, so the result is 13, which is then included in the third variable. Thus, data scientists can define variables to contain the data and write Python programs based on the algorithm designed for each data mining technique.

To determine variables, letters, numbers, or underscores can be used, but it cannot begin with numbers like 1number. However, variable determination should be easy for data scientists to recall. Therefore, data scientists can begin programming in Python with the following syntax.

variable = "alphabetic data"

variable = numeric data

Based on the provided syntax, data scientists have the ability to store both alphabetical and numerical data within variables. Subsequently, they can showcase this data using the "print" command, as illustrated in Figure 1 below.

Figure 1. Example of variable determination

```
name = "Jirapon Sunkpho"
age = 50
print(name)
print(age)

Jirapon Sunkpho
50
```

In the illustration, the variable named "name" contains the alphabetical data "Jirapon Sunkpho," while the variable "age" contains the numerical data, which is 50. Subsequently, the data stored within these variables represent output using the "print" command. Once data scientists have populated the variables with data, they can also conduct mathematical operations on these variables to process the data, with the following grammatical syntax.

variable = variable arithmetic operator variable

Using the syntax provided, data scientists can store numerical data within variables. These variables are then subjected to mathematical operations to yield a result. Subsequently, the result is exhibited using the print command, as demonstrated in Figure 2.

Figure 2. An example of using variables to perform arithmetic operation

```
num1 = 5
num2 = 8
num3 = num1 + num2
print(num3)

13
```

In this example, variable "num1" holds the value 5 while variable "num2" holds the value 8. Upon adding the numbers stored in "num1" and "num2," the result is 13, which is then assigned to "num3" and displayed using the print command. According to the distinction between alphabetic and numeric variables within Python, variable types used in computations are categorized as "float," representing real numbers like 0.5, and "int," representing integers such as 5. Data scientists can inspect the data type within a variable using the syntax provided.

print(type(variable))

From the syntax provided, data scientists can utilize the "type" command to examine the data type within a variable, aligning with the workings of the print statement as demonstrated below.

Figure 3. Types of variables

```
ex = 6
print(type(ex))

ed = 9.0
print(ed)

<class 'int'>
9.0
```

As shown in Figure 3, the variable "ex" holds the number 6 while the variable "ed" contains the number 9.0. Upon utilizing the print(type()) command to exhibit the data type, the result indicates an integer, signifying that variable "ex" contains integer-like data. Conversely, when displaying the datum within variable "ed," it appears as the decimal number 9.0. If data scientists wish to alter the variable type for data processing, programs can be scripted following the syntax provided below.

print(int(variable))

print(float(variable))

From the syntax, data scientists can use ***int*** command to convert ***float*** variables into ***int***, and use ***float*** command to convert ***int*** variable into ***float*** as shown below.

Figure 4. Converting the data type

```
ed = 9.0
ex = 6
print(int(ed))
print(float(ex))

9
6.0
```

As shown in Figure 4, variable "ed" contains the number 9.0, identified as a float or real number, while variable "ex" contains 6, recognized as an int or integer. Data scientists possess the capability to convert data types. For "ed", the print(int(ed)) command is employed to convert the data type from float to int, resulting in the change from 9.0 to 9. Conversely, for "ex", the print(float(ex)) command is utilized to convert the data type from int to float, resulting in the change from 6 to 6.0.

A. Mathematical Operators

Regarding the manipulation of variables containing numerical values within Python, mathematical operators are made available for data scientists to utilize in tandem with the algorithms of various data mining techniques.

Table 1. Mathematical operators in Python

operator	Meaning	example
+	plus	a+b
-	minus	a-b
*	multiply	a*b
/	divide	a/b
%	Modulus	a%b
**	exponentiation	a**b

In Python, there is a specific sequence for interpreting mathematical operators, wherein the Interpreter executes calculations for multiplication, division, addition, and subtraction, respectively. Consequently, when data scientists develop computational algorithms for each model, they cannot rely on the formula being deciphered in the usual sequence, proceeding from left to right. Instead, it is imperative to consider the sequence in which the interpreter parses the language to ensure accurate results in data analysis. An illustrative example of data sequencing is provided below.

Figure 5. An example of a mathematical operation

```
a = 5
b = 3
c = 4
d = 6
e = 2
f = a + b - c * d / e
g = (((a+b)-c)*d)/e
print(f)
print(g)

-4.0
12.0
```

In Figure 5, variable "a" holds the number 5, variable "b" holds the number 3, variable "c" holds the number 4, variable "d" holds the number 6, and variable "e" holds the number 2. Mathematical calculations are then executed, commencing with multiplication, followed by division, addition, and subtraction, until yielding a result of -4.0. Additionally, data scientists have the capability to organize mathematical operations using parentheses, prioritizing addition, subtraction, multiplication, and division in sequence, ultimately resulting in 12.0. Apart from performing mathematical operations with variables, Python also offers other types of operations to streamline programming tasks.

Table 2. Syntax and configuration examples within Python variables

Operators used to assign variable values	**Example**	**Writing a set of commands without using operators for configuration**
=	c = 3	c = 3
+=	c += 3	c = c + 3
-=	c -= 3	c = c - 3
*=	c *= 3	c = c * 3
/=	c /= 3	c = c / 3
%=	c %= 3	c = c % 3
//=	c //= 3	c = c // 3
**=	c **= 3	c = c ** 3

As shown in Table 2, data scientists have the ability to alter the configuration format to streamline programming tasks. For instance, the expression "c = c + 3" implies taking the value within variable c, adding 3 to it, and then assigning the result back to variable c. Data scientists can condense this operation by writing programs in the form "c += 3" to achieve the same processing outcome as demonstrated in the example below.

Figure 6. Converting the configuration style

```
h = 0
g = 0
h = h + 3
print(h)
g += 3
print(g)

3
3
```

In the example, variables "h" and "g" initially have a value of 0. Subsequently, "h" is incremented by 3 using the expression "h = h + 3", resulting in "h" being set to 3. This writing style is then streamlined to "g += 3", yielding the same outcome, with "g" also equaling 3. Data scientists have the ability to modify their programming style in this manner to effectively reduce programming time.

B. Logical Operators

Data scientists can manipulate data within variables using logical data types, typically represented as True and False, in accordance with specified processing conditions.

Table 3. Logical operators within Python

Logical operators	meaning	example
and	True and True are resulted as True. Otherwise, it is false in all cases.	a and b
or	False or False are resulted as False Otherwise, it is true in all cases.	a or b
not	True and False values within a variable are transformed into the opposite values.	not a

As shown in Table 3, when data scientists aim to handle Boolean data, they can craft a program as demonstrated below.

Figure 7. Logical data processing

```
a = True
b = True
c = a and b
print(c)
d = a or b
print(d)
f = not a
print(f)
```

```
True
True
False
```

As depicted in Figure 7, the logical values of variables “a” and “b” are both assigned as True. The logical operator “and” is then applied to variables “a” and “b”, resulting in True. Subsequently, this outcome is stored in variable “c”, and the result is displayed as True via the print command. This is because “True and True” always yields True; otherwise, it is False in all cases.

When variables “a” and “b” are processed with the logical operator “or”, and the resulting data are stored in variable “d”, the outcome is True. This is because “False or False” is False; otherwise, it is True in all cases. Lastly, the command “not a” transforms the value True into False. This result is then assigned to variable “f” and displayed through the print command.

C. Comparative Operations

Whenever data scientists aim to compare the values stored within variables, they can utilize comparative operations. If the outcome of the comparison is true, it will be assigned a value of True; otherwise, if the result is false, it will be assigned a value of False, as outlined in Table 4.

Table 4. Comparative operators

Operators	meaning	example
>	The greater-than sign “>” is employed to compare values within variables. The outcome is True if the value in the first variable is greater than the value in the second variable; otherwise, it is False in all cases.	a > b
<	The less-than sign “<” is utilized to compare values within variables. The result is True if the value in the first variable is less than the value in the second variable; otherwise, it is False in all cases.	a < b
==	The equals sign “==” yields True when the values inside both variables are equal; otherwise, it returns False in all cases.	a == b
!=	The not equals sign “!=” produces True when the values inside the two variables are not equal; otherwise, it returns False in all cases.	a != b
>=	Either the greater-than sign “>” or the equal sign “=” can be used to compare values within variables. The result is True if the value in the first variable is greater than or equal to the value in the second variable; otherwise, it is False in all cases.	a >= b
<=	Either the less-than sign “<” or the equal sign “=” is employed to compare values within variables. The result is True if the value in the first variable is less than or equal to the value in the second variable; otherwise, it is False in all cases.	a <= b

From the tables provided, data scientists can compare values within variables by programming as demonstrated in the example below (Figure 8).

Figure 8. An example of using comparison operators

```
a = 20
b = 10
c = a > b
print(c)
d = a < b
print(d)

True
False
```

In the example, variable “a” holds the number 20, and variable “b” holds the number 10. If “a” is greater than “b”, the result is True because the value in variable “a” is indeed greater than the value in variable “b”. Conversely, when “a” is less than “b”, the result is False because the value in variable “a” is not greater than the value in variable “b”.

CONDITIONAL OPERATIONS

When data scientists aim to employ logical and comparative operators to instruct a digital device to execute a specific action or to repeat it, they can utilize the following control commands.

1. *if* Condition

When data scientists operate a digital device for logic and comparison operations, they can program it according to the following syntax.

if condition:

command

Based on the syntax provided, an operation occurs when the result of a condition is True. Data scientists can write a program as follows.

Figure 9. Using if command

```
a = 10
if a == 10:
  print("Digital Transformation")

Digital Transformation
```

As shown in Figure 9, variable "a" holds the number 10, and the "if" command is utilized to compare whether the value in variable "a" is equal to 10 or not. When executing the "if" command and the result is True, the command after the colon is subsequently executed. In this case, it is to display the message "Digital Transformation" through the print command.

If data scientists intend to operate a digital device when the result is False, it can be programmed with the following syntax:

if condition:

command

else:

command

From the syntax provided, when the result is True, the command set will execute the command after the colon. If it is False, the command set will execute the command after the "else:" command. Data scientists can write a program as follows:

Figure 10. Operation when getting a false result

```
a = 9
if a == 10:
  print("Digital Transformation")
else:
  print("College of Innovation")

College of Innovation
```

As shown in Figure 10, if the condition results in False, data scientists can operate a digital device by writing a set of commands after the "else" command. For instance, if variable "a" has a value of 9 and the command checks whether it is equal to 10, the result is False. Consequently, the device is activated after the "else" command, and the phrase "College of Innovation" is displayed using the print command.

If data scientists wish to establish more complex conditions for instructing digital devices to function, they can write a program using the following syntax:

if condition:
command
elif condition:
command
elif condition:
command
else:
command

Based on the syntax provided, data scientists can create multiple choices of commands. If the result of the first condition is True, the first set of commands will be executed. Alternatively, if the result is False, the program will proceed to evaluate the second condition. If the second condition is True, the corresponding statement is executed. If False, the program moves on to compare the third condition. If the third condition is True, the corresponding statement is executed. Finally, if all previous conditions are False, the last statement is executed. Data scientists can write a program as follows:

Figure 11. Example of using complex conditions

```
a = 5
if a > 10:
  print("Digital Transformation")
elif a > 8 :
  print("College of Innovation")
elif a > 6:
  print("Business Analytics")
else:
  print("Design Thinking")

Design Thinking
```

In this example, the data scientists have defined a total of 4 alternative commands, with variable "a" initialized to 5. The first condition checks whether the value in variable "a" is greater than 10. If this condition results in False, the program proceeds to check the second condition, which verifies if the value in variable "a" is greater than 8. If this condition also results in False, the program then evaluates the third condition to determine if the value in variable "a" is greater than 6. If this condition is False as well, the command set following the "else:" statement is executed, displaying the word "Design Thinking".

2. Loop

When data scientists anticipate iterative operations, they can utilize either of the loop statements within Python: the for statement or the while statement.

A. *For* Loop

The syntax of the *for* loop can be divided into two types: *for* Loop 1, which iterates over a specified range, and *for* Loop 2, which iterates over the values contained within a variable as illustrated by the following syntax.

for Loop 1: Using the ***for*** command along with specifying the range

for i in range(n):

command

From the syntax provided, scientists are required to assign an ending point so that the *for* loop repeats the specified cycles. The program can be written as shown in the following example.

Figure 12. Iteration using the for command, for Loop 1

```
n = 5
for a in range(n):
  print("Digital Transformation")

Digital Transformation
Digital Transformation
Digital Transformation
Digital Transformation
Digital Transformation
```

As shown in Figure 12, the data scientists specify a range of data by setting the variable "n" to 5. Subsequently, they utilize a *for* loop to output the term "Digital Transformation" five times. In this type of loop, an explicit initialization is not required, and the iteration will continue according to the configured cycle's end.

for Loop 2: Iteration to show values inside variables

for i in variable:

command

When iterating with the *for* command using the *for* Loop 2 method, data scientists can iterate over the data contained within variables, and can write the program as follows:

Figure 13. Iterating using the for command, for Loop 2 method

```
n = [1,2,3,4,5]
for i in n:
  print(n)

[1, 2, 3, 4, 5]
[1, 2, 3, 4, 5]
[1, 2, 3, 4, 5]
[1, 2, 3, 4, 5]
[1, 2, 3, 4, 5]
```

As shown in Figure 13, the data scientists store the numbers 1 through 5 into variable "n". They then use the *for* command to display the value inside variable "n" five times, based on the number contained within variable "n". Additionally, data scientists can employ the loop in text rendering, where the command set will execute according to the loop cycle, which is equal to the number within the variable.

B. *While* Loop

When data scientists intend to iterate while the conditional result is True, they can utilize the *while* command for iteration with the following syntax.

Initialization of variables

while variable default condition:

command

Increasing or decreasing the value of the initialized variables

From the syntax provided, data scientists initialize the variables used for iteration control. Then, the *while* command is employed to check the condition. If the result of the condition is True, the specified command is executed. Subsequently, the value within the variable is incremented or decremented to evaluate the condition again. If the result of the conditional check turns out to be False, the loop is exited. The program can be written as shown in the example below.

Figure 15. Using the while statement

```
i = 1

while i <= 10:
    print(i)
    i += 1
    if i == 5:
      break
```

```
1
2
3
4
```

In the example, data scientists initialize variable "i". The *while* command then checks if the value inside variable "i" is less than or equal to 10. If the result is True, it displays the value inside variable "i" using the print command. Afterwards, the value of variable "i" is incremented to continue creating loops until the value inside variable "i" is not greater than or equal to 10. If the result of the condition is False, the iteration will be exited.

C. Exiting the loops with the *Break* command

When data scientists utilize the while command for iterative operations, and they intend to exit the loop prematurely, the *break* command can be employed as demonstrated in the following syntax.

```
while True:
command
adding the iterative value
if condition:
break
```

From the syntax provided, data scientists can operate a digital device to iterate while the value obtained through the while command is true, incrementally increasing the value to perform iteration. The loop exits when the while command is checked and the value is False. If data scientists wish to add conditions to exit the loop, they can create conditions using the if command and then utilize the break command to exit the loop if the value checked through the if command is True. A program can be written as follows:

Figure 16. Exiting the loops with the break command

```
i = 1

while i <= 10:
    print(i)
    i += 1
    if i == 5:
      break
```

```
1
2
3
4
```

In this example, the data scientists initialize the variable "i" to 1 and repeatedly iterate while the value inside the variable "i" is less than or equal to 10. The value of "i" is continually incremented until it reaches a value where the condition becomes False. However, data scientists can exit the loop prematurely using the *break* command when the value inside the variable "i" equals 5.

D. Excluding processing within the loop with the *Continue* command

When data scientists employ the *for* loop command, they can skip certain iterations if they meet defined conditions by using the continue command, as shown in the following syntax.

if condition:

continue

command

From the syntax provided, data scientists have the ability to skip the execution of the command set if the value obtained from the condition is True. They can achieve this by utilizing *continue command*. Subsequently, they execute the command when the condition is False. A program can be written as follows:

Figure 17. Skipping the loops with the continue command

```
for i in range(10):
    if i == 5:
        continue
    print(i)
```

```
0
1
2
3
4
6
7
8
9
```

In the example, the data scientists utilize a for loop to iterate through numbers from 0 to 9. The loop iterates to represent the value in variable "i" only if the value obtained in the for loop is True, which corresponds to the specified data range. The *continue command* is employed to skip the execution of commands when the value inside the variable "i" is 5. As a result, when executing the command set, numbers from 0 to 9 are displayed except for 5. This corresponds to the exception of executing the command set through the use of *continue command*.

BASIC OF DATA STRUCTURE

When data scientists aim to store multiple data within a single variable or import a dataset from a computer into Python, they utilize command sets to manage and access data within different types of data structures.

1. List

Data scientists can pack multiple amounts of data into the ***List*** variable. The syntax for creating ***List*** is as follows.

variable = [data, data, …, data]

From the syntax, a single variable acts as ***List*** by storing multiple data in square brackets. Data scientists can create ***List*** as follows.

Figure 18. Creating list figure

```
i = [1, 3, 5, 7, 9 ]
print(i)
```

```
[1, 3, 5, 7, 9]
```

In the example, data scientists can create the variable “i” to store all five numeric data, which consist of 1, 3, 5, 7, and 9 respectively. Subsequently, they can display these data using the print command.

2. Managing data within *List*

Data scientists can utilize commands to access and manipulate data within a list, such as adding data to a list, replacing existing data, or deleting data, using the following syntax.

Syntax 1: Adding data to ***list***, Method 1
variable += [‘data’, ‘data’]

According to Syntax 1, data scientists can use a list variable to add new data into the list using the symbol +=. The newly added data will come after the previously added data.

Syntax 2: Adding data to ***list***, Method 2
variable.append('data')

According to Syntax 2, data scientists can add data to the end of the current data by using the .append command. Data scientists can choose to use either Syntax 1 or Syntax 2 in their programming.

Syntax 3: Replacing the existing data
variable[data location] = "data"

According to Syntax 3, when data scientists intend to replace existing data within a list, they can refer to the data location within the list and insert the new data into it.

Syntax 4: Deleting data within the ***list***
variable[data range] = [ ]

According to Syntax 4, data scientists can specify the location of the data to be deleted and replace it with a blank value. Subsequently, the appended data of the deleted data will fill the empty position. Data scientists can program all the four syntaxes as follows:

Figure 19. Managing data within list

```
staffs = ['Jirapon', 'Sarawut', 'Chayakrit', 'Kannapa']
print(staffs)

staffs += ['Kom', 'Noppol']
print(staffs)

staffs.append('Jiroj')
print(staffs)

staffs[5] ="Jibby"
print(staffs)

staffs[1:3] = []
print(staffs)
```

```
['Jirapon', 'Sarawut', 'Chayakrit', 'Kannapa']
['Jirapon', 'Sarawut', 'Chayakrit', 'Kannapa', 'Kom', 'Noppol']
['Jirapon', 'Sarawut', 'Chayakrit', 'Kannapa', 'Kom', 'Noppol', 'Jiroj']
['Jirapon', 'Sarawut', 'Chayakrit', 'Kannapa', 'Kom', 'Jibby', 'Jiroj']
['Jirapon', 'Kannapa', 'Kom', 'Jibby', 'Jiroj']
```

In the example, data scientists create a list variable called "staffs" containing "Jirapon" data in position 0, "Sarawut" data in position 1, "Chayakrit" data in position 2, and "Kannapa" data in position 3. These data are then displayed using the print command.

Next, "Kom" data is added to position 4 and "Noppol" data to position 5 using the += operator, and the updated data is displayed using the print command. The "Kom" and "Noppol" data are appended to the existing data within the list. Subsequently, data scientists add "Jiroj" data to position 6 using the .append command, and then display it via the print command.

When data scientists intend to replace the data in position 5, formerly "Noppol," with the data "Jibby," they refer to the position of the data and put the new data to replace it. The updated data are then displayed using the print command. Finally, data scientists determine that the locations of data to be deleted are positions 1 and 2. These data are then replaced. As indicated by the print command, the deletion of an item from a list is performed one position before the final digit of the deletion position.

3. Dictionary Key and Values

When data scientists wish to create a variable that can hold multiple types of data, they can write a program using the following syntax.Syntax 1: Creating a dictionary

variable = {key: value}, ..., {key: value}

According to Syntax 1, data scientists can create a dictionary consisting of a set of data that acts as keys and values, both of which can be either numeric or alphabetic.

Syntax 2: Adding data into the dictionary
variable[key] = value

From syntax 2, data scientists can add key and value data to the dictionary by appending the existing data.

Syntax 3: Removing data from the dictionary
del variable[key]

From Syntax 3, data scientists can delete data within a dictionary using the del command, specifying the keys to be deleted. After execution, the specified keys and their corresponding values are removed from the dictionary.

Syntax 4: Displaying data of all keys and values within a dictionary
variable.keys()
variable.values()

With Syntax 4, data scientists can display all data in a dictionary by printing all keys and their corresponding values using the print command.

With these four syntaxes, data scientists can write programs to manipulate dictionaries, as demonstrated in the example.

Figure 20. Manipulating the dictionary

```
students = {"Jirapa": 123, "Janira": 567, "Yonrada": 891}
print(students)

students["Jirakan"] = 345
print(students)

del students['Jirapa']
print(students)

print(students.keys())

print(students.values())
```

```
{'Jirapa': 123, 'Janira': 567, 'Yonrada': 891}
{'Jirapa': 123, 'Janira': 567, 'Yonrada': 891, 'Jirakan': 345}
{'Janira': 567, 'Yonrada': 891, 'Jirakan': 345}
dict_keys(['Janira', 'Yonrada', 'Jirakan'])
dict_values([567, 891, 345])
```

In the example, data scientists create a dictionary named "students" by filling it with data consisting of three sets of letter keys and numeric values. The dictionary is then displayed. Next, a new set of data is added to the dictionary before displaying it again. The newly added data are appended to the existing data.

Subsequently, data scientists delete data from the dictionary by referring to the keys using the del command. In the example, the data scientists refer to the "Jirapa" key, so after re-rendering the data, the "Jirapa" key and its corresponding value, "123," are removed from the dictionary.

Data scientists can display all of the keys in a dictionary using the .keys() method and retrieve only the values of all data within a dictionary using the .values() method.

4. Searching for data with keywords

When scientists store large amounts of data in variables that function as lists or dictionaries, they can search for the data using the following syntax.

Syntax 1: Searching for data from the list
"keyword" in variable

According to Syntax 1, data scientists can search for data within a list and display it using the print command.

Syntax 2: Searching for data from the dictionary
'keyword' in variable

Using Syntax 2, data scientists can search for data within a dictionary and display it using the print command.

With both syntaxes, data scientists can program the search for data in the list and the dictionary as follows.

Figure 21. Searching data with keywords

```
staffs_list = ["Sunkpho", "Ramjan", "Campiranon"]

print("Ramjan" in staffs_list)

staffs_dict = {"Sunkpho":1, "Ramjan":2, "Campiranon":3}

print('Sunkpho' in staffs_dict)


True
True
```

In the example, data scientists create a list containing "Sunkpho," "Ramjan," and "Campiranon" data respectively. They then search for "Ramjan" within the staffs_list variable and display the result using the print command. The result is True, indicating that the data are contained within the list.

Next, a dictionary is created containing data such as "Sunkpho:1," "Ramjan:2," and "Campiranon:3." Subsequently, "Sunkpho" is searched within the staffs_dict variable, which acts as a dictionary. The result is True, indicating that the datum is indeed contained in the dictionary.

IMPORTING DATA INTO A COMMAND SET (FILE I/O)

When data scientists intend to prepare data for processing using various techniques, they can use commands within Python to read data by inputting the data via the keyboard and creating .txt format files.

1. Importing data into the command set via a keyboard

In cases where data scientists intend to input data into the command set via a keyboard, they can write a program using the following syntax.

variable = input("alt text")

From the syntax provided, data scientists can write a program to input data into the command set via the keyboard, as demonstrated in the example below.

Figure 22. Importing data into the command set via keyboard

```
aa = input("Please enter number")
print(aa)
```

```
Please enter number20
20
```

In this example, data scientists input data into variables via a keyboard using the input command. Specifically, the number 20 is inserted into variable "aa," and the value inside variable "aa" is displayed on the keyboard.

2. Creating and manipulating text files

Data scientists can create a .txt (Text File) which supports writing data into that file. They can also read the written data from the file and display it on a screen. The syntax for writing and reading data within the file is as follows.

Syntax 1: Writing data into the ***text file***
file variable = open("file name ***.txt", "w+"***)
file variable ***.write***("data")
file variable. ***close***()

Based on Syntax 1, data scientists can create a .txt file by specifying the file name and using the "w+" mode to write data into the text file with the open function. The file object is then assigned to a variable to hold the file. Data scientists can use the .write() method to write data to the file and the .close() method to close the file.

Syntax 2: Reading data from the ***text file***
file variable = open("file name ***.txt", "r+"***)
variable = file variable.***read***(character count)
print (variable)
File variable.***close***()

According to Syntax 2, data scientists can open a file using the open function, specifying the "r+" mode to read data from the Text File. The data from the Text File are then imported into a variable using the .read method, and the data are displayed using the Print command. Finally, the file is closed with the close() method.

Data scientists can write a program to create a file, write data, and read from a text file as shown in the example below.

Figure 23. Creating a file, writing and reading data from a text file

```
aa = open("aa.txt", "w+")
aa.write( "Digital Transformation and Innovation")
aa.close()

bb = open("aa.txt","r+")
str = bb.read(40)
print("Output are : ", str)
bb.close()

Output are :  Digital Transformation and Innovation
```

As shown in Figure 23, data scientists create a file named "aa" using the open function. They use the "w+" mode to write data into the Text File via the .write method. In the example, data scientists write the "Digital Transformation and Innovation" data into the Text File, and then close the file using the .close() method.

Data scientists can then reopen the "aa" file, using the "r+" mode to read the data in the text file. They load the file into the "bb" variable and execute the .read() command, which reads all 40 characters. Later, the data are stored in the "str" variable, which displays the data using the print statement. Finally, the file is closed again with the .close() method.

EXCEPTION HANDLING

In cases where an error occurs during processing, causing the program to stop working, data scientists can use Exception Handling to handle the error and allow the program to continue processing. The syntax for Exception Handling is as follows.

Try:

command
except, type of exception:
command
else:
command

According to the syntax, data scientists encapsulate all commands to be processed inside a try block. If an error occurs during processing, it is handled inside the except block. If no error occurs, the commands inside the else block are executed.

The except block handles errors specified by the programmer, such as IOError (which occurs when the command set is unable to open a file) or SyntaxError (which is caused by a syntax error in the program).

Data scientists can write a command set covered by Exception Handling as demonstrated in the example.

Figure 24. Using exception handling in cases where the command fails to open the text file

```
try:
    aa = open("dd.txt", "r+")
    aa.write("Test")
except IOError:
    print("I could not find a text file")
else:
    print("Everything correct")
    aa.close()

I could not find a text file
```

As shown in the example, data scientists write a command set within a try block to open and read a text file named "dd.txt," which has not been created before. Consequently, the IOError exception condition is met, causing the program to execute the print statement "I could not find a text file" and terminate.

In another scenario, if the statement within the try block is valid and no error occurs, it will be executed as follows:

Figure 25. Using exception handling in cases where the command set can open files

```
try:
    aa = open("aa.txt", "r+")
    aa.write("Test")
except IOError:
    print("I could not find a text file")
else:
    print("Everything Correct")
    aa.close()

Everything Correct
```

As depicted in Figure 25, the command successfully opens the Text File named "aa.txt," which is a pre-existing file. Subsequently, the command is executed within the else block, which displays the statement "Everything Correct" and then closes the file using the .close() method.

CONCLUSION

Data scientists can utilize Python as an open-source tool for processing big data, thereby reducing the costs associated with digital resource investments. Python offers libraries that provide a comprehensive set of commands for data processing, making it a powerful tool in the field of data science. As a result, Python has become a fundamental language that scientists should learn for future studies.

This book introduces the basic commands that data scientists need to study before writing programs to manipulate data and display it in various formats.

Google Colab is a software editor that allows users to write Python commands. It also provides libraries that store command sets for data mining processing. Data scientists can conduct experiments, write command sets, and test them via the web without the need to install any software on their computers.

EXERCISES

1. Create a Python program to prompt the user for two numbers via the keyboard. Then, perform addition, subtraction, multiplication, and division operations on these numbers and display the results on the screen.

2. Develop a Python program to obtain the weight of pork from the user via the keyboard. Next, calculate the total price the customer needs to pay for the pork by multiplying the weight with the price per pound, which is $2.
3. Design a program for a hamburger restaurant to facilitate customer orders:
    - If the customer requests a beef hamburger (press 1), prompt them to enter the number of hamburgers. Then, calculate the total price based on $4 per hamburger and display it.
    - If the customer requests a pork hamburger (press 2), prompt them to enter the number of hamburgers. Then, calculate the total price based on $3 per pork hamburger and display it.
    - If the customer inputs any other number, display an alert message saying "Please choose between 1 and 2."
4. Create a program to input scores from the keyboard and display the corresponding letter grade:
    - For scores between 80 and 100, display "A".
    - For scores between 70 and 79, display "B".
    - For scores between 60 and 69, display "C".
    - For scores between 50 and 59, display "D".
    - For scores between 0 and 49, display "F".
    - If the score is above 100 or below 0, show the message "Please enter your score from 0 to 100".

Allow the user to choose whether to redo the process by pressing "Y" or exit by pressing "Q" using a *while* loop.

REFERENCES

Bader, D. (2018). *Python tricks: The book.* Dan Bader.

Bowles, M. (2015). *Machine learning in Python: Essential techniques for predictive analysis*. Wiley. DOI: 10.1002/9781119183600

Hill, C. (2015). *Learning scientific programming with Python*. Cambridge University Press. DOI: 10.1017/CBO9781139871754

Joshi, P. (2017). *Artificial intelligence with Python: A comprehensive guide to building intelligent apps for Python beginners and developers*. Packt Publishing Ltd.

Lubanovic, B. (2019). *Introducing Python: Modern computing in simple packages* (2nd ed.). O'Reilly Media, Inc.

Mueller, J. (2018). *Beginning programming with Python* (2nd ed.). John Wiley & Sons.

Raschka, S., & Mirajalili, V. (2018). *Python machine learning: Machine learning and deep learning with Python, scikit-learn, and TensorFlow* (2nd ed.). Packt Publishing.

Reges, S., Obourn, A., & Stepp, M. (2019). *Building Python programs* (1st ed.). Pearson.

Sneeringer, L. (2016). *Professional Python*. WROX/John Wiley & Sons.

Stewart, J. (2017). *Python for scientists* (2nd ed.). Cambridge University Press. DOI: 10.1017/9781108120241

Sunkpho, S., & Ramjan, S. (2020). *Introduction to Python programming for data science*. Thammasat Press.

Tananatong, T., & Ramjan, S. (2022). *Data visualization design and development for data science*. Thammasat Press.

Zelle, J. M. (2010). *Python programming: An introduction to computer science* (2nd ed.). Beedle & Associates.

Chapter 10
Data Analytics With Python

ABSTRACT

It is crucial for junior data scientists to learn computer programming as data science software packages may not always cater to the requirements of data analysis. Python provides a vast library of algorithms for data analysis, including NumPy, Pandas, Matplotlib, Seaborn, and Scikit-learn. NumPy and Pandas aid in organizing datasets as part of the pre-processing stage while Matplotlib and Seaborn offer a range of data visualization commands. These visualization tools are instrumental in data exploration processes, such as creating histograms and scatter plots, and displaying data mining results like cluster analysis outcomes. Scikit-learn is a popular library in the data science industry that offers various data mining commands for regression, decision constructs, and cluster analysis, covering both supervised and unsupervised learning. Therefore, junior data scientists must learn Python programming for data science applications, especially when using software packages that require editing the model using Python commands.

INTRODUCTION

In today's world, various tools facilitate data analysis throughout the workflow. These include data extraction tools, survey tools, preparation tools, data analysis tools with data mining techniques, and data visualization tools. Each step of the process is supported by readily available software, including both standalone applications and programming languages. Python stands out as a versatile tool that supports the entire workflow. It enables data analysis tasks such as dataset manipulation, importation routines, the development of data visualizations, and analysis using data mining techniques through its extensive library ecosystem (Massaron & Mueller, 2015: Mueller & Massaron, 2019).

DOI: 10.4018/979-8-3693-6001-9.ch010

NUMPY LIBRARY

The NumPy library offers a collection of commands that data scientists can utilize to manipulate imported datasets within Python's command environment. This library is specifically designed to organize data into a format suitable for processing with data mining techniques.

1. Array

Python supports storing data in arrays, organized into rows and columns. Array variables can accommodate data of one or more dimensions. The structure is as follows:

Table 1. 1-dimension array

	Column 0
Row 0	0,0
Row 1	1,0
Row 2	2,0
Row.	.
Row.	.
Row n	n,0

As shown in Table 1, data scientists can store data as a 1-dimensional array with records starting from 1 row and 1 column. Inside array variables, the location of the data is specified at row 0 and column 0.

For example, the number 2 might be contained in row 0 and column 0. When data scientists store more than 1 column, a 2-dimensional array variable can be created with the following structure:

Table 2. 2-dimension array

	Column 0	Column 1	Column 2	Column .	Column .	Column n
Row 0	0,0	0,1	0,2	0,.	0,.	0,n
Row 1	1,0	1,1	1,2	1,.	1,.	1,n
Row 2	2,0	2,1	2,2	2,.	2,.	2,n
Row .	.,0	.,1	.,2	.,.	.,.	.,n
Row .	.,0	.,1	.,2	.,.	.,.	.,n
Row n	n,0	n,1	n,2	n,.	n,.	n,n

As shown in Table 2, data scientists can store data in multiple rows and columns simultaneously. For example, the numeric data 25 may be positioned in Row 5, Column 3. By storing data in this manner, data scientists can design data structures with good memory management.

Therefore, when manipulating datasets that require array variables to store data, data scientists can execute commands from the NumPy library with the following syntax:

import numpy as the variable that executes command sets

Array variable = the variable that executes the ***.array*** command([data,data..data])

From the syntax, data scientists can utilize the '**.array**' command from the NumPy library to create array variables, which can be implemented as demonstrated in the example below.

Figure 1. Using commands to create array variables

```
import numpy as mm
a = mm.array([5,6,7])
print(a)
```

```
[5 6 7]
```

As shown in Figure 1, the data scientist utilizes the '.array' command from the NumPy library. The variable 'mm' executes the command to generate array data consisting of 5, 6, and 7. Subsequently, the data are stored in variable 'a' and displayed using the print command.

When data scientists aim to store data as a 2-dimensional array, they can also utilize the '**.array**' command from the NumPy library. The syntax for this operation is as follows:

import numpy as the variable that executes command sets

Array variable = the variable that executes the ***.array*** command([(data,data..data), (data,data..data)])

From the syntax, data scientists can add the second data. In Python, the data inside the parentheses are counted as 1 row.

Figure 2. Using commands to create a 2-dimension array

```
import numpy as mm
a = mm.array([(5,6,7),(8,9,10)])
print(a)
```

```
[[ 5  6  7]
 [ 8  9 10]]
```

As shown in Figure 2, data scientists utilize the variable 'mm' to invoke the '.array' command from the NumPy library, generating two datasets: 5, 6, 7 as in set 1, and 8, 9, 10 as in set 2. Subsequently, the data are assigned to variable 'a' and displayed using the print command.

2. Creating array data with *.arange*

Within the NumPy library, data scientists can utilize the '.arange' command to generate a series of numbers and create array variables for various purposes. The syntax for this command is as follows:

import numpy as the variable that executes command sets

print(variable that executes the ***.arange*** command(number of numbers))

Based on the syntax, data scientists utilize a variable to invoke the '.arange' command from the NumPy library, specifying a number, and then display the generated series of numbers using the print command. The series starts from 0 and continues up to the specified number minus one. A program demonstrating this functionality could be written as shown in the example below.

Figure 3. Creating an array dataset with .arange

```
import numpy as np
print(np.arange(5))
```

```
[0 1 2 3 4]
```

As shown in Figure 3, data scientists utilize the np variable to invoke the '.arange' command from the NumPy library. They then create a dataset consisting of five arrays starting from 0 and ending at 4. Finally, they display the generated dataset using the print command.

3. The *.reshape* command

After data scientists have created an array dataset with the '.arange' command, they can arrange the data into specified row and column sizes by using the .reshape command from the NumPy library as shown in the following syntax:

import numpy as the variable that executes command sets

print(variable to execute ***.arange***(numbers***).reshape***(numbers of rows, numbers of columns)

After creating a dataset with the '.arange' command, data scientists can adjust the data into the specified row and column format using the '.reshape' command.

Figure 4. Compiling data with .reshape

```
import numpy as np
a = np.arange(10).reshape(5,2)
print(a)

[[0 1]
 [2 3]
 [4 5]
 [6 7]
 [8 9]]
```

By creating a dataset containing 10 numbers from 0 to 9 with the '.arange' command, the scientists compile the data using the '.reshape' command to have 5 rows and 2 columns, pack the data into variable a, and then display the data via the print command. When compiling data with the '.reshape' command, data scientists must take into account the size of the data.

4. The *.linspace* command

Not only can the '.arange' statement be used to create an array of datasets, but the '.linspace' command from the NumPy library can also be employed to generate periodic datasets.

import numpy as the variable that executes a set of instructions

the variables that execute ***.linspace*** (initial number, end number, data frequency)

From the syntax, data scientists invoke the '.linspace' command, specifying the start and end numbers of the generated dataset, as well as the number of data points to be evenly distributed within that range. The program is written as follows:

Figure 5. Creating a dataset with .linspace command

```
import numpy as np
print(np.linspace(7, 15, 3))

[ 7. 11. 15.]
```

As shown in Figure 5, data scientists utilize the np variable to invoke the '.linspace' command from the NumPy library, generating a data range starting from 7 and ending at 15 with a frequency of 3. Therefore, the generated data points are 7, 11, and 15, respectively.

5. Changing data types in *array* variables

When data scientists prepare array data, they can utilize the 'dtype' command to modify the data types within array variables. If the current data type is an integer and needs to be changed to a real number, it can be specified as 'float'. Conversely, if the data type is a real number and needs to be changed to an integer, it can be specified as 'int', as shown in the following syntax:

import numpy as the variable that executes a set of commands

array variables = the variables that execute ***.array***([[(data,data..data), (data,data.. data)]], dtype= 'data type')

From the syntax, after the scientists create an array-like dataset, they can change the data type using 'dtype', as demonstrated in the example below.

Figure 6. Changing the data type

```
import numpy as mm
ee = mm.array([[5.8,6.2],[7.1,8.3]],dtype='int')
print(ee.dtype)
print(ee)
```

```
int64
[[5 6]
 [7 8]]
```

As presented in Figure 6, data scientists create an array dataset with all real numbers. They then use the 'dtype' command to convert a real number into an integer. Upon checking the data type using the 'dtype' command and printing the result, it shows as 'int64', indicating that the data inside the variable have been converted into integers. The entire results are then displayed through a print statement.

6. Mathematical Operations within *array*

When data scientists wish to perform mathematical operations on data, they can use array variables containing datasets to execute the operations, as shown in the following syntax:

> ***import numpy*** as the variable that executes command sets
> Array variables = the variable that executes ***.array***([data])
> Array variables = the variable that executes ***.array***([data])
> variable = array variable mathematical operators ***array*** variables

From the syntax, scientists can utilize the created array variables to conduct mathematical operations like addition, subtraction, multiplication, and division by implementing the following program:

Figure 7. Mathematical Operation of array variables

```
import numpy as mm
ee = mm.array([7,4])
cc = mm.arange(2)
c = ee - cc
print(c)

[7 3]
```

After creating the 1st array variable with datasets 7 and 4, and the 2nd array variable with datasets 0 and 1, the data within these variables undergo mathematical subtraction. The result is then stored in variable c. Specifically, 7 is subtracted by 0 to yield 7, and 4 is subtracted by 1 to yield 3.

7. Creating *array* variables with *.random* command

Data scientists can generate datasets using the '.random' function from the NumPy library, which produces random numbers within the range of 0 to 1, as shown in the syntax below.

> ***import numpy*** as the variable that executes the command
> variable = the variable that executes the ***.random.random*** command([number of rows, number of columns])

From the provided syntax, scientists can generate datasets with values between 0 and 1 within an array variable using the '.random' command. They can then specify the number of rows and columns for the array. To illustrate, consider the following example:

Figure 8. Creating a dataset with .random command

```
import numpy as np
a = np.random.random([3,4])
print(a)

array([[0.52256213, 0.88143325, 0.52947593, 0.04102454],
       [0.01393007, 0.5033998 , 0.18646051, 0.31449915],
       [0.74056756, 0.42395087, 0.12502817, 0.93248877]])
```

As shown in Figure 8, data scientists utilize the 'np' variable to invoke the '.random' command from the NumPy library. They generate a dataset ranging from 0 to 1 with 3 rows and 4 columns, and then output the data using the print command.

8. Summarizing Array Data

After data scientists have created array datasets, they can summarize that data with commands such as '.sum' to combine numeric data within the array variable, '.min' to find the smallest number within the array variable, and '.max' to find the largest number in the array variable as seen in the following syntax.

> ***import numpy*** as the variable that executes a set of commands
> Array variable = the variable that executes ***.array***([data,data..data])
> ***print***(array variable.sum())
> ***print***(array variable.min())
> ***print***(array variable.max())

From the syntax, data scientists can sum up the elements and find the largest and smallest values from the array variable. The program can be written as shown in the example below.

Figure 9. Summarizing data in array variables

```
import numpy as np
a = np.array([1,3,5,7,9])
print(a.sum())
print(a.min())
print(a.max())
```

```
25
1
9
```

As shown in Figure 9, data scientists create an array variable consisting of 1, 3, 5, 7, and 9, respectively. They then use the '.sum' command to calculate the sum of the data, resulting in 25. Next, they utilize the '.min' command to find the smallest value, which is 1, and the '.max' command to find the largest value, which is 9.

9. Indexing and Slicing

When data scientists need to access specific data points within an array, they can reference the location where the data are stored and manipulate the data by slicing the array. The syntax for slicing data in Python is as follows:

> ***import numpy*** as the variable that executes a set of commands
> Array variable = the variable that executes ***.array***([data,data..data])
> Array variable[location of data]
> Array variable[start position:end position:display frequency)

From the provided syntax, data scientists can reference specific locations within an array to access and manipulate the data stored at those locations. By specifying the start and end indices, along with the step size, they can extract data from the array at regular intervals. Below is an example program demonstrating the usage of slicing to access data within an array:

Figure 10. Accessing data locations and intermittent displays

```
import numpy as mm
a = mm.array([5,4,3,2,1,5,4,3,2,1])
print(a[3])
print(a[1:7:2])

2
[4 2 5]
```

As shown in Figure 10, the scientists initialize an array variable containing the data: 5, 4, 3, 2, and 1. By specifying the index position 3, they access the value stored at that location, which is the number 2. This value is then displayed using a print command.

Next, the data within positions 1 to 7 are accessed using slicing, with a step size of 2. This means that data are extracted from every second position within the specified range. The resulting values, 4, 2, and 5, are displayed using print commands.

10. Vectorization

When data scientists undertake Attribute Transformation during the preparation process, they can utilize the .vectorize command from the NumPy library. Vectorization involves employing small data, often referred to as Broadcast, to conduct calculations on the dataset, thereby altering the data. The syntax for this operation is as follows:

> ***import numpy*** as the variable that executes the command
> variable = the variable that executes ***.vectorize***(computing function)

Based on the syntax provided, data scientists can utilize the '.vectorize' command to perform calculations on a small dataset. Below is an example demonstrating how to implement this operation in a program:

Figure 11. Vectorization

```
def abc(d, e):
  if d > e:
    return d - e
  else:
    return d + e

import numpy as np
mm = np.vectorize(abc)
print(mm([4, 3, 2, 1], 2))

[2 1 4 3]
```

As shown in Figure 11, the data scientists utilize the np variable to execute the vectorize command from the NumPy library. Within this command, the abc function is invoked, encapsulating all the data into the mm variable. The function takes the values 4, 3, 2, and 1 as the d parameter, and 2 as the e parameter. It performs a conditional operation: if the value inside variable d is greater than the value in variable e, it subtracts the returned values; otherwise, it adds them. As a result, the calculated values are 2, 1, 4, and 3, respectively. This illustrates how the vectorize command can be employed to process data efficiently.

PANDAS LIBRARY

When data scientists manipulate and process data using mining techniques, Pandas is a crucial library utilized for storing command sets.

1. Series and Data Frames

Whenever data scientists import data or create datasets within Python, the datasets are then referred to as DataFrames, with the columns within the dataset being called Series. Each row of data is referred to as an Instance, and individual data points are called Data Objects. Data scientists can create a Series using the following syntax:

Import pandas as series variables
Series variables.Series([data,data, ….])

From the syntax, data scientists use the '.Series' command to create a single column of data as follows:

Figure 12. Creating a series

```
import pandas as pd
pd.Series(['Jirapon Sunkpho', 'Sarawut Ramjan', 'Kanapan Pongponrat'])

0       Jirapon Sunkpho
1        Sarawut Ramjan
2    Kanapan Pongponrat
dtype: object
```

As shown in Figure 12, data scientists utilize the pd variable to call the '.Series' command from the pandas library to generate the data within the Series. When scientists aim to create multiple Series and amalgamate them into a Data Frame, they can do so by following the syntax below:

Import pandas as the variable that invokes commands
variables that invoke ***.DataFrame***({ column name: series variable})

From the syntax, data scientists can utilize the '.DataFrame' command from the pandas library, specifying the column name and the generated series variable. The program can be written as follows:

Figure 13. Creating a data frame

```
import pandas as pd
c = pd.Series(['Digital Transformation', 'Service Innovation', 'Creative Industry'])
stu = pd.Series([60, 60, 120])

pd.DataFrame({ 'Curiculums': c, 'Number of Students': stu })
```

	Curiculums	Number of Students
0	Digital Transformation	60
1	Service Innovation	60
2	Creative Industry	120

As shown in Figure 13, data scientists have created two series: one containing data on three courses and the other containing the number of students in each academic year. The '.DataFrame' command is then utilized to name the series and connect them, combining all the series into a DataFrame.

2. Importing data into the command set

The Pandas Library facilitates data import by allowing the importation of datasets from a computer into Python. Data can also be imported from the internet into Python. The process of importing data from a computer into a command set can be implemented using the following syntax:

import pandas as the variable that invokes commands

Data Frame variables = Variables that invoke ***csv***('file source address')

From the provided syntax, data scientists can import CSV files by specifying the file path and then importing the data into DataFrame variables. This can be accomplished in Google Colab using the following programming approach:

Figure 14. Importing data from computer into command set

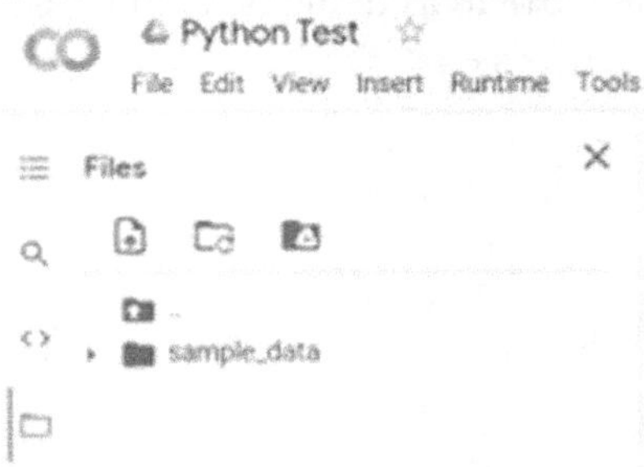

As shown in Figure 14, scientists click on "Upload to Session Storage" in Google Colab, and then specify the file location. They can then select the desired file to import into Google Colab. In this example, the file named "chol.txt" is chosen

Figure 15. Entering the file address

As shown in Figure 15, data scientists can right-click on the "chol.txt" file and copy its address. They can then use this file address in their Python program to import the data into Google Colab as demonstrated in the example.

Figure 16. Importing data from a computer into Google Colab

```
import pandas as pd
cc=pd.read_csv("/content/chol.txt")
print(cc)
```

```
       AGE HEIGHT WEIGHT CHOL SMOKE BLOOD MORT
0           20 176 77 195 nonsmo b alive
1            53 167 56 250 sigare o dead
2            44 170 80 304 sigare a dead
3           37 173 89 178 nonsmo o alive
4           26 170 71 206 sigare o alive
..                                    ...
195           35 174 57 222 pipe a alive
196         38 172 91 227 nonsmo b alive
197         26 170 60 167 sigare a alive
198         39 165 74 259 sigare o alive
199            49 178 81 275 pipe b alive

[200 rows x 1 columns]
```

As shown in Figure 16, data scientists utilize the '.read_csv' command to import the dataset from the "chol.txt" file into Google Colab. The imported dataset is then stored in the variable 'cc', and the data are displayed using the print command.

If scientists wish to import any dataset available on the internet, they can do so by importing the file address into Google Colab without the need to upload it. The program can be written according to the following syntax:

import pandas as the variable that invokes commands

Data Frame variable = Variable that invoke ***csv***('Internet file source address')

From the syntax, data scientists can specify the URL of a dataset available on the internet to import and process the data by writing a program similar to the example provided.

Figure 17. Importing data on the Internet into datasets

```
import pandas as pd
cc=pd.read_csv("https://download.mlcc.google.com/mledu-datasets/california_housing_train.csv")
print(cc)
```

```
       longitude  latitude  ...  median_income  median_house_value
0        -114.31     34.19  ...         1.4936             66900.0
1        -114.47     34.40  ...         1.8200             80100.0
2        -114.56     33.69  ...         1.6509             85700.0
3        -114.57     33.64  ...         3.1917             73400.0
4        -114.57     33.57  ...         1.9250             65500.0
...          ...       ...  ...            ...                 ...
16995    -124.26     40.58  ...         2.3571            111400.0
16996    -124.27     40.69  ...         2.5179             79000.0
16997    -124.30     41.84  ...         3.0313            103600.0
16998    -124.30     41.80  ...         1.9797             85800.0
16999    -124.35     40.54  ...         3.0147             94600.0

[17000 rows x 9 columns]
```

As shown in Figure 17, data scientists copy the URL of the dataset using the read_csv command from the Pandas library.

3. Indexing, Selecting and Filtering

After importing a dataset into Python, data scientists can manipulate the data by accessing each Series within the DataFrame, following the syntax below.

variable = the variable that executes command [“named ***Series***”]

From the syntax, data scientists can reference a specific series within a DataFrame, assign its instances to a variable, and then display them, as illustrated in the example.

Figure 18. Data accessibility (indexing)

```
import pandas as pd
cc=pd.read_csv("/content/sample_data/california_housing_test.csv")
ff=cc["median_income"]
print(ff)
```

```
0       6.6085
1       3.5990
2       5.7934
3       6.1359
4       2.9375
         ...
2995    1.1790
2996    3.3906
2997    2.2895
2998    3.2708
2999    8.5608
Name: median_income, Length: 3000, dtype: float64
```

Figure 18 demonstrates how scientists can index or access the series named “median_income” to display the data from all data frames. In other cases, scientists can access multiple series from the same data frame simultaneously.

Figure 19. Selecting data

```
import pandas as pd
cc=pd.read_csv("/content/sample_data/california_housing_test.csv")
ff=cc[["median_income","total_bedrooms","population"]]
print(ff)
```

```
      median_income  total_bedrooms  population
0            6.6085           661.0      1537.0
1            3.5990           310.0       809.0
2            5.7934           507.0      1484.0
3            6.1359            15.0        49.0
4            2.9375           244.0       850.0
...             ...             ...         ...
2995         1.1790           642.0      1258.0
2996         3.3906          1082.0      3496.0
2997         2.2895           201.0       693.0
2998         3.2708            14.0        46.0
2999         8.5608           263.0       753.0

[3000 rows x 3 columns]
```

According to Figure 19, data scientists can add the series intended for display using an extra layer of square brackets to cover multiple series simultaneously. In the example, scientists access the series including "median_income," "total_bedrooms," and "population."

When displaying all data, scientists can also perform filtering to select only the data involved in processing. The program can be written as presented in the following example:

Figure 20. Filtering

```
import pandas as pd
cc=pd.read_csv("/content/sample_data/california_housing_test.csv")
ff = cc[cc['population'] > 1429]
print(ff)
```

```
      longitude  latitude  ...  median_income  median_house_value
0       -122.05     37.37  ...         6.6085            344700.0
2       -117.81     33.78  ...         5.7934            270500.0
8       -122.84     38.40  ...         3.6696            194400.0
9       -118.02     34.08  ...         2.3333            164200.0
13      -117.03     32.97  ...         4.5625            231200.0
...         ...       ...  ...            ...                 ...
2982    -118.28     34.08  ...         3.1607            182000.0
2984    -117.59     33.88  ...         2.6111            107000.0
2987    -121.97     37.29  ...         5.3294            300300.0
2990    -118.23     34.09  ...         2.6923            150000.0
2996    -118.14     34.06  ...         3.3906            237200.0

[1103 rows x 9 columns]
```

As shown in Figure 20, scientists are able to filter data to select only instances with the series named "population" greater than 1,429. From the sample, the number of instances has dropped from a total of 3,000 to 1,103.

4. Data Processing in the Data Frame
   A. Data Processing within the Data Frame

When data scientists intend to operate on the data within the series and the variables acting as broadcast or small data, they can access the series variable and create broadcast variables to perform mathematical operations by writing the following program.

Figure 21. Using broadcast along with series variables

```
import pandas as pd
cc=pd.read_csv("/content/sample_data/california_housing_test.csv")
ff = cc['population']
b = 1000
c = ff - b
print(c)
```

```
0        537.0
1       -191.0
2        484.0
3       -951.0
4       -150.0
         ...
2995     258.0
2996    2496.0
2997    -307.0
2998    -954.0
2999    -247.0
Name: population, Length: 3000, dtype: float64
```

As shown in Figure 21, the scientists access the Series named "population," create a broadcast variable with a value of 1000, place it inside variable "b," then subtract the values of all data objects within the series from variable "b," and present the result through print commands.

B. Sorting data within a Data Frame

In the data survey process, data scientists can sort all instances within a dataset based on a particular series to explore trends and patterns in the data. The program can be written as shown in the example.

Figure 22. Sorting instances with series

```
import pandas as pd
cc=pd.read_csv("/content/sample_data/california_housing_test.csv")
cc.sort_values(by='median_house_value')
```

	longitude	latitude	housing_median_age	total_rooms	total_bedrooms	population	households	median_income	median_house_value
2001	-117.16	32.71	52.0	845.0	451.0	1230.0	375.0	1.0918	22500.0
1031	-123.08	40.40	10.0	365.0	102.0	140.0	49.0	1.7969	37500.0
2740	-119.97	36.44	18.0	1128.0	237.0	772.0	220.0	2.1771	39200.0
734	-117.65	35.00	36.0	1184.0	316.0	672.0	241.0	1.9107	39800.0
2555	-122.06	37.39	22.0	1236.0	290.0	413.0	274.0	3.6875	40000.0
...	...	...	...	...	...	...	...	...	...
1563	-118.44	33.98	21.0	18132.0	5419.0	7431.0	4930.0	5.3359	500001.0
1561	-122.06	37.27	16.0	1612.0	221.0	567.0	208.0	10.5793	500001.0
1510	-122.43	37.79	52.0	6186.0	1566.0	2065.0	1374.0	5.8543	500001.0
2738	-118.45	33.96	24.0	3097.0	791.0	1075.0	639.0	5.7230	500001.0
2999	-119.63	34.42	42.0	1765.0	263.0	753.0	260.0	8.5608	500001.0

3000 rows × 9 columns

As shown in Figure 22, data scientists utilize the '.sort_values' command to sort instances based on a particular series, facilitating the exploration of data patterns and trends. In the example, the dataset is sorted according to the series named median_house_value, arranging the data from the smallest to the largest values.

C. Dealing with missing values

Before proceeding with data analysis using data mining techniques, it is crucial for data scientists to survey and prepare the data, which involves checking for missing values within the data objects. To accomplish this, data scientists can write a program to detect and handle missing values by either eliminating the incomplete data objects or filling them with alternative values. The program can be structured as follows:

```
import numby
from numpy import nan as NA
```

Based on the syntax provided, data scientists utilize the 'NaN' command from the NumPy library in conjunction with other commands from the Pandas library to identify data containing NA or missing values. Subsequently, they replace those values with NaN as demonstrated in the example.

Figure 23. Verifying missing values

```
import pandas as pd
import numpy
from numpy import nan as NA

a = pd.Series([2,NA,4,5])
b = pd.Series([6,7,8,NA])
c = pd.Series([10,NA,12,13])

data = pd.DataFrame({'A':a,'B':b,'C':c})
data
```

	A	B	C
0	2.0	6.0	10.0
1	NaN	7.0	NaN
2	4.0	8.0	12.0
3	5.0	NaN	13.0

As shown in Figure 23, data scientists utilize the NaN command from the NumPy library to handle missing values in their dataset. By examining data containing NA text or missing values and replacing them with NaN, they demonstrate this process using three series, each containing NA-formatted data. Subsequently, they create a Data Frame from these series and display it, effectively replacing all NA-formatted data with NaN.

Programming in this manner enables data scientists to identify missing values within a dataset. To survey and prepare the data effectively, data scientists may opt to address these missing values by either removing incomplete data entries from the dataset or imputing them with alternative values. This process can be implemented using the following syntax.

variable = dataset variable.***dropna()***
variable = variable.***reset_index***(drop=True)

From the provided syntax, data scientists utilize the '.dropna()' command to eliminate data entries formatted as NaN. Subsequently, the '.reset_index(drop=True)' command is employed to reorganize the cleaned dataset. This process can be implemented as demonstrated in the following example.

Figure 24. Eliminating incomplete data

```
import pandas as pd
import numpy
from numpy import nan as NA

a = pd.Series([2,NA,4,5])
b = pd.Series([6,7,8,NA])
c = pd.Series([10,NA,12,13])

data = pd.DataFrame({'A':a,'B':b,'C':c})
dataclean = data.dropna()
dataclean = dataclean.reset_index(drop=True)
dataclean
```

	A	B	C
0	2.0	6.0	10.0
1	4.0	8.0	12.0

In the scenario depicted in Figure 24, data scientists extract the NaN-formatted data from the Data Frame stored in the 'data' variable. Subsequently, they utilize the '.dropna()' command to eliminate the NaN-formatted entries from the data frame, storing the cleaned data frame in the 'dataclean' variable. Next, they restructure the data frame using the '.reset_index(drop=True)' command, ensuring that only complete data entries remain. Finally, they display the result.

In this case, data scientists opt to fill incomplete data, such as by replacing it with the mean or substituting it with nominal values. The syntax for filling incomplete data with the mean is as follows:

variable = fillna(data.mean())variable.

From the syntax provided, data scientists utilize the '.fillna(data.mean())' command to fill incomplete data with the mean. This can be implemented as shown in the example below:

Figure 25. Filling missing values with the mean

```
import pandas as pd
import numpy
from numpy import nan as NA

a = pd.Series([2,NA,4,5])
b = pd.Series([6,7,8,NA])
c = pd.Series([10,NA,12,13])

data = pd.DataFrame({'A':a,'B':b,'C':c})
datamean = data.fillna(data.mean())
datamean
```

	A	B	C
0	2.000000	6.0	10.000000
1	3.666667	7.0	11.666667
2	4.000000	8.0	12.000000
3	5.000000	7.0	13.000000

As shown in Figure 25, the data scientists compute the mean of each series to generate an average. Subsequently, they use the 'fillna(data.mean())' command to fill the missing values in each series with its respective mean. Finally, they display all the data.

D. Dealing with Duplicate Data

In the process of surveying and preparing data, another aspect that scientists need to consider is how to handle duplicate data. Therefore, the initial step is to check whether the dataset imported into the Python command contains any duplicate data. This can be achieved using the following syntax.

variable.duplicated(keep=False)

From the syntax, data scientists can utilize the '.duplicated(keep=False)' command to determine whether the data objects within the data frame are duplicates. If the value is True, it indicates duplication while False indicates that the data object is unique. The program can be implemented as follows.

Figure 26. Verifying duplicate data

```
import pandas as pd
import numpy

a = pd.Series([1,4,4,7,7,10,10,13,16])
b = pd.Series([2,5,5,8,18,11,11,14,17])
c = pd.Series([3,6,6,9,9,12,12,15,9])

data = pd.DataFrame({'A':a,'B':b,'C':c})
print(data.duplicated(keep=False))
```

```
0    False
1     True
2     True
3    False
4    False
5     True
6     True
7    False
8    False
dtype: bool
```

	A	B	C
0	1	2	3
1	4	5	6
2	4	5	6
3	7	8	9
4	7	18	9
5	10	11	12
6	10	11	12
7	13	14	15
8	16	17	9

As shown in Figure 26, after creating a data frame from a series, data scientists check for duplicate data using the '.duplicated(keep=False)' command, and display the result through a print statement. Upon execution of the dataset, they find a total of four duplicates, indicated by the True value in the result.

After examining the duplicate data, data scientists can reduce this duplication while maintaining the integrity of the data frame structure in the data preparation process. The program can be written as follows:

variable.drop_uplicates(inplace=True)

The syntax allows data scientists to utilize the '.drop_duplicates(inplace=True)' command for reducing duplicate data. This program can be implemented as shown in the following example.

Figure 27. Reducing duplicate data

```
import pandas as pd
import numpy

a = pd.Series([1,4,4,7,7,10,10,13,16])
b = pd.Series([2,5,5,8,18,11,11,14,17])
c = pd.Series([3,6,6,9,9,12,12,15,9])

data = pd.DataFrame({'A':a,'B':b,'C':c})
data.drop_duplicates(inplace=True)
data
```

	A	B	C
0	1	2	3
1	4	5	6
3	7	8	9
4	7	18	9
5	10	11	12
7	13	14	15
8	16	17	9

As shown in Figure 27, data scientists utilize the '.drop_duplicates(inplace=True)' command to minimize data duplication. Following the execution of this command set, the duplication is reduced while preserving the structure of the data frame. The goal is to address data duplication issues, ensuring data integrity for analysis purposes.

E. Dealing with Outliers

Data scientists can identify outliers within datasets imported into Python commands, which typically consist of unusually high or low values. These outliers have the potential to skew the average value of a feature, thereby distorting the patterns and trends observed in the analyzed data. Consequently, they can introduce inaccuracies in data analysis results.

Therefore, data scientists can calculate z-values, which standardize the distribution of each feature within the dataset to a normal curve. If a data point falls beyond 3 standard deviations (SD) from the mean, either positively or negatively, it is identified as an outlier. Below is an example program demonstrating this approach.

Figure 28. Detecting outliers

```
import pandas as pd
import numpy as np
df = pd.read_csv("http://www.mosaic-web.org/go/datasets/galton.csv")

def z_score(high):
  outlierlimit = 3
  m = np.mean(high)
  sd = np.std(high)
  z = [(x - m) / sd for x in high]
  return np.where(np.abs(z) > outlierlimit)

for i in z_score(df.height)[0]:
  print(df[i:i+1])
print()

    family  father  mother sex  height  nkids
125     35    71.0    69.0   M    78.0      5
    family  father  mother sex  height  nkids
288     72    70.0    65.0   M    79.0      7
    family  father  mother sex  height  nkids
672    155    68.0    60.0   F    56.0      7
```

Data scientists import data into a command set and examine each data point within the data frame to determine if it qualifies as an outlier based on its z-value. This is achieved by applying the z-value algorithm to the data and checking if the resulting value exceeds 3 standard deviations from the mean. If the intention is to identify deficient-valued data points, the threshold is changed to -3 standard deviations. Subsequently, the command set filters and displays instances with z-values greater than 3, allowing scientists to identify potential outliers. However, it is advisable for scientists to consult domain experts to contextualize their findings and ensure accurate interpretations.

DEVELOPING DATA VISUALIZATION WITH MATPLOTLIB AND SEABORN LIBRARIES

Data scientists have the capability to create data visualizations to address the objectives of data exploration and presentation (Healy, 2018; Pajankar, 2021). Through the development of data visualizations, they can delve into data patterns encompassing trends and distributions. In Python, the Matplotlib and Seaborn libraries offer a range of commands that empower scientists to craft insightful visualizations for exploring data (Healy, 2018; Pajankar, 2021).

1. Line Chart

Data scientists have the capability to create line graphs composed of two datasets utilizing the .plot command from the Matplotlib library.

import matplotlib.pyplot as variable that executes a command set
Variable that executes the .plot([axis data x],[y-axis data])
Variables that run the .show() routine.

Based on the syntax, data scientists obtain the variable to execute the .plot command within the matplotlib.pyplot library to generate a line graph. Subsequently, the outcome is displayed using the .show() command. A program to create a graph is outlined below.

Figure 29. Creating a line graph

```
import matplotlib.pyplot as cc
cc.plot([2,5,6,7,9,12],
        [3,2,8,3,7,8])
cc.show()
```

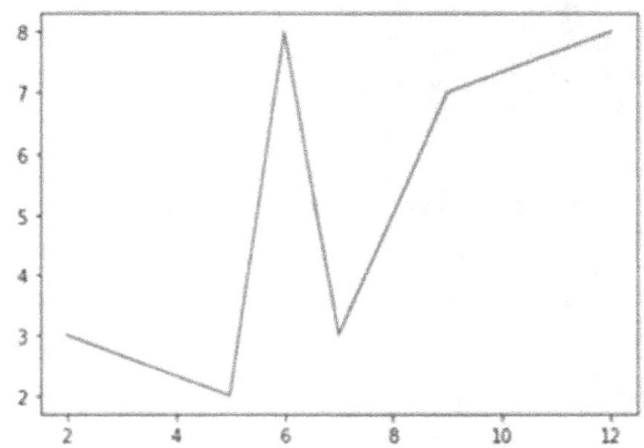

In the figure, data scientists utilize the variable 'cc' to execute the '.plot' command within the matplotlib.pyplot library. Subsequently, they organize the data for the x and y axes to generate a line graph, which is then displayed using the '.show()' command. If data scientists wish to enhance the line graph by including visual guidelines and annotating each part of the graph, they can create the program as illustrated in the following syntax:

import matplotlib.pyplot as variable that executes a command set
from matplotlip import style
style.use("ggplot")
Variable that executes .plot([axis data x],[y-axis data])
plt.title("Graphic label")
plt.xlabel("x-axis label")
plt.ylable("y-axis label")

Based on the syntax, the scientists import the 'style' command from the matplotlib library and assign the ggplot format. Then, they use the 'plt.title' command to create the graph label, 'plt.xlabel' command to create the x-axis label, 'plt.ylabel' command to create the y-axis label, and incorporate visual guidelines. The program is structured as illustrated in the following example.

Figure 30. Creating a ggplot patterned line graph

```
import matplotlib.pyplot as cc
from matplotlib import style
style.use("ggplot")
cc.plot([2,5,6,7,9,12],
        [3,2,8,3,7,8])
plt.title("Relationship of COVID-19 with Tourism")
plt.xlabel("COVID-19")
plt.ylabel("Tourism")
```

```
Text(0, 0.5, 'Tourism')
```

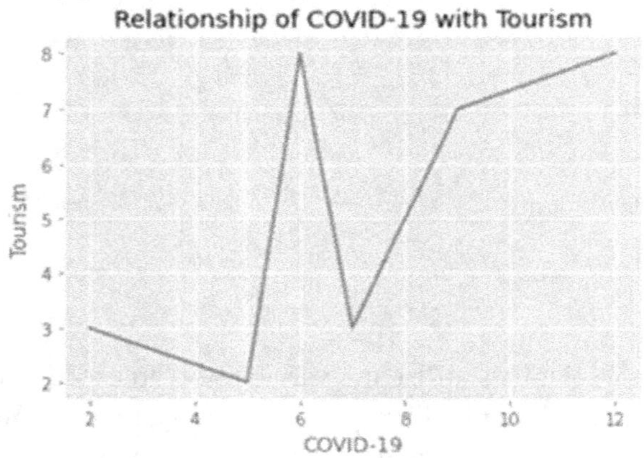

As shown in Figure 30, data scientists utilize the ggplot pattern to implement guidelines and to add graph titles and labels for the x- and y-axis. The graph represents quantitative data arranged based on clustered data. For example, it can demonstrate the correlation between COVID-19 incidence and tourism numbers, with quantitative data from 2020 and 2021 displayed as follows:

Figure 31. Presenting quantitative data by clustering

```
import matplotlib.pyplot as cc
from matplotlib import style
style.use("ggplot")
cc.plot([2,5,6,7,9,12],
        [3,2,8,3,7,8],
       label = 2020)
cc.plot([4,7,8,9,12,14],
        [5,4,10,5,9,10],
       label = 2021)
plt.title("Relationship of COVID-19 with Tourism")
plt.xlabel("COVID-19")
plt.ylabel("Tourism")
plt.legend()
```

```
<matplotlib.legend.Legend at 0x7fef66419750>
```

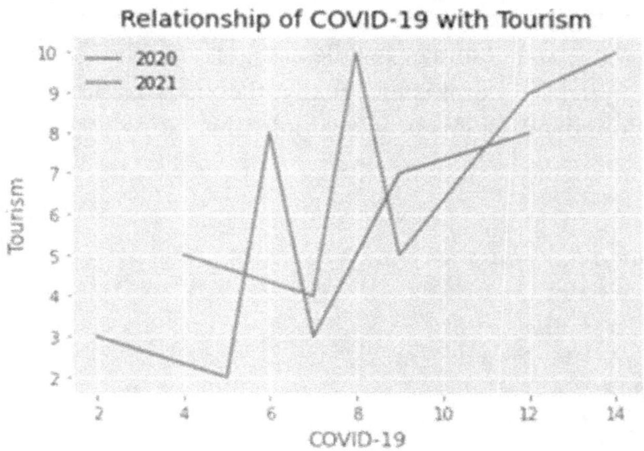

As shown in Figure 31, data scientists establish two data clusters representing the years 2020 and 2021, facilitating a comparison of COVID-19 incidence with tourism rates. Within each dataset, labels are assigned to differentiate data, implemented through the plt.legend() command, which generates data labels. The line graph for 2020 is depicted in orange while the line graph for 2021 is represented in blue.

2. Bar Chart

Data scientists have the capability to create bar charts by combining quantitative data with data utilized for classification. The program structure is outlined in the following syntax:

import numpy as nv
Import matplotlib.pyplot as a variable that runs the command to create a graph
Series acting as the x-axis = [data]
Series acting as the y-axis = [data]
variable that controls graphing = variable that executes the graphing command (len(Series acting as the y-axis)
variables that run commands to create graphs .bar(variables that control graph creation, Series that act as axes)
variables that run commands to create graphs .xticks(variables that control graphing, Series acting on the x-axis)
variables that execute the command to create graphs .show()

In the provided syntax, data scientists can establish a Series for both the x and y axes. The '.arange(len())' command quantifies the number of data points derived from the Series serving as the x-axis. Quantitative data representation can be accomplished using the '.bar' command while categorizing the data display can be achieved with the '.xticks()' command. Finally, the visualization can be rendered using the '.show' command. Below is an example illustrating how the program can be composed:

Figure 32. Creating a bar chart

```
import numpy as cc
import matplotlib.pyplot as p
x = ['Cat','Dog','Lion','Monkey']
y = [30,40,50,60]
ee = cc.arange(len(x))
p.bar(ee,y)
p.xticks(ee,x)
p.show()
```

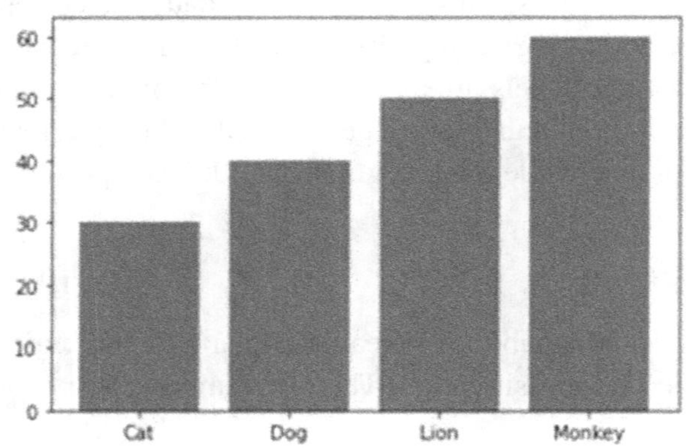

As shown in Figure 32, data scientists utilize the '.arange' command from the NumPy library to count and compile a bar chart with data-classifying variables. Subsequently, the variable 'p' executes a command to create a bar graph from the matplotlib.pyplot library. Upon generating data for the x-axis (types of animals) and y-axis (quantity of each animal), they create a bar chart based on the y-axis data and display them categorized by data types on the x-axis using the '.show()' command.

When data scientists aim to add descriptions to the bar chart, they can write a program similar to the following example.

Figure 33. Adding details to the bar chart

```
import matplotlib.pyplot as cc
cc.bar(
['cat','dog','lion','monkey'],
[30,40,50,60],
label = "Animal Quantity",
align = "center"
)
p.title("Animal in a Zoo")
p.xlabel("Animal Types")
p.ylabel("Quantity")
p.legend()
```

```
<matplotlib.legend.Legend at 0x7fd82ccc6ed0>
```

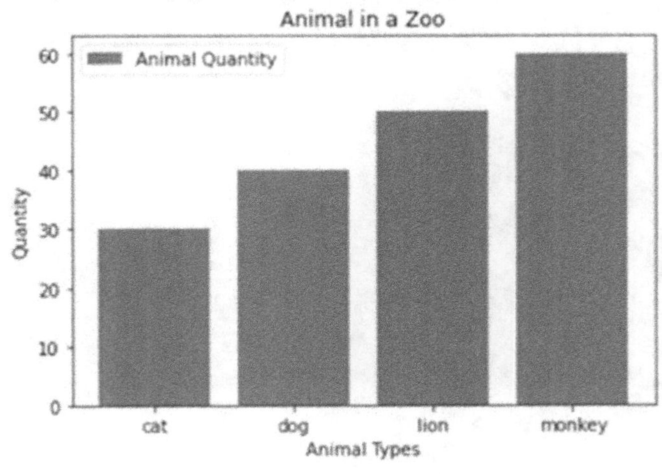

Data scientists can enhance the graph with more detailed descriptions. The graph can be titled using the '.title' command, followed by describing the x-axis with the 'p.xlabel' command, the y-axis with the 'p.ylabel' command, and finally, adding a legend for the bars using the 'p.legend()' command.

In cases where scientists aim to compare quantitatively-divided data and data categorized into two classifications, such as the number of zoo animals in 2020 and 2021, and the animal species, they can write programs to display the results as follows.

Figure 34. Creating two data sets to compare in the bar chart

```
import matplotlib.pyplot as cc
cc.bar(
['cat','dog','lion','monkey'],
[30,40,50,60],
label = "Animal Quantity 2020",
color = 'g',
align = "center",
alpha = 0.5
)

cc.bar(
['cat','dog','lion','monkey'],
[60,80,100,120],
label = "Animal Quantity 2021",
color = 'm',
align = "center",
alpha = 0.5
)

p.title("Animal in a Zoo")
p.xlabel("Animal Types")
p.ylabel("Quantity")
p.legend()
```

```
<matplotlib.legend.Legend at 0x7fd82cb40790>
```

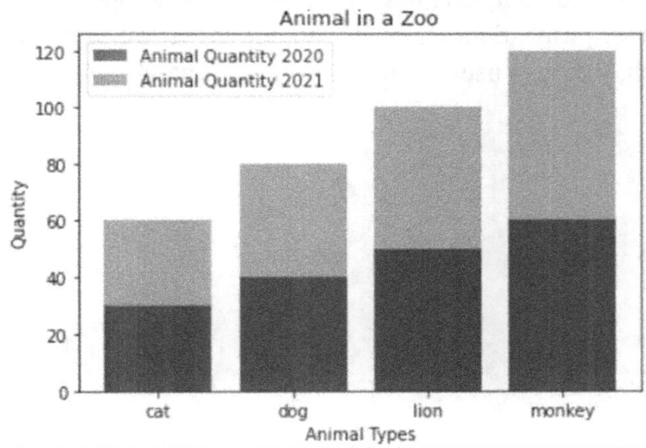

As shown in Figure 34, data scientists create two datasets representing the number of animals according to their types in 2020 and 2021. The bars representing 2020 data are shown in green while those for 2021 data are displayed in purple with a color intensity of 0.5. Despite the bars for both years being overlapped, it is evident that the 2021 data are depicted as having higher volume.

3. Pie Chart

To make a quantitative comparison of data in percentages by dividing the display by data types, data scientists can create a pie chart using the following syntax:

```
import matplotlib.pyplot as variables that execute the command
storage variable for categorization = [data used for categorization]
quantitative storage variables = [quantitative data]
variables that use pie command (quantitative storage variables,
labels = storage variables for categorization
autopct = "data display in percentage")
p.title("chart explaining Data")
p.show()
```

In the provided syntax, data scientists utilize a variable to execute the '.pie' command from the 'matplotlib.pyplot' library to create a pie chart. They prepare the data for categorization and quantification by defining storage variables for both. These variables are then used to generate the pie chart, with the categorization data stored in the 'labels' variable and the quantitative data in the 'sizes' variable. The percentages are displayed alongside the labels using the 'autopct' parameter.

To add a title to the graph, data scientists can utilize the 'plt.title' command, and to display the graph, they can use the 'plt.show()' command.

Figure 35. Creating a pie chart

```
import matplotlib.pyplot as cc
music = ["Mozart","Beethoven","Chopin","Wagner"]

r = [90,80,70,60]
cc.pie(r,
       labels = music,
       autopct = "%.1f%%")
cc.title("Popular Music in the World")
cc.show()
```

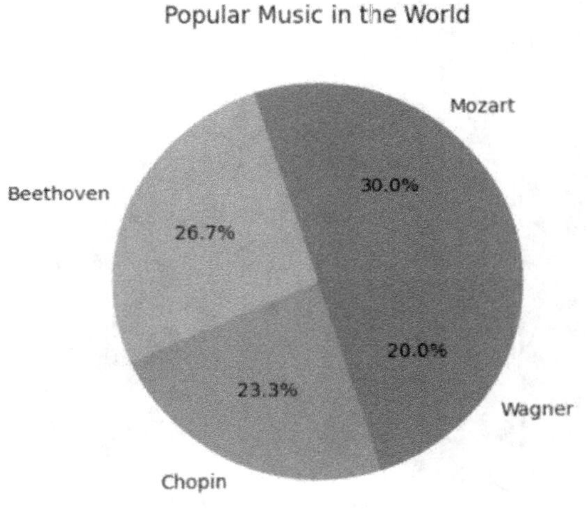

As shown in Figure 35, the scientists prepare the data for categorization and store the data in the 'music' variable. They also generate quantitative data and store the data in the 'r' variable. The purpose of the pie chart is to illustrate the percentage distribution of the total data.

When creating the pie chart, both the quantitative and categorization data are used to represent the proportions, and the result is displayed in percentage form using the 'autopct' command.

The sample pie chart depicts the proportion of popular classical songs worldwide. If the scientists wish to emphasize a specific proportion in the pie chart, they can write a program as follows:

Figure 36. The focus display of a particular aspect in the pie chart

```
import matplotlib.pyplot as cc
music = ["Mozart","Beethoven","Chopin","Wagner"]

r = [90,80,70,60]
e = [0,0.3,0,0.1]
cc.pie(r,
      labels = music,
      explode = e,
      autopct = "%.1f%%")
cc.title("Popular Music in the World")
cc.show()
```

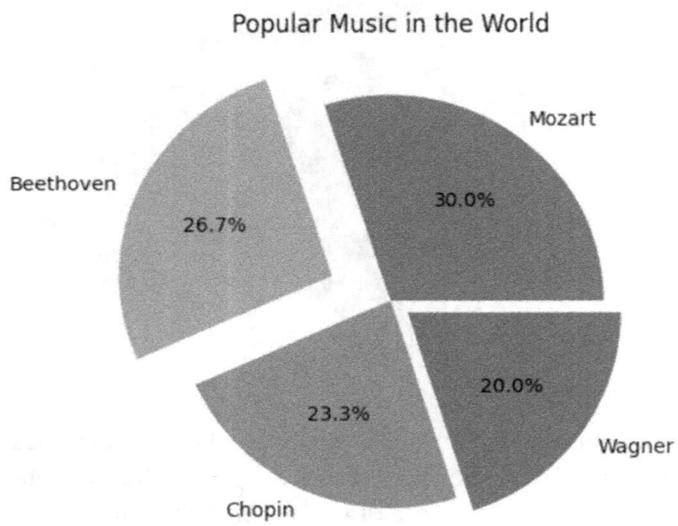

As shown in Figure 36, data scientists can adjust the position of specific portions on the pie chart to visually separate them from the rest of the proportions, enabling a focused display of desired data. This adjustment can be achieved using the ‘explode’ parameter when creating the pie chart.

When scientists aim to provide additional context for the data types represented on the graph by including legends, they can write a program similar to the following example:

Figure 37. Adding a legend to the pie chart

```
import matplotlib.pyplot as cc
music = ["Mozart","Beethoven","Chopin","Wagner"]

r = [90,80,70,60]
e = [0,0.3,0,0.1]
cc.pie(r,
       labels = music,
       explode = e,
       autopct = "%.1f%%")
cc.title("Popular Music in the World")
cc.legend()
cc.show()
```

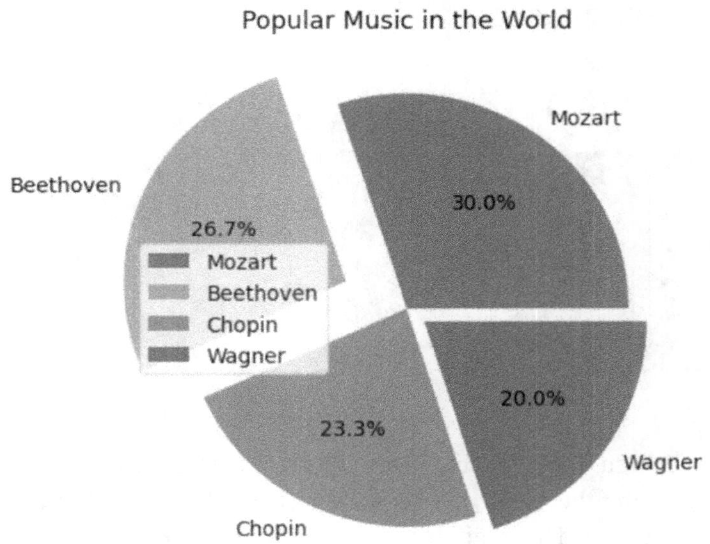

As shown in Figure 37, data scientists can utilize the classification datasets to create a legend for a pie chart using the '.legend()' command. In the example provided, a legend is generated to illustrate the colors representing different proportions classified within the datasets.

4. Histogram

Histograms are employed to examine the distribution of data, with the x-axis representing the frequency of data within a range, and the y-axis depicting the quantitative values corresponding to the same feature. As a result, histograms are constructed based on data from a single feature.

> import matplotlib.pyplot as variable that executes the command
> data containing variable = [data]
> variable that executes ***.hist***(data containing variable)

From the provided syntax, data scientists can populate variables with data and utilize the '.hist' command from the 'matplotlib.pyplot' library to generate a histogram. Below is an example demonstrating how to write the program:

Figure 38. Creating a histogram

```
import pandas as pd
import matplotlib.pyplot as plt
cc = pd.read_csv("/content/sample_data/california_housing_train.csv")
x = cc['median_income']
plt.hist(x)

(array([1833., 6100., 5020., 2466.,  891.,  368.,  152.,   79.,   42.,
          49.]),
 array([ 0.4999 ,  1.94992,  3.39994,  4.84996,  6.29998,  7.75   ,
         9.20002, 10.65004, 12.10006, 13.55008, 15.0001 ]),
 <a list of 10 Patch objects>)
```

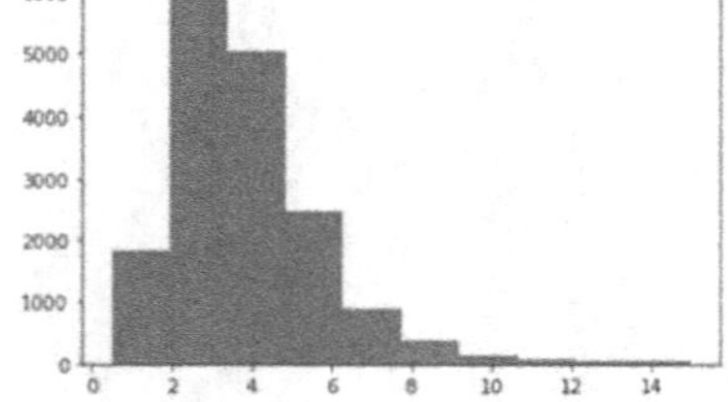

As shown in Figure 38, data scientists import the dataset named 'california_housing_train.csv' using the '.read_csv' command from the Pandas library. They then access the feature named 'median_income' and assign it to a variable x. Subsequently, they create a histogram using the '.hist' command. In this example, the frequency range of the data is depicted on the x-axis, derived from the 'median_income' feature while the y-axis represents the frequency or count of data points falling within each range. This enables the scientists to analyze the distribution of the 'median_income' feature during the data survey process.

The Seaborn library offers the '.distplot' command to data scientists, allowing them to create a graph combining a histogram with a line dispersion display. The syntax for using this command is as follows:

```
import seaborn as graphing variable
variable = data
graphing variable.displot(variable, kde=True)
```

Figure 39. Creating a density plot along with a histogram

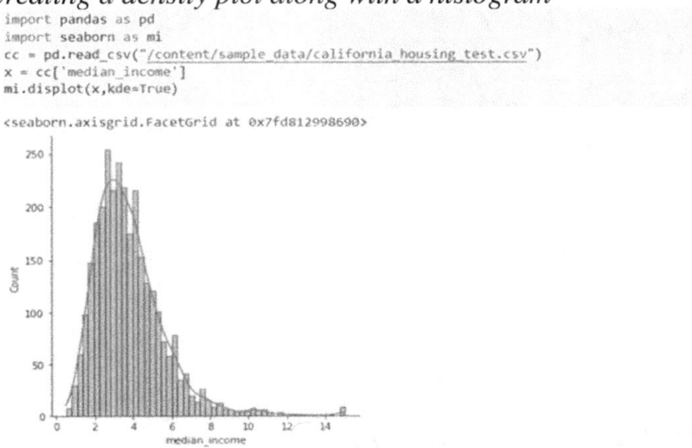

As shown in Figure 39, scientists use the '.distplot' command to construct a histogram showcasing the distribution of the dataset. They insert the dataset named California_housing_test.csv into the command and assign the feature named median_income to the variable x. This allows them to create a histogram using the '.distplot' command, providing insights into the distribution of data through both bar and line formats.

5. Density Plot

Data scientists create a density plot to explore the distribution of the data. They use the Seaborn library's '.kdeplot' command and insert the dataset named California_housing_test.csv. Then, they specify the feature named median_income to be analyzed. This creates a density plot where the y-axis represents the probability of the feature, providing insights into how the data are distributed.

```
import seaborn as graphing variable
variable = data
graphing variable.kdeplot(variable)
```

From the syntax, data scientists can create a Density Plot using the '.kdeplot' command from the Seaborn library.

Figure 40. Creating density plot

```
import pandas as pd
import seaborn as mi
cc = pd.read_csv("/content/sample_data/california_housing_train.csv")
x = cc['median_income']
mi.kdeplot(x)

<matplotlib.axes._subplots.AxesSubplot at 0x7fd81e82a1d0>
```

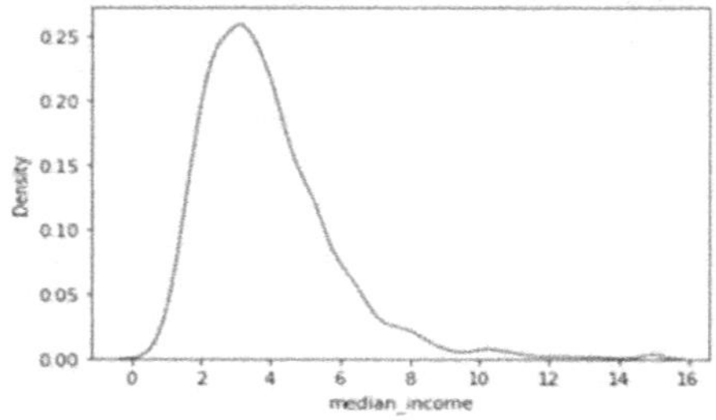

As shown in Figure 40, data scientists generate a Density Plot for data exploration by executing the .kdeplot command from the Seaborn library. In the example, the dataset "california_housing_train.csv" is imported, and the feature named "median_income" is assigned to the variable "x" to create the Density Plot. The x-axis represents data frequency while the y-axis represents the probability of the same feature.

6. Creating Box Plot

Data scientists can initially explore five statistics: the minimum value, the 25th percentile value, the median value, the 75th percentile value, and the maximum value, from the analyzed feature. These statistics can be represented in a Box Plot, which visualizes quantitative data along with its distribution.

> import seaborn as variable that executes a command set
> storage variable = command executing variable(data).
> data.boxplot(x= 'x-axis Feature', y= 'y-axis Feature', data = storage variable, order = [display of each type]

From the syntax, data scientists can create a Box Plot using the '.boxplot' command available in the Seaborn library. They specify the feature used for creating the x-axis, representing the classification data, and the feature used for creating the y-axis, representing quantitative data. The dataset is then passed into the Box Plot and rendered accordingly.

Figure 41. Creating box plot

```
import seaborn as mi
ee = mi.load_dataset('iris')
mi.boxplot(x='species', y = 'sepal_length', data = ee, order=["virginica","setosa","versicolor"] )

<matplotlib.axes._subplots.AxesSubplot at 0x7fd811e23650>
```

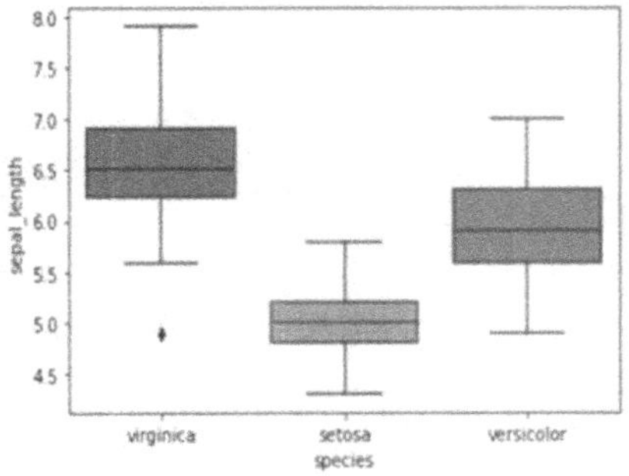

As shown in Figure 41, the scientists load a sample dataset in Python called iris by using the 'load_dataset' function from the Seaborn library, storing it in the variable 'ee', and then creating a Box Plot. The x-axis displays the feature named species, representing the names of Iris flower species while the y-axis displays the feature named sepal_length, representing the length of the Iris flower petal. The data from the 'ee' variable are then plotted in the Box Plot, organized according to the Iris species: virginica, setosa, and versicolor.

The Box Plot visually represents various statistical measures for each Iris flower species, including outliers, the smallest value, the 25th percentile, the median (50th percentile), the 75th percentile, and the largest value. It provides data scientists with insights into the distribution of data across different Iris cultivars, facilitating further analysis and classification using data mining techniques.

7. Scatter Plot

In the survey process, data scientists can utilize quantitative data from two or more features to generate a scatter plot, which visually depicts the relationship between the selected data points. Scatter plots are particularly useful for identifying outliers within the dataset.

import seaborn as variable that executes the command
variable = variable that executes the command(data)

data.regplot(x= Feature that creates the x-axis, y =Feature that creates the y-axis)

From the syntax, data scientists can generate a scatter plot to analyze the relationship between data points using the '.regplot' command available in the Seaborn library. This command allows for the visualization of the relationship between quantitative data from two or more features.

Figure 42. Creating scatter plot

```
import seaborn as mi
ee = mi.load_dataset('iris')
mi.regplot(x=ee["sepal_length"], y = ee["sepal_width"])

<matplotlib.axes._subplots.AxesSubplot at 0x7fd811d37690>
```

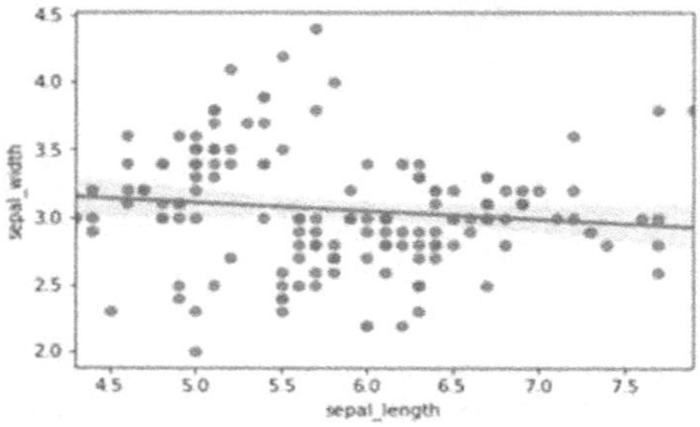

As shown in Figure 42, scientists utilize the Seaborn library's '.regplot' command to generate a scatter plot based on two features, namely sepal_length and sepal_width, sourced from the iris sample dataset. This scatter plot visually represents the relationship between the data points derived from these two features. Additionally, scientists can identify any outliers present within the scatter plot.

FEATURE ENCODING

When data scientists import a dataset into their programming environment to prepare it for analysis, they often employ techniques such as Label Encoding and One Hot Encoding.

1. Label Encoding by adding feature names and monitoring for incomplete data.

In situations where data scientists encounter datasets lacking feature names for use in data analysis, or containing incomplete data, they can address these issues by writing a program using the following syntax:

import pandas as the variable that executes commands
variable = [feature name data]
dataset storage variable = (header = None, names = variables, na_values= "?")
the variable that holds dataset.head()

From the provided syntax, data scientists utilize a variable to execute the '.read_csv' command from the pandas library. Subsequently, they assign the data within the variable as the feature names in the dataset and replace any missing values represented by '?' with NaN. The program can be implemented as follows:

Figure 43. Adding a feature name and monitoring for incomplete data

```
import pandas as pd
h = ["Number1", "Number 2", "Normalization"]

df = pd.read_csv("https://archive.ics.uci.edu/ml/machine-learning-databases/autos/imports-85.data",
                 header = None, names = h,na_values="?")
df.head()
```

			Number1	Number 2	Normalization
9.0	111.0	5000.0	21	27	13495.0
		5000.0	21	27	16500.0
9.0	154.0	5000.0	19	26	16500.0
10.0	102.0	5500.0	24	30	13950.0
8.0	115.0	5500.0	18	22	17450.0

3	NaN	alfa-romero	gas	std	two
1	NaN	alfa-romero	gas	std	two
2	164.0	audi	gas	std	four

In the provided scenario, the data scientists utilize the 'pd' variable to execute the '.read_csv' command from the pandas library to import the dataset "imports-85.data" into the command set. They then create a dataset to be used for naming features and store it in the variable 'names'. Additionally, they specify 'na_values="??"', indicating that any data object resembling a question mark should be replaced with NaN.

The '.head()' command is then used to display the first few rows of the dataset, revealing that the created dataset is indeed used for naming features. However, prior to naming features, it is crucial for data scientists to explore both the number of features and the nature of the data objects within each feature to facilitate effective programming and analysis.

2. Label Encoding by converting letters to numbers

In many cases, data scientists receive datasets containing textual information, such as gender, province, and region, which are used for classification. However, data mining techniques require numerical data for analysis. Hence, data scientists need to convert these textual categories into numerical values while preserving their classification properties. This can be accomplished using the following syntax.

replacement data storage variable = {"Text Data Object": Number}
dataset variable.replace(replacement data storage variable)

From the syntax, data scientists can specify a text data object representing categories within the dataset. They then assign numerical values to these categories while ensuring that the numerical values retain the classification properties of the original text. The program can be written as follows:

Figure 44. Turning texts into numbers

```
import pandas as pd
da = pd.DataFrame(["Cat","Lion","Dog"])
print(da)
convert = {"Cat": 1,"Lion": 2, "Dog": 3}
da.replace(convert)
```

```
      0
0   Cat
1  Lion
2   Dog
```

	0
0	1
1	2
2	3

As shown in Figure 44, the scientists use the variable 'pd' to execute the '.DataFrame' command from the Pandas library, creating a dataset containing 'Cat', 'Lion', and 'Dog'. This dataset is stored in the variable da and printed using the 'print' command. Next, they specify the numbers to replace the text data objects and store them in the 'convert' variable. The text is then replaced with numbers using the '.replace' command.

3. One Hot Encoding

In Label Encoding, each category is assigned a unique number, but this may imply ordinality that does not exist in the data. One Hot Encoding creates dummy variables for each category, which can better represent categorical data without imposing any ordinal relationship.

> Import pandas as dataset variables
> data storage variable = dataset variable.DataFrame({'data category':[data]})
> dataset variable.get_dummies(data storage variable, prefix=['data category'])

From the syntax, data scientists can create a DataFrame that stores data categories covering all data objects. They then quantify the text to be counted as quantitative data. Subsequently, dummy variables are created with numbers, consisting of 0 indicating no data and 1 indicating data presence.

Figure 45. Creating dummy data set from text

```
import pandas as pd
da = pd.DataFrame({'Animal': ['Cat', 'Dog', 'Lion','Lion','Lion']})
print(da)
pd.get_dummies(da,prefix=['Animal'])
```

```
  Animal
0    Cat
1    Dog
2   Lion
3   Lion
4   Lion
```

	Animal_Cat	Animal_Dog	Animal_Lion
0	1	0	0
1	0	1	0
2	0	0	1
3	0	0	1
4	0	0	1

As shown in Figure 45, the scientists create a DataFrame containing animal categories: Cat, Dog, Lion, Lion, and Lion. They display the result using the print command. When the data are transformed into dummy variables using the .get_dummies command, the resulting table shows the frequency of each category encountered. For example, if Lion appears three times in the original data, it is represented as a frequency of 3 in the dummy dataset with the value 1. This transformation quantifies text data by counting the frequency of occurrences.

4. Scikit-Learn Library

Python provides the Scikit-Learn library, which offers a set of commands for data mining. Data scientists can import datasets into the library and utilize mining commands to analyze them. Data analysis with machine learning (ML) can be approached in two main ways:

- Supervised learning involves splitting the dataset into two sets. The first set is used to train the machine to recognize patterns in the data while the second set is reserved for testing the accuracy of the trained model. Supervised learning techniques include regression, neural networks, and deep learning. These techniques not only forecast or classify data, but also assess the accuracy of predictions and classifications by comparing them with actual data, resulting in a closer alignment with reality.
- Unsupervised learning involves applying data mining techniques without instructing the machine to learn specific patterns. Clustering and Association Rule Mining are examples of unsupervised learning techniques.

The Scikit-Learn library offers a command set for data mining in both forms: Supervised learning and unsupervised learning. Data scientists can experiment with the commands provided by the Scikit-Learn library as demonstrated below.

Linear Regression Analysis examines the relationship between two features within a supervised learning model, necessitating the division of data into two sets: Train Set and Test Set (Sonu & Suyampulingam, 2021). Data scientists utilize the LinearRegression command from the Scikit-Learn library to perform regression analysis. They define features and target variables and then generate a scatter plot from the actual dataset. The model learns from the dataset by fitting it with the .fit command, enabling predictions for further analysis. Finally, the predicted values are used to create a Prediction Line on the Scatter Plot. To assess the accuracy of the predictions compared to the actual data, data scientists can use the Scikit-Learn library, following the example provided below.

Figure 46. Linear regression analysis

```
import matplotlib.pyplot as p
from sklearn.linear_model import LinearRegression

h = [[160], [165], [170], [173], [180]]
w = [[60], [65], [72], [75], [80]]
p.scatter(h, w)
p.title('Relationship of high and weight of 5 students')
p.xlabel('Student hight')
p.ylabel('Student weight')


model = LinearRegression()
model.fit(X=h, y=w)

w = model.predict([[175]])
print(w)

p.plot(h,model.predict(h))
```

```
[[75.97598628]]
[<matplotlib.lines.Line2D at 0x7fb6af4a6080>]
```

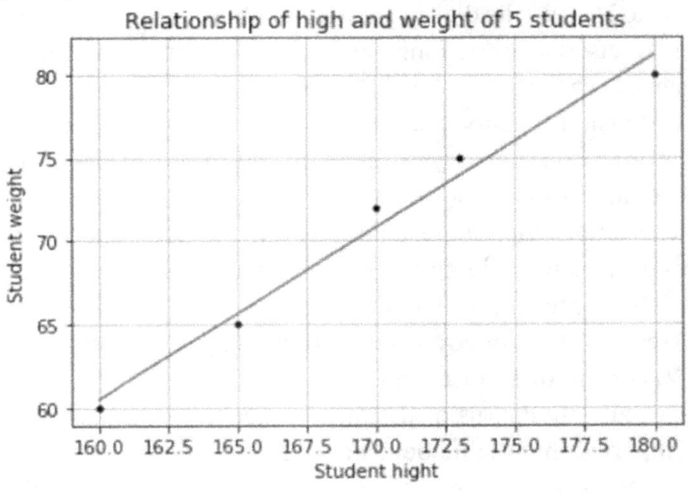

As shown in the graph above, the scientists have created a feature for height and a target variable for weight. A Scatter Plot is then generated, depicting data points where the x-axis represents height and the y-axis represents weight. The LinearRegression() command from the Scikit-Learn library is utilized to train the machine learning model with the height and weight datasets.

Using supervised learning regression analysis, the scientists predict the weight corresponding to a height of 175 cm. The result, 75.97 kg, is displayed using the print command. Subsequently, all forecasted data are used to generate a Prediction Line, demonstrating the proximity of the forecasted data to the actual data.

CLASSIFICATION

Data classification falls under the umbrella of supervised learning in data mining wherein data are partitioned into two segments: one for training the machine and the other for testing purposes. Target variables are defined as the outcomes of data classification. The inquiries align with methodologies employed in data analysis, such as categorizing bank customers based on their ability to repay loans or identifying coffee shop patrons likely to visit other coffee establishments. Decision trees are among the data mining techniques categorized as data classification methods (Cheewaprakobkit, 2019). Data scientists can utilize the sample dataset from 'sklearn.datasets' to conduct experiments in large data processing. They can then employ classification techniques by importing 'DecisionTreeClassifier()' from the tree module to classify the data using decision 'trees'. This involves partitioning the data into two sets: one for training the machine learning model and the other for testing its accuracy. The 'train_test_split' command from 'sklearn.model_selection' facilitates this division. Finally, data scientists can evaluate the accuracy of their data analysis using the 'accuracy_score' command from 'sklearn.metrics'.

While processing the data, scientists encapsulate decision tree techniques into variables. Subsequently, the sample dataset is split into two sets. The first set comprises features utilized for training machine learning models and their corresponding target variables, accounting for 60 percent of all instances while the second set encompasses features employed for testing along with their target variables, constituting 40 percent of all instances.

After categorizing the data using the decision tree technique, the data for machine learning are imported into the model using the '.fit' command. Subsequently, the data for testing, along with the model trained for learning, are classified using the '.predict' command. The effectiveness of data classification is then assessed using the 'accuracy_score' command, comparing the test target variables with the classified data. The results are presented using the 'print' command in the final step. Additionally, data scientists can visualize the results of data classification using decision trees by employing the 'tree.plot.tree' command.

To implement this, data scientists can run the program on the iris dataset, which comprises attributes such as petal width, petal length, sepal width, and sepal length, totaling 150 instances. The program is designed to classify the Iris cultivars, including Setosa, Versicolor, and Virginica, which are assigned as target variables. Below is an example of how the program can be written:

Figure 47. Programming for data analysis with decision trees

```
from sklearn.datasets import load_iris
from sklearn import tree
from sklearn import metrics
from sklearn.externals.six import StringIO
from sklearn.model_selection import train_test_split
from sklearn.metrics import accuracy_score
import seaborn as sns
import pandas as pd
import pydotplus
from IPython.display import Image

iris = load_iris()
sns.set
df = pd.DataFrame(iris.data)
df.columns = iris.feature_names
df.loc[:,'target'] = pd.Series(iris.target_names[iris.target])
sns.pairplot(df, hue='target')

model = tree.DecisionTreeClassifier()

x_trian, x_test, y_trian, y_test = train_test_split(iris.data,iris.target,test_size = 0.4)

model.fit(x_trian,y_trian)
expected = y_test
predicted = model.predict(x_test)
acc=accuracy_score(y_test,predicted)
print(acc)

dot_data = StringIO()
tree.export_graphviz(model, out_file=dot_data,
                     feature_names=iris.feature_names,
                     class_names=iris.target_names,
                     filled = True, rounded =True,
                     special_characters = True)
graph = pydotplus.graph_from_dot_data(dot_data.getvalue())
Image(graph.create_png())
```

As shown in Figure 47, data scientists have segmented the programming into three main parts:

1. Development of visual data using the Scatter Matrix for data exploration.
2. Data analysis employing the decision tree technique.
3. Displaying the accuracy of data analysis and data classification results obtained with decision trees.

Part 1: Data scientists load the iris dataset using load_iris(), create a DataFrame from it, and generate a Scatter Matrix visualization using the .pairplot command. The visualization includes features such as petal width, petal length, sepal width, and sepal length, along with the target variable, which is the Iris flower species. The resulting visualization is displayed in the image below.

Figure 48. Scatter matrix visualization for data exploration

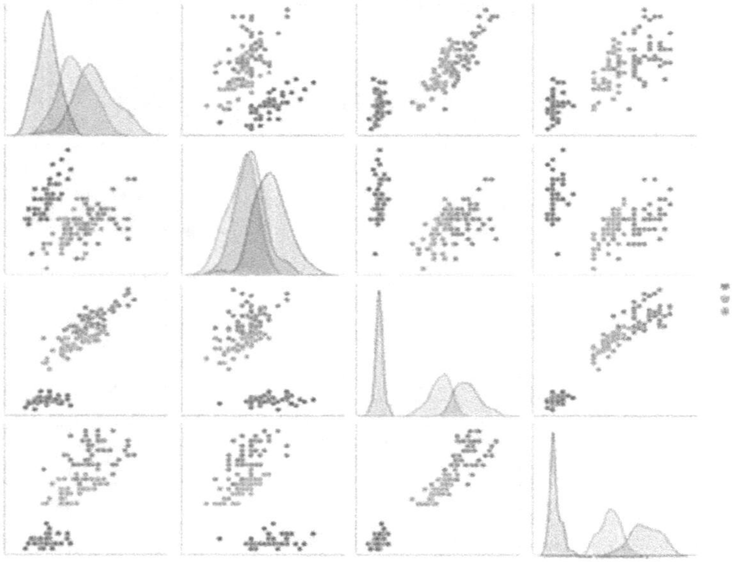

Part 2: Data scientists initialize a decision tree model using the tree.DecisionTreeClassifier command and then split the dataset into two parts: one for training the machine learning model (iris.data) and the other for testing (iris.target). The split is made with 60% of the data for training and 40% for testing. Each dataset contains features related to the characteristics of Iris flowers and their respective cultivars.

The machine learning dataset is then fed into the model using the .fit method, and the data are classified using the .predict command, applying the test features to the model. The accuracy of the classification is evaluated using the accuracy_score command, comparing the target variable data from the testing dataset with the results obtained from the classification. Upon executing the command set, the accuracy of the model is determined as follows:

Figure 49. Accuracy of data analysis with decision trees

```
0.9166666666666666
```

As shown in Figure 49, it can be observed that the accuracy of the data analysis is 91.66%, indicating a high level of accuracy and alignment with the actual data.

In Part 3, the scientists construct decision trees derived from the data analysis conducted in Part 2. They utilize the tree.export_graphviz command to generate a graphical representation of the analysis results. This graph illustrates the classification of Iris flower cultivars based on the features and target variables.

Figure 50. Decision tree model

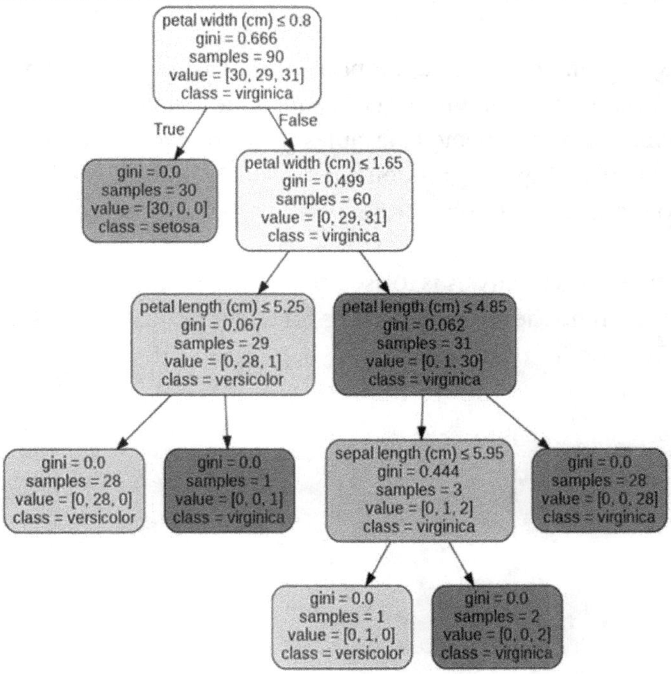

REGRESSION

When tasked with analyzing quantitatively correlated data, such as customer revenue and product sales, scientists can employ regression analysis to understand and predict the relationship. Regression analysis is a form of data mining technique falling under supervised learning, requiring data to be divided into two sets: one for training the model and the other for testing its accuracy.

Although this book has previously covered programming for simple regression analysis, this section will delve into programming for multiple linear regression and polynomial regression to enhance the understanding of regression analysis.

1. Multiple Linear Regression

In this scenario, when scientists aim to predict target variable outcomes using two or more feature data, they utilize multiple regression analysis (Rathaur, Kamath, & Ghanekar, 2020). Data scientists can delve into programming using multiple regression analysis techniques to predict target variables utilizing two or more features. The sample program is structured into three parts:

1. Feature Selection: to choose appropriate variables for data analysis.
2. Visualization: represented in a 3D Scatter Plot format to visually explore the data derived from the selected variables in the previous section.
3. Application of multiple regression analysis techniques to analyze the data pertaining to the target variables.

The objective of this analysis is to ascertain which features influence daily rental pricing and determine the optimal pricing for accommodation each day. Below is an example program for this purpose.

Figure 51. Multiple regression analysis

```
import matplotlib.pyplot as plt
import numpy as np
import pandas as pd
from sklearn.linear_model import LinearRegression
from sklearn.model_selection import train_test_split

df = pd.read_csv('/content/AB_NYC_2019.csv')
print(df.corr().abs().nlargest(3,'price').index)

fig = plt.figure(figsize=(18,15))
ax = fig.add_subplot(111, projection='3d')
ax.scatter(df['availability_365'],df['longitude'],df['price'],c='b')
ax.set_xlabel("availability_365")
ax.set_ylabel("longitude")
ax.set_zlabel("price")
plt.show()

x = pd.DataFrame(np.c_[df['availability_365'], df['longitude']],
                 columns = ['availability_365','longitude'])
y = df['price']
x_train, x_test, y_train, y_test = train_test_split(x,y,test_size=0.3)

model = LinearRegression()
model.fit(x_train,y_train)

price_perday = model.predict(x_test)
print(price_perday)

print('R-Sqaured: %.4f' % model.score(x_test,y_test))

Index(['price', 'longitude', 'availability_365'], dtype='object')
```

As depicted in Figure 51, the data scientists have structured the program into three distinct parts.

Part 1: Data scientists initiate the program by utilizing the read_csv command from the Pandas library to import the dataset into the instruction set. Subsequently, they conduct a correlation analysis between all features and the target variable, which in this case is the rental price per day, employing the .corr() command. The top three correlated features are identified as follows: “price” (target variable), “longitude” (property's location), and “availability_365” (number of days of service per year). This meticulous process, known as feature selection, enables data scientists to identify the most influential features for analysis. They can leverage this approach in collaboration with domain experts, stakeholders, or inquiries to pinpoint the features that significantly impact their performance. The results of this data analysis are as follows:

Figure 52. Feature selection operation

```
Index(['price', 'longitude', 'availability_365'], dtype='object')
```

Part 2: Once the data scientists have identified the features suitable for predicting target variables, they proceed to examine the data by plotting both features and target variables. This visualization aids in understanding the data distribution and identifying any outliers. To depict the relationships between the variables in a 3D format, a 3D Scatter Plot visualization is employed. In this visualization, each data point is represented by its values on the x, y, and z axes. Specifically, the feature "availability_365" is plotted on the x-axis, the longitude on the y-axis, and the target variable "price" on the z-axis. This approach allows for a comprehensive exploration of the data and facilitates the visualization of the relationships among the variables.

Figure 53. Surveying data with 3D scatter plot

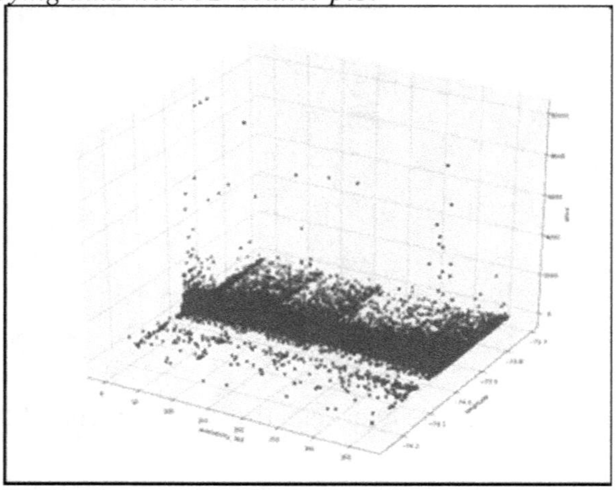

Part 3: Data Analysis with Multiple Regression Analysis

In this phase, data scientists perform data analysis using multiple regression analysis techniques. They first compile the features "availability_365" and "longitude" into a DataFrame, which is then assigned to the variable x to represent the observations. By combining features in this manner, they prepare the data for analysis with multiple regression. Next, the target variable, "price," is assigned to the variable y. The dataset comprising x and y is then split into two subsets: 60% for training the machine learning model and 40% for testing the model's performance. The model is instantiated using LinearRegression(), and the machine is trained on the training features and target variable. Subsequently, the data scientists utilize the model to predict daily accommodation prices. The .predict command is employed with the test features, and the predictions are displayed using the print command. The accuracy of the predictions is evaluated using the R-squared metric, which yields a value of 0.0274. This indicates a low level of accuracy, suggesting that the predicted values do not closely align with the actual data. The results of the analysis are depicted in the accompanying figure.

Figure 54. Forecast results and model accuracy values

```
[175.51704094 157.10322755 131.13947656 ...  84.28931985 131.47634801
 200.62518158]
R-Sqaured: 0.0274
```

To analyze data using multiple regression analysis techniques in Python, the LinearRegression() command is utilized similar to simple regression analysis. However, before analyzing with the target variables, multiple features are combined to create a DataFrame.

2. Polynomial Regression

When data scientists observe data through scatter plots and find that the data are not linear, they can utilize polynomial regression analysis techniques for more accurate predictions as suggested by Gong and Zhang (2021). Data scientists begin by defining a matrix to accommodate the data object within a feature variable, specifying the number of degrees for PolynomialFeatures. Subsequently, they employ the .fit_transform command to transform the data object into a matrix format, facilitating the forecasting of target variable values. This process enables them to generate a graph that visualizes the intersection of the actual data with the prediction line derived from the forecast, exhibiting high accuracy. Below is an example program demonstrating this process:

Figure 55. Programming with polynomial regression analysis technique

```
import matplotlib.pyplot as plt
from sklearn.linear_model import LinearRegression
from sklearn.model_selection import train_test_split
from sklearn.preprocessing import PolynomialFeatures

polynomail_features = PolynomialFeatures(degree = 2)

h = [[1.5],[2],[3],[4],[5],[6]]
w = [[1.5],[2.5],[4],[4],[4.5],[5]]

h_poly = polynomail_features.fit_transform(h)
print(h_poly)

model = LinearRegression()
model.fit(h_poly,w)

weight = model.predict(h_poly)
print(weight)

plt.scatter(h,w)
plt.plot(h, weight)
plt.show()

print('R-Sqaured: %.4f' % model.score(h_poly,w))
```

As shown in Figure 55, data scientists demonstrate the transformation of standard data into matrix form using the PolynomialFeatures command, adhering to the equation Y = B0 + B1X + B2X2. In this example, Degree is specified as 2, indicating that the matrix, ranging from 0 to 2, totals to 3. Subsequently, the values within the variable h are converted into this format before being assigned to the variable h_poly. The outcome of the data transformation is presented as follows:

Figure 56. Results of data processing with PolynomailFeatures

```
[[ 1.    1.5   2.25]
 [ 1.    2.    4.  ]
 [ 1.    3.    9.  ]
 [ 1.    4.   16.  ]
 [ 1.    5.   25.  ]
 [ 1.    6.   36.  ]]
```

Data scientists integrate the h_poly variable, serving as a feature, with the w variable, acting as the target variable. Utilizing the. fit command, the machine is trained to learn from this combined dataset. Subsequently, data analysis is conducted using the LinearRegression() command, followed by prediction with the h_poly variable. The forecasted outcome is then displayed using the print command.

Figure 57. Forecast results with polynomial regression analysis

```
[[1.71496131]
 [2.40472915]
 [3.52566638]
 [4.30180567]
 [4.73314703]
 [4.81969046]]
```

To demonstrate the effectiveness of the data analysis, data scientists generate a scatter plot using the initial variables h and w. Subsequently, a Prediction Line is generated using the forecasted data alongside the variable h_poly, which has been transformed using PolynomialFeatures to capture the underlying patterns. The accuracy of the analysis is then evaluated using the .score command, yielding a high accuracy rate of 94.74%, as depicted in Figure 58 below.

Figure 58. Results of data analysis by polynomial regression analysis technique

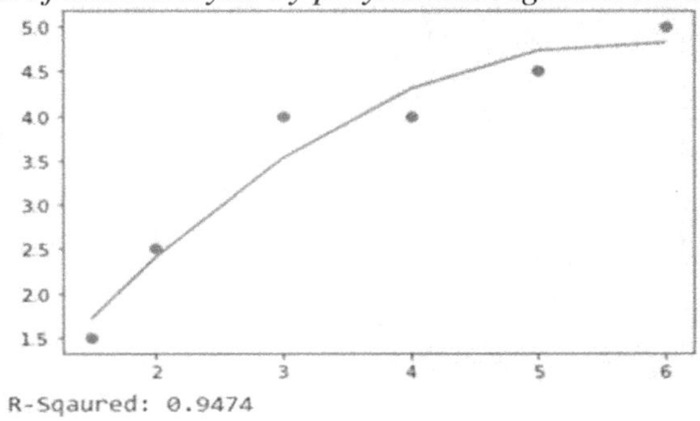

Polynomial regression analysis involves transforming data into matrix format, allowing for the utilization of non-linear features to analyze target variable data using the LinearRegression() command. As demonstrated by the samples, the forecasted results exhibit high accuracy.

FEATURE EXTRACTION

Data mining techniques rely on computational methods to process datasets, providing answers to specific questions. However, these techniques typically require numerical data. Often, data scientists receive datasets that contain text or images which cannot be directly used in data mining. To address this, feature extraction is employed to convert text or images into a numeric format, enabling their use in computational processes during data preparation. The Scikit-Learn library offers datasets that facilitate feature extraction for this purpose.

1. Sklearn.Feature_Extraction

The Scikit-Learn library offers a package called 'Sklearn.Feature_Extraction', which contains a collection of commands for feature extraction. Data scientists can utilize the '.fit_transform' command along with the dataset and the '.toarray()' command to convert all text into numbers in the form of an array. Additionally, they can display the feature names within the dataset using the '.get_feature_names()' command. Below is an example program for Feature Extraction:

Figure 59. Using the DicVectorizer command

```
from sklearn.feature_extraction import DictVectorizer

vec = DictVectorizer()

m = [{'Province':'Bangkok','Covid-19':200},
     {'Province':'Chiang Mai','Covid-19':300},
     {'Province':'Lampang','Covid-19':10}]

print(vec.fit_transform(m).toarray())
print(vec.get_feature_names())

[[200.   1.   0.   0.]
 [300.   0.   1.   0.]
 [ 10.   0.   0.   1.]]
['Covid-19', 'Province=Bangkok', 'Province=Chiang Mai', 'Province=Lampang']
```

As shown in Figure 59, data scientists utilize the 'DictVectorizer()' command to initialize the 'vec' variable for manipulating the data. They then create a dataset consisting of both text and numeric values and store it in the variable 'm'. Next, they convert this dataset into a numeric array using the '.fit_transform().toarray()' commands applied to the variable 'm'. Upon execution, the result obtained is a complete numeric array. Following this, the feature names are displayed using the 'get_feature_names' command. The output of the execution includes the text "Covid=19" and a list of provinces, namely Bangkok, Chiang Mai, and Lampang, which represent the text data.

2. Sklearn.Featue_Extraction.Text

When data scientists receive lengthy text or sentence datasets and aim to convert them into a numerical representation, they can utilize the 'CountVectorizer' command from the 'sklearn.feature_extraction.text' package. Data scientists utilize the 'CountVectorizer' command from the 'sklearn.feature_extraction.text' package. They create a variable to convert text into numeric data using the 'CountVectorizer(analyzer='word')' command. The variables are then employed to process the data within the dataset with the '.fit_transform().toarray()' command, and the feature names within the dataset are displayed with the '.get_feature_names()' command. Data scientists can write the syntax as shown in the example below.

Figure 60. Using CounVectorizer command

```
from sklearn.feature_extraction.text import CountVectorizer
d = ['College of Innovation is the leader of innovation',
     'in Thailand. Besides, There are many Professor',
     ' who expert in digital transformation and ',
     'service design.']
vec = CountVectorizer(analyzer='word')
print(vec.fit_transform(d).toarray())
print(vec.get_feature_names())

[[0 0 0 1 0 0 0 0 2 1 1 0 2 0 0 0 1 0 0 0]
 [0 1 1 0 0 0 0 1 0 0 0 1 0 1 0 1 0 1 0 0]
 [1 0 0 0 0 1 1 1 0 0 0 0 0 0 0 0 0 0 1 1]
 [0 0 0 0 1 0 0 0 0 0 0 0 0 0 1 0 0 0 0 0]]
['and', 'are', 'besides', 'college', 'design', 'digital', 'expert', 'in'
```

As shown in Figure 60, the scientists utilize the 'CountVectorizer(analyzer='word')' command to define the 'vec' variable for processing the data. Subsequently, the dataset stored in a variable is inserted into the '.fit_transform().toarray()' command to convert text into numeric data in an array format. The '.get_feature_names()' command is then employed to retrieve feature names from the source dataset, which are displayed using the print command.

3. Feature Hashing

If data scientists aim to ascertain the number of data objects converted from text into numeric data within the 'sklearn.feature_extraction' package, they can utilize the 'FeatureHasher' command. Data scientists employ the 'FeatureHasher' command from the 'sklearn.feature_extraction' package, specifying the number of data objects after processing. Subsequently, they utilize the '.transform' command to convert the data, displaying it in array format via the '.toarray()' command.

Figure 61. Using FeatureHasher

```
from sklearn.feature_extraction import FeatureHasher
hash = FeatureHasher(n_features=10)
Animal = [{'Lion': 1, 'Tiger':2, 'Cat':4}]
data = hash.transform(Animal)
data.toarray()

array([[-1.,  0.,  4., -2.,  0.,  0.,  0.,  0.,  0.,  0.]])
```

As shown in Figure 61, data scientists utilize the 'FeatureHasher' command from the 'sklearn.feature_extraction' package by defining the 'hash' variable to process the data, setting 'n_features' to a value of 10. This indicates that after processing, there will be ten numeric data objects. Subsequently, the dataset is stored in the 'Animal' variable, and the data are transformed into a numeric format using the '.transform()' command. Finally, the transformed data are stored in the 'data' variable and displayed as an array using the '.toarray()' command.

CONCLUSION

When embarking on Python for big data analysis, data scientists should acknowledge the plethora of libraries available to facilitate their work, such as Pandas, NumPy, SciPy, and Scikit-Learn. Beyond merely grasping commands and programming techniques, familiarity with data mining becomes essential for selecting the appropriate technique to tackle specific problems. Python supports the exploration of data through visualization and its preparation. Serving as a tool for data science processes and big data analytics, Python optimizes digital resource usage. Moreover, this book leverages Google Colab tools, enabling data scientists to write and test Python commands directly via a web browser, eliminating the need to install software editors and interpreters for libraries on their local computers.

EXERCISES

1. Write a program to generate a data frame from a dataset like this:
2. Write a program to create a dataframe from a dataset containing values 16, 20, and NA. Replace NA values with the mean of 16 and 20.
3. Write a program to perform one-hot encoding using the data provided in the following table:

Colors
Red
Red
Yellow
Green
Pink

4. Explain the distinction in data analysis approaches between Supervised Learning and Unsupervised Learning.

5. From the dataset that includes mileage and oil data, apply polynomial regression analysis to predict oil levels based on distance.

   Distance [2.5,4.6,5.6,3.2,6.6,3.1,3.2,3.3,4.5]

   Oil[2.2,5.5,5.2,4.1,4.2,4.4,3.2,2.2,1.4]

REFERENCES

Cheewaprakobkit, P. (2019). *Predicting student academic achievement by using the decision tree and neural network techniques*. Asia-Pacific International University.

Gong, Y., & Zhang, P. (2021). Predictive analysis and research of Python usage rate based on polynomial regression model. *2021 3rd International Conference on Artificial Intelligence and Advanced Manufacture (AIAM)*, 266–270.

Healy, K. (2018). *Data visualization: A practical introduction*. Princeton University Press.

Massaron, L., & Mueller, J. (2015). *Python for data science for dummies*. John Wiley & Sons, Inc.

Mueller, J., & Massaron, L. (2019). *Python for data science* (2nd ed.). John Wiley & Sons, Inc.

Pajankar, A. (2021). *Practical Python data visualization: A fast track approach to learning data visualization with Python*. Apress. DOI: 10.1007/978-1-4842-6455-3

Rathaur, S., Kamath, N., & Ghanekar, U. (2020). Software defect density prediction based on multiple linear regression. *2020 Second International Conference on Inventive Research in Computing Applications (ICIRCA)*, 434–439. DOI: 10.1109/ICIRCA48905.2020.9183110

Sonu, S. B., & Suyampulingam, A. (2021). Linear regression-based air quality data analysis and prediction using Python. *2021 IEEE Madras Section Conference (MASCON)*, 1–7. DOI: 10.1109/MASCON51689.2021.9563432

Chapter 11
Introduction to R Programming

ABSTRACT

This chapter serves as a comprehensive introduction to R programming, a widely used language for statistical computing and data analysis. Covering its history, features, and significance across various fields, including statistics, data science, and machine learning, the chapter aims to equip readers with fundamental skills to effectively utilize R. Beginning with practical aspects like installation and setup of RStudio IDE, we introduce basic concepts such as data types, variables, and operations. Subsequently, we explore data manipulation, visualization using ggplot2, and programming concepts like control structures and functions. Through examples and exercises, readers gain hands-on experience in writing R scripts and using conditional statements and loops. Finally, the chapter summarizes key concepts and provides guidance on further learning resources, empowering beginners to confidently embark on their journey in mastering R programming for data analysis tasks.

OVERVIEW OF R

A. What is R?

R is a powerful and versatile programming language specifically designed for statistical computing and data analysis (Lafaye de Micheaux, Drouilhet, & Liquet, 2013). Developed by Ross Ihaka and Robert Gentleman at the University of Auckland in the early 1990s, R was created to address the shortcomings of existing statistical software and provide researchers, statisticians, and data analysts with a free, open-source tool for analyzing data (Ihaka, 1994). At its core, R is a programming language that offers extensive capabilities for data manipulation, statistical

DOI: 10.4018/979-8-3693-6001-9.ch011

analysis, visualization, and machine learning. Its syntax is concise and expressive, making it easy to perform complex data operations and create sophisticated visualizations. R is widely used across various industries and academic fields for tasks such as data exploration, hypothesis testing, regression analysis, time series analysis, and predictive modeling (Derryberry, 2014: dos Santos, 2023). Its flexibility and extensibility are further enhanced by the vast ecosystem of packages available through the Comprehensive R Archive Network (CRAN), which provides thousands of contributed packages covering a wide range of statistical techniques and data manipulation tools (Mora et. al., 2020).

B. History and development of R

The development of R began in 1993 when Ihaka and Gentleman released the initial version of the language to the public. Since then, R has undergone continuous development and refinement, driven by contributions from a global community of users, developers, and researchers. One of the key milestones in R's development was the establishment of the Comprehensive R Archive Network (CRAN) in 1997. CRAN serves as the central repository for R packages, providing users with easy access to a vast collection of packages for data analysis, visualization, and machine learning. Over the years, R has evolved into a mature and robust language, with regular updates and releases introducing new features, improvements, and bug fixes. Today, R is widely recognized as one of the leading programming languages for statistical computing and data analysis, with a large and active community of users and developers worldwide.

C. Features and capabilities of R

R offers a rich set of features and capabilities that make it a powerful tool for data analysis and statistical computing. Some of the key features of R include the following:

1. Data Manipulation: R provides a wide range of functions and packages for manipulating data, including filtering, sorting, aggregating, and transforming datasets.
2. Statistical Analysis: R offers extensive support for statistical analysis, with built-in functions and packages for hypothesis testing, regression analysis, time series analysis, and more.
3. Data Visualization: R includes powerful tools for creating visualizations, including base graphics, lattice graphics, and the popular ggplot2 package, which allows users to create highly customizable and publication-quality plots.

4. Machine Learning: R provides a range of packages for machine learning, including the caret, randomForest, and xgboost packages, which allow users to build and train machine learning models for classification, regression, and clustering tasks.
5. Reproducible Research: R supports the concept of reproducible research, allowing users to document and share their analyses in a transparent and reproducible manner using tools such as R Markdown and knitr.

Overall, R's rich ecosystem of packages, its powerful capabilities for data manipulation and analysis, and its active community make it a valuable tool for researchers, data analysts, and statisticians across various fields.

IMPORTANCE OF LEARNING R

A. Growing popularity and adoption of R

In recent years, the popularity and adoption of R have experienced significant growth, driven by several factors. One key factor is the increasing demand for data analysis and statistical computing skills across industries. As organizations seek to leverage data to gain insights and make informed decisions, the need for tools like R that enable sophisticated data analysis and visualization has grown exponentially (Pandey, Srivastava & Verma, 2017: Min, & Zhou, 2021). Additionally, the rise of data science as a discipline has contributed to the growing popularity of R. Data scientists and analysts rely on R's rich set of features and packages for tasks such as exploratory data analysis, predictive modeling, and machine learning. The versatility and flexibility of R make it well-suited for tackling complex data analysis challenges in a wide range of domains. Furthermore, the open-source nature of R and its active community of users and developers have played a significant role in its increasing adoption. The availability of thousands of contributed packages through the Comprehensive R Archive Network (CRAN) allows users to extend R's functionality and address specific needs in their projects.

B. Applications of R in various fields

R finds applications across various fields, including statistics, data analysis, machine learning, and more. In the field of statistics, R is widely used for hypothesis testing, regression analysis, time series analysis, and multivariate analysis. Its rich set of statistical functions and packages make it a preferred tool for statisticians and researchers. In data analysis, R is used for tasks such as data cleaning, transformation, and visualization. The ggplot2 package, for example, provides a powerful and flexible framework for creating a wide range of visualizations, including scatter plots, bar charts, and heatmaps. In the field of machine learning, R is used for building and training machine learning models for tasks such as classification, regression, and clustering. Packages like caret, randomForest, and xgboost provide tools for model training, evaluation, and tuning, making R a popular choice among data scientists and machine learning practitioners. R is also used in academia for teaching and research purposes. Its intuitive syntax and extensive documentation make it accessible to students and researchers in various disciplines, from social sciences to biology and beyond.

Overall, the demand for R programmers is expected to continue growing as organizations increasingly rely on data-driven decision-making, creating abundant career opportunities in various industries and sectors.

GETTING STARTED WITH R

BASIC CONCEPTS IN R

In this section, we will cover fundamental concepts that form the backbone of R programming. Whether you are new to R or looking to refresh your knowledge, this section will provide you with a solid understanding of essential concepts for working effectively with R.

A. Data Types and Objects

1. In R, data types are fundamental building blocks used to store and manipulate data. The main data types in R include the following:

Numeric data types represent numerical values, such as integers or floating-point numbers. For example:

Figure 1. Numeric data in R script

```
x <- 10
y <- 3.14
```

Character data types represent text strings. They are enclosed in quotation marks (either single or double). For example:

Figure 2. Character data in R script

```
name <- "Sarawut Ramjan"
city <- 'chiang Mai'
```

Logical data types represent Boolean values, which can be either TRUE or FALSE. For example:

Figure 3. Logical data in R script

```
is_raining <- TRUE
has_license <- FALSE
```

R also supports other data types such as complex numbers, raw vectors, and factors although they are less commonly used in everyday programming.

2. Vectors, matrices, arrays, lists, and data frames

R provides several data structures to organize and manipulate data efficiently:

Vectors are one-dimensional arrays that can hold elements of the same data type. They can be created using the 'c()' function. For example:

Figure 4. Vector in R script

```
numeric_vector <- c(1, 2, 3, 4, 5)
character_vector <- c("apple", "banana", "orange")
```

Matrices are two-dimensional arrays that can hold elements of the same data type. They can be created using the 'matrix()' function. For example:

Figure 5. Matrix function

```
numeric_matrix <- matrix(1:6, nrow = 2, ncol = 3)
```

Arrays are multi-dimensional extensions of matrices. They can hold elements of the same data type. Arrays can be created using the 'array()' function. For example:

Figure 6. Array in R script

```
numeric_array <- array(1:12, dim = c(2, 3, 2))
```

Lists are versatile data structures that can hold elements of different data types. They can be created using the 'list()' function. For example:

Figure 7. List in R script

```
my_list <- list(name = "Sirawadee", age = 30, is_student = TRUE)
```

Data frames are two-dimensional data structures that can hold elements of different data types. They are similar to tables in a relational database or spreadsheets. Data frames can be created using the 'data.frame()' function. For example:

Figure 8. Data frames in R script

```
df <- data.frame(name = c("Sarawut", "Sirawadee", "Sirarat"),
                 age = c(16,17,18),
                 is_student = c(FALSE, TRUE, FALSE))
```

These data structures are essential for organizing and manipulating data in R. Understanding their characteristics and how to work with them is crucial for effective data analysis and programming in R.

B. Variables and Assignment

1. Assigning values to variables

In R, variables are used to store data values that can be referenced and manipulated throughout a script or session. To assign a value to a variable, you use the assignment operator '<-' or the equals sign '='.

Figure 9. Assigning values to variables

```
# Assigning values to variables using the assignment operator (<-)
x <- 10
y <- "Sirawadee Ramjan"

# Assigning values to variables using the equals sign (=)
z = TRUE
```

2. Naming conventions and best practices

When naming variables in R, it is essential to follow certain conventions and best practices to ensure readability and maintainability of your code. Here are some guidelines to consider:

- Descriptive Names: choose variable names that accurately describe the data they represent. This makes your code easier to understand and maintain.

Figure 10. Descriptive names

```
# Descriptive variable names
num_apples <- 10
message <- "Welcome to R programming!"
```

Use of Lowercase Letters: variable names in R are case-sensitive, but it is a common convention to use lowercase letters for variable names to distinguish them from function names.

Figure 11. Use of lowercase letters

```
# Lowercase variable names
total_sales <- 1000
```

Avoid Reserved Words: avoid using reserved words or built-in function names as variable names to prevent conflicts and confusion.

Figure 12. Avoid reserved words

```
# Avoid using reserved words as variable names
if <- 5  # This will result in an error
```

Consistent Naming Style: choose a consistent naming style and stick to it throughout your codebase. Whether you prefer snake_case or camelCase, consistency is key.

Figure 13. Consistent naming style

```
# Consistent naming style (snake_case)
user_age <- 30

# Consistent naming style (camelCase)
totalSales <- 1000
```

By following these naming conventions and best practices, you can write clean, readable, and maintainable R code that is easy to understand and collaborate on.

C. Basic Operations

1. Arithmetic operations

Arithmetic operations in R allow you to perform calculations on numeric values. The basic arithmetic operators are '+' (addition), '-' (subtraction), '*' (multiplication), '/' (division), and

'^' (exponentiation).

Figure 14. Arithmetic operations in R

```
# Arithmetic operations
x <- 10
y <- 5

# Addition
result_addition <- x + y  # Result: 15

# Subtraction
result_subtraction <- x - y  # Result: 5

# Multiplication
result_multiplication <- x * y  # Result: 50

# Division
result_division <- x / y  # Result: 2

# Exponentiation
result_exponentiation <- x ^ y  # Result: 100000
```

2. Comparison and logical operations

Comparison and logical operations in R are used to compare values and evaluate conditions. The comparison operators include '<' (less than), '>' (greater than), '==' (equal to), '!=' (not equal to), '<=' (less than or equal to), and '>=' (greater than or equal to). Logical operators include '&' (logical AND), '|' (logical OR), and '!' (logical NOT).

Figure 15. Comparison and logical operations in R

```
# Comparison operations
a <- 10
b <- 20

# Less than
result_less_than <- a < b  # Result: TRUE

# Greater than
result_greater_than <- a > b  # Result: FALSE

# Equal to
result_equal_to <- a == b  # Result: FALSE

# Not equal to
result_not_equal_to <- a != b  # Result: TRUE

# Less than or equal to
result_less_than_or_equal_to <- a <= b  # Result: TRUE

# Greater than or equal to
result_greater_than_or_equal_to <- a >= b  # Result: FALSE

# Logical operations
c <- TRUE
d <- FALSE

# Logical AND
result_logical_and <- c & d  # Result: FALSE

# Logical OR
result_logical_or <- c | d  # Result: TRUE

# Logical NOT
result_logical_not <- !c  # Result: FALSE
```

3. Vectorized operations

Vectorized operations in R allow you to perform operations on entire vectors or arrays at once, making code more concise and efficient.

Figure 16. Vectorized operations in R

```
# Vectorized operations
vector1 <- c(1, 2, 3)
vector2 <- c(4, 5, 6)

# Element-wise addition
result_vector_addition <- vector1 + vector2  # Result: c(5, 7, 9)

# Element-wise multiplication
result_vector_multiplication <- vector1 * vector2  # Result: c(4, 10, 18)
```

Vectorized operations are particularly useful when working with large datasets or arrays as they allow for efficient computation without the need for explicit looping over individual elements.

WORKING WITH DATA IN R

A. Importing Data

1. Reading data from various file formats

Reading data from different file formats is a common task in data analysis with R. The 'read.csv()' function is commonly used to read data from CSV files while the 'read_excel()' function from the 'readxl' package is used for Excel files.

Figure 17. Reading data from Excel file

```
# Reading data from a CSV file
data <- read.csv("file.csv")

# Install and load the readxl package
install.packages("readxl")
library(readxl)

# Reading data from an Excel file
data <- read_excel("file.xlsx")
```

2. Loading built-in datasets

R comes with several built-in datasets that can be used for practice and learning purposes. These datasets are accessible using the 'data()' function.

Figure 18. Reading data from built-in dataset

```
# Loading a built-in dataset
data("mtcars")

# View the dataset
head(mtcars)
```

Other commonly used built-in datasets include 'iris', 'mtcars', 'ChickWeight', and 'airquality'. These datasets are often used in examples and tutorials to demonstrate various data analysis techniques.

B. Data Exploration and Manipulation

1. Summary statistics and basic data exploration

Summary statistics provide a concise overview of the characteristics of a dataset, such as measures of central tendency, dispersion, and distribution. The 'summary()' function provides a quick summary of numeric variables while 'str()' displays the structure of the dataset.

Figure 19. Summary statistics with R script

```
# Summary statistics
summary(mtcars)

# Structure of the dataset
str(mtcars)
```

2. Subsetting, filtering, and indexing data

Subsetting, filtering, and indexing data allow you to extract specific subsets of data based on certain criteria. You can use square brackets '[ ]' to subset rows and columns of a dataset.

Figure 20. Subsetting, filtering, and indexing data in R

```
# Subsetting rows based on condition
subset_data <- mtcars[mtcars$mpg > 20, ]

# Filtering rows based on condition
filter_data <- mtcars[mtcars$mpg > 20 & mtcars$cyl == 6, ]

# Indexing specific columns
index_data <- mtcars[, c("mpg", "cyl")]
```

3. Adding, removing, and modifying columns

You can add, remove, and modify columns in a dataframe using various functions and operators.

Figure 21. Adding, removing, and modifying columns in R

```
# Adding a new column
mtcars$new_col <- mtcars$mpg * 0.43

# Removing a column
mtcars$hp <- NULL

# Modifying a column
mtcars$wt <- mtcars$wt * 1000  # Convert weight to grams
```

These operations allow you to manipulate the structure and content of your dataset to better suit your analysis needs.

C. Data Visualization

Data visualization is a crucial aspect of data analysis, allowing for the exploration and communication of insights effectively. In R, the 'ggplot2' package is widely used for creating a variety of plots with customizable aesthetics.

1. Introduction to ggplot2 for creating plots

The 'ggplot2' package follows the grammar of graphics, making it intuitive to create complex plots by adding layers of visualization elements.

Figure 22. Example of scatter plot with R coding

```
# Load ggplot2 library
library(ggplot2)

# Example dataset
data <- data.frame(
  x = c(1, 2, 3, 4, 5),
  y = c(2, 3, 5, 7, 11)
)

# Create a scatter plot
ggplot(data, aes(x = x, y = y)) +
  geom_point() +
  labs(title = "Scatter Plot", x = "X-axis", y = "Y-axis")
```

Figure 23. Example of scatter plot in R

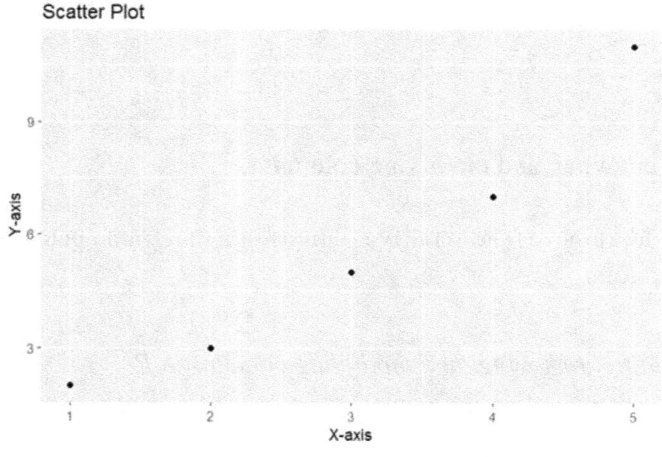

2. Creating basic plots

The ggplot2 allows for the creation of various types of plots, including scatter plots, histograms, bar plots, and more. A histogram is a graphical representation of the distribution of numerical data, showing the frequency of values within pre-defined bins.

Figure 24. Histogram example for basic plots

```
# Create a histogram
ggplot(data, aes(x = y)) +
  geom_histogram(binwidth = 1, fill = "skyblue", color = "black") +
  labs(title = "Histogram", x = "Values", y = "Frequency")
```

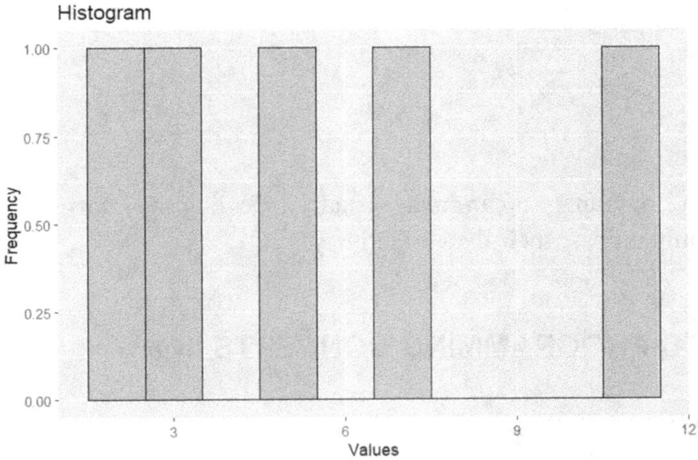

In this example, we create a histogram of the ‘y’ variable from our dataset ‘data’. We specify the ‘binwidth’ parameter to control the width of the bins in the histogram. The ‘fill’ and ‘color’ parameters are used to customize the fill and outline the colors of the bars, respectively.

3. Customizing plot aesthetics and appearance

The ggplot2 provides extensive options for customizing the appearance of plots, including colors, themes, labels, and annotations.

Figure 25. Customizing plot aesthetics and appearance with R coding

```
# Customizing plot aesthetics
ggplot(data, aes(x = x, y = y)) +
  geom_point(color = "red", size = 3, shape = 17) +
  theme_minimal() +
  labs(title = "Customized Scatter Plot", x = "X-axis", y = "Y-axis")
```

Figure 26. Example of customized scatter plot in R

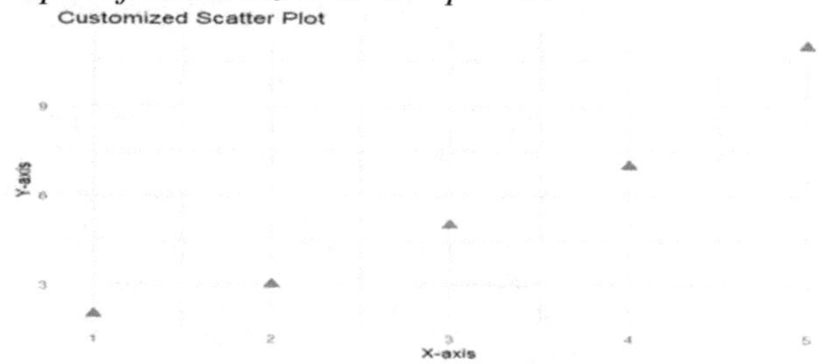

By leveraging ggplot2, data analysts can create visually appealing and informative plots to explore and communicate their data effectively.

INTRODUCTION TO PROGRAMMING CONCEPTS IN R

A. Control Structures

Control structures in R allow for the execution of specific code blocks based on certain conditions or for a certain number of iterations. They include conditional statements and loops.

1. Conditional statements

Conditional statements are used to execute different blocks of code based on whether a specified condition evaluates to 'TRUE' or 'FALSE'.

Figure 27. If-else condition in R

```
# Example of if-else statement
x <- 10

if (x > 0) {
  print("x is positive")
} else if (x < 0) {
  print("x is negative")
} else {
  print("x is zero")
}
```

In this example, if the value of x is greater than 0, the message "x is positive" is printed. If x is less than 0, "x is negative" is printed. Otherwise, if x equals 0, "x is zero" is printed.

2. Loops

Loops are used to iterate over a sequence of values or until a specified condition is met.

Figure 28. Loop in R

```
# Example of for loop
for (i in 1:5) {
  print(paste("Iteration:", i))
}

# Example of while loop
x <- 5
while (x > 0) {
  print(x)
  x <- x - 1
}
```

In the first example, a *for* loop iterates over the sequence of values from 1 to 5, printing each value along with the iteration number. In the second example, a *while* loop is used to print the value of 'x' while it is greater than 0, decrementing 'x' by 1 in each iteration.

Control structures are essential for implementing logic and flow control in R scripts, allowing for more dynamic and flexible code execution.

B. Functions

Functions in R allow for the encapsulation of reusable code blocks that perform specific tasks. They facilitate code organization, modularity, and reusability.

1. Writing and using functions in R

You can define your own functions in R using the function() keyword. Here is an example:

Figure 29. Function in R

```
# Define a function to calculate the square of a number
square <- function(x) {
  return(x^2)
}

# Use the function to calculate the square of 5
result <- square(5)
print(result)  # Output: 25
```

In this example, the 'square()' function takes one argument 'x' and returns its square. You can then call this function with a specific value to calculate its square.

2. Built-in functions and libraries

R comes with a wide range of built-in functions that perform common operations. Additionally, there are many libraries (also known as packages) available in R that provide additional functions for various tasks. You can use the 'library()' function to load a specific library into your R session and access its functions.

Figure 30. Example of built-in functions in R

```
# Load the ggplot2 library for data visualization
library(ggplot2)

# Use a built-in function to generate random numbers
random_numbers <- rnorm(100, mean = 0, sd = 1)
print(random_numbers)
```

In this example, the 'rnorm()' function generates 100 random numbers from a normal distribution with a mean of 0 and a standard deviation of 1. The 'print()' function is then used to display the generated numbers.

Functions are a fundamental concept in R programming, allowing you to encapsulate logic, improve code readability, and promote code reuse.

C. Error Handling

Error handling in R allows you to manage unexpected situations and handle errors gracefully. This section covers techniques for handling errors and exceptions, as well as debugging techniques.

1. Handling errors and exceptions in R

R provides several mechanisms for handling errors and exceptions:

Try-Catch Blocks, you can use 'tryCatch()' to attempt an expression and handle any resulting error or exception.

Figure 31. Try-catch blocks

```
# Example of tryCatch() for error handling
tryCatch({
  result <- 10 / 0  # Attempt to divide by zero
}, error = function(e) {
  print("Error occurred:")
  print(e$message)
})
```

In this example, if an error occurs during the execution of the expression inside the 'tryCatch()' block, the error message will be captured and printed.

2. Debugging techniques

Debugging in R involves identifying and fixing errors in your code. Some useful debugging techniques include the following:

- Print Statements: inserting 'print()' statements at strategic points in your code to print variable values and track the flow of execution.

Figure 32. Using print() statements for debugging

```
# Example of using print() statements for debugging
x <- 5
print(x)
```

- Interactive Debugging: RStudio provides a built-in debugger that allows you to set breakpoints, step through code execution and inspect variable values interactively.
- Browser Function: you can insert the browser() function at any point in your code to pause execution and enter an interactive debugging mode.

Figure 33. Interactive debugging

```
# Example of using browser() for interactive debugging
my_function <- function(x) {
  browser()
  y <- x * 2
  return(y)
}
```

These techniques help you to identify and fix errors in your code, ensuring that your programs run smoothly and produce accurate results.

CONCLUSION

Throughout this chapter, we have delved into the core concepts of R programming, covering its historical background, versatile features, and wide-ranging applications across diverse domains like statistics, data analysis, and machine learning. We have guided readers through the process of installing R and setting up RStudio, the preferred IDE for R development. Exploring fundamental concepts such as data types, variables, operations, and data manipulation has provided a solid grounding in R programming essentials. Moreover, we have introduced the art of data visualization using tools like ggplot2, enabling readers to gain insights from their datasets. Finally, we have explored programming constructs like control structures, functions, error handling, and debugging, empowering readers to write efficient and robust R code. By internalizing these key concepts, readers are poised to embark on their R programming journey with confidence, ready to tackle data analysis challenges head-on.

EXERCISE

1. Write a program that calculates the sum of two numbers and prints the result.
2. Create a vector with the numbers 1 to 10 and print it.
3. Load the built-in dataset "mtcars" and display the first few rows.
4. Write a function that takes two numbers as input and returns their product.
5. Plot a simple line graph with the points (1, 2), (2, 4), (3, 6), (4, 8), and (5, 10).

REFERENCES

Derryberry, D. R. (2014). *Basic data analysis for time series with R*. John Wiley & Sons, Inc. DOI: 10.1002/9781118593233

dos Santos, D. F. D., de Faria, P. R., Travençolo, B. A. N., & do Nascimento, M. Z. (2023). Influence of data augmentation strategies on the segmentation of oral histological images using fully convolutional neural networks. *Journal of Digital Imaging*, *36*(4), 1608–1623. DOI: 10.1007/s10278-023-00814-z PMID: 37012446

Ihaka, R., & Gentleman, R. (1994). *R: A language for data analysis and graphics*. Dept. of Statistics, School of Mathematical and Information Sciences, University of Auckland.

Lafaye de Micheaux, P., Drouilhet, R., & Liquet, B. (2013). *The R software: Fundamentals of programming and statistical analysis*. Springer. DOI: 10.1007/978-1-4614-9020-3

Min, S. H., & Zhou, J. (2021). smplot: An R package for easy and elegant data visualization. *Frontiers in Genetics*, *12*, 802894. Advance online publication. DOI: 10.3389/fgene.2021.802894 PMID: 34976028

Mora, C. M., Sicilia, M., García, B. E., & Sánchez, A. S. (2020). Evolution and prospects of the Comprehensive R Archive Network (CRAN) package ecosystem. *Journal of Software (Malden, MA)*, *32*(11), 1–14. DOI: 10.1002/smr.2270

Pandey, R., Srivastava, N., & Verma, K. (2017). Data visualization through R and Azure for scaling machine training sets. *2017 7th International Conference on Communication Systems and Network Technologies (CSNT)*, 345–349. DOI: 10.1109/CSNT.2017.8418564

Chapter 12
R Programming for Data Scientists

ABSTRACT

The chapter "R Programming for Data Scientists" provides a comprehensive guide for both novice and experienced data scientists seeking to utilize R for data analysis. It begins with an overview of R's significance in the data science domain and progresses to cover fundamental R programming concepts, data manipulation techniques, and advanced statistical analysis methods. Readers will learn to create insightful visualizations using ggplot2, perform statistical analysis, and explore data mining techniques such as association rule mining, clustering, classification, and anomaly detection. Advanced topics that include working with dates, writing functions, and integrating machine learning are also discussed. Throughout the chapter, practical examples and case studies demonstrate R's practical application in solving real-world data science challenges. By chapter end, readers will have gained proficiency in R programming and acquired the skills necessary to excel in data analysis tasks.

INTRODUCTION TO R PROGRAMMING FOR DATA SCIENTISTS

Get ready to dive into the world of data science with our new chapter on "Introduction to R Programming for Data Scientists"! Discover the power of R as a versatile tool for data analysis, visualization, and statistical modeling. Whether you are a beginner or an experienced data professional, this chapter will equip you with essential R programming concepts tailored specifically for data science applications. Learn to manipulate data, create stunning visualizations, perform statistical analysis, and explore advanced topics such as machine learning, all within the familiar environment of R (Bruce, Bruce, & Gedeck, 2020: Barman, Beckman & Chebaro, 2022: Llaudet, & Imai, 2023: Shilane, Crecchio & Lorenzetti, 2024).

DOI: 10.4018/979-8-3693-6001-9.ch012

A. Importance of R in data science

In the dynamic landscape of data science, where the volume and complexity of data are ever-expanding, the choice of programming language plays a pivotal role in enabling efficient data analysis, modeling, and visualization. Among the myriad of languages available, R stands out as a powerhouse tool tailored specifically for the needs of data scientists (Harry, 2021: R Statistical Programing Software for Data Science, 2021: Ditta & Woodward, 2022: Mailund, 2022). Its significance in the field of data science cannot be overstated, owing to several key factors.

Rich Ecosystem of Packages: R boasts an extensive repository of packages tailored to various data science tasks, covering data manipulation, statistical analysis, machine learning, and visualization. These packages provide ready-made functions and algorithms, allowing data scientists to streamline their workflows and focus on deriving insights from data rather than reinventing the wheel.

Statistical Prowess: R has its roots in statistical computing, making it inherently well-suited for statistical analysis and hypothesis testing. With a wide array of built-in statistical functions and packages, R empowers data scientists to perform complex statistical analyses with ease, ensuring robust and accurate insights into data patterns and relationships.

Powerful Visualization Capabilities: visualizing data is crucial for gaining insights and communicating findings effectively. R excels in this aspect with its ggplot2 package, which offers unparalleled flexibility and customization options for creating high-quality visualizations. From simple scatter plots to intricate multi-panel plots, R enables data scientists to craft visually compelling representations of data that facilitate meaningful interpretation.

Community Support and Collaboration: R benefits from a vibrant and supportive community of data scientists, statisticians, and programmers who contribute to its development and maintenance. This community-driven ecosystem fosters collaboration, knowledge sharing, and the continuous improvement of R's capabilities, ensuring that it remains at the forefront of data science innovation.

Integration with Other Tools and Technologies: R seamlessly integrates with other tools and technologies commonly used in the data science workflow, such as SQL databases, Hadoop, and Spark. This interoperability allows data scientists to leverage R's strengths in conjunction with other tools, enabling them to tackle diverse data analysis challenges efficiently.

B. Overview of R's capabilities for data analysis

R stands as a stalwart in the realm of data analysis, offering a comprehensive suite of tools and functionalities tailored to meet the diverse needs of data scientists. Its versatility and robustness make it a go-to choice for professionals across various industries. Let's delve into the key capabilities that R brings to the table for data analysis:

Data Manipulation – R provides powerful functions for reshaping, filtering, and merging datasets, streamlining data preprocessing.
Statistical Analysis – With strong statistical computing roots, R supports both basic and advanced statistical analyses for data exploration and interpretation.
Visualization – R excels in data visualization, particularly with ggplot2, enabling the creation of insightful and detailed graphics.
Machine Learning – R offers extensive machine learning packages for classification, regression, clustering, and dimensionality reduction.
Interactivity & Reproducibility – R allows real-time data exploration and supports reproducible workflows for transparent research documentation.
Integration & Extensibility – R integrates with SQL, Hadoop, and Spark while allowing users to develop custom functions and packages for specialized tasks.

In summary, R's capabilities for data analysis are extensive and multifaceted, making it an indispensable tool for data scientists seeking to extract actionable insights from data. As we delve deeper into R programming in this chapter, we will explore these capabilities in greater detail, equipping you with the knowledge and skills to leverage R effectively for your data analysis endeavors.

C. Brief comparison with other programming languages commonly used in data science

In the bustling landscape of data science, multiple programming languages vie for attention, each offering unique features and advantages. Let's briefly compare R with other prominent languages commonly used in data science:

- **Python –** A widely used language known for its simplicity, versatility, and extensive libraries for machine learning (e.g., scikit-learn, TensorFlow). While R excels in statistical analysis and visualization, Python offers broader applications, including AI and automation.
- **SQL –** A powerful language for querying relational databases but limited in statistical analysis and visualization. R provides specialized tools for in-depth data exploration and modeling.

- **Julia –** A high-performance language combining elements of R and Python, ideal for numerical computing (Migran, Anna & Dmitry, 2023). However, its ecosystem is still evolving compared to R and Python.

The choice of language depends on specific tasks and user preferences. R is ideal for statistical analysis and visualization, while integrating it with Python or SQL can enhance productivity in data science workflows.

DATA MANIPULATION AND CLEANING IN R

Data Manipulation and Cleaning in R explores essential preprocessing techniques to refine datasets for analysis. This chapter covers R's powerful tools for importing, cleaning, and reshaping data, handling missing values, and addressing outliers. Whether you're a beginner or an experienced data scientist, you'll gain the skills to prepare data for insightful analysis with confidence.

A. Data cleaning techniques

Data cleaning is a critical step in the data analysis process, ensuring that datasets are accurate and reliable for analysis. In R, handling missing values and dealing with outliers are common tasks. Let's demonstrate how to perform these techniques with an example dataset.

1. Handling missing value is essential in data preprocessing to maintain data quality and accuracy. Missing values can result from data collection errors, equipment failures, or human mistakes. Ignoring them can lead to biased results, so proper handling is crucial. R provides effective techniques to address missing values, ensuring data integrity for analysis.

Figure 1. Handling missing values in R

```
library(tidyverse)

# Example dataset with missing values
data <- tibble(
  id = c(1, 2, 3, 4, 5),
  age = c(25, 30, NA, 40, 45),
  income = c(50000, 60000, NA, 70000, 80000)
)

# View the dataset
print(data)

# Remove rows with missing values
clean_data <- na.omit(data)

# View the cleaned dataset
print(clean_data)
```

As shown in Figure 1, the command lines are as follows:

- library(tidyverse): This line loads the tidyverse package, which is a collection of R packages designed for data science tasks. It includes popular packages like ggplot2 for data visualization and dplyr for data manipulation.
- data <- tibble(...): This line creates a dataset named "data" using the tibble() function from the tidyverse package. The dataset consists of three variables: "id", "age", and "income". The "id" variable contains numeric IDs, the "age" variable contains ages with one missing value (NA), and the "income" variable contains income values with one missing value (NA).
- print(data): This line prints the "data" dataset to the console, allowing you to inspect its contents.
- clean_data <- na.omit(data): This line removes rows with missing values (NA) from the "data" dataset using the na.omit() function. It creates a new dataset named "clean_data" containing only the rows with complete data (i.e., no missing values).
- print(clean_data): This line prints the "clean_data" dataset to the console, allowing you to view the cleaned dataset without missing values.

Overall, this code demonstrates how to create a dataset with missing values, remove rows with missing values, and view the resulting cleaned dataset using R and the tidyverse package as shown in Figure 2.

Figure 2. Result of handling missing values in R

```
# A tibble: 4 × 3
     id   age income
  <dbl> <dbl>  <dbl>
1     1    25  50000
2     2    30  60000
3     4    40  70000
4     5    45  80000
```

Overall, the choice of handling missing values depends on factors such as the amount of missing data, the underlying data generating process, the nature of the analysis, and the goals of the study. It is important to carefully consider the implications of each approach and select the most suitable method based on the specific characteristics of the dataset and the analytical objectives.

2. Dealing with outliers is essential for accurate data analysis. Outliers may result from measurement errors, data entry mistakes, or genuine anomalies. Improper handling can distort analysis and bias results. R provides effective methods to identify and address outliers, ensuring reliable statistical and predictive modeling.

Figure 3. Dealing with outliers in R

```
# Filter out outliers based on the z-score of the 'age' variable
outliers <- data %>%
  filter(abs(scale(age)) > 2)  # Adjust threshold as needed

# View identified outliers
print(outliers)

# Remove outliers from the dataset
clean_data <- data %>%
  filter(abs(scale(age)) <= 2)  # Adjust threshold as needed

# View the cleaned dataset
print(clean_data)
```

As shown in Figure 3, the command lines are as follows:

- The code filters out outliers from the 'data' dataframe based on the absolute value of the z-score of the 'age' variable being greater than 2. The threshold of 2 can be adjusted as needed depending on the specific context and requirements.
- The identified outliers are stored in a dataframe named 'outliers'.

- The code then removes the outliers from the 'data' dataframe, creating a new dataframe named 'clean_data' containing only the rows where the absolute value of the z-score of the 'age' variable is less than or equal to 2.
- Finally, both the identified outliers and the cleaned dataset are printed to the console for inspection.

After executing the code, the third instance was excluded from the dataset, and the result appears as shown in Figure 4 below.

Figure 4. Result of dealing with outliers in R

```
# A tibble: 4 × 3
     id   age income
  <dbl> <dbl>  <dbl>
1     1    25  50000
2     2    30  60000
3     4    40  70000
4     5    45  80000
```

The choice of approach for dealing with outliers depends on factors such as the nature of the data, the specific analytical goals, and the potential impact of outlier removal or transformation on the analysis results. It is essential to carefully consider the implications of each approach and to select the most appropriate method based on the characteristics of the dataset and the objectives of the analysis.

B. Reshaping and transforming data

Reshaping and transforming data are often necessary to structure data in a format suitable for analysis. Let's demonstrate how to reshape and transform data using an example dataset.

1. Reshaping data in R involves restructuring the layout of datasets to better suit the desired analysis or presentation format. This process is often necessary when data is stored in a wide format but needs to be transformed into a long format or vice versa. Reshaping data allows for easier manipulation, visualization, and analysis.

Figure 5. Reshaped data in R

```
# Example dataset
wide_data <- tibble(
  id = c(1, 2, 3),
  variable1 = c(10, 20, 30),
  variable2 = c(100, 200, 300)
)

# Reshape data from wide to long format
long_data <- pivot_longer(wide_data, cols = -id, names_to = "variable", values_to = "value")

# View the reshaped data
print(long_data)# Example dataset
wide_data <- tibble(
  id = c(1, 2, 3),
  variable1 = c(10, 20, 30),
  variable2 = c(100, 200, 300)
)

# Reshape data from wide to long format
long_data <- pivot_longer(wide_data, cols = -id, names_to = "variable", values_to = "value")

# View the reshaped data
print(long_data)
```

As shown in Figure 5, the command lines are as follows:

- wide_data <- tibble(...): this line creates a dataset named "wide_data" using the tibble() function. The dataset contains three variables: "id", "variable1", and "variable2". Each variable is represented by a vector of values provided within the c() function.
- long_data <- pivot_longer(wide_data, cols = -id, names_to = "variable", values_to = "value"): this line reshapes the "wide_data" dataset from wide to long format using the pivot_longer() function. The cols = -id argument specifies that all columns except for the "id" column should be reshaped. The names_to = "variable" argument specifies the name of the new variable that will contain the column names from the wide format, and the values_to = "value" argument specifies the name of the new variable that will contain the values corresponding to each column.
- print(long_data): this line prints the reshaped dataset "long_data" to the console, allowing you to inspect its contents. The dataset now has a longer format, with each row representing a unique observation, and the "variable" column indicating the original variable name while the "value" column contains the corresponding values from the wide format.

After executing the code, the data are reshaped as shown in Figure 6.

Figure 6. Result of reshaped data in R

```
# A tibble: 6 × 3
     id variable  value
  <dbl> <chr>     <dbl>
1     1 variable1    10
2     1 variable2   100
3     2 variable1    20
4     2 variable2   200
5     3 variable1    30
6     3 variable2   300
```

Overall, reshaping data in R is a fundamental data manipulation task that allows for more efficient analysis and visualization of complex datasets. By understanding and implementing appropriate reshaping techniques, data scientists can transform their data into a format that best suits their analytical needs and facilitates further exploration and interpretation.

2. Transforming data involves modifying or converting the structure or values of the dataset to better suit the requirements of the analysis or to meet specific objectives. This process is essential for preparing the data for further analysis, visualization, or modeling. Transformations can include a wide range of operations, such as converting data types, creating new variables, scaling or standardizing variables, or aggregating data at different levels of granularity.

Figure 7. Transforming data in R

```
# Example dataset
data <- tibble(
  id = c(1, 2, 3),
  age = c(25, 30, 35)
)

# Transform age variable to categorical variable
data <- mutate(data, age_category = case_when(
  age < 30 ~ "Young",
  age >= 30 ~ "Old"
))

# View the transformed data
print(data)
```

As shown in Figure 7, the command lines are as follows:

- data <- tibble(...): this line creates a dataset named "data" using the tibble() function. The dataset contains two variables: "id" and "age". The "id" variable contains numeric IDs, and the "age" variable contains numeric values representing ages.
- data <- mutate(data, age_category = case_when(...)): this line uses the mutate() function from the dplyr package to create a new variable named "age_category" in the "data" dataset. The case_when() function is used to specify conditions for assigning values to the new variable based on the values of the existing "age" variable. If the "age" is less than 30, the value of "age_category" is assigned as "Young"; if the "age" is greater than or equal to 30, the value of "age_category" is assigned as "Old".
- print(data): This line prints the transformed dataset "data" to the console, allowing you to inspect its contents. The dataset now contains the original variables "id" and "age", as well as the new variable "age_category", which categorizes individuals into "Young" or "Old" based on their age.

Overall, these command lines demonstrate how to transform a numeric variable into a categorical variable based on specified conditions using the mutate() function in R. This type of transformation is commonly used for data preprocessing and analysis tasks. After executing the code, the data are transformed as shown in Figure 8.

Figure 8. Result of transforming data in R

```
# A tibble: 3 x 3
     id   age age_category
  <dbl> <dbl> <chr>
1     1    25 Young
2     2    30 Old
3     3    35 Old
```

Overall, transforming data is a fundamental step in the data analysis process, allowing data scientists to prepare and structure the data in a way that facilitates meaningful analysis and interpretation. By employing appropriate transformation techniques, data scientists can uncover insights, identify patterns, and derive actionable conclusions from the data.

C. Using the dplyr package for efficient data manipulation

Data manipulation is essential in data science for cleaning, transforming, and integrating data for analysis. It enhances feature engineering, supports data exploration through filtering and summarization, and prepares data for visualization. The **dplyr** package in R provides efficient functions for these tasks. Below is an example of how to use **dplyr** for data manipulation.

Figure 9. Data manipulation in R

```
# Example dataset
data <- tibble(
  id = c(1, 2, 3, 4),
  age = c(25, 30, 35, 40),
  income = c(50000, 60000, 70000, 80000)
)

# Filter rows based on condition
filtered_data <- data %>%
  filter(age > 30)

# View the filtered data
print(filtered_data)

# Group data by age and calculate mean income
summary_data <- data %>%
  group_by(age) %>%
  summarise(mean_income = mean(income))

# View the summary data
print(summary_data)
```

As shown in Figure 9, the command lines are as follows:

- data <- tibble(...): this line creates a dataset named "data" using the tibble() function. The dataset contains three variables: "id", "age", and "income". Each variable is represented by a vector of values provided within the c() function.
- filtered_data <- data %>% filter(age > 30): this line filters the "data" dataset to include only rows where the "age" variable is greater than 30. The %>% operator (pipe operator) is used to chain the filter() function to the dataset. The resulting filtered dataset is stored in a new object named "filtered_data".
- print(filtered_data): this line prints the filtered dataset "filtered_data" to the console, allowing you to inspect the rows that meet the filtering condition.
- summary_data <- data %>% group_by(age) %>% summarise(mean_income = mean(income)): this line groups the "data" dataset by the "age" variable and calculates the mean income for each age group. The group_by() function is used to specify the grouping variable, and the summarise() function calculates summary statistics within each group. The resulting summary data, containing the mean income for each age group, is stored in a new object named "summary_data".

- print(summary_data): this line prints the summary data “summary_data” to the console, displaying the mean income for each age group.

Overall, these command lines demonstrate how to filter rows based on a condition, and how to group data and calculate summary statistics using the dplyr package in R. After executing the code, the data are manipulated as shown in Figure 10.

Figure 10. Result of data manipulation in R

```
# A tibble: 4 × 2
    age mean_income
  <dbl>       <dbl>
1    25       50000
2    30       60000
3    35       70000
4    40       80000
```

Overall, data manipulation is a fundamental step in the data science workflow, allowing us to clean, transform, integrate, explore, and analyze data effectively, ultimately leading to informed decision-making and actionable insights.

DATA VISUALIZATION WITH R

Explore the principles and techniques of data visualization in R, from basic plots to advanced interactive visualizations. This section equips both beginners and experts with the skills to transform raw data into compelling visuals that reveal insights and support informed decision-making.

A. Creating basic plots (scatter plots, bar plots, histograms)

In this section, we will explore the fundamentals of creating basic plots using ggplot2 in R. Whether you are visualizing relationships between variables, comparing categorical data, or exploring the distribution of numeric variables, ggplot2 provides a simple yet powerful framework for generating a variety of plots.

1. Scatter plots are a fundamental tool for visualizing relationships between two continuous variables. With ggplot2, creating a scatter plot is straightforward. Simply specify the variables to be plotted on the x and y axes, and use the ‘geom_point()’ function to add points to the plot.

Figure 11. Scatter plot with R

```
library(ggplot2)

# Load the murders dataset
data("murders", package = "ggplot2")

# Create a scatter plot of murders with population on the x-axis and total on the y-axis
ggplot(murders, aes(x = population, y = total)) +
  geom_point() +
  labs(x = "Population", y = "Total Murders") +
  ggtitle("Scatter Plot of Murders by Population")
```

As shown in Figure 11, the command lines are as follows:

- library(ggplot2): this line loads the ggplot2 package into the R session, allowing us to use its functions for data visualization.
- data("murders", package = "ggplot2"): this line loads the "murders" dataset from the ggplot2 package into the R session. The "murders" dataset contains information about murders in US states, including variables such as population and total murders.
- ggplot(murders, aes(x = population, y = total)): this line initializes a ggplot object with the "murders" dataset as the data source and specifies the aesthetic mappings (aes) for the plot. It sets the x-axis to represent the "population" variable and the y-axis to represent the "total" variable.
- geom_point(): this line adds a layer to the ggplot object, specifying that the plot should be displayed as a scatter plot with points representing each observation.
- labs(x = "Population", y = "Total Murders"): this line adds labels to the x-axis and y-axis of the plot, specifying the names of the variables being plotted.
- ggtitle("Scatter Plot of Murders by Population"): this line adds a title to the plot, providing a descriptive title for the visualization.

Overall, these command lines create a scatter plot of murders with population on the x-axis and total murders on the y-axis, using the "murders" dataset from the ggplot2 package in R. After executing the code, the scatter plot appears as shown in Figure 12.

Figure 12. Example of scatter plot with R

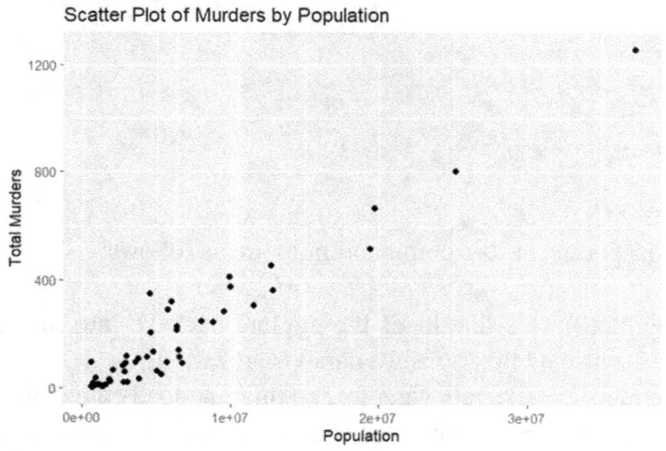

2. Bar plots are commonly used for visualizing the distribution of categorical data or comparing the frequency or proportion of different categories. To create a bar plot in ggplot2, specify the categorical variable to be plotted on the x-axis and use the 'geom_bar()' function to add bars to the plot.

Figure 13. Bar plot with R

```
# Create a bar plot of murders by region
ggplot(murders, aes(x = region, fill = region)) +
  geom_bar() +
    labs(x = "Region", y = "Number of Murders") +
    ggtitle("Bar Plot of Murders by Region")
```

As shown in Figure 13, the command lines are as follows:

- ggplot(murders, aes(x = region, fill = region)): this line initializes a ggplot object with the "murders" dataset as the data source. It specifies the aesthetic mappings (aes) for the plot, setting the x-axis to represent the "region" variable and the fill color of the bars to also represent the "region" variable.
- geom_bar(): this line adds a layer to the ggplot object, specifying that the plot should be displayed as a bar plot. By default, geom_bar() counts the number of observations in each category and creates a bar for each category.

- labs(x = "Region", y = "Number of Murders"): this line adds labels to the x-axis and y-axis of the plot, specifying the names of the variables being plotted.
- ggtitle("Bar Plot of Murders by Region"): this line adds a title to the plot, providing a descriptive title for the visualization.

Overall, these command lines create a bar plot of murders by region using the "murders" dataset in R with ggplot2. Each bar represents the number of murders in a specific region, and the regions are distinguished by different fill colors. After executing the code, the bar plot appears as shown in Figure 14.

Figure 14. Example of bar plot with R

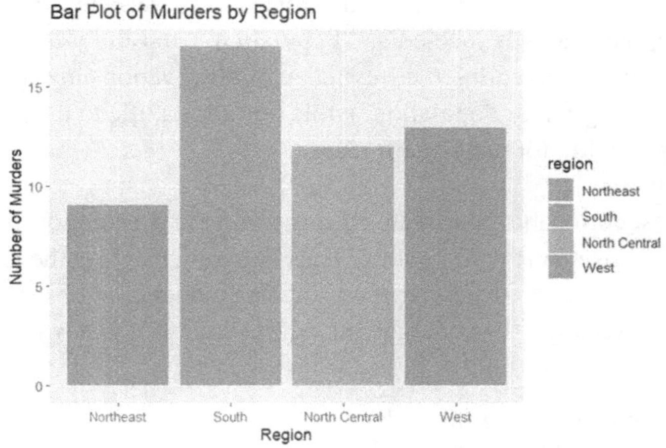

3. Histograms are used to visualize the distribution of a single numeric variable by dividing it into bins or intervals and representing the frequency or density of observations within each bin. To create a histogram in ggplot2, specify the numeric variable to be plotted and use the 'geom_histogram()' function.

Figure 15. Histogram with R

```
# Create a histogram of population
ggplot(murders, aes(x = population)) +
  geom_histogram(binwidth = 1000000, fill = "skyblue", color = "black") +
  labs(x = "Population", y = "Frequency") +
  ggtitle("Histogram of Population")
```

As shown in Figure 15, the command lines are as follows:

- ggplot(murders, aes(x = population)): this line initializes a ggplot object with the "murders" dataset as the data source. It specifies the aesthetic mappings (aes) for the plot, setting the x-axis to represent the "population" variable.
- geom_histogram(binwidth = 1000000, fill = "skyblue", color = "black"): this line adds a layer to the ggplot object, specifying that the plot should be displayed as a histogram using the geom_histogram() function. The binwidth argument sets the width of the bins in the histogram. Additionally, the fill argument specifies the fill color of the bars, and the color argument specifies the color of the borders of the bars.
- labs(x = "Population", y = "Frequency"): this line adds labels to the x-axis and y-axis of the plot, specifying the names of the variables being plotted. In this case, the x-axis is labeled as "Population", and the y-axis is labeled as "Frequency", representing the frequency of observations in each bin.
- ggtitle("Histogram of Population"): this line adds a title to the plot, providing a descriptive title for the visualization.

Overall, these command lines create a histogram of the "population" variable using the "murders" dataset in R with ggplot2. The histogram displays the distribution of population across states, with bars representing the frequency of observations within each bin. After executing the code, the histogram appears as shown in Figure 16.

Figure 16. Example of histogram in R

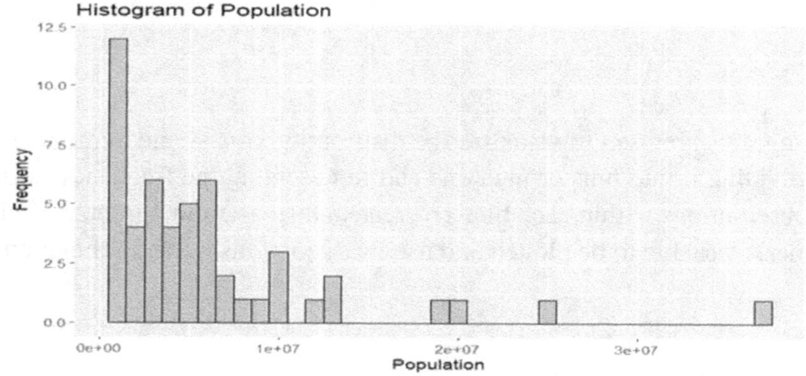

B. Customizing plots with themes, colors, and annotations

Customization plays a vital role in enhancing the visual appeal and interpretability of plots. In R, the ggplot2 package provides extensive options for customizing plots, allowing users to tailor visualizations to their specific needs and preferences. This section explores how to customize plots with themes, colors, and annotations to create visually stunning and informative visualizations.

Themes allow users to modify the overall appearance of plots, including elements such as fonts, grid lines, and background colors. ggplot2 provides several built-in themes, such as 'theme_gray()', 'theme_minimal()', and 'theme_bw()', each offering a different aesthetic style. Custom themes can also be created by specifying individual theme elements.

Color choices play a crucial role in distinguishing between different elements in a plot and conveying information effectively. ggplot2 allows users to customize colors for various plot components, including points, lines, bars, and backgrounds. Colors can be specified using hexadecimal codes, color names, or predefined color palettes.

Annotations provide additional context or information to plots, helping to highlight important features or insights. Annotations can include text labels, arrows, shapes, or lines, and can be added to specific plot locations using functions like 'geom_text()', 'geom_label()', or 'annotate()'.

For example, we can create a scatter plot of the murder rate against population using the murders dataset from the 'dslabs' package. We customize the plot by setting the color of the points to red, adding axis labels, setting a plot title, and applying the minimal theme to the plot. These customization options help to improve the clarity and visual appeal of the visualization, making it easier to interpret and understand as shown in Figure 17.

Figure 17. Customizing plots in R

```
library(ggplot2)
library(dslabs)

# Load the dataset from dslabs package
data("murders", package = "dslabs")

# Create a scatter plot of murder rate against population
ggplot(murders, aes(x = population, y = total)) +
  geom_point(color = "red") +  # Set point color to red
  labs(x = "Population", y = "Total Murders") +  # Set axis labels
  ggtitle("Scatter Plot of Total Murders by Population") +  # Set plot title
  theme_minimal()  # Apply minimal theme to the plot
```

As shown in Figure 17, the command lines are as follows:

- library(ggplot2): this line loads the ggplot2 package into the R session, providing access to functions and capabilities for creating plots.

- library(dslabs): this line loads the dslabs package into the R session. The dslabs package contains various datasets used for teaching and learning data science concepts.
- data("murders", package = "dslabs"): this line loads the "murders" dataset from the dslabs package into the R session. The "murders" dataset contains information about murders in US states, including variables such as population and total murders.
- ggplot(murders, aes(x = population, y = total)) +: this line initializes a ggplot object with the "murders" dataset as the data source. It specifies the aesthetic mappings (aes) for the plot, setting the x-axis to represent the "population" variable and the y-axis to represent the "total" variable.
- geom_point(color = "red") +: this line adds a layer to the ggplot object, specifying that the plot should be displayed as a scatter plot with points representing each observation. The color argument sets the color of the points to red.
- labs(x = "Population", y = "Total Murders") +: this line adds labels to the x-axis and y-axis of the plot, specifying the names of the variables being plotted.
- ggtitle("Scatter Plot of Total Murders by Population") +: this line adds a title to the plot, providing a descriptive title for the visualization.
- theme_minimal(): this line applies the minimal theme to the plot, modifying the overall appearance of the plot by adjusting elements such as fonts, grid lines, and background colors to create a minimalistic style.

Overall, these command lines create a scatter plot of total murders against population using the "murders" dataset in R with ggplot2. The plot is customized with red points, axis labels, a plot title, and a minimal theme to enhance its visual appeal and interpretability. After executing the code, the customizing plot appears as shown in Figure 18.

Figure 18. Example of customizing plots in R

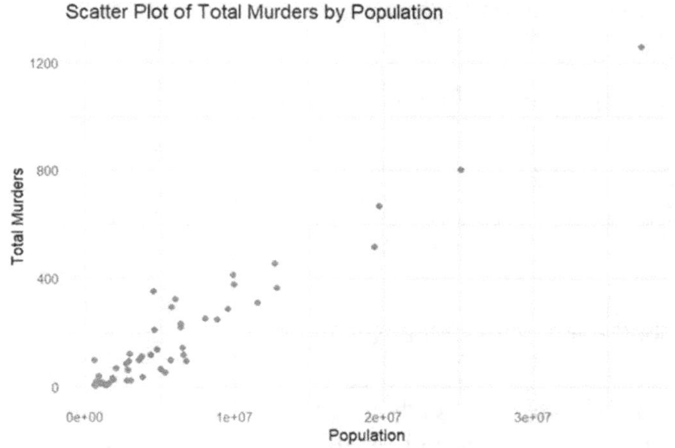

C. Visualizing relationships and patterns in data

Visualizing relationships and patterns in data is crucial during the data exploration step for several reasons:

- **Identifying Patterns** – Detect trends and structures in data that may not be obvious from raw numbers.
- **Spotting Outliers** – Easily identify anomalies that may indicate unique or unexpected phenomena.
- **Understanding Relationships** – Visualize variable interactions to aid predictive modeling and decision-making.
- **Exploring Complex Data** – Uncover hidden dependencies in multi-variable datasets.
- **Communicating Insights** – Present findings clearly to stakeholders for easier interpretation.
- **Hypothesis Generation** – Discover unexpected patterns that inspire new research questions.

In summary, visualizing relationships and patterns in data is essential for gaining a deeper understanding of the data, identifying trends and outliers, exploring complex datasets, communicating findings, and generating hypotheses. It is a critical step in the data exploration process that can lead to valuable insights and actionable recommendations. Therefore, data scientists can visualize a relationship between features by data visualization as shown in Figure 9.

Figure 19. Data exploration with scatter plot in R

```
library(ggplot2)

# Create a scatter plot of car weight against miles per gallon (mpg)
ggplot(mtcars, aes(x = wt, y = mpg)) +
  geom_point(color = "green") +  # Set point color to green
  labs(x = "Car Weight", y = "Miles per Gallon (mpg)") +  # Set axis labels
  ggtitle("Scatter Plot of Car Weight vs. Miles per Gallon (mpg)") +  # Set plot title
  theme_minimal()  # Apply minimal theme to the plot
```

As shown in Figure 19, the command lines are as follows:

- library(ggplot2): this line loads the ggplot2 package into the R session, providing access to functions and capabilities for creating plots.
- ggplot(mtcars, aes(x = wt, y = mpg)) +: this line initializes a ggplot object with the mtcars dataset as the data source. It specifies the aesthetic mappings (aes) for the plot, setting the x-axis to represent the "wt" (car weight) variable and the y-axis to represent the "mpg" (miles per gallon) variable.
- geom_point(color = "green") +: this line adds a layer to the ggplot object, specifying that the plot should be displayed as a scatter plot with points representing each observation. The color argument sets the color of the points to green.
- labs(x = "Car Weight", y = "Miles per Gallon (mpg)") +: this line adds labels to the x-axis and y-axis of the plot, specifying the names of the variables being plotted.
- ggtitle("Scatter Plot of Car Weight vs. Miles per Gallon (mpg)") +: this line adds a title to the plot, providing a descriptive title for the visualization.
- theme_minimal(): this line applies the minimal theme to the plot, modifying the overall appearance of the plot by adjusting elements such as fonts, grid lines, and background colors to create a minimalistic style.

After executing the code, the data exploration appears as shown in Figure 20.

Figure 20. Example of data exploration with scatter plot in R

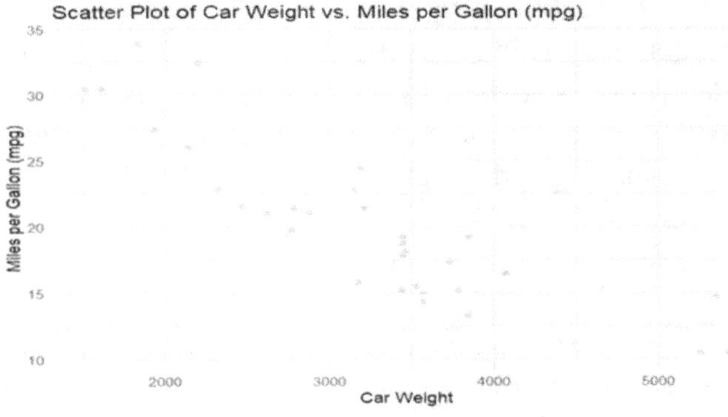

The provided code creates a scatter plot as shown in Figure 20 to visualize the relationship between car weight and miles per gallon (mpg) using the mtcars dataset. Let's discuss how this visualization can be used to explore relationships between features and its impact on data explanation.

1. Exploring Relationships, by plotting **car weight** against **miles per gallon**, we can visually explore their relationship using a scatter plot. This helps identify patterns, such as a potential negative linear relationship where heavier cars may have lower fuel efficiency. Additionally, clusters or outliers in the plot can offer further insights into data distribution and trends.
2. Impact on Data Explanation, A **scatter plot** provides a clear, intuitive way to communicate the relationship between **car weight** and **miles per gallon**, making it easier for stakeholders to understand trends without complex statistics. This visualization aids in **data-driven decision-making**, such as evaluating trade-offs in vehicle design or purchasing considerations based on fuel efficiency.

Overall, the scatter plot provides a powerful tool for exploring relationships between features in the data and conveying insights to others in a clear and interpretable manner. It enhances our ability to understand and explain the underlying patterns and dynamics within the dataset, facilitating informed decision-making and analysis.

STATISTICAL ANALYSIS WITH R

Explore statistical analysis in R, whether you're a beginner or an expert. This section covers descriptive statistics, hypothesis testing, regression analysis, and advanced methods to extract meaningful insights. Unlock R's full potential for data-driven decision-making and elevate your analytical skills.

A. Descriptive statistics

Descriptive statistics are essential for understanding the characteristics of a dataset. They provide a summary overview of the data, including measures of central tendency (such as mean, median, and mode) and measures of dispersion (such as range, variance, and standard deviation). Let's explore these concepts further with an example dataset and R coding:

Figure 21. Descriptive statistics with R

```
# Example dataset
data <- c(10, 15, 20, 25, 30, 35, 40, 45, 50)

# Summary statistics
summary_stats <- summary(data)
print(summary_stats)

# Measures of central tendency
mean_value <- mean(data)
median_value <- median(data)
mode_value <- table(data)[which.max(table(data))]  # Calculate mode
print(paste("Mean:", mean_value))
print(paste("Median:", median_value))
print(paste("Mode:", mode_value))

# Measures of dispersion
range_value <- range(data)
variance_value <- var(data)
sd_value <- sd(data)
print(paste("Range:", range_value))
print(paste("Variance:", variance_value))
print(paste("Standard Deviation:", sd_value))
```

As shown in Figure 21, we have a simple dataset containing numeric values. We then calculate various descriptive statistics using R:

- Summary Statistics: we use the summary() function to generate summary statistics, including minimum, 1st quartile, median, mean, 3rd quartile, and maximum values.
- Measures of Central Tendency: we compute the mean, median, and mode of the dataset to understand its central tendency. The mode is calculated by finding the most frequent value using the table() function.

- Measures of Dispersion: we determine the range, variance, and standard deviation to assess the spread or dispersion of the data.

These descriptive statistics provide valuable insights into the characteristics of the dataset, aiding in data exploration and decision-making processes as shown in Figure 22.

Figure 22. Example of descriptive statistics with R

```
   Min. 1st Qu.  Median    Mean 3rd Qu.    Max.
     10      20      30      30      40      50
[1] "Mean: 30"
[1] "Mode: 1"
[1] "Range: 10" "Range: 50"
[1] "Variance: 187.5"
[1] "Standard Deviation: 13.6930639376292"
```

B. Inferential statistics

Inferential statistics allow us to make inferences or predictions about a population based on a sample of data. Two fundamental techniques in inferential statistics are hypothesis testing and confidence intervals.

1. **Hypothesis testing** is a method used to evaluate a claim or hypothesis about a population parameter based on sample data. It involves setting up null and alternative hypotheses, calculating a test statistic, and determining the likelihood of observing the results if the null hypothesis were true. Let's conduct a hypothesis test using an example dataset from the R library.

The hypothesis being tested is whether there is a significant difference in the mean miles per gallon (mpg) between cars with four cylinders and cars with six cylinders.

The null hypothesis H_0 would typically state that there is no difference in the mean mpg between the two groups:

H_0: $\mu_{mpg\_4cyl} = \mu_{mpg\_6cyl}$

Where: $\mu_{mpg_{4cyl}}$ represents the population mean mpg for cars with 4 cylinders, and $\mu_{mpg_{6cyl}}$ represents the population mean mpg for cars with 6 cylinders.

The alternative hypothesis H_1 would then suggest that there is a difference in the mean mpg between the two groups:

$H_1: \mu_{mpg\_4cyl} \neq \mu_{mpg\_6cyl}$

The 't.test()' function in R will conduct a two-sample t-test to assess whether the observed difference in sample means is statistically significant, based on the assumptions of the test. The result of the test will indicate whether there is sufficient evidence to reject the null hypothesis in favor of the alternative hypothesis.

Figure 23. T-Test with R coding

```
data("mtcars")

# Filter the dataset to include only cars with 4 or 6 cylinders
mtcars_filtered <- subset(mtcars, cyl %in% c(4, 6))

t_test_result <- t.test(mpg ~ cyl, data = mtcars_filtered)
print(t_test_result)
```

As shown in Figure 23, we use the mtcars dataset from the R library to compare the mean miles per gallon (mpg) between cars with four and six cylinders. We conduct a two-sample t-test to determine if there is a significant difference in the mean mpg between the two groups as shown in Figure 24.

Figure 24. Example of T-test result from R execution

```
        Welch Two Sample t-test

data:  mpg by cyl
t = 4.7191, df = 12.956, p-value = 0.0004048
alternative hypothesis: true difference in means between group 4 and group 6 is not equal to 0
95 percent confidence interval:
  3.751376 10.090182
sample estimates:
mean in group 4 mean in group 6
       26.66364        19.74286
```

The Welch Two Sample t-test compares the mean miles per gallon (mpg) between cars with four cylinders and cars with six cylinders. Here is the interpretation of the results:

- Test Statistic (t-value): the calculated t-value is 4.7191. This value indicates the magnitude of the difference between the means of the two groups relative to the variability within each group.
- Degrees of Freedom (df): the degrees of freedom associated with the t-distribution is 12.956. This value is used to determine the critical value for the t-test and the precision of the estimate.

- p-value: the p-value associated with the t-test is 0.0004048. This p-value is less than the commonly used significance level of 0.05, indicating strong evidence against the null hypothesis. Therefore, we reject the null hypothesis and conclude that there is a statistically significant difference in the mean mpg between cars with four and six cylinders.
- Confidence Interval: the 95% confidence interval for the difference in means between the two groups is (3.751376, 10.090182). This interval provides a range of plausible values for the true difference in means. Specifically, we are 95% confident that the true difference in mean mpg between cars with four and six cylinders lies between approximately 3.75 and 10.09.
- Sample Estimates: the sample mean mpg for cars with four cylinders is 26.66364, and the sample mean mpg for cars with six cylinders is 19.74286. This provides insight into the central tendency of the data for each group.

In summary, the results of the Welch Two Sample t-test indicate a statistically significant difference in the mean mpg between cars with four and six cylinders, with cars with four cylinders having a higher mean mpg compared to cars with six cylinders.

2. **Confidence intervals** provide a range of values that are likely to contain the true population parameter with a certain level of confidence. They are calculated based on sample data and provide a measure of the precision of an estimate. Let's calculate a confidence interval for the mean miles per gallon (mpg) of cars with four cylinders using the same example dataset. As shown in Figure 23, we add a confident intervals calculation with R coding as Figure 25.

Figure 25. Confident intervals with R

```
ci <- t.test(mtcars$mpg[mtcars$cyl == 4])$conf.int
print(ci)
```

As shown in Figure 25, we calculate a 95% confidence interval for the mean mpg of cars with four cylinders using the t.test() function. The resulting confidence interval provides a range of values within which we can be 95% confident that the true mean mpg of cars with four cylinders lies as shown in Figure 26.

Figure 26. Result of confident intervals with R

```
[1] 23.63389 29.69338
attr(,"conf.level")
[1] 0.95
```

The result is 23.63389 and 29.69338 indicates that the 95% confidence interval for the mean miles per gallon (mpg) of cars with four cylinders is between approximately 23.63 and 29.69. We are 95% confident that the true mean mpg of cars with four cylinders falls within the range of approximately 23.63 to 29.69 miles per gallon. This means that if we were to repeat the sampling process multiple times and calculate a confidence interval for each sample, approximately 95% of these intervals would contain the true population mean mpg. The 'conf.level' attribute confirms that the confidence level associated with this interval is 95%, which aligns with the typical confidence level used for such analyses.

MACHINE LEARNING WITH R

Explore machine learning in R, from basics to advanced techniques. Learn to implement regression, classification, clustering, and more for real-world applications. This section equips you with the skills to leverage R for predictive modeling and data-driven decision-making.

A. Overview of machine learning algorithms available in R

R offers a rich ecosystem of machine learning algorithms that cater to various tasks, including regression, classification, clustering, and dimensionality reduction. An overview of some commonly used machine learning algorithms available in R is presented as follows:

- **Linear Regression** is a supervised learning algorithm used for predicting a continuous target variable based on one or more input features. In R, you can implement linear regression using the 'lm()' function.
- **Logistic Regression** is a classification algorithm used for binary classification tasks. It models the probability of a binary outcome based on input features. In R, logistic regression can be implemented using the 'glm()' function with the appropriate family argument.
- **Decision Trees** are versatile supervised learning algorithms that can be used for both classification and regression tasks. They partition the feature space

into regions and make predictions based on the majority class or average value in each region. R provides several packages, such as 'rpart' and 'tree', for building decision tree models.

- **Random Forest** is an ensemble learning algorithm that combines multiple decision trees to improve predictive performance and reduce overfitting. It generates a forest of trees and aggregates their predictions to make more accurate predictions. In R, you can use the 'randomForest' package to implement random forest models.
- **Support Vector Machine** (SVM) is a powerful supervised learning algorithm used for classification and regression tasks. It finds the optimal hyperplane that separates classes in the feature space or approximates a nonlinear decision boundary using kernel functions. R provides the 'e1071' package for SVM implementation.
- **K-Nearest Neighbors** (KNN) is a simple and intuitive algorithm used for classification and regression tasks. It makes predictions based on the majority class or average value of the k nearest neighbors in the feature space. R offers the 'class' package for KNN implementation.
- **K-Means Clustering** is an unsupervised learning algorithm used for clustering similar data points into groups or clusters. It partitions the data into k clusters based on the similarity of data points. R provides the 'stats' package for implementing K-means clustering.
- **Principal Component Analysis** (PCA) is a dimensionality reduction technique used to reduce the dimensionality of high-dimensional data while preserving most of its variance. It identifies the principal components that capture the maximum variance in the data. R offers PCA implementation through the 'stats' package.

These are just a few examples of the machine learning algorithms available in R. Depending on your specific task and data characteristics, you can choose the most appropriate algorithm and leverage the extensive R ecosystem to build robust and efficient machine learning models.

B. Supervised learning techniques

Supervised learning is a branch of machine learning where algorithms learn from labeled data to make predictions or decisions. In R, a wide range of supervised learning techniques are available for various tasks, including regression and classification. An overview of some popular supervised learning techniques in R is presented below.

1. Classification

For a beginner in R programming, a straightforward and intuitive classification technique to start with is Decision Trees. Decision trees are easy to understand and interpret, making them ideal for beginners. They also provide insights into how decisions are made, making them valuable for exploratory data analysis. Decision trees are suitable for beginners for the following reasons:

- Intuitive Concept: decision trees mimic human decision-making processes, where each node represents a decision based on input features, and each branch represents possible outcomes.
- No Assumptions About Data: decision trees do not make any assumptions about the distribution of the data or the relationship between variables, making them flexible and applicable to various types of datasets.
- Easy to Implement: implementing decision trees in R is straightforward thanks to libraries like rpart (Recursive Partitioning and Regression Trees) and tree, which provide simple functions for building decision tree models.
- Visualization: decision trees can be easily visualized, allowing beginners to understand the underlying decision-making process and interpret the model's results effectively.

With decision trees, beginners can gain hands-on experience in building and interpreting machine learning models in R while learning fundamental concepts such as feature selection, splitting criteria, and model evaluation. Once comfortable with decision trees, beginners can gradually explore more advanced classification techniques in R.

Let's use the popular Iris dataset, which is included in the datasets package in R, to demonstrate building a decision tree model. We will then interpret the results of the decision tree.

Figure 27. Decision tree with R

```
library(rpart)
library(rpart.plot)
library(datasets)

# Load the Iris dataset
data(iris)

# Build the decision tree model
model <- rpart(Species ~ ., data = iris)

# Visualize the decision tree with better formatting
rpart.plot(model, type = 4, extra = 1, tweak = 1.2)
```

As shown in Figure 27, the command lines are as follows:

- Load required libraries: these lines load the necessary R packages (rpart, rpart.plot, and datasets) into the current R session. These packages provide functions for building decision trees (rpart), visualizing decision trees (rpart. plot), and accessing datasets, including the Iris dataset (datasets).
- Load the Iris dataset: this line loads the Iris dataset into the R environment. The Iris dataset is a dataset that contains measurements of iris flowers along with their species (setosa, versicolor, or virginica).
- Build the decision tree model: this line builds a decision tree model using the rpart() function. The formula Species ~ . specifies that the species variable should be predicted based on all other variables in the dataset (. indicates all other variables).
- Visualize the decision tree with better formatting: this line generates a more visually appealing plot of the decision tree model using the rpart.plot() function. We specify type = 4 to display the actual number of observations in each terminal node, extra = 1 to display additional information such as error rates and class distributions, and tweak = 1.2 to adjust the spacing between nodes for better readability.

These commands load the required libraries, load the Iris dataset, build a decision tree model, and visualize the resulting tree with better formatting, providing insights into the relationships between input features and the target variable (species of iris flowers). After executing the code, the data mining result is displayed as shown in Figure 28.

Figure 28. Example of decision tree result by R

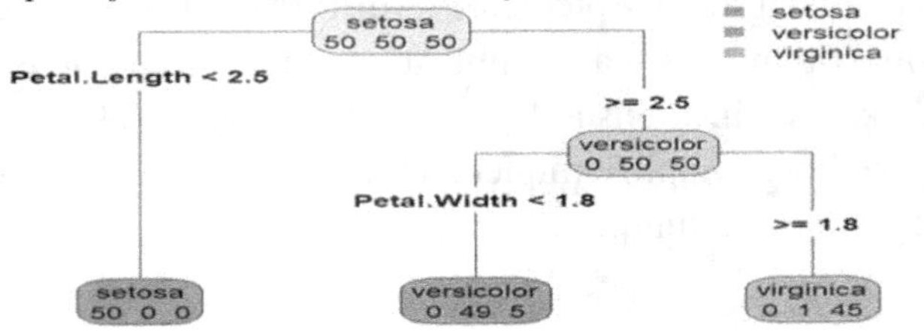

As shown in Figure 28, the interpreting results are as follows:

- **Root Node**: the top node of the decision tree represents the entire dataset. It shows the variable and split criterion that best separates the classes (in this case, species of iris flowers).
- **Internal Nodes** nodes represent decisions based on input features. Each node shows the splitting variable and the threshold value used for the split.
- **Branches** emanating from each node represent the possible outcomes of the decision. They lead to subsequent nodes or terminal nodes (leaves).
- **Terminal Nodes** (Leaves) represent the final decision or prediction. They show the predicted class or species based on the majority class of observations in that node.
- **Predictions**: the number of observations and the predicted class are displayed in each terminal node. For example, if a terminal node shows "Setosa (n = 50)", it means that all 50 observations in that node belong to the Setosa species.
- **Model Complexity:** the depth and structure of the tree determine its complexity. A deeper tree may capture more intricate patterns but risks overfitting the training data.

Interpreting the decision tree involves understanding how the model splits the feature space based on input variables to classify observations into different classes. It provides insights into the relationships between input features and the target variable, helping to identify important predictors and understand the decision-making process of the model.

2. Regression

Simple linear regression is an **easy-to-understand** technique for predicting a continuous variable using a single predictor. Its **intuitive concept** models relationships with a straight-line fit, making it accessible for beginners. The **clear interpretation** of coefficients and visualizations aids in understanding variable relationships. R's **built-in tools**, like lm(), simplify implementation, providing a **strong foundation** for advanced regression techniques.

Figure 29. Simple linear regression with R

```r
library(datasets)
library(ggplot2)
library(caret)

# Load the mtcars dataset (example dataset from R library)
data(mtcars)

# Fit a simple linear regression model
model <- lm(mpg ~ wt, data = mtcars)

# Make predictions
predictions <- predict(model, newdata = mtcars)

# Calculate model performance metrics
r_squared <- summary(model)$r.squared
rmse <- sqrt(mse)

# Visualize the relationship with a scatter plot and regression line
ggplot(mtcars, aes(x = wt, y = mpg)) +
  geom_point() +  # Add scatter plot points
  geom_smooth(method = "lm", se = FALSE, color = "blue") +  # Add regression line
  labs(x = "Car Weight (wt)", y = "Miles per Gallon (mpg)", title = "Car Weight vs. Miles per Gallon") +
  theme_minimal() +  # Apply a minimal theme
  geom_text(aes(label = paste("R-squared", round(r_squared, 3), "\nRMSE", round(rmse, 3))),
            x = max(mtcars$wt), y = min(mtcars$mpg), hjust = 1, vjust = 0, color = "red", size = 3)
```

As shown in Figure 29, the command lines are as follows:

- library(datasets): this command loads the datasets package, which contains various example datasets including the mtcars dataset that we'll use for this analysis.
- library(ggplot2): this command loads the ggplot2 package, which is a powerful plotting library in R used for creating visualizations.
- library(caret): this command loads the caret package, which is a comprehensive toolkit for machine learning in R. We'll use it later for calculating model performance metrics.
- data(mtcars): this command loads the mtcars dataset into the R environment. It is a built-in dataset in R containing data about different car models.
- model <- lm(mpg ~ wt, data = mtcars): this command fits a simple linear regression model using the lm() function. It predicts the miles per gallon (mpg) based on the car weight (wt) using the mtcars dataset.
- predictions <- predict(model, newdata = mtcars): this command makes predictions using the linear regression model (model) on the same dataset (mtcars). It calculates the predicted values of mpg based on the car weight (wt).
- r_squared <- summary(model)$r.squared: this command calculates the coefficient of determination (R-squared) for the linear regression model. It measures the proportion of variance in the dependent variable (mpg) that is explained by the independent variable (wt).
- rmse <- sqrt(mse): this line seems to be missing the calculation of mse (Mean Squared Error). We need to calculate mse before calculating rmse.

- The ggplot() function creates a scatter plot of the mtcars dataset, where the x-axis represents car weight (wt) and the y-axis represents miles per gallon (mpg). We then add points to the plot using geom_point().
- geom_smooth(method = "lm", se = FALSE, color = "blue"): this command adds a regression line to the plot using geom_smooth(). We specify method = "lm" to indicate that we want to fit a linear regression line. The se = FALSE argument disables the display of standard error bands around the line, and color = "blue" sets the color of the line to blue.
- labs(x = "Car Weight (wt)", y = "Miles per Gallon (mpg)", title = "Car Weight vs. Miles per Gallon"): this command sets the labels for the x-axis, y-axis, and plot title using the labs() function.
- theme_minimal(): this command applies a minimal theme to the plot, which removes unnecessary background elements and grid lines, resulting in a clean and simple appearance.
- geom_text(aes(label = paste("R-squared", round(r_squared, 3), "\nRMSE", round(rmse, 3))), x = max(mtcars$wt), y = min(mtcars$mpg), hjust = 1, vjust = 0, color = "red", size = 3): this command adds text annotations to the plot using geom_text(). It displays the R-squared and RMSE (Root Mean Squared Error) values at a specified location on the plot. The hjust = 1 and vjust = 0 arguments adjust the horizontal and vertical alignment of the text, and color = "red" sets the color of the text to red.

After executing the code, the regression result is as displayed in Figure 30.

Figure 30. The result of simple linear regression with R

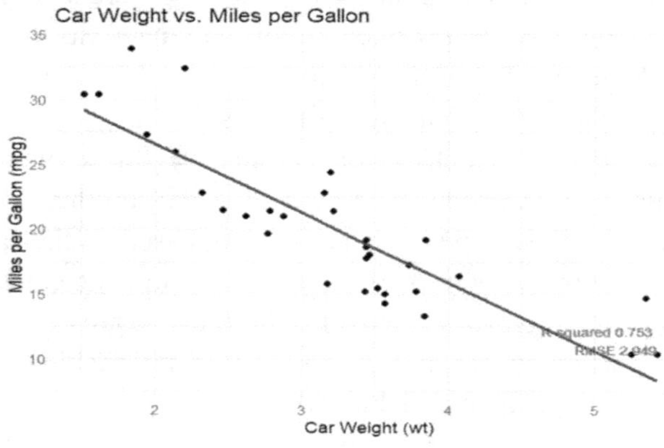

As shown in Figure 30, the provided R code conducts a simple linear regression analysis using the mtcars dataset, aiming to predict the miles per gallon (mpg) of cars based on their weight (wt). Here is the interpretation of the results:

- Regression Model Fit: the regression model's coefficients are estimated using the least squares method. It produces an equation of the form: mpg = b0 + b1 * wt, where b0 is the intercept and b1 is the slope coefficient for the weight (wt) variable.
- Model Performance Metrics, R-squared: The coefficient of determination (R-squared) indicates the proportion of variance in the dependent variable (mpg) explained by the independent variable (wt). In this case, the R-squared value is calculated to be approximately 0.753, suggesting that around 75.3% of the variability in mpg can be explained by wt. RMSE (Root Mean Squared Error): The RMSE measures the average deviation between the observed mpg values and the predicted values from the regression model. In this case, the RMSE value indicates the average prediction error of the model.
- Visualization: the scatter plot with a blue regression line illustrates the relationship between car weight (wt) and miles per gallon (mpg). Each point represents a car from the mtcars dataset, where the x-coordinate corresponds to the car weight and the y-coordinate represents the observed miles per gallon. The regression line represents the best-fitting linear relationship between the two variables. Additionally, the plot includes red text annotations displaying the R-squared and RMSE values. These annotations provide insights into the model's performance directly on the plot, making it easier to interpret.

Overall, the regression analysis suggests a moderately strong relationship between car weight and miles per gallon as indicated by the relatively high R-squared value. The regression line visually captures the general trend in the data while the performance metrics offer quantitative measures of the model's goodness of fit.

C. Unsupervised learning techniques

Discover the power of unsupervised learning techniques in R. In this section, we will delve into the world of data exploration and pattern discovery without labeled outcomes. Uncover hidden structures and relationships within your data using clustering and dimensionality reduction. Stay tuned for practical demonstrations, insightful explanations, and hands-on examples to unlock the potential of unsupervised learning with R.

1. Clustering

Clustering is an **unsupervised learning** technique that groups similar data points without predefined labels, making it ideal for **exploratory analysis**. Its **simplicity** and **intuitive nature** make it beginner-friendly, requiring minimal preprocessing. R provides **user-friendly packages** like stats and cluster, enabling easy implementation of clustering algorithms for pattern recognition.

Figure 31. Clustering with R

```
library(datasets)
library(cluster)
library(ggplot2)

# Load the iris dataset
data(iris)

# Selecting relevant columns for clustering
iris_features <- iris[, -5]  # Exclude the species column (last column)

# Perform k-means clustering
kmeans_model <- kmeans(iris_features, centers = 3, nstart = 25)

# Visualize the clusters
ggplot(iris, aes(x = Sepal.Length, y = Petal.Length, color = factor(kmeans_model$cluster))) +
  geom_point() +
  labs(x = "Sepal Length", y = "Petal Length", color = "Cluster") +
  ggtitle("K-means Clustering of Iris Dataset")
```

As shown in Figure 31, the actions are as follows:

- We load the necessary libraries: datasets for accessing the iris dataset, cluster for clustering algorithms, and ggplot2 for visualization.
- We load the iris dataset, which contains information about iris flowers, including sepal and petal measurements.
- We select relevant columns (sepal and petal measurements) for clustering by excluding the species column as clustering is an unsupervised learning technique and does not require labeled data.
- We perform k-means clustering using the kmeans() function, specifying the number of clusters (centers) as 3 and the number of random starts (nstart) as 25.
- We visualize the clusters using a scatter plot, with sepal length on the x-axis, petal length on the y-axis, and each point colored according to its assigned cluster. This allows us to visually inspect the clustering results and identify any patterns or clusters in the data.

This code provides a simple example of clustering using the k-means algorithm on the iris dataset and visualizes the clustering results using ggplot2, making it easy to understand and implement for beginners. After executing the code, the clustering result is displayed as shown in Figure 32.

Figure 32. Result from clustering with R

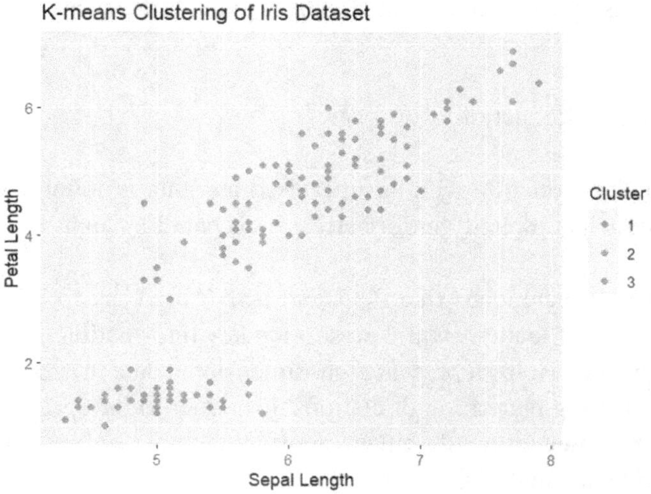

From Figure 32, we can interpret the following:

- Cluster Separation: the scatter plot shows distinct clusters of data points, each represented by a different color. In this case, we used the k-means algorithm to partition the iris dataset into three clusters based on sepal and petal measurements.
- Cluster Characteristics: we can observe that the data points within each cluster tend to be close to each other and distant from points in other clusters. This indicates that the clustering algorithm has successfully identified groups of data points with similar characteristics.
- Cluster Centers: the center of each cluster, represented by the centroid, is not explicitly shown in the plot but is calculated by the k-means algorithm. These cluster centers represent the mean of the feature values for all data points assigned to the cluster.
- Cluster Interpretation: based on domain knowledge or further analysis, we can interpret the clusters and understand what each cluster represents. For example, in the context of the iris dataset, each cluster may correspond to a different species of iris based on their sepal and petal measurements.
- Evaluation: while visual inspection provides an initial understanding of the clustering results, it is important to conduct further evaluation, such as silhouette analysis or cluster validation metrics, to assess the quality of the clustering and determine the optimal number of clusters.

Overall, the data visualization of clustering allows us to identify patterns, structure, and relationships within the data, facilitating exploratory analysis and insight generation.

2. Dimensionality Reduction

Dimensionality reduction with unsupervised learning is suitable for beginners practicing R due to its simplicity and effectiveness in handling high-dimensional data.

- **Simplicity** – Techniques like PCA and t-SNE are easy to implement in R, reducing dataset features while preserving key information.
- **Visualization** – Helps represent high-dimensional data in a lower-dimensional space, making patterns and relationships easier to interpret.
- **Feature Engineering** – Identifies important features, aiding in model performance and data analysis.
- **Computational Efficiency** – Reduces computational complexity, improving processing speed and resource usage.
- **Unsupervised Nature** – Works without labeled data, making it accessible for beginners unfamiliar with supervised learning.

Overall, dimensionality reduction with unsupervised learning offers a valuable tool for beginners practicing R to preprocess, explore, and gain insights from high-dimensional datasets in a straightforward and intuitive manner.

Figure 33. Dimensionality reduction with R

```
library(datasets)
library(ggplot2)
library(pracma)

# Load the iris dataset
data(iris)

# Selecting relevant columns for PCA
iris_features <- iris[, -5]  # Exclude the species column (last column)

# Perform PCA
pca_result <- princomp(iris_features, cor = TRUE)


# Plot PCA components
biplot(pca_result)
```

As shown in Figure 33, the command lines are as follows:

- Load required libraries: this line loads the necessary R packages (datasets, ggplot2, and pracma) that contain functions and datasets needed for the analysis.

- Load the iris dataset: this line loads the iris dataset, which is a built-in dataset in R containing measurements of iris flowers. This dataset will be used for the PCA analysis.
- Selecting relevant columns for PCA: this line extracts the relevant columns from the iris dataset for the PCA analysis. It removes the last column (Species), which contains the species labels of the iris flowers as PCA is an unsupervised technique and does not require labeled data.
- Perform PCA: this line applies the Principal Component Analysis (PCA) algorithm to the selected columns of the iris dataset. It computes the principal components and their loadings based on the correlation matrix of the data.
- Plot PCA components: this line plots the results of the PCA analysis using a biplot. A biplot displays both the principal components and the original variables in a single plot, allowing for the visualization of relationships between variables and the contribution of variables to each principal component.

Each line of the code performs a specific task, from loading necessary packages and data to conducting the PCA analysis and visualizing the results. Together, these lines form a comprehensive analysis pipeline for exploring the structure of the iris dataset using PCA. After executing the code, the dimensionality reduction result is displayed in Figure 34.

Figure 34. Result of dimensionality reduction with R

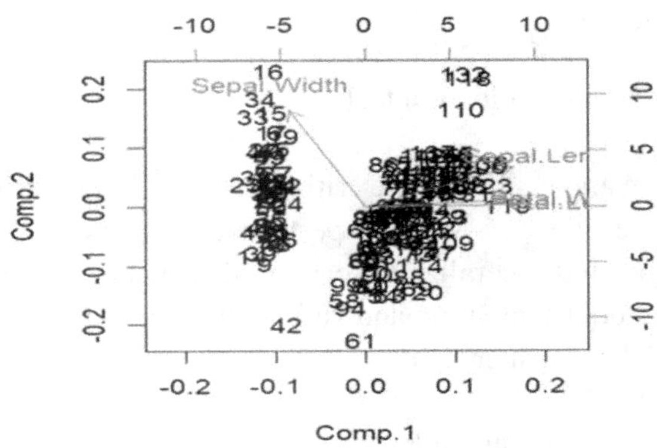

From Figure 34, we can interpret the following:

- Principal Components: the biplot displays arrows representing the principal components (PC1 and PC2) as vectors in the feature space. These principal components capture the directions of maximum variance in the original feature space.

- Variable Loadings: the length and direction of each arrow indicate the contribution and direction of each original variable (sepal length, sepal width, petal length, and petal width) to the principal components. Variables with longer arrows contribute more to the corresponding principal component.
- Variable Relationships: the angle between arrows represents the correlation or relationship between variables. Variables pointing in similar directions have positive correlations while variables pointing in opposite directions have negative correlations.
- Cluster Structure: data points (iris samples) are plotted in the biplot space, and their positions relative to the arrows indicate their projections onto the principal components. Points that are close together in the biplot space share similar patterns of variation across the original variables.
- Outliers: outliers or extreme observations may appear as data points located far from the main cluster of points. These outliers represent samples that deviate significantly from the overall pattern of variation in the dataset.

Overall, the biplot provides insights into the structure and relationships within the iris dataset, allowing us to visualize how the original variables contribute to the principal components and how samples are distributed in the reduced-dimensional space defined by the principal components. This visualization aids in understanding the underlying structure of the data and identifying potential patterns or clusters among the iris samples.

D. Model evaluation and validation techniques

Model evaluation and validation are critical steps in the machine learning workflow. These processes aim to assess the performance of predictive models and to ensure their reliability and generalization capabilities. In this section, we will explore the importance of model evaluation and validation and discuss various techniques used to assess model performance using R.

1. Cross Validation Technique in R

Cross-validation is a widely used technique in machine learning and statistical modeling for assessing the performance of predictive models. It involves partitioning the dataset into multiple subsets, training the model on a portion of the data (training set), and evaluating its performance on the remaining data (validation set).

This process is repeated multiple times, with different subsets used for training and validation, to obtain robust estimates of model performance.

K-fold cross-validation is one of the most common cross-validation techniques. In K-fold cross-validation, the dataset is divided into K equal-sized folds or subsets. The model is trained K times, each time using K-1 folds as the training set and the remaining fold as the validation set. The performance of the model is then averaged across the K iterations to obtain a single estimate of its performance.

In R, the caret package provides convenient functions for performing K-fold cross-validation. The 'trainControl()' function allows you to specify the cross-validation method, including the number of folds (K). The 'train()' function can then be used to train the model using cross-validation.

Figure 35. K-fold cross-validation with R

```
library(caret)
data(iris)

# Specify cross-validation parameters
ctrl <- trainControl(method = "cv", number = 10)

# Train the model using K-fold cross-validation
model <- train(Species ~ ., data = iris, method = "rf", trControl = ctrl)

# View the cross-validation results
summary(model)
```

As shown in Figure 35, the command lines are as follows:

- library(caret): this command loads the caret package, which provides functions for training and evaluating predictive models in R. The caret package is a comprehensive package widely used for machine learning tasks, including cross-validation.
- data(iris): this command loads the iris dataset, a built-in dataset in R that contains measurements of iris flowers. The iris dataset is commonly used for demonstrating machine learning algorithms and techniques.
- ctrl <- trainControl(method = "cv", number = 10): this line creates a control object (ctrl) for specifying cross-validation parameters. Here, we are using the K-fold cross-validation (method = "cv") with number = 10 folds. This means the dataset will be divided into 10 equal-sized folds for cross-validation.
- model <- train(Species ~ ., data = iris, method = "rf", trControl = ctrl): this command trains a random forest (method = "rf") model using the Species column as the target variable and all other columns as predictor variables (.) from the iris dataset. The train() function from the caret package is used, and the cross-validation parameters specified in the ctrl object are passed via the trControl argument.

- summary(model): this command displays a summary of the cross-validation results for the trained model. It provides information such as the mean and standard deviation of performance metrics across the cross-validation folds, including accuracy, Kappa, and ROC metrics, depending on the model and task. This summary helps assess the model's performance and identify potential areas for improvement.

    After executing the code, the K-fold cross-validation result is displayed as shown in Figure 36.

Figure 36. Result from K-fold cross-validation in R

```
                 Length Class      Mode
call                4   -none-     call
type                1   -none-     character
predicted         150   factor     numeric
err.rate         2000   -none-     numeric
confusion          12   -none-     numeric
votes             450   matrix     numeric
oob.times         150   -none-     numeric
classes             3   -none-     character
importance          4   -none-     numeric
importanceSD        0   -none-     NULL
localImportance     0   -none-     NULL
proximity           0   -none-     NULL
ntree               1   -none-     numeric
mtry                1   -none-     numeric
forest             14   -none-     list
y                 150   factor     numeric
test                0   -none-     NULL
inbag               0   -none-     NULL
xNames              4   -none-     character
problemType         1   -none-     character
tuneValue           1   data.frame list
obsLevels           3   -none-     character
param               0   -none-     list
```

As shown in Figure 36, after performing K-fold cross-validation with a random forest model on the iris dataset, the results provide insights into the model's performance across the different folds.

- Accuracy: the accuracy metric indicates the proportion of correctly classified instances out of the total instances in each fold. Higher accuracy values indicate better performance.
- Kappa: Cohen's Kappa statistic measures the agreement between the predicted and actual classes, considering the possibility of agreement occurring by chance. A Kappa value close to 1 indicates strong agreement beyond chance.
- Accuracy SD: this represents the standard deviation of accuracy across the different folds. A smaller standard deviation suggests more consistency in model performance.
- Kappa SD: similarly, the standard deviation of Kappa values across folds provides insight into the consistency of agreement between predicted and actual classes.

- Resampling results: each fold's accuracy and Kappa values are provided individually, allowing for a detailed examination of the model's performance on different subsets of the data.

Overall, by examining the mean accuracy, Kappa, and their standard deviations across folds, we can assess the model's robustness and generalization capabilities. If the model demonstrates consistent and high performance across all folds, it indicates that the model is reliable and can generalize well to unseen data. Additionally, comparing the resampling results across different models or hyperparameters can help in model selection and optimization.

Leave-One-Out cross-validation (LOOCV) is a special case of K-fold cross-validation where K equals the number of samples in the dataset. In LOOCV, each sample is used as the validation set once while the remaining samples are used for training. This process is repeated for each sample, and the model's performance is evaluated by averaging the results across all iterations.

In R, 'LOOCV' can be performed using the same 'caret' package with the 'method = "LOOCV"' parameter in the 'trainControl()' function.

Figure 37. Leave-One-Out cross-validation (LOOCV) in R

```
library(caret)
data(iris)

# Specify LOOCV as the cross-validation method
ctrl <- trainControl(method = "LOOCV")

# Train the model using Leave-One-Out cross-validation
model <- train(Species ~ ., data = iris, method = "rf", trControl = ctrl)

# View the cross-validation results
summary(model)
```

As shown in Figure 37, the command lines are as follows:

- library(caret): this line loads the caret package, which is a comprehensive package in R for training and evaluating machine learning models. It provides functions for various tasks such as data preprocessing, model training, and performance evaluation.
- data(iris): this command loads the built-in iris dataset into the R environment. The iris dataset contains measurements of iris flowers, making it a popular dataset for practicing machine learning algorithms and techniques.
- ctrl <- trainControl(method = "LOOCV"), here, we create a control object named ctrl using the trainControl() function from the caret package. We specify the cross-validation method as "LOOCV" (Leave-One-Out Cross-

Validation). This technique involves using each observation in the dataset as a validation set once while using the rest of the data for training.

- model <- train(Species ~ ., data = iris, method = “rf”, trControl = ctrl), this line trains a random forest model (method = “rf”) using the Species column as the target variable and all other columns as predictor variables (.) from the iris dataset. The train() function from the caret package is used for model training, and the trControl argument specifies the cross-validation method (ctrl).
- summary(model), finally, this command displays a summary of the cross-validation results for the trained model. It provides information such as the mean and standard deviation of performance metrics across the cross-validation folds, including accuracy, Kappa, and ROC metrics, depending on the model and task. This summary helps assess the model's performance and identify potential areas for improvement.

After executing the code, the Leave-One-Out cross-validation (LOOCV) result is displayed as shown in Figure 38.

Figure 38. Result of Leave-One-Out cross-validation (LOOCV) in R

```
                Length Class      Mode
call               4   -none-     call
type               1   -none-     character
predicted        150   factor     numeric
err.rate        2000   -none-     numeric
confusion         12   -none-     numeric
votes            450   matrix     numeric
oob.times        150   -none-     numeric
classes            3   -none-     character
importance         4   -none-     numeric
importanceSD       0   -none-     NULL
localImportance    0   -none-     NULL
proximity          0   -none-     NULL
ntree              1   -none-     numeric
mtry               1   -none-     numeric
forest            14   -none-     list
y                150   factor     numeric
test               0   -none-     NULL
inbag              0   -none-     NULL
xNames             4   -none-     character
problemType        1   -none-     character
tuneValue          1   data.frame list
obsLevels          3   -none-     character
param              0   -none-     list
```

From the summary of the model trained using Leave-One-Out Cross-Validation (LOOCV) with a random forest algorithm on the iris dataset as shown in Figure 38, we can interpret the results as follows:

- Accuracy: the accuracy metric indicates the proportion of correctly classified instances out of the total instances. In LOOCV, each observation serves as a validation set once, and accuracy represents the overall performance of the model in correctly predicting the class labels. Higher accuracy values indicate better model performance.
- Kappa: Cohen's Kappa statistic measures the agreement between the predicted and actual classes, considering the possibility of agreement occurring by chance. It provides a more robust measure of classification performance, especially when the class distribution is imbalanced. A Kappa value close to 1 indicates strong agreement beyond chance.
- Accuracy SD: this represents the standard deviation of accuracy across the different iterations of LOOCV. A smaller standard deviation suggests more consistency in model performance across different validation sets.
- Kappa SD: similarly, the standard deviation of Kappa values across iterations provides insights into the consistency of agreement between predicted and actual classes.
- Resampling results: each iteration of LOOCV provides accuracy and Kappa values, allowing for a detailed examination of the model's performance on individual observations. This helps in identifying any patterns or trends in model predictions and assessing the model's reliability.

Overall, by analyzing the summary of the model trained with LOOCV, we can evaluate the model's performance, understand its robustness, and identify potential areas for improvement. If the model demonstrates high accuracy and Kappa values with low variability, it indicates that the model is reliable and can generalize well to unseen data.

Both K-fold cross-validation and Leave-One-Out cross-validation are effective techniques for estimating the performance of predictive models and selecting optimal model parameters in R. They help to prevent overfitting and provide reliable estimates of model performance on unseen data.

2. Model Performance Metrics in R

In machine learning, evaluating the performance of a model is crucial to assessing its effectiveness and suitability for the task at hand. Various performance metrics provide insights into different aspects of a model's performance. In R, several common performance metrics are widely used, each serving a specific purpose and offering unique insights into model performance.

- **Accuracy** – Measures the proportion of correctly classified instances but can be misleading for imbalanced datasets.
- **Precision** – Calculates true positives among predicted positives, crucial when false positives are costly (e.g., fraud detection).
- **Recall** – Identifies true positives among actual positives, important for minimizing false negatives (e.g., disease detection).
- **F1-score** – Harmonic mean of precision and recall, useful for imbalanced datasets where both metrics are equally important.
- **ROC-AUC** – Evaluates a model's ability to distinguish between classes across thresholds, ideal for binary classification tasks.

A demonstration of how to compute and interpret these performance metrics using an example dataset in R is presented below:

Figure 39. Model performance matrix in R

```
library(caret)
library(pROC)
library(titanic)
data("titanic_train")
# Remove rows with missing values
titanic_train <- na.omit(titanic_train)
# Convert Survived variable to factor
titanic_train$Survived <- factor(titanic_train$Survived)
# Train a classification model (e.g., logistic regression)
model <- train(Survived ~ Pclass + Sex + Age + SibSp + Parch + Fare + Embarked,
               data = titanic_train,
               method = "glm",
               family = "binomial")
# Make predictions
predictions <- predict(model, newdata = titanic_train)

# Compute confusion matrix
conf_matrix <- confusionMatrix(predictions, titanic_train$Survived)

# Compute accuracy
accuracy <- conf_matrix$overall['Accuracy']

# Compute precision
precision <- conf_matrix$byClass['Pos Pred Value']

# Compute recall (sensitivity)
recall <- conf_matrix$byClass['Sensitivity']

# Compute F1-score
f1_score <- (2 * precision * recall) / (precision + recall)

# Print performance metrics
cat("Accuracy:", accuracy, "\n")
cat("Precision:", precision, "\n")
cat("Recall:", recall, "\n")
cat("F1-Score:", f1_score, "\n")
```

As shown in Figure 39, the command lines are as follows:

- library(caret): this line loads the caret package, which provides functions for training and evaluating classification and regression models.
- library(pROC): this line loads the pROC package, which provides functions for computing and visualizing ROC curves and AUC.
- library(titanic): this line loads the titanic package, which contains the Titanic dataset.
- data("titanic_train"): this line loads the Titanic training dataset into the R environment.
- titanic_train <- na.omit(titanic_train): this line removes rows with missing values from the Titanic training dataset.
- titanic_train$Survived <- factor(titanic_train$Survived): this line converts the "Survived" variable to a factor, which is required for classification modeling in R.
- model <- train(Survived ~ Pclass + Sex + Age + SibSp + Parch + Fare + Embarked, data = titanic_train, method = "glm", family = "binomial"): this line trains a logistic regression model using the train function from the caret package. It predicts the "Survived" variable based on other variables such as passenger class, sex, age, etc.
- predictions <- predict(model, newdata = titanic_train): this line makes predictions using the trained logistic regression model on the Titanic training dataset.
- conf_matrix <- confusionMatrix(predictions, titanic_train$Survived): this line computes the confusion matrix to evaluate the classification performance of the model.
- accuracy <- conf_matrix$overall['Accuracy']: this line extracts the overall accuracy from the confusion matrix.
- precision <- conf_matrix$byClass['Pos Pred Value']: this line extracts the precision (positive predictive value) from the confusion matrix.
- recall <- conf_matrix$byClass['Sensitivity']: this line extracts the recall (sensitivity) from the confusion matrix.
- f1_score <- (2 * precision * recall) / (precision + recall): this line calculates the F1-score, which is the harmonic mean of precision and recall.
- cat("Accuracy:", accuracy, "\n"): this line prints the accuracy metric.
- cat("Precision:", precision, "\n"): this line prints the precision metric.
- cat("Recall:", recall, "\n"): this line prints the recall metric.
- cat("F1-Score:", f1_score, "\n"): this line prints the F1-score metric.

After executing the code, the model performance matrix result is displayed as shown in Figure 40.

Figure 40. Result of model performance matrix in R

```
> cat("Accuracy:", accuracy, "\n")
Accuracy: 0.8011204
> cat("Precision:", precision, "\n")
Precision: 0.8147321
> cat("Recall:", recall, "\n")
Recall: 0.8608491
> cat("F1-Score:", f1_score, "\n")
F1-Score: 0.837156
```

As shown in Figure 40, the results of the model performance metrics are interpreted as follows:

- The accuracy metric indicates the overall correctness of the model's predictions. In this case, it represents the proportion of correctly predicted outcomes (both survived and not survived) out of all predictions made by the model. For example, if the accuracy is 0.80, it means that the model correctly predicted 80% of the outcomes in the dataset.
- Precision measures the proportion of true positive predictions (correctly predicted survived cases) out of all positive predictions made by the model. It indicates how reliable the model is when it predicts that a passenger survived. For example, if the precision is 0.75, it means that out of all the instances the model predicted as survived, 75% of them actually survived.
- Recall, also known as sensitivity or true positive rate, measures the proportion of true positive predictions (correctly predicted survived cases) out of all actual positive cases in the dataset. It indicates the model's ability to correctly identify passengers who actually survived. For example, if the recall is 0.80, it means that the model correctly identified 80% of the passengers who actually survived.
- The F1-score is the harmonic mean of precision and recall. It provides a balanced measure of the model's performance by considering both precision and recall. A high F1-score indicates that the model has both high precision and high recall, meaning it can make accurate predictions while capturing a significant portion of the positive cases.

CONCLUSION

In conclusion, this journey through R programming for data scientists has equipped you with essential skills and techniques to tackle various challenges in data analysis and manipulation. From importing data to reshaping and transforming it, you have learned how to handle missing values, outliers, and efficiently manipulate data using packages like dplyr. With the power of ggplot2, you have explored the art of data visualization, from basic plots to customized visualizations that reveal intricate patterns and relationships in your data. Moving into statistical analysis, you have mastered descriptive and inferential statistics, delving into regression analysis to uncover deeper insights from your datasets. In the realm of machine learning, you have been introduced to a diverse array of algorithms for both supervised and unsupervised learning, gaining insights into model evaluation and validation techniques to ensure the robustness of your predictive models. With these skills in your arsenal, you are well-prepared to embark on your journey as a proficient data scientist, equipped to tackle real-world data challenges and drive impactful insights and decisions.

EXERCISES AND QUESTIONS

1. Describe two common techniques for handling missing values in R.
2. How does the ggplot2 package contribute to data visualization in R? Provide an example of a plot that can be created using ggplot2.
3. Explain the significance of performing hypothesis testing in inferential statistics. Provide an example scenario where hypothesis testing might be applied.
4. Can you differentiate between supervised and unsupervised learning techniques in machine learning? Provide examples of each.
5. Discuss the importance of model evaluation and validation techniques in machine learning. How might these techniques be used to improve the performance of predictive models?

REFERENCES

Barman, A., Beckman, L. S., & Chebaro, Y. (2022). Interdisciplinary computing education: An introductory programming and data science course for postdoctoral researchers in the biosciences. *2022 IEEE Frontiers in Education Conference (FIE)*, 1–8. DOI: 10.1109/FIE56618.2022.9962737

Bruce, P. C., Bruce, A., & Gedeck, P. (2020). *Practical statistics for data scientists: 50+ essential concepts using R and Python* (2nd ed.). O'Reilly Media, Inc.

Ditta, A. S., & Woodward, A. M. (2022). Technology or tradition? A comparison of students' statistical reasoning after being taught with R programming versus hand calculations. *Scholarship of Teaching and Learning in Psychology*. Advance online publication. DOI: 10.1037/stl0000327

Harry, H. (2021). *R (Programming Language)*. Facts On File.

Llaudet, E., & Imai, K. (2023). *Data analysis for social science: A friendly and practical introduction*. Princeton University Press.

Mailund, T. (2022). *Beginning data science in R 4: Data analysis, visualization, and modelling for the data scientist* (2nd ed.). Apress. DOI: 10.1007/978-1-4842-8155-0

Migran, N. G., Anna, V. K., & Dmitry, S. K. (2023). Julia language features for processing statistical data. *Discrete and Continuous Models and Applied Computational Science*, *31*(1), 5–26. DOI: 10.22363/2658-4670-2023-31-1-5-26

R statistical programming software for data science. (2021). *Business Expert Press*.

Shilane, D., Crecchio, N. D., & Lorenzetti, N. L. (2024). Some pedagogical elements of computer programming for data science: A comparison of three approaches to teaching the R language. *Teaching Statistics*, *46*(1), 24–37. DOI: 10.1111/test.12361

Compilation of References

Abbas, A., Prayitno, P., Butarbutar, F., Nurkim, N., Prumanto, D., Dewadi, F. M., Hidayati, N., & Windarto, A. P. (2021). Implementation of clustering unsupervised learning using K-means mapping techniques. *IOP Conference Series. Materials Science and Engineering*, *1088*(1), 012004. DOI: 10.1088/1757-899X/1088/1/012004

Abdul Aziz, A., & Starkey, A. (2020). Predicting supervise machine learning performances for sentiment analysis using contextual-based approaches. *IEEE Access : Practical Innovations, Open Solutions*, *8*, 17722–17733. DOI: 10.1109/ACCESS.2019.2958702

Abu-Soud, S. M. (2019). A novel approach for dealing with missing values in machine learning datasets with discrete values. *2019 International Conference on Computer and Information Sciences (ICCIS)*, 1–5. DOI: 10.1109/ICCISci.2019.8716430

Adeniyi, D. A., Wei, Z., & Yongquan, Y. (2016). Automated web usage data mining and recommendation system using K-Nearest Neighbor (KNN) classification method. *Applied Computing & Informatics*, *12*(1), 90–108. DOI: 10.1016/j.aci.2014.10.001

Aditya, G. M., Hoode, A., Anvesh Rai, K., Biradar, G., Ajay Kumara, M., Manoj Kumar, M. V., Prashanth, B. S., Sneha, H. R., & Shivadarshan, S. L. (2021). Machine learning-based platform and recommendation system for food ordering services within premises. *2021 2nd Global Conference for Advancement in Technology (GCAT)*, 1–8.

Aggarwal, C. C. (2018). *Neural networks and deep learning: A textbook*. Springer. DOI: 10.1007/978-3-319-94463-0

Agrawal, R., & Srikant, R. (1994). Fast algorithms for mining association rules. *Proceedings of the 20th International Conference on Very Large Data Bases (VLDB)*, Santiago, Chile, September 12–15.

Almasoud, A. M., Al-Khalifa, H. S., & Al-Salman, A. S. (2019). Handling big data scalability in biological domain using parallel and distributed processing: A case of three biological semantic similarity measures. *BioMed Research International, 2019*, 1–20. DOI: 10.1155/2019/6750296 PMID: 30809545

Andrews, F. M., & Messenger, R. C. (1973). *Multivariate nominal scale analysis: A report on a new analysis technique and a computer program*. University of Michigan.

Angiulli, F., & Fassetti, F. (2021). Uncertain distance-based outlier detection with arbitrarily shaped data objects. *Journal of Intelligent Information Systems, 57*(1), 1–24. DOI: 10.1007/s10844-020-00624-7

Atanasovski, M., Kostov, M., Arapinoski, B., & Spirovski, M. (2020). K-nearest neighbor regression for forecasting electricity demand. *2020 55th International Scientific Conference on Information, Communication and Energy Systems and Technologies (ICEST), 110–113.*

Baby, S. S., & Reddy, S. L. (2021). End-to-end product recommendation system with improvements in Apriori algorithm. *2021 Third International Conference on Inventive Research in Computing Applications (ICIRCA)*, 1357–1361. DOI: 10.1109/ICIRCA51532.2021.9544981

Bader, D. (2018). *Python tricks: The book*. Dan Bader.

Barman, A., Beckman, L. S., & Chebaro, Y. (2022). Interdisciplinary computing education: An introductory programming and data science course for postdoctoral researchers in the biosciences. *2022 IEEE Frontiers in Education Conference (FIE)*, 1–8. DOI: 10.1109/FIE56618.2022.9962737

Başarslan, M. S., & Argun, İ. D. (2018). Classification of a bank data set on various data mining platforms. *2018 Electric Electronics, Computer Science, Biomedical Engineerings' Meeting (EBBT)*, 1–4.

Bataineh, A. Q., Mushtaha, A. S., Abu-AlSondos, I. A., Aldulaimi, S. H., & Abdeldayem, M. (2024). Ethical & legal concerns of artificial intelligence in the healthcare sector. In *2024 ASU International Conference in Emerging Technologies for Sustainability and Intelligent Systems (ICETSIS)* (pp. 491–495). IEEE. DOI: 10.1109/ICETSIS61505.2024.10459438

Bayram, E., & Nabiyev, V. (2020). Image segmentation by using K-means clustering algorithm in Euclidean and Mahalanobis distance calculation in camouflage images. *2020 28th Signal Processing and Communications Applications Conference (SIU)*, 1–4.

Bell, J. (2015). *Machine learning: Hands-on for developers and technical professionals*. John Wiley & Sons.

Ben Ncir, C.-E., Hamza, A., & Bouaguel, W. (2021). Parallel and scalable Dunn Index for the validation of big data clusters. *Parallel Computing*, *102*, 102. DOI: 10.1016/j.parco.2021.102751

Beohar, D., & Rasool, A. (2021). Handwritten digit recognition of MNIST dataset using deep learning state-of-the-art artificial neural network (ANN) and convolutional neural network (CNN). *2021 International Conference on Emerging Smart Computing and Informatics (ESCI)*, 542–548. DOI: 10.1109/ESCI50559.2021.9396870

Berman, J. J. (2018). *Principles and practice of big data: Preparing, sharing, and analyzing complex information* (2nd ed.). Academic Press/Elsevier.

Bilal, M., Ali, G., Iqbal, M. W., Anwar, M., Malik, M. S. A., & Kadir, R. A. (2022). Auto-Prep: Efficient and automated data preprocessing pipeline. *IEEE Access : Practical Innovations, Open Solutions*, *10*, 107764–107784. DOI: 10.1109/ACCESS.2022.3198662

Bing, L., Yiming, M., & Lee, R. (2001). Analyzing the interestingness of association rules from the temporal dimension. *Proceedings 2001 IEEE International Conference on Data Mining (ICDM 2001)*, 377–384. DOI: 10.1109/ICDM.2001.989542

Bowles, M. (2015). *Machine learning in Python: Essential techniques for predictive analysis*. Wiley. DOI: 10.1002/9781119183600

Bramer, M. (2016). *Principle of data mining* (3rd ed.). Springer-Verlag London Ltd. DOI: 10.1007/978-1-4471-7307-6

Bruce, P. C., Bruce, A., & Gedeck, P. (2020). *Practical statistics for data scientists: 50+ essential concepts using R and Python* (2nd ed.). O'Reilly Media, Inc.

Bunjongprasoet, P., & Ramjan, S. (2021). *Prediction road and period of time for road accidents in Bangkok*. Independent Study. College of Innovation: Thammasat University.

Cai, S., Sun, R., Hao, S., Li, S., & Yuan, G. (2016). An efficient outlier detection approach on weighted data stream based on minimal rare pattern mining. *China Communications*, *16*(10), 83–99. DOI: 10.23919/JCC.2019.10.006

Cardona, J. A. S., & Gomez, G. C. H., & Lopez Trujillo, M. (2014). Knowledge discovery process in the open government Colombian model. *2014 9th Computing Colombian Conference (9CCC), 96–102*.

Carlson, K., Livermore, M. A., & Rockmore, D. N. (2020). The problem of data bias in the pool of published U.S. appellate court opinions. *Journal of Empirical Legal Studies, 17*(2), 224–261. DOI: 10.1111/jels.12253

Cheewaprakobkit, P. (2019). *Predicting student academic achievement by using the decision tree and neural network techniques*. Asia-Pacific International University.

Chen, Q., & Qin, J. (2021). Research and implementation of movie recommendation system based on deep learning. *2021 IEEE International Conference on Computer Science, Electronic Information Engineering and Intelligent Control Technology (CEI)*, 225–228. DOI: 10.1109/CEI52496.2021.9574461

Chiarini, T. M., Kohli, R., & Forsgren, N. (2021). Theories in flux: Reimagining theory building in the age of machine learning. *Management Information Systems Quarterly, 45*(1), 455–459.

Chinnarasri, C., Nonsawang, S., & Supharatid, S. (2012). *Application of artificial neural networks for river stage forecasting in Hatyai. King Mongkut's University of Technology Thonburi*. KMUTT.

Choi, H., Kim, J., Joe, S., & Gwon, Y. (2021). Evaluation of BERT and ALBERT sentence embedding performance on downstream NLP tasks. *2020 25th International Conference on Pattern Recognition (ICPR)*, 5482–5487. DOI: 10.1109/ICPR48806.2021.9412102

Chow, T. W. S., & Cho, S.-Y. (2007). *Neural networks and computing: Learning algorithms and applications*. Imperial College Press. DOI: 10.1142/p487

Dai, H., Zhang, S., Wang, L., & Ding, Y. (2016). Research and implementation of big data preprocessing system based on Hadoop. *2016 IEEE International Conference on Big Data Analysis (ICBDA)*, 1–5. DOI: 10.1109/ICBDA.2016.7509802

Damatie, E. M., Eleyan, A., & Bejaoui, T. (2024). Real-time email phishing detection using a custom DistilBERT model. *2024 International Symposium on Networks, Computers and Communications (ISNCC)*, 1–6. DOI: 10.1109/ISNCC62547.2024.10759011

Derryberry, D. R. (2014). *Basic data analysis for time series with R*. John Wiley & Sons, Inc. DOI: 10.1002/9781118593233

Ditta, A. S., & Woodward, A. M. (2022). Technology or tradition? A comparison of students' statistical reasoning after being taught with R programming versus hand calculations. *Scholarship of Teaching and Learning in Psychology*. Advance online publication. DOI: 10.1037/stl0000327 dos Santos, D. F. D., de Faria, P. R., Travençolo, B. A. N., & do Nascimento, M. Z. (2023). Influence of data augmentation strategies on the segmentation of oral histological images using fully convolutional neural networks. *Journal of Digital Imaging*, *36*(4), 1608–1623. DOI: 10.1007/s10278-023-00814-z PMID: 37012446

Du, J. (2021). Research on enterprise information security and privacy protection in big data environment. In *2021 3rd International Conference on Machine Learning, Big Data and Business Intelligence (MLBDBI)* (pp. 324–327). IEEE. DOI: 10.1109/MLBDBI54094.2021.00067

Dubey, S., Jain, S. K., Gautam, P., & Sonare, S. (2024). Impact of water pollutants in River Narmada using RapidMiner tool. *2024 IEEE 13th International Conference on Communication Systems and Network Technologies (CSNT)*, 808–811. DOI: 10.1109/CSNT60213.2024.10546204

Emon, M. I., Shahiduzzaman, M., Rakib, M. R. H., Shathee, M. S. A., Saha, S., Kamran, M. N., & Fahim, J. H. (2021). Profile-based course recommendation system using association rule mining and collaborative filtering. *2021 International Conference on Science & Contemporary Technologies (ICSCT)*, 1–5. DOI: 10.1109/ICSCT53883.2021.9642633

Fernando, T., Gammulle, H., Denman, S., Sridharan, S., & Fookes, C. (2021). Deep learning for medical anomaly detection - A survey. *ACM Computing Surveys*, *54*(7), 1–37. DOI: 10.1145/3464423

Ghorpade, V. G., & Koneru, V. S. (2021). Pattern recognition neural network model for experimental-based compressive strength graded self-compacting concrete. *Materials Today: Proceedings*, *43*(2), 795–799. DOI: 10.1016/j.matpr.2020.06.175

Ghous, H., & Kovács, L. (2020). Efficiency comparison of Python and RapidMiner. *Multidiszciplináris Tudományok*, *10*(3), 212–220. DOI: 10.35925/j.multi.2020.3.26

Ginting, S. W., Hartati, R. S., Sudarma, M., & Swamardika, I. B. A. (2021). Clustering of earthquake and volcanic eruption trauma survivor groups using K-means algorithm. *2021 International Conference on Smart-Green Technology in Electrical and Information Systems (ICSGTEIS)*, 69–73. DOI: 10.1109/ICSGTEIS53426.2021.9650357

Glass, D. H. (2013). Confirmation measures of association rule interestingness. *Knowledge-Based Systems*, *44*, 65–77. DOI: 10.1016/j.knosys.2013.01.021

Gong, Y., & Zhang, P. (2021). Predictive analysis and research of Python usage rate based on polynomial regression model. *2021 3rd International Conference on Artificial Intelligence and Advanced Manufacture (AIAM)*, 266–270.

Gong, S., Ye, H.-W., & Zhu, X. (2009). Item-based collaborative filtering recommendation using self-organizing map. *2009 Chinese Control and Decision Conference (CCDC)*, 4029–4031. DOI: 10.1109/CCDC.2009.5192713

Govindaraj, V., Thiyagarajan, A., Rajasekaran, P., Zhang, Y., & Krishnasamy, R. (2020). Automated unsupervised learning-based clustering approach for effective anomaly detection in brain magnetic resonance imaging (MRI). *IET Image Processing, 14*(14), 3516–3526. DOI: 10.1049/iet-ipr.2020.0597

Greco, S., Słowiński, R., & Szczęch, I. (2016). Measures of rule interestingness in various perspectives of confirmation. *Information Sciences, 346–347*, 216–235. DOI: 10.1016/j.ins.2016.01.056

Grütter, R. (2019). A framework for assisted proximity analysis in feature data. *Journal of Geographical Systems, 21*(3), 367–394. DOI: 10.1007/s10109-019-00304-3

Guo, C., Zhang, M., & Chen, H. (2021). Suitability of low-field nuclear magnetic resonance (LF-NMR) combining with back-propagation artificial neural network (BP-ANN) to predict printability of polysaccharide hydrogels 3D printing. *International Journal of Food Science & Technology, 56*(5), 2264–2272. DOI: 10.1111/ijfs.14844

Gupta, A., Sahayadhas, A., & Gupta, V. (2020). Proposed techniques to design speed-efficient data warehouse architecture for fastening knowledge discovery process. *2020 IEEE Third International Conference on Artificial Intelligence and Knowledge Engineering (AIKE)*, 200–201. DOI: 10.1109/AIKE48582.2020.00039

Harry, H. (2021). *R (Programming Language)*. Facts On File.

Haviluddin, I. M., Putra, G. M., Puspitasari, N., Setyadi, H. J., Dwiyanto, F. A., Wibawa, A. P., & Alfred, R. (2020). A performance comparison of Euclidean, Manhattan and Minkowski distances in K-means clustering. *2020 6th International Conference on Science in Information Technology (ICSITech)*, 184–188.

Healy, K. (2018). *Data visualization: A practical introduction*. Princeton University Press.

Hernandez-Suarez, A., Sanchez-Perez, G., Toscano-Medina, K., Martinez-Hernandez, V., Sanchez, V., & Perez-Meana, H. (2018). A web scraping methodology for bypassing Twitter API restrictions.

Hill, C. (2015). *Learning scientific programming with Python*. Cambridge University Press. DOI: 10.1017/CBO9781139871754

Hodijah, A., & Setijohatmo, U. T. (2021). Analysis of frequent itemset generation based on trie data structure in Apriori algorithm. *Telkomnika, 19*(5), 1553–1564. DOI: 10.12928/telkomnika.v19i5.19273

Hong, G., & Nan, G. (2021). Research and application of a multidimensional association rules mining algorithm based on Hadoop. *2021 IEEE International Conference on Parallel & Distributed Processing with Applications, Big Data & Cloud Computing, Sustainable Computing & Communications, Social Computing & Networking (ISPA/BDCloud/SocialCom/SustainCom)*, 636–643. DOI: 10.1109/ISPA-BDCloud-SocialCom-SustainCom52081.2021.00093

Ihaka, R., & Gentleman, R. (1994). *R: A language for data analysis and graphics*. Dept. of Statistics, School of Mathematical and Information Sciences, University of Auckland.

Inmon, W. H., & Lindstedt, D. (2015). *Data architecture: A primer for the data scientist—Big data, data warehouse, and data vault*. Morgan Kaufmann/Elsevier.

Jafari, R. (2022). *Hands-on data preprocessing in Python: Learn how to effectively prepare data for successful data analytics*. Packt Publishing.

Jaleel, Q., & Ali, I. H. (2022). Facial behavior analysis-based DeepFake video detection using GAN discriminator. *2022 International Conference on Data Science and Intelligent Computing (ICDSIC)*, 36–40. DOI: 10.1109/ICDSIC56987.2022.10075660

Jamalludin, M. D., Muljono, F., Shidik, G. F., & Fanani, A. Z. Purwanto, & Al Zami, F. (2021). Implementation of feature selection using gain ratio towards improved accuracy of support vector machine (SVM) on YouTube comment classification. *2021 International Seminar on Application for Technology of Information and Communication (ISemantic)*, 28–31.

Jiang, S., Jiang, T., & Wang, L. (2020). Secure and efficient cloud data deduplication with ownership management. *IEEE Transactions on Services Computing, 13*(6), 1152–1165.

John, J., & Sherif, B. V. (2022). Comparative analysis on different DeepFake detection methods and semi-supervised GAN architecture for DeepFake detection. *2022 Sixth International Conference on I-SMAC (IoT in Social, Mobile, Analytics and Cloud) (I-SMAC)*, 516–521. DOI: 10.1109/I-SMAC55078.2022.9987265

Johnny, O., & Trovati, M. (2020). Big data inconsistencies and incompleteness: A literature review. *International Journal of Grid and Utility Computing, 5*(5), 705. DOI: 10.1504/IJGUC.2020.110057

Joshi, P. (2017). *Artificial intelligence with Python: A comprehensive guide to building intelligent apps for Python beginners and developers*. Packt Publishing Ltd.

Junaidi, A., Tanjung, N. A. F., Wijayanto, S., Lasama, J., & Iskandar, A. R. (2021). Overfitting problem in images classification for egg incubator using convolutional neural network. *2021 9th International Conference on Cyber and IT Service Management (CITSM)*, 1–7.

Jyothi, P. N., Lakshmi, D. R., & Rao, K. V. S. N. R. (2020). A supervised approach for detection of outliers in healthcare claims data. *Journal of Engineering Science & Technology Review*, *13*(1), 204–213. DOI: 10.25103/jestr.131.25

Kamukwamba, Y., & Chunxiao, L. (2021). A novel algorithm using content-based filtering technology in Apache Spark for big data analysis. *2021 4th International Conference on Artificial Intelligence and Big Data (ICAIBD)*, 22–26.

Karthik, M. G., & Krishnan, M. B. M. (2021). Detecting internet of things attacks using post pruning decision tree-synthetic minority over sampling technique. *International Journal of Intelligent Engineering & Systems*, *14*(4), 105–114. DOI: 10.22266/ijies2021.0831.10

Khan, S. A., & Ali Rana, Z. (2019). Evaluating performance of software defect prediction models using area under precision-recall curve (AUC-PR). *2019 2nd International Conference on Advancements in Computational Sciences (ICACS)*, 1–6.

Khatter, H., Arif, S., Singh, U., Mathur, S., & Jain, S. (2021). Product recommendation system for e-commerce using collaborative filtering and textual clustering. *2021 Third International Conference on Inventive Research in Computing Applications (ICIRCA)*, 612–618. DOI: 10.1109/ICIRCA51532.2021.9544753

Kim, W., Yeo, K. M., Jeong, W. C., Park, S. H., Park, J. D., & Moon, Y. B. (2024). Masked background and object image-based data augmentation method. In *2024 15th International Conference on Information and Communication Technology Convergence (ICTC)* (pp. 1329–1331). IEEE. DOI: 10.1109/ICTC62082.2024.10827114

Kumar, P., Ganapathy, G., & Kang, J.-J. (2021). A hybrid mod K-means clustering with mod SVM algorithm to enhance the cancer prediction. *International Journal of Internet. Broadcasting and Communication*, *13*(2), 231–243.

Kusumawardhani, N. K., Nasrun, M., & Setianingsih, C. (2019). Web recommended system library book selection using item-based collaborative filtering method. *2019 IEEE International Conference on Engineering, Technology and Education (TALE)*, 1–8. DOI: 10.1109/TALE48000.2019.9225960

Kyaw, K. S., & Limsiroratana, S. (2019). Case study: Knowledge discovery process using computation intelligence with feature selection approach. *2019 17th International Conference on ICT and Knowledge Engineering (ICT&KE).*

Lafaye de Micheaux, P., Drouilhet, R., & Liquet, B. (2013). *The R software: Fundamentals of programming and statistical analysis.* Springer. DOI: 10.1007/978-1-4614-9020-3

Lakshmi Devi, R., & Samundeeswari, V. V. (2021). Detection and automated classification of brain tumor types in MRI images using convolutional neural network with grid search optimization. *2021 Fifth International Conference on I-SMAC (IoT in Social, Mobile, Analytics and Cloud) (I-SMAC)*, 1280–1284. DOI: 10.1109/I-SMAC52330.2021.9640670

Lawal, M. M., Ibrahim, H., Sani, N. F. M., & Yaakob, R. (2020). Analyses of indexing techniques on uncertain data with high dimensionality. *IEEE Access : Practical Innovations, Open Solutions*, *8*, 74101–74117. DOI: 10.1109/ACCESS.2020.2988487

LeCun, Y., Cortes, C., & Burges, J. C. C. (2021). The MNIST database of handwritten digits. Retrieved from http://yann.lecun.com/exdb/mnist/

Li, J., Horiguchi, Y., & Sawaragi, T. (2020). Data dimensionality reduction by introducing structural equation modeling to machine learning problems. In *2020 59th Annual Conference of the Society of Instrument and Control Engineers of Japan (SICE)* (pp. 826–831). IEEE. DOI: 10.23919/SICE48898.2020.9240323

Li, Z. (2024). A feature engineering strategy for data-driven predictive models of educational building's electricity consumption. In *2024 7th International Conference on Advanced Algorithms and Control Engineering (ICAACE)* (pp. 542–546). IEEE. DOI: 10.1109/ICAACE61206.2024.10549389

Li, K., Li, J., Liu, S., Li, Z., Bo, J., & Liu, B. (2019). GA-iForest: An efficient isolated forest framework based on genetic algorithm for numerical data outlier detection. *Transactions of Nanjing University of Aeronautics & Astronautics*, *36*(6), 1026–1038.

Liu, L. (2021). Design of human resource management information system based on decision tree algorithm. *2021 Global Reliability and Prognostics and Health Management (PHM-Nanjing)*, 1–6.

Liu, L., & Ding, H. (2011). Modeling China Telecom customer churn prediction based on CRISP-DM. In *2011 International Conference on E-Business and E-Government (ICEE)* (pp. 1–4). IEEE. DOI: 10.1109/ICEBEG.2011.5884504

Liu, Y.-Y., Li, L., Liu, Y.-S., Chan, P.-W., Zhang, W.-H., & Zhang, L. (2021). Estimation of precipitation induced by tropical cyclones based on machine-learning-enhanced analogue identification of numerical prediction. *Meteorological Applications, 28*(2), e1978. DOI: 10.1002/met.1978

Llaudet, E., & Imai, K. (2023). *Data analysis for social science: A friendly and practical introduction*. Princeton University Press.

Lourenco, J., & Varde, A. S. (2020). Item-based collaborative filtering and association rules for a baseline recommender in e-commerce. *2020 IEEE International Conference on Big Data (Big Data)*, 4636–4645. DOI: 10.1109/BigData50022.2020.9377807

Lubanovic, B. (2019). *Introducing Python: Modern computing in simple packages* (2nd ed.). O'Reilly Media, Inc.

Mailund, T. (2022). *Beginning data science in R 4: Data analysis, visualization, and modelling for the data scientist* (2nd ed.). Apress. DOI: 10.1007/978-1-4842-8155-0

Mandhare, H. C., & Idate, S. R. (2017). A comparative study of cluster-based outlier detection, distance-based outlier detection, and density-based outlier detection techniques. *2017 International Conference on Intelligent Computing and Control Systems (ICICCS)*, 931–935. DOI: 10.1109/ICCONS.2017.8250601

Maneechaeye, P., & Ramjan, S. (2023). Analyzing factors influencing safety behaviors among Thai flight crews: A supervised machine learning approach. *15th National Conference on Administration and Management*.

Maslan, A., Mohamad, K. M. B., & Mohd Foozy, F. B. (2020). Feature selection for DDoS detection using classification machine learning techniques. *IAES International Journal of Artificial Intelligence, 9*(1), 137–145. DOI: 10.11591/ijai.v9.i1.pp137-145

Massaron, L., & Mueller, J. (2015). *Python for data science for dummies*. John Wiley & Sons, Inc.

Mat, T. M., Lajis, A., & Nasir, H. (2018). Text data preparation in RapidMiner for short free text answer in assisted assessment. *2018 IEEE 5th International Conference on Smart Instrumentation, Measurement and Application (ICSIMA)*, 1–4.

Mesner, O. C., & Shalizi, C. R. (2021). Conditional mutual information estimation for mixed, discrete, and continuous data. *IEEE Transactions on Information Theory, 67*(1), 464–484. DOI: 10.1109/TIT.2020.3024886

Migran, N. G., Anna, V. K., & Dmitry, S. K. (2023). Julia language features for processing statistical data. *Discrete and Continuous Models and Applied Computational Science, 31*(1), 5–26. DOI: 10.22363/2658-4670-2023-31-1-5-26

Miller, A. I. (2019). Ian Goodfellow's generative adversarial networks: AI learns to imagine. In *The artist in the machine: The world of AI-powered creativity* (pp. 87–98). MIT Press. DOI: 10.7551/mitpress/11585.003.0015

Min, S. H., & Zhou, J. (2021). smplot: An R package for easy and elegant data visualization. *Frontiers in Genetics, 12*, 802894. Advance online publication. DOI: 10.3389/fgene.2021.802894 PMID: 34976028

Mishra, A., & Vats, A. (2021). Supervised machine learning classification algorithms for detection of fracture location in dissimilar friction stir welded joints. *Frattura e Integrita Strutturale, 15*(58), 242–253. DOI: 10.3221/IGF-ESIS.58.18

Mladenova, T. (2021). A feature-weighted rule for the k-nearest neighbor. *2021 5th International Symposium on Multidisciplinary Studies and Innovative Technologies (ISMSIT)*, 493–497.

Mnich, K., Polewko-Klim, A., Kitlas Golinska, A., Lesinski, W., & Rudnicki, W. R. (2020). Super learning with repeated cross validation. *2020 International Conference on Data Mining Workshops (ICDMW)*, 629–635. DOI: 10.1109/ICDMW51313.2020.00089

Mohan, L., Jain, S., Suyal, P., & Kumar, A. (2020). Data mining classification techniques for intrusion detection system. *2020 12th International Conference on Computational Intelligence and Communication Networks (CICN)*, 351–355.

Montesdeoca, B., Luengo, J., Maillo, J., García-Gil, D., García, S., & Herrera, F. (2019). A first approach on big data missing values imputation. *IoTBDS 2019 - Proceedings of the 4th International Conference on Internet of Things, Big Data and Security*, 315–323.

Mora, C. M., Sicilia, M., García, B. E., & Sánchez, A. S. (2020). Evolution and prospects of the Comprehensive R Archive Network (CRAN) package ecosystem. *Journal of Software (Malden, MA), 32*(11), 1–14. DOI: 10.1002/smr.2270

Mueller, J. (2018). *Beginning programming with Python* (2nd ed.). John Wiley & Sons.

Mueller, J., & Massaron, L. (2019). *Python for data science* (2nd ed.). John Wiley & Sons, Inc.

Nigam, H., Biswas, P., Raj, J. S., Iliyasu, A. M., Bestak, R., & Baig, Z. A. (2021). Web scraping: From tools to related legislation and implementation using Python.

Padhy, S. K., Singh, A. K., & Vetrivelan, P. (2022). Item-based collaborative filtering blockchain for secure movie recommendation system. *Lecture Notes in Electrical Engineering, 792*, 937–948. DOI: 10.1007/978-981-16-4625-6_93

Pajankar, A. (2021). *Practical Python data visualization: A fast track approach to learning data visualization with Python*. Apress. DOI: 10.1007/978-1-4842-6455-3

Pandey, R., Srivastava, N., & Verma, K. (2017). Data visualization through R and Azure for scaling machine training sets. *2017 7th International Conference on Communication Systems and Network Technologies (CSNT)*, 345–349. DOI: 10.1109/CSNT.2017.8418564

Panopoulos, I., Nikolaidis, S., Venieris, S. I., & Venieris, I. S. (2023). Exploring the performance and efficiency of transformer models for NLP on mobile devices. *2023 IEEE Symposium on Computers and Communications (ISCC)*, 1–4. DOI: 10.1109/ISCC58397.2023.10217850

Parkavi, A., Jawaid, A., Dev, S., & M. S., V. (2018). The patterns that don't exist: Study on the effects of psychological human biases in data analysis and decision making. In *2018 3rd International Conference on Computational Systems and Information Technology for Sustainable Solutions (CSITSS)* (pp. 193–197). IEEE. DOI: 10.1109/CSITSS.2018.8768554

Paruechanon, P., & Sriurai, W. (2019). Applying association rule to risk analysis for student-dropout in Information Technology program. *Journal of Science and Science Education*, *1*(2), 123–133.

Pecioski, D., Gavriloski, V., Domazetovska, S., & Ignjatovska, A. (2023). An overview of reinforcement learning techniques. *2023 12th Mediterranean Conference on Embedded Computing (MECO)*, 1–4. DOI: 10.1109/MECO58584.2023.10155066

Phan, Q.-T., Wu, Y.-K., & Phan, Q.-D. (2021). An overview of data preprocessing for short-term wind power forecasting. *2021 7th International Conference on Applied System Innovation (ICASI)*, 121–125.

Phoha, S., & Ramjan, S. (2023). *Sentiment analysis model for customer classification based on JCI service standards: A case study from Thailand*. Independent Study. College of Innovation: Thammasat University.

Punhani, R., Arora, V. P. S., Sabitha, S., & Kumar Shukla, V. (2021). Application of clustering algorithm for effective customer segmentation in e-commerce. *2021 International Conference on Computational Intelligence and Knowledge Economy (ICCIKE)*, 149–154. DOI: 10.1109/ICCIKE51210.2021.9410713

Puspasari, B. D., Damayanti, L. L., Pramono, A., & Darmawan, A. K. (2021). Implementation K-means clustering method in job recommendation system. *2021 7th International Conference on Electrical, Electronics and Information Engineering (ICEEIE)*, 1–6.

Puspitasari, D. I., Kholdani, A. F. R., Dharmawati, A., Rosadi, M. E., & Dhuhita, W. M. P. (2021). Stroke disease analysis and classification using decision tree and random forest methods. *2021 Sixth International Conference on Informatics and Computing (ICIC)*, 1–4. Alam, M. G. R., Hussain, S., Islam Mim, M. M., & Islam, M. T. (2021). Telecom customer behavior analysis using naïve Bayes classifier. *2021 IEEE 4th International Conference on Computer and Communication Engineering Technology (CCET)*, 308–312. DOI: 10.1109/ICIC54025.2021.9632906

R statistical programming software for data science. (2021). *Business Expert Press*.

Rahman, B., Warnars, H. L. H. S., Sabarguna, B. S., & Budiharto, W. (2021). Heart disease classification model using k-nearest neighbor algorithm. *2021 Sixth International Conference on Informatics and Computing (ICIC)*, 1–4. DOI: 10.1109/ICIC54025.2021.9632918

Ramirez-Hernandez, J., Juarez-Sandoval, O.-U., Hernandez-Gonzalez, L., Hernandez-Ramirez, A., & Olivares-Dominguez, R.-S. (2020). Voltage control based on a back-propagation artificial neural network algorithm. *2020 IEEE International Autumn Meeting on Power, Electronics and Computing (ROPEC)*, 1–6. DOI: 10.1109/ROPEC50909.2020.9258699

Raschka, S., & Mirajalili, V. (2018). *Python machine learning: Machine learning and deep learning with Python, scikit-learn, and TensorFlow* (2nd ed.). Packt Publishing.

Rathaur, S., Kamath, N., & Ghanekar, U. (2020). Software defect density prediction based on multiple linear regression. *2020 Second International Conference on Inventive Research in Computing Applications (ICIRCA)*, 434–439. DOI: 10.1109/ICIRCA48905.2020.9183110

Reges, S., Obourn, A., & Stepp, M. (2019). *Building Python programs* (1st ed.). Pearson.

Ren, X. (2021). Application of Apriori association rules algorithm to data mining technology to mining e-commerce potential customers. *2021 International Wireless Communications and Mobile Computing (IWCMC)*, 1193–1196.

Rezaeijo, S. M., Hashemi, B., Mofid, B., Bakhshandeh, M., Mahdavi, A., & Hashemi, M. S. (2021). The feasibility of a dose painting procedure to treat prostate cancer based on mpMR images and hierarchical clustering. *Radiation Oncology (London, England)*, *16*(1), 1–16. DOI: 10.1186/s13014-021-01906-2 PMID: 34544468

Riswanto, E., Robi'in, B., & Suparyanto, . (2019). Mobile recommendation system for culinary tourism destination using KNN (K-nearest neighbor). *Journal of Physics: Conference Series*, *1201*(1), 012039. DOI: 10.1088/1742-6596/1201/1/012039

Romero, M. P., Parry, J., Prosser, A., Upton, P., Rees, E., Tearne, O., Arnold, M., Chang, Y.-M., Brunton, L. A., Stevens, K., & Drewe, J. A. (2019). Decision tree machine learning applied to bovine tuberculosis risk factors to aid disease control decision making. *Preventive Veterinary Medicine*, 175. PMID: 31812850

Sabau Popa, C. D., Popa, D. N., Bogdan, V., & Simut, R. (2021). Composite financial performance index prediction – A neural networks approach. *Journal of Business Economics and Management*, *22*(2), 277–296. DOI: 10.3846/jbem.2021.14000

Salıcı, M., & Ölçer, Ü. E. (2024). Impact of transformer-based models in NLP: An in-depth study on BERT and GPT. *2024 8th International Artificial Intelligence and Data Processing Symposium (IDAP)*, 1–6. DOI: 10.1109/IDAP64064.2024.10710796

Salman, W. A. K., & Sadkhan, S. B. (2021). Proposed association rules mining algorithm for sensors data streams. *2021 1st Babylon International Conference on Information Technology and Science (BICITS)*, 76–81.

Samasiri, P. (2020). Visual representations of different family structures using an interactive data exploration technique. *2020 1st International Conference on Big Data Analytics and Practices (IBDAP), 1–5.*

Samsani, S. (2016). An RST-based efficient preprocessing technique for handling inconsistent data. *2016 IEEE International Conference on Computational Intelligence and Computing Research (ICCIC)*, 1–8. DOI: 10.1109/ICCIC.2016.7919591

Santos, G. R. (2023). *Data wrangling with R: Load, explore, transform and visualize data for modeling with tidyverse libraries*. Packt Publishing.

Shao, L., Mahajan, A., Schreck, T., & Lehmann, D. J. (2017). Interactive regression lens for exploring scatter plots. *Computer Graphics Forum*, *36*(3), 157–166. DOI: 10.1111/cgf.13176

Shilane, D., Crecchio, N. D., & Lorenzetti, N. L. (2024). Some pedagogical elements of computer programming for data science: A comparison of three approaches to teaching the R language. *Teaching Statistics*, *46*(1), 24–37. DOI: 10.1111/test.12361

Shrestha, R. B., Razavi, M., & Prasad, P. W. (2020). An unsupervised machine learning technique for recommendation systems. *2020 5th International Conference on Innovative Technologies in Intelligent Systems and Industrial Applications (CITISIA), 1–9.*

Sneeringer, L. (2016). *Professional Python*. WROX/John Wiley & Sons.

Snineh, S. M., Amrani, N. E. A., Youssfi, M., Bouattane, O., & Daaif, A. (2021). Detection of traffic anomaly in highways by using recurrent neural network. *2021 Fifth International Conference on Intelligent Computing in Data Sciences (ICDS)*, 1–6. DOI: 10.1109/ICDS53782.2021.9626741

Song, J., Yu, Q., & Bao, R. (2019). The detection algorithms for similar duplicate data. In *2019 6th International Conference on Systems and Informatics (ICSAI)* (pp. 1534–1542). IEEE. DOI: 10.1109/ICSAI48974.2019.9010154

Song, H., Fu, Y., Saket, B., & Stasko, J. (2021). Understanding the effects of visualizing missing values on visual data exploration. *2021. IEEE Visualization Conference : VIS*, 161–165.

Sonu, S. B., & Suyampulingam, A. (2021). Linear regression-based air quality data analysis and prediction using Python. *2021 IEEE Madras Section Conference (MASCON)*, 1–7. DOI: 10.1109/MASCON51689.2021.9563432

SPSS IncInternational Consortium. (2000). *CRISP-DM 1.0: Free document offers step-by-step guidance for data mining projects*. Business Wire.

Sriwiboon, N. (2020). Improvement the performance of the chest X-ray image classification with convolutional neural network model by using image augmentations technique for COVID-19 diagnosis. *The Journal of King Mongkut's University of Technology North Bangkok, 31*(1), 109–117. DOI: 10.14416/j.kmutnb.2020.10.002

Stewart, J. (2017). *Python for scientists* (2nd ed.). Cambridge University Press. DOI: 10.1017/9781108120241

Sunkpho, J., & Ramjan, S. (2020). Predicting condominium price in Bangkok using web mining technique. *Srinakharinwirot Research and Development (Journal of Humanities and Social Sciences), 12*(24).

Sunkpho, J., & Ramjan, S. (2020). Predicting condominium price in Bangkok using web mining techniques. *Srinakharinwirot Research and Development (Journal of Humanities and Social Sciences), 12*(24).

Sunkpho, S., & Ramjan, S. (2020). *Introduction to Python programming for data science*. Thammasat Press.

Susanti, S. P., & Azizah, F. N. (2017). Imputation of missing value using dynamic Bayesian network for multivariate time series data. *2017 International Conference on Data and Software Engineering (ICoDSE)*, 1–5. DOI: 10.1109/ICODSE.2017.8285864

Tai, Y., Sun, Z., & Yao, Z. (2021). Content-based recommendation using machine learning. *2021 IEEE 31st International Workshop on Machine Learning for Signal Processing (MLSP)*, 1–4.

Tananatong, T., & Ramjan, S. (2022). *Data visualization design and development for data science*. Thammasat Press.

Tanantong, T. (2021). *Data mining*. Retrieved from https://www.skilllane.com/courses/tuxsa-Data-Mining-Algorithms/chapter

Tanantong, T., & Ramjan, S. (2021). An association rule mining approach to discover demand and supply patterns based on Thai social media data. *International Journal of Knowledge and Systems Science, 12*(2), April–June 2021.

Tanantong, T., & Ramjan, S. (2022). *Data visualization for data science* (1st ed.). Thammasat Press.

Telikani, A., Shahbahrami, A., & Gandomi, A. H. (2021). High-performance implementation of evolutionary privacy-preserving algorithm for big data using GPU platform. *Information Sciences*, *579*, 251–265. DOI: 10.1016/j.ins.2021.08.006

Thammasiri, S., & Ramjan, S. (2021). *Corrosion under insulation severity prediction for Carron steel in marine environment using data science methodology*. Independent Study. College of Innovation: Thammasat University.

Thangakumar, J., & Kommina, S. B. (2020). Ant colony optimization-based feature subset selection with logistic regression classification model for education data mining. *International Journal of Advanced Science and Technology*, *29*(3), 5821–5834.

Thankachan, T., Prakash, K. S., & Jothi, S. (2021). Artificial neural network modeling to evaluate and predict the mechanical strength of duplex stainless steel during casting. *Sadhana*, *46*(4), 1–12. DOI: 10.1007/s12046-021-01742-w

Thongjor, N. (2017). Understanding the data classification: k-nearest neighbours. Retrieved August 9, 2021, from https://www.babelcoder.com/blog/articles/k-nearest-neighbors

Toumi, A., Gribaa, N., & Ben Abdessalem Karaa, W. (2021). Mining biomedical texts based on statistical method and association rules. *2021 International Conference of Women in Data Science at Taif University (WiDSTaif)*, 1–4. DOI: 10.1109/WiDSTaif52235.2021.9430200

Vichi, M., Ritter, G., & Giusti, A. (2013). *Classification and data mining*. Springer Verlag.

Wafa, H. A., Aminuddin, R., Ibrahim, S., Mangshor, N. N. A., & Wahab, N. I. F. A. (2021). A data visualization framework during pandemic using the Density-Based Spatial Clustering with Noise (DBSCAN) machine learning model. *2021 IEEE 11th International Conference on System Engineering and Technology (ICSET)*, 1–6.

Wang, J., Sato, K., Guo, S., Chen, W., & Wu, J. (2019). Big data processing with minimal delay and guaranteed data resolution in disaster areas. *IEEE Transactions on Vehicular Technology*, *68*(4), 3833–3842. DOI: 10.1109/TVT.2018.2889094

Wayan Priscila Yuni Praditya, N., Erna Permanasari, A., & Hidayah, I. (2021). Designing a tourism recommendation system using a hybrid method (collaborative filtering and content-based filtering). *2021 IEEE International Conference on Communication, Networks and Satellite (COMNETSAT)*, 298–305. DOI: 10.1109/COMNETSAT53002.2021.9530823

Wijaya, Y. A., Kurniady, D. A., Setyanto, E., Tarihoran, W. S., Rusmana, D., & Rahim, R. (2021). Davies Bouldin Index algorithm for optimizing clustering case studies mapping school facilities. *TEM Journal*, *10*(3), 1099–1103. DOI: 10.18421/TEM103-13

Yadalam, T. V., Gowda, V. M., Kumar, V. S., Girish, D., & M., N. (2020). Career recommendation systems using content-based filtering. *2020 5th International Conference on Communication and Electronics Systems (ICCES)*, 660–665.

Yager, R. R. (2020). Ordinal scale-based uncertainty models for AI. *Information Fusion*, *64*, 92–98. DOI: 10.1016/j.inffus.2020.06.010

Yang, F.-J. (2019). An extended idea about decision trees. *2019 International Conference on Computational Science and Computational Intelligence (CSCI)*, 349–354. DOI: 10.1109/CSCI49370.2019.00068

Yingzhuo, X., & Xuewen, W. (2021). Research on community consumer behavior based on association rules analysis. *2021 6th International Conference on Intelligent Computing and Signal Processing (ICSP)*, 1213–1216.

Zelle, J. M. (2010). *Python programming: An introduction to computer science* (2nd ed.). Beedle & Associates.

Zhang, H., Zhang, L., & Jiang, Y. (2019). Overfitting and underfitting analysis for deep learning-based end-to-end communication systems. *2019 11th International Conference on Wireless Communications and Signal Processing (WCSP)*, 1–6.

Zhang, C., & Zhang, S. (2002). *Association rule mining: Models and algorithms*. Springer Berlin Heidelberg. DOI: 10.1007/3-540-46027-6

Zhou, Y., Yan, S., Wang, C., Zheng, K., & Zhu, L. (2021). Position monitoring system based on hierarchical clustering. *2021 26th IEEE Asia-Pacific Conference on Communications (APCC)*, 111–114.

About the Authors

Sarawut Ramjan, a Ph.D. graduate in Computer and Engineering Management from Assumption University in 2006, served as a lecturer at North-Chiang Mai University for nine years. Currently, he is an Associate Professor specializing in Digital Transformation and Innovation at Thammasat University, a role he has occupied for the past six years.

Jirapon Sunkpho, a graduate in Civil Engineering with a specialization in Computer-Aided Engineering from Carnegie Mellon University, currently holds the position of Associate Professor specializing in Digital Transformation and Innovation at Thammasat University. Additionally, he serves as the Vice Rector in Digital at Thammasat University.

Index

M

O

P

R

S

T

www.ingramcontent.com/pod-product-compliance
Lightning Source LLC
LaVergne TN
LVHW080341011026
849161LV00009B/2144